SWORD ORATORIA

TAKASHI YAGI

ORIGINAL STORY FUJINO OMORI
CHARACTER DESIGN KIYOTAKA HAIMURA
SUZUHITO YASUDA

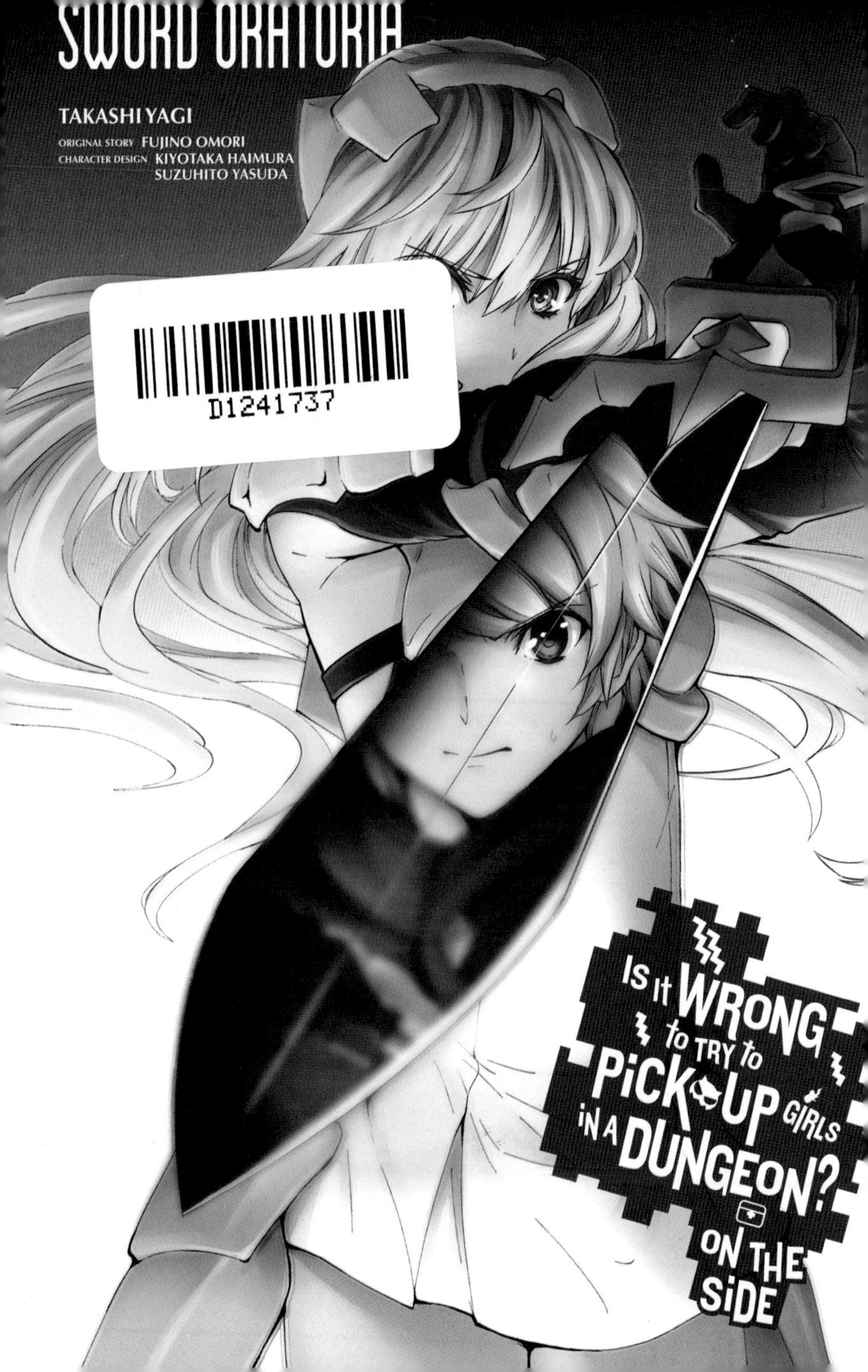

IS IT WRONG TO TRY TO PICK UP GIRLS IN A DUNGEON? ON THE SIDE

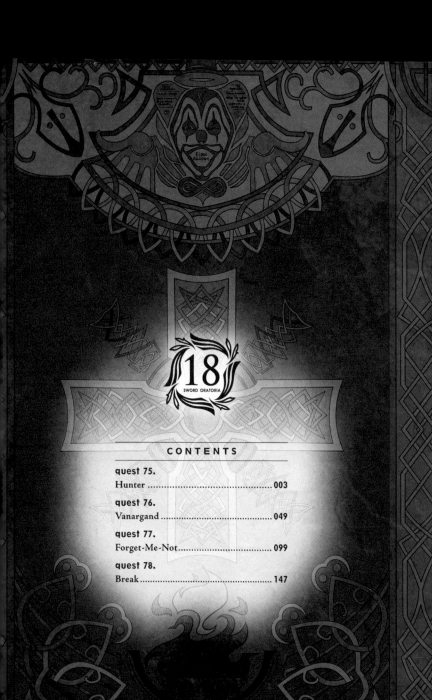

18
SWORD ORATORIA

CONTENTS

quest 75.
Hunter 003

quest 76.
Vanargand 049

quest 77.
Forget-Me-Not 099

quest 78.
Break 147

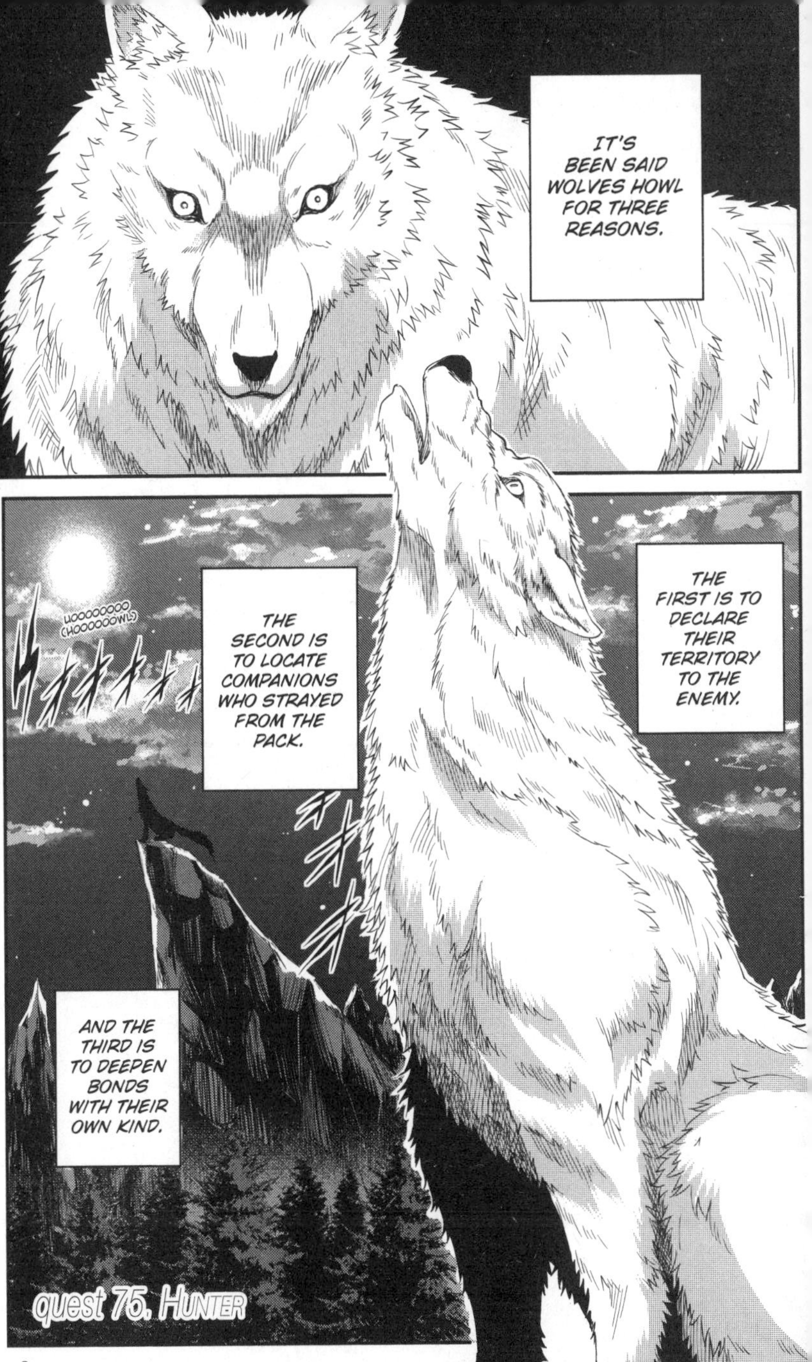
IT'S BEEN SAID WOLVES HOWL FOR THREE REASONS.
THE FIRST IS TO DECLARE THEIR TERRITORY TO THE ENEMY.
THE SECOND IS TO LOCATE COMPANIONS WHO STRAYED FROM THE PACK.
HOOOOOOOOO
(HOOOOOOWL)
AND THE THIRD IS TO DEEPEN BONDS WITH THEIR OWN KIND.
quest 75. Hunter

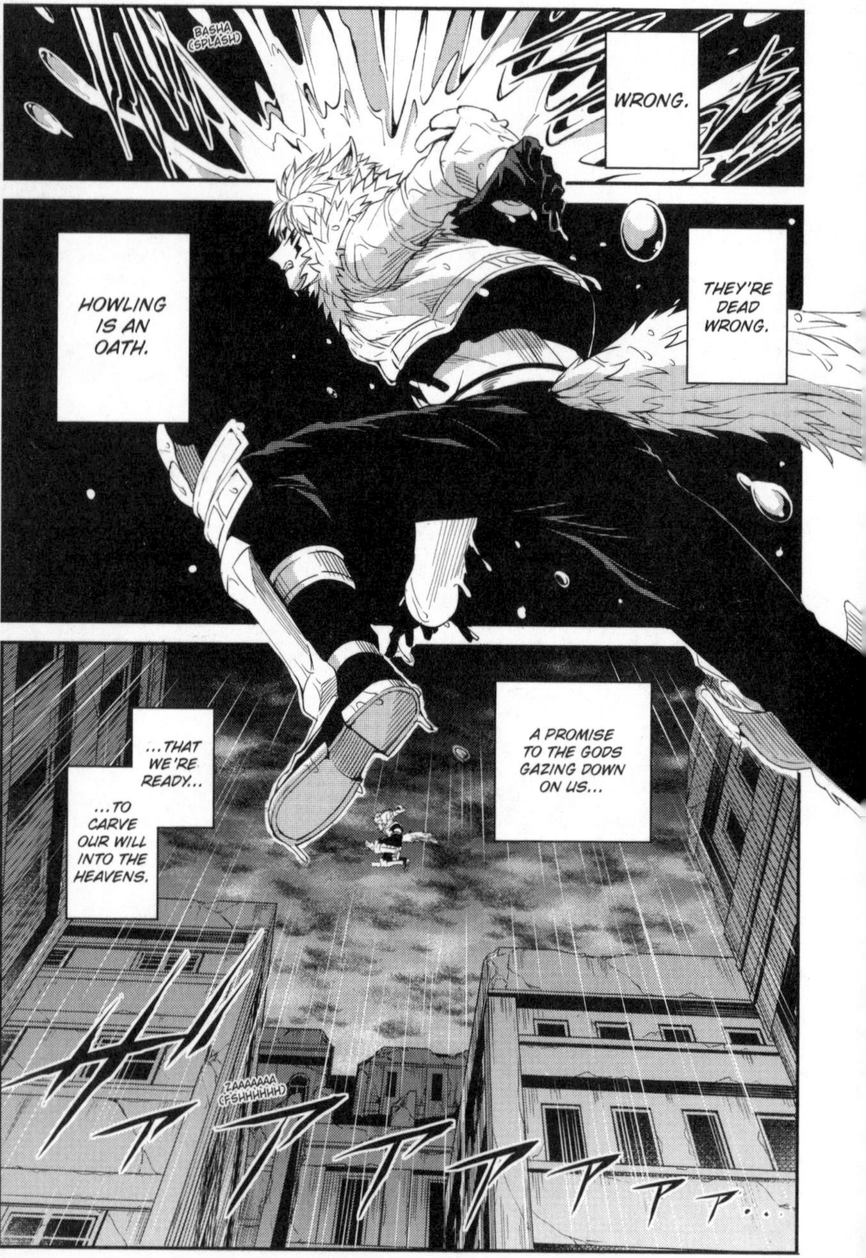
WRONG.
BASHA (SPLASH)
THEY'RE DEAD WRONG.
HOWLING IS AN OATH.
A PROMISE TO THE GODS GAZING DOWN ON US...
...THAT WE'RE READY...
...TO CARVE OUR WILL INTO THE HEAVENS.
ZAAAAAAA (FSHHHHHHH)

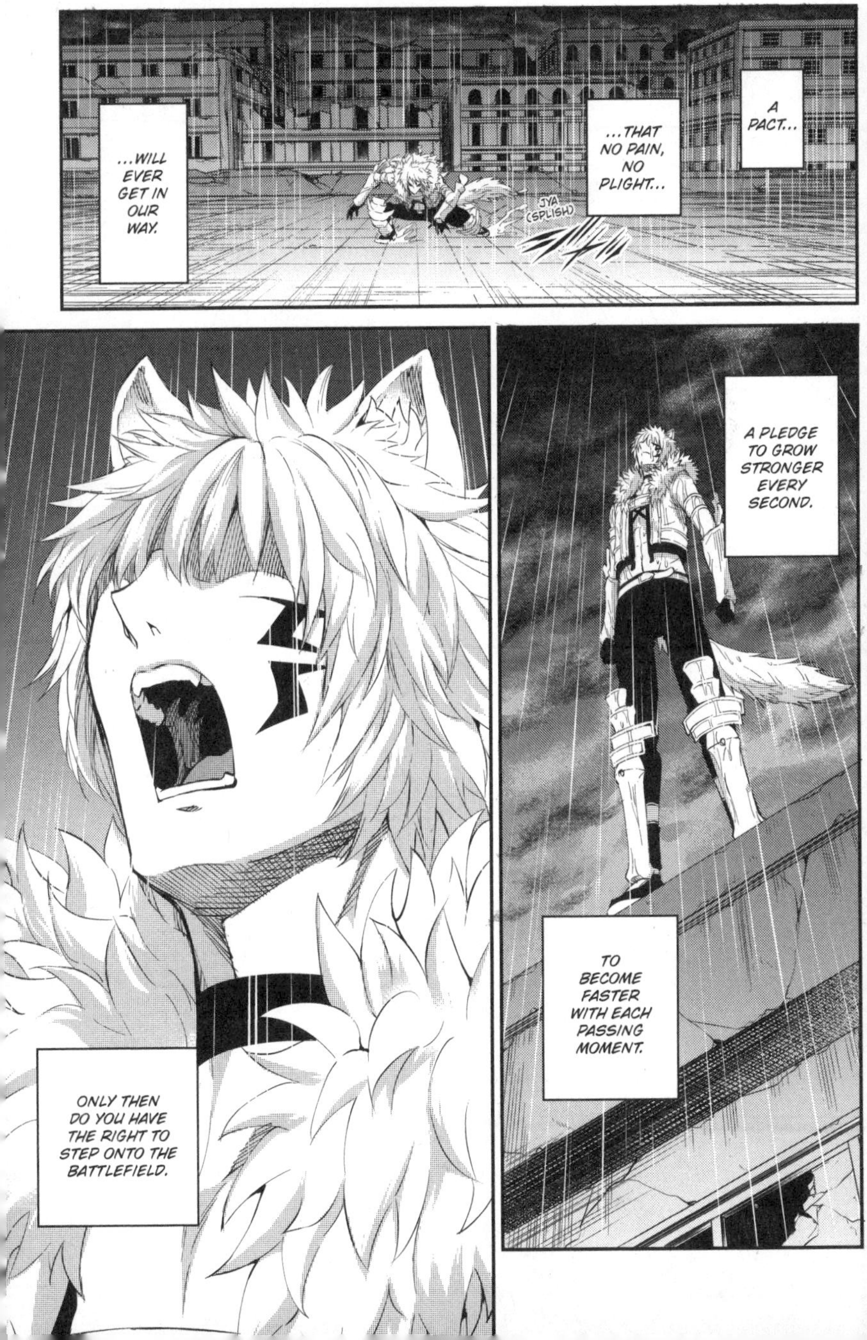
A PACT...
...THAT NO PAIN, NO PLIGHT...
JYA (SPLISH)
...WILL EVER GET IN OUR WAY.
A PLEDGE TO GROW STRONGER EVERY SECOND.
TO BECOME FASTER WITH EACH PASSING MOMENT.
ONLY THEN DO YOU HAVE THE RIGHT TO STEP ONTO THE BATTLEFIELD.

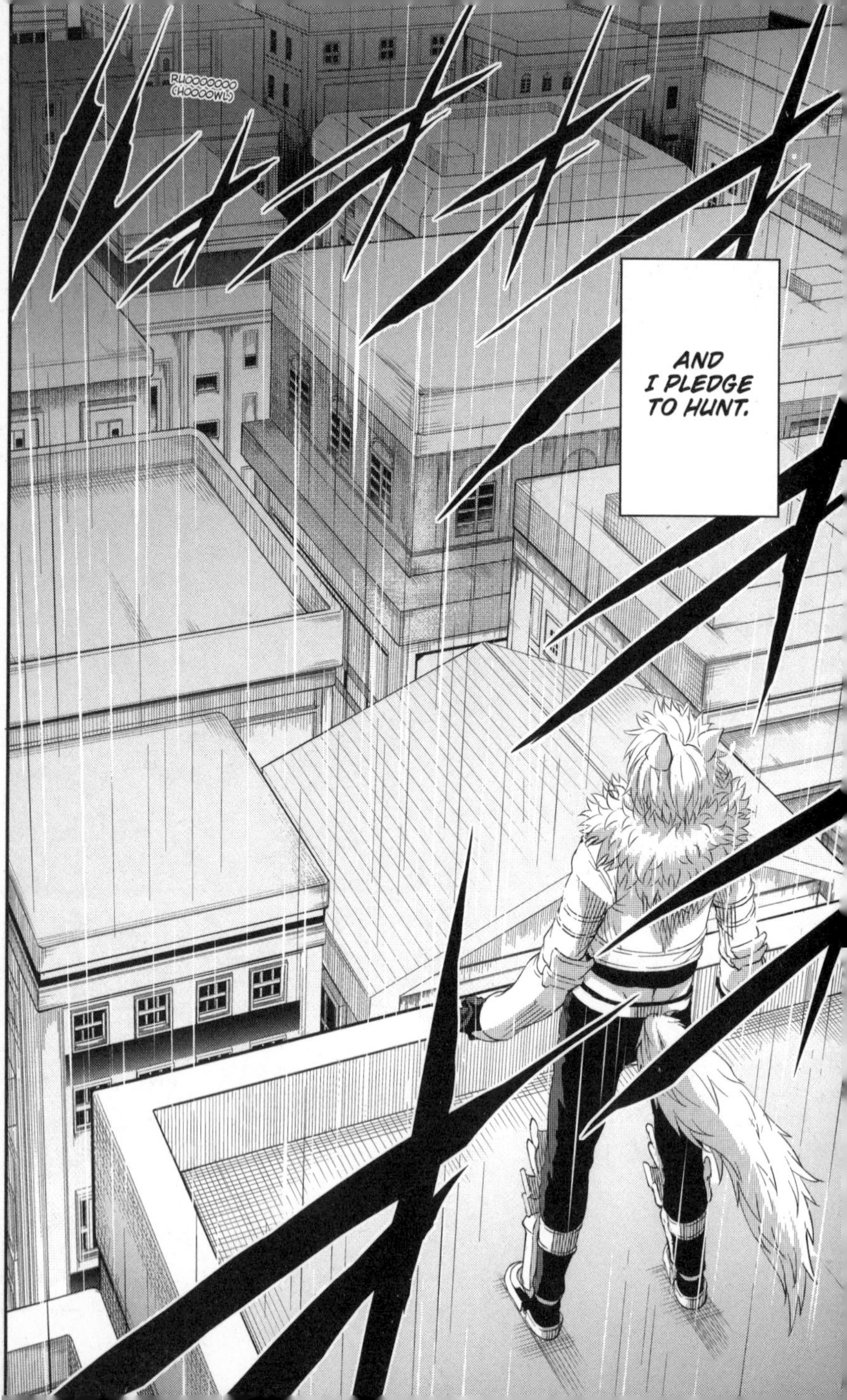
AND I PLEDGE TO HUNT.
RUOOOOOOO (HOOOOWL)

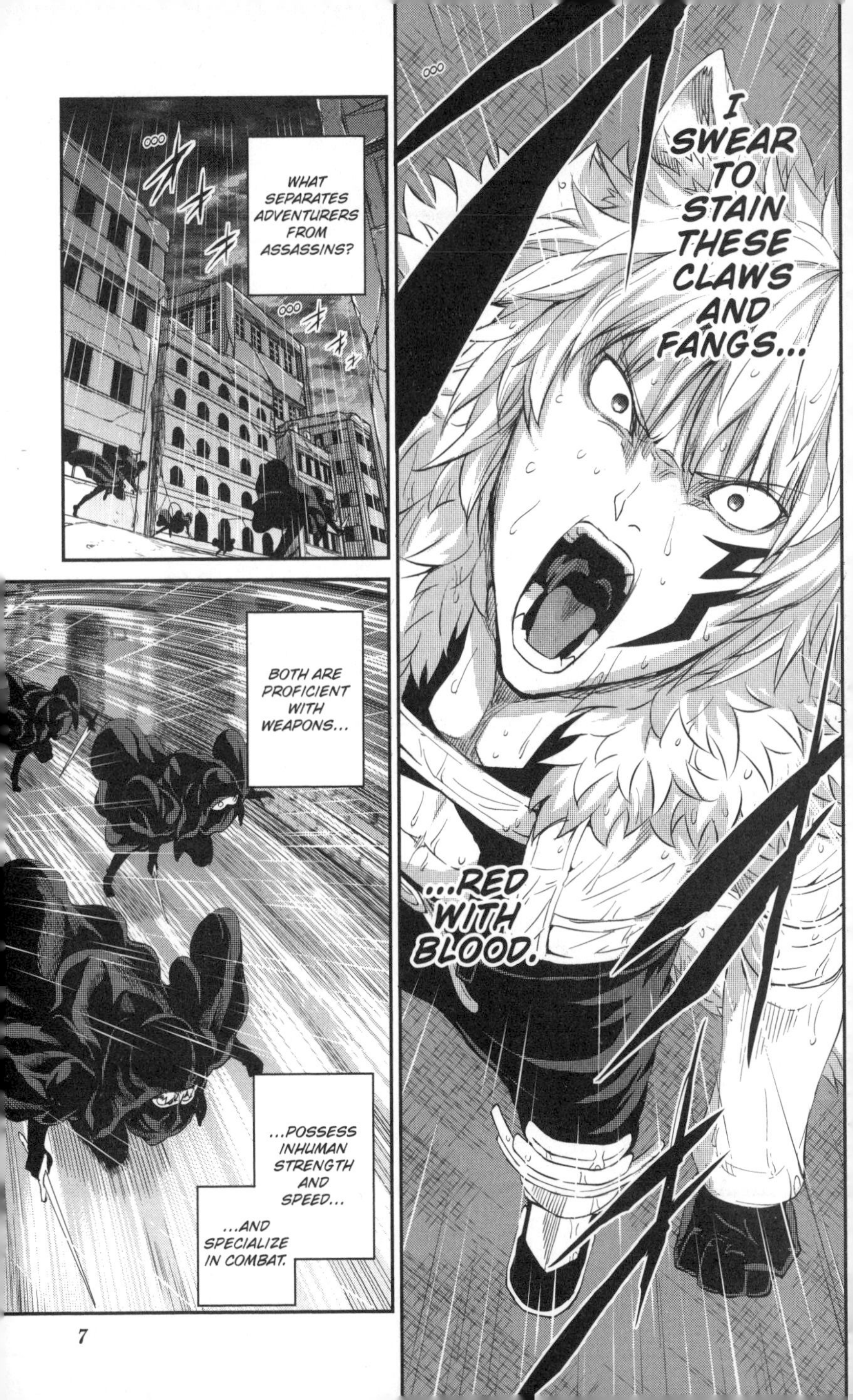
I SWEAR TO STAIN THESE CLAWS AND FANGS...
...RED WITH BLOOD.
WHAT SEPARATES ADVENTURERS FROM ASSASSINS?
BOTH ARE PROFICIENT WITH WEAPONS...
...POSSESS INHUMAN STRENGTH AND SPEED...
...AND SPECIALIZE IN COMBAT.

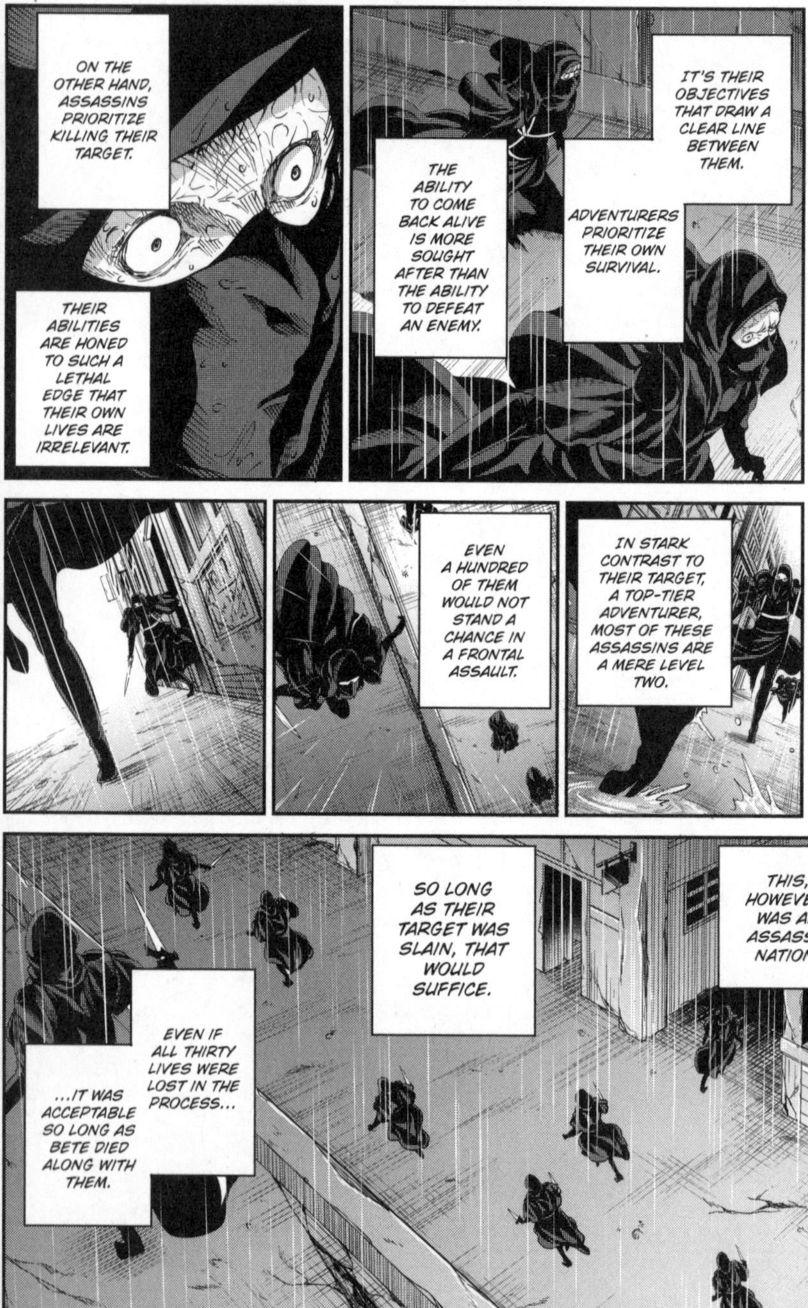
IT'S THEIR OBJECTIVES THAT DRAW A CLEAR LINE BETWEEN THEM.
ADVENTURERS PRIORITIZE THEIR OWN SURVIVAL.
THE ABILITY TO COME BACK ALIVE IS MORE SOUGHT AFTER THAN THE ABILITY TO DEFEAT AN ENEMY.
ON THE OTHER HAND, ASSASSINS PRIORITIZE KILLING THEIR TARGET.
THEIR ABILITIES ARE HONED TO SUCH A LETHAL EDGE THAT THEIR OWN LIVES ARE IRRELEVANT.
IN STARK CONTRAST TO THEIR TARGET, A TOP-TIER ADVENTURER, MOST OF THESE ASSASSINS ARE A MERE LEVEL TWO.
EVEN A HUNDRED OF THEM WOULD NOT STAND A CHANCE IN A FRONTAL ASSAULT.
THIS, HOWEVER, WAS AN ASSASSI-NATION.
SO LONG AS THEIR TARGET WAS SLAIN, THAT WOULD SUFFICE.
EVEN IF ALL THIRTY LIVES WERE LOST IN THE PROCESS...
...IT WAS ACCEPTABLE SO LONG AS BETE DIED ALONG WITH THEM.

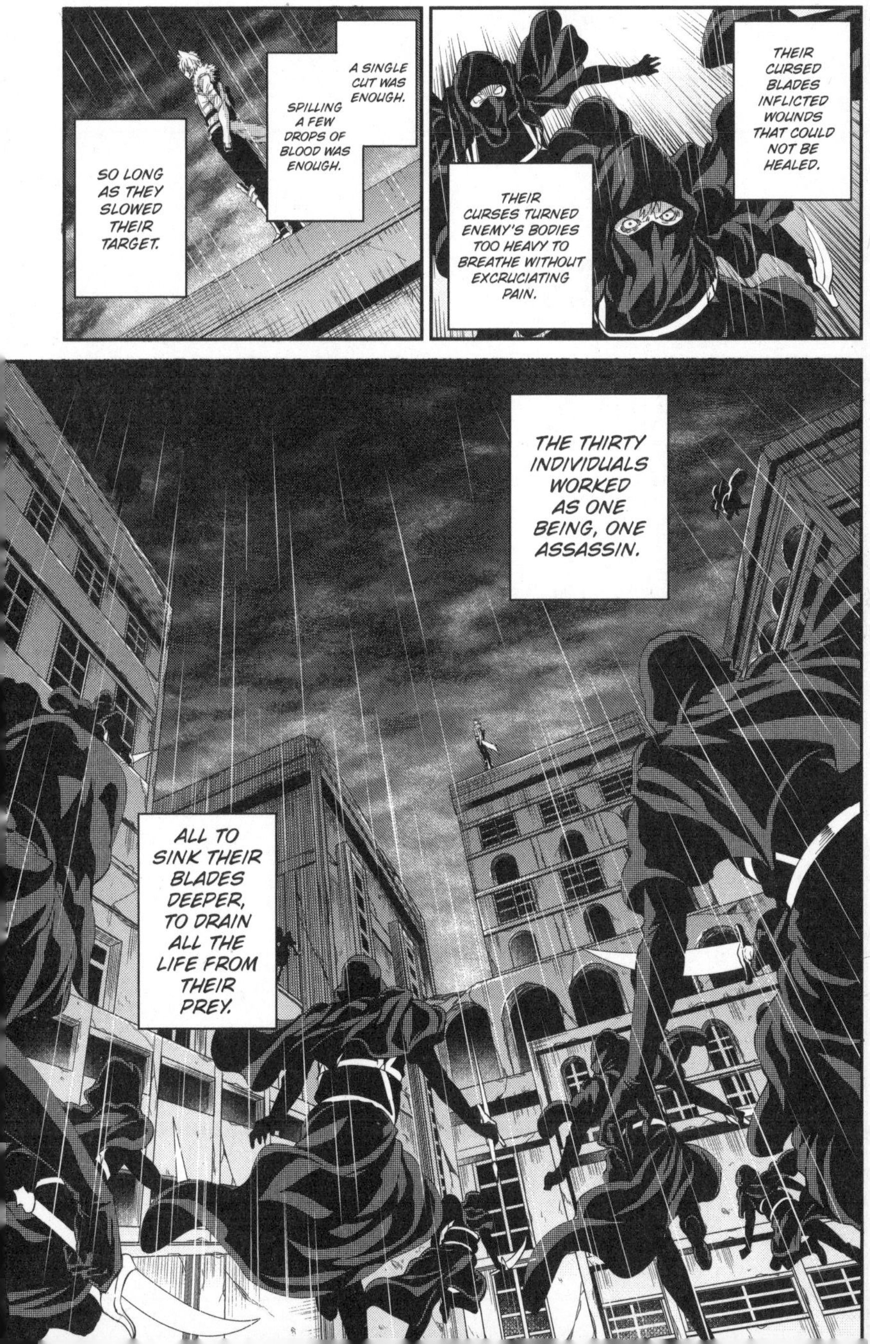
THEIR CURSED BLADES INFLICTED WOUNDS THAT COULD NOT BE HEALED.
THEIR CURSES TURNED ENEMY'S BODIES TOO HEAVY TO BREATHE WITHOUT EXCRUCIATING PAIN.
A SINGLE CUT WAS ENOUGH.
SPILLING A FEW DROPS OF BLOOD WAS ENOUGH.
SO LONG AS THEY SLOWED THEIR TARGET.
THE THIRTY INDIVIDUALS WORKED AS ONE BEING, ONE ASSASSIN.
ALL TO SINK THEIR BLADES DEEPER, TO DRAIN ALL THE LIFE FROM THEIR PREY.

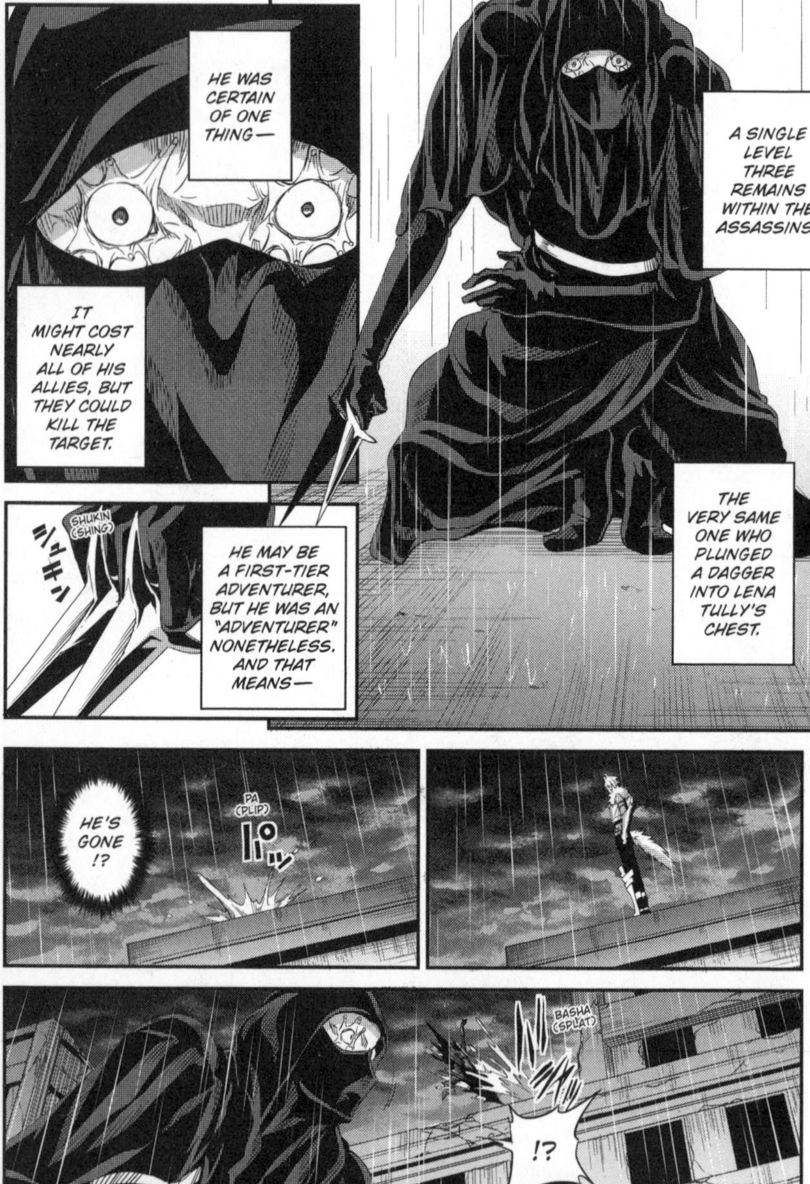
A SINGLE LEVEL THREE REMAINS WITHIN THE ASSASSINS.
THE VERY SAME ONE WHO PLUNGED A DAGGER INTO LENA TULLY'S CHEST.
HE WAS CERTAIN OF ONE THING—
IT MIGHT COST NEARLY ALL OF HIS ALLIES, BUT THEY COULD KILL THE TARGET.
SHUKIN (SHING)
HE MAY BE A FIRST-TIER ADVENTURER, BUT HE WAS AN "ADVENTURER" NONETHELESS. AND THAT MEANS—
PA (PLIP)
HE'S GONE !?
BASHA (SPLAT)
!?

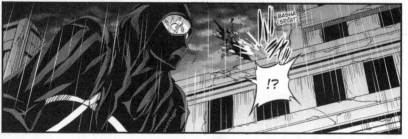

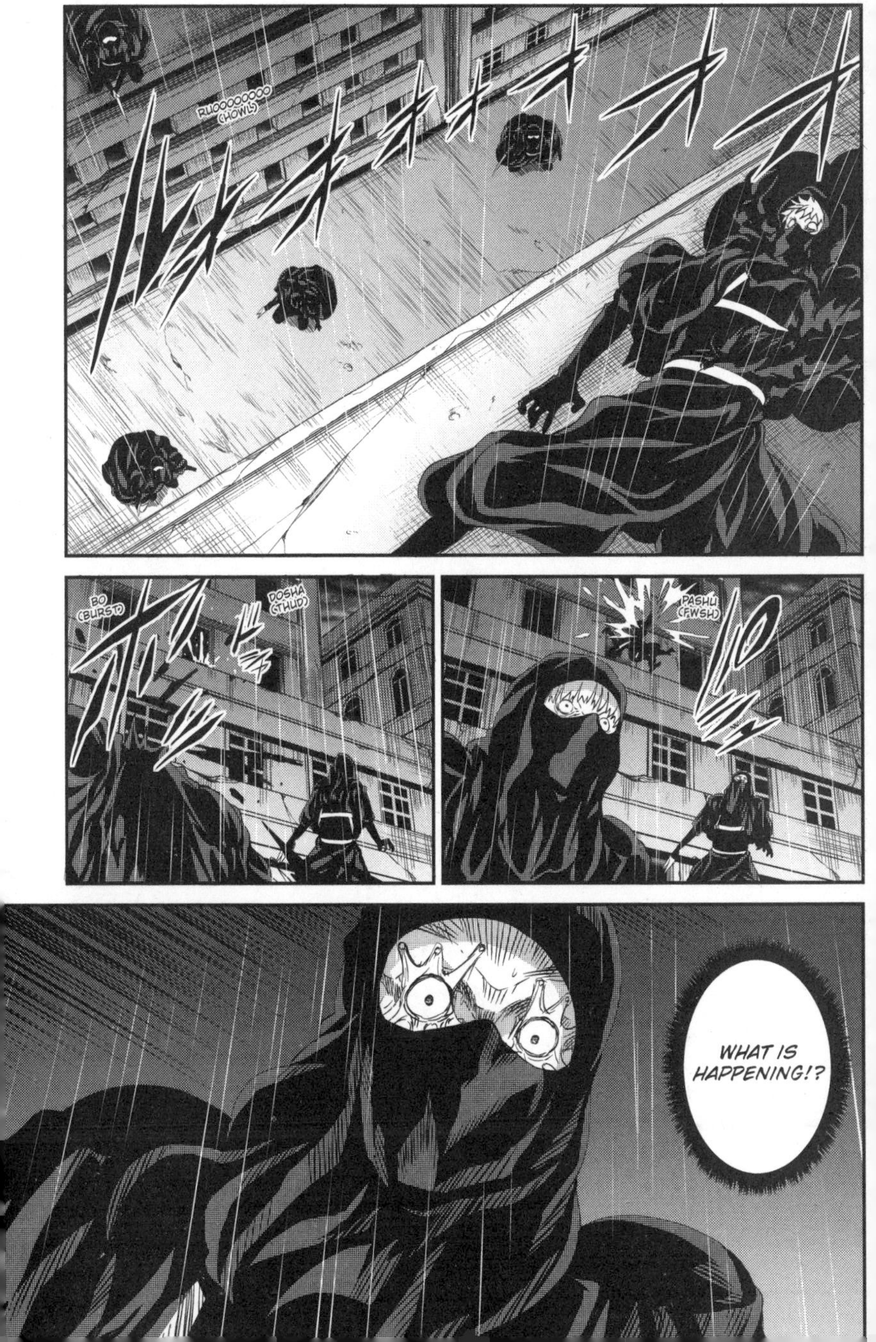
RUOOOOOOOOO (HOWL)
PASHU (FWSH)
DOSHA (THUD)
BO (BURST)
WHAT IS HAPPENING!?

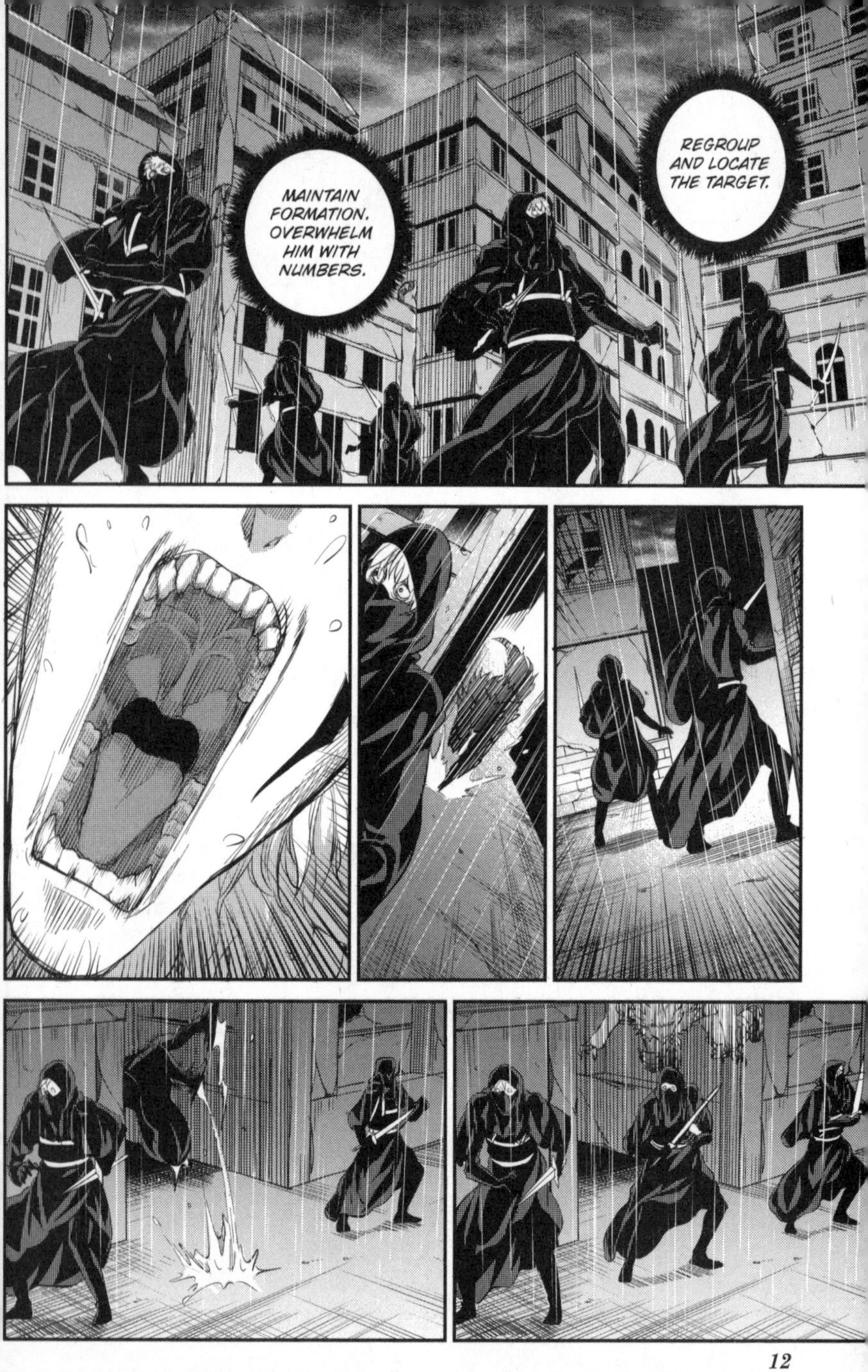
REGROUP AND LOCATE THE TARGET.
MAINTAIN FORMATION. OVERWHELM HIM WITH NUMBERS.

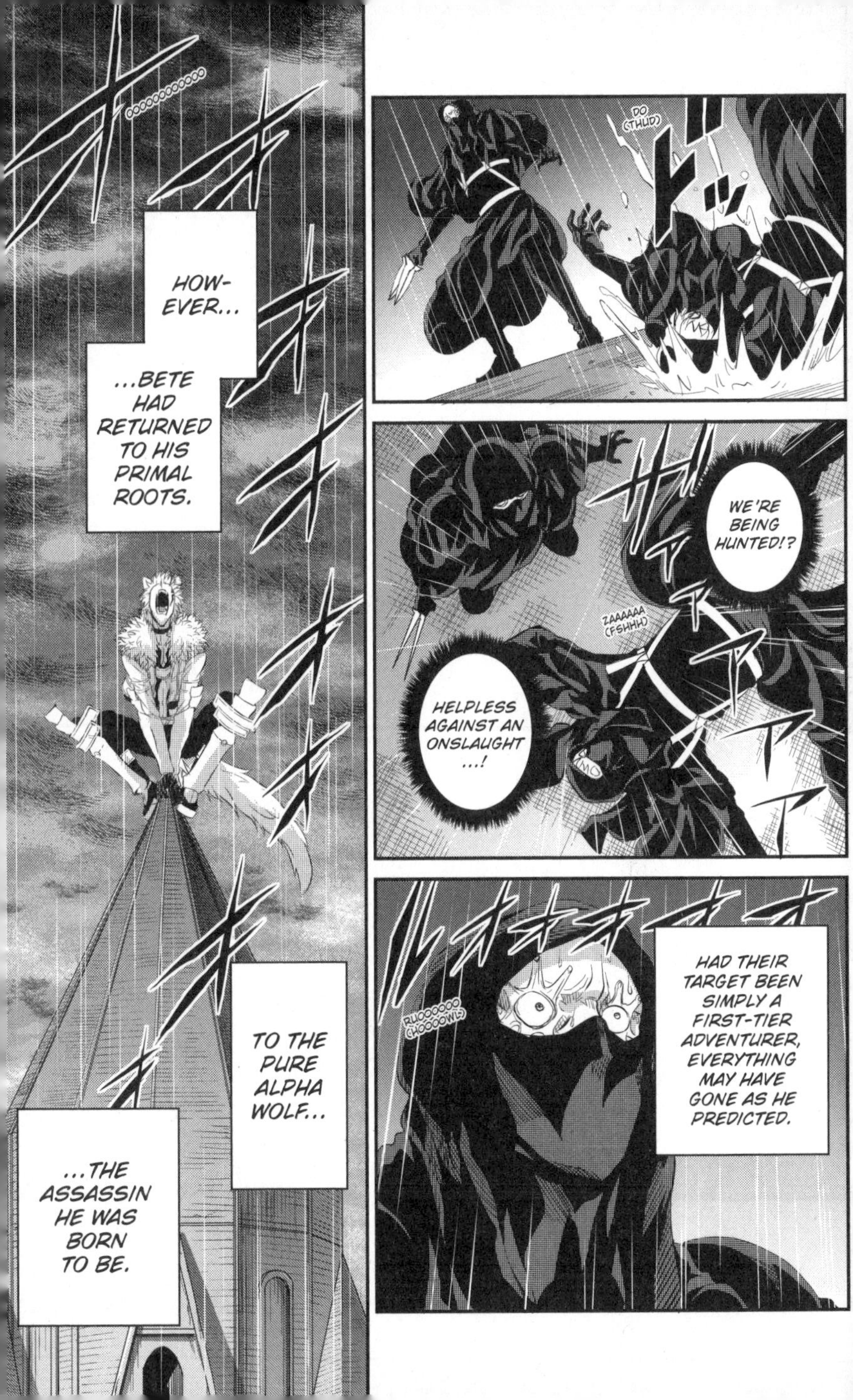
DO (THUD)
WE'RE BEING HUNTED!?
ZAAAAAA (FSHHH)
HELPLESS AGAINST AN ONSLAUGHT ...!
HAD THEIR TARGET BEEN SIMPLY A FIRST-TIER ADVENTURER, EVERYTHING MAY HAVE GONE AS HE PREDICTED.
RUOOOOOO (HOOOOWL)
OOOOOOOOOOOO
HOW-EVER...
...BETE HAD RETURNED TO HIS PRIMAL ROOTS.
TO THE PURE ALPHA WOLF...
...THE ASSASSIN HE WAS BORN TO BE.

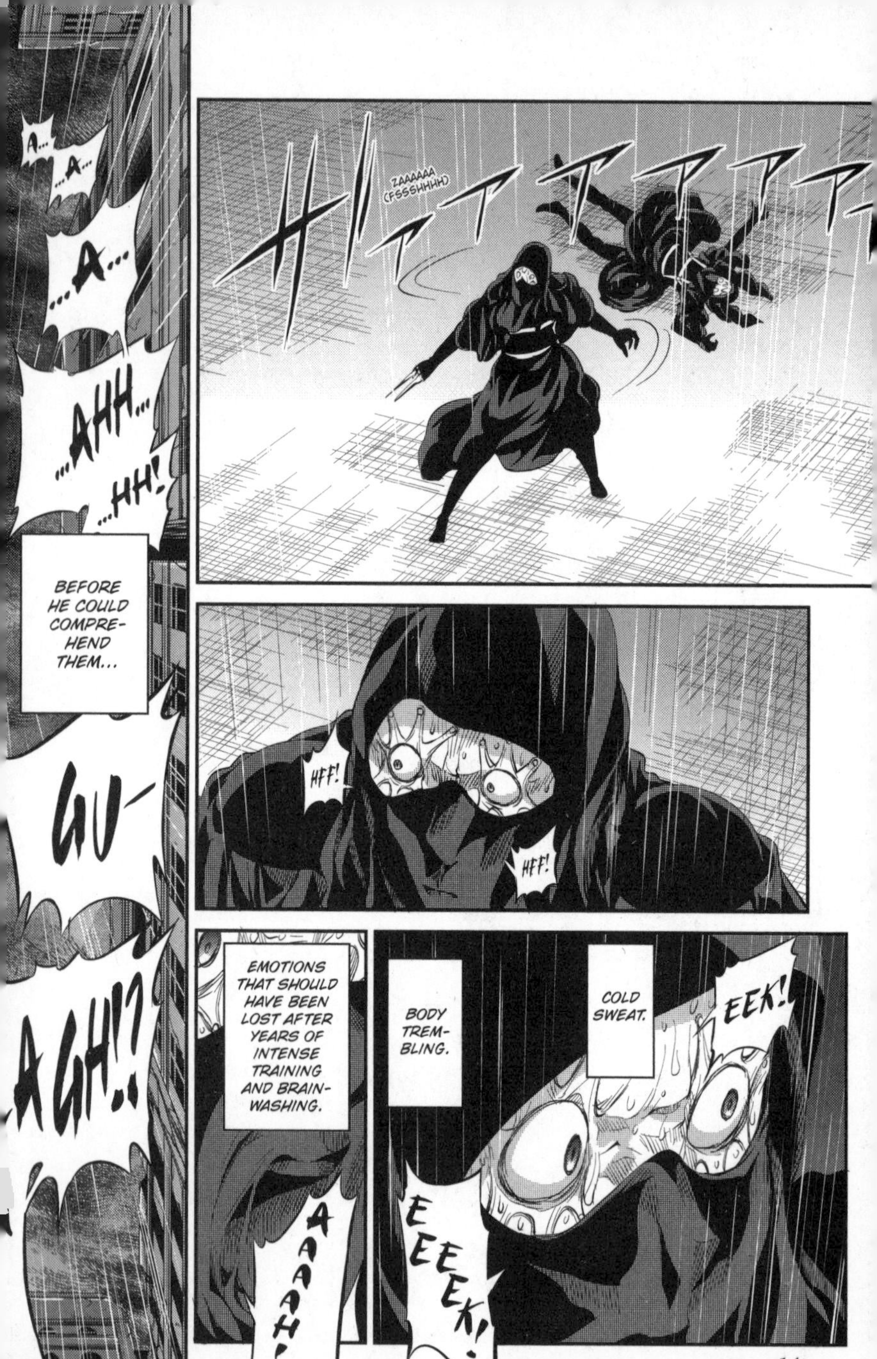
ZAAAAAA (FSSSHHHH)
HFF!
HFF!
COLD SWEAT.
EEK!
BODY TREMBLING.
EEEEK!
EMOTIONS THAT SHOULD HAVE BEEN LOST AFTER YEARS OF INTENSE TRAINING AND BRAIN-WASHING.
AAAAAH!
A... ...A... ...A...
...AHH... ...HH!
BEFORE HE COULD COMPRE-HEND THEM...
GU- ...AGH!?

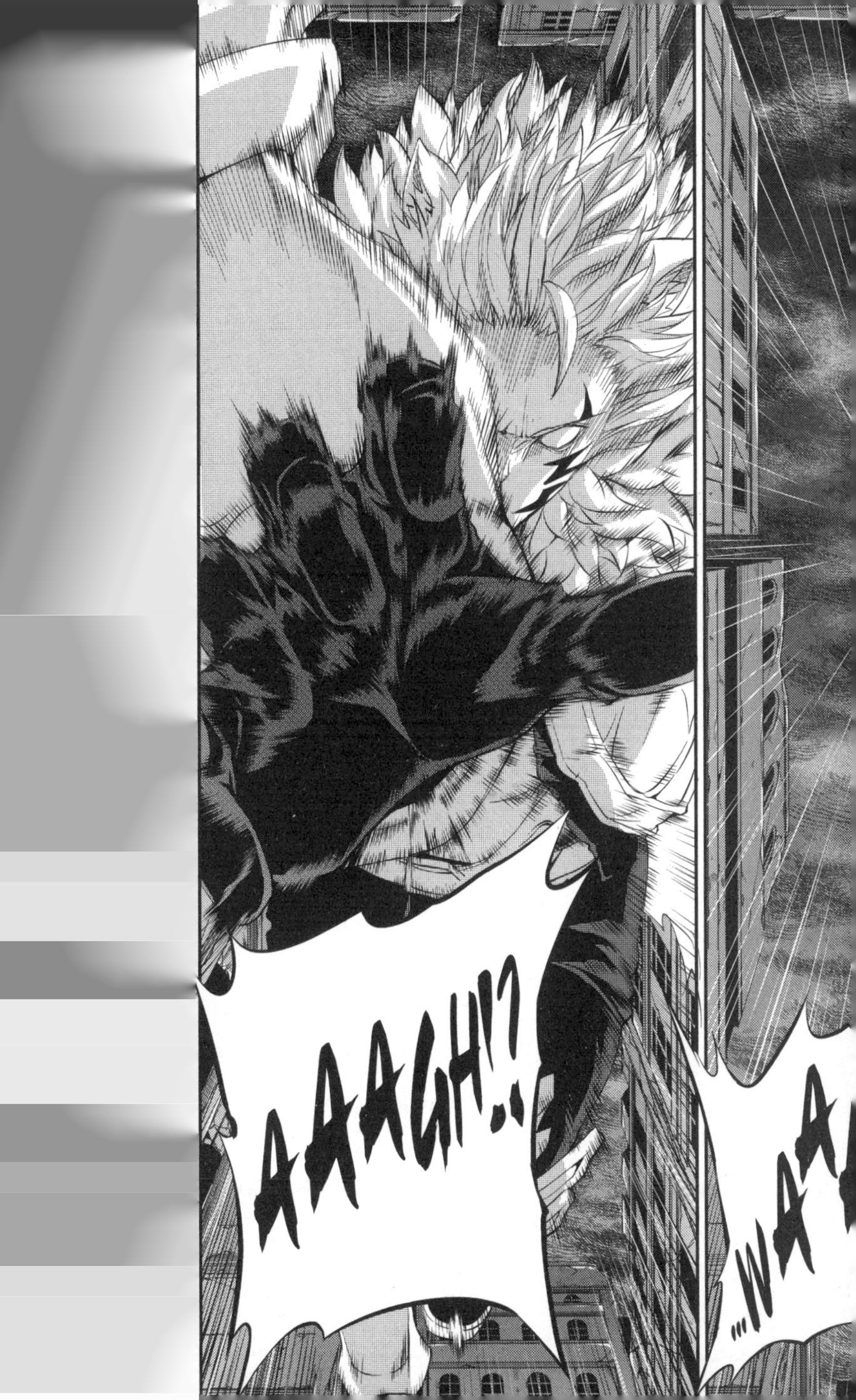
...WAA
AAAGH!?..

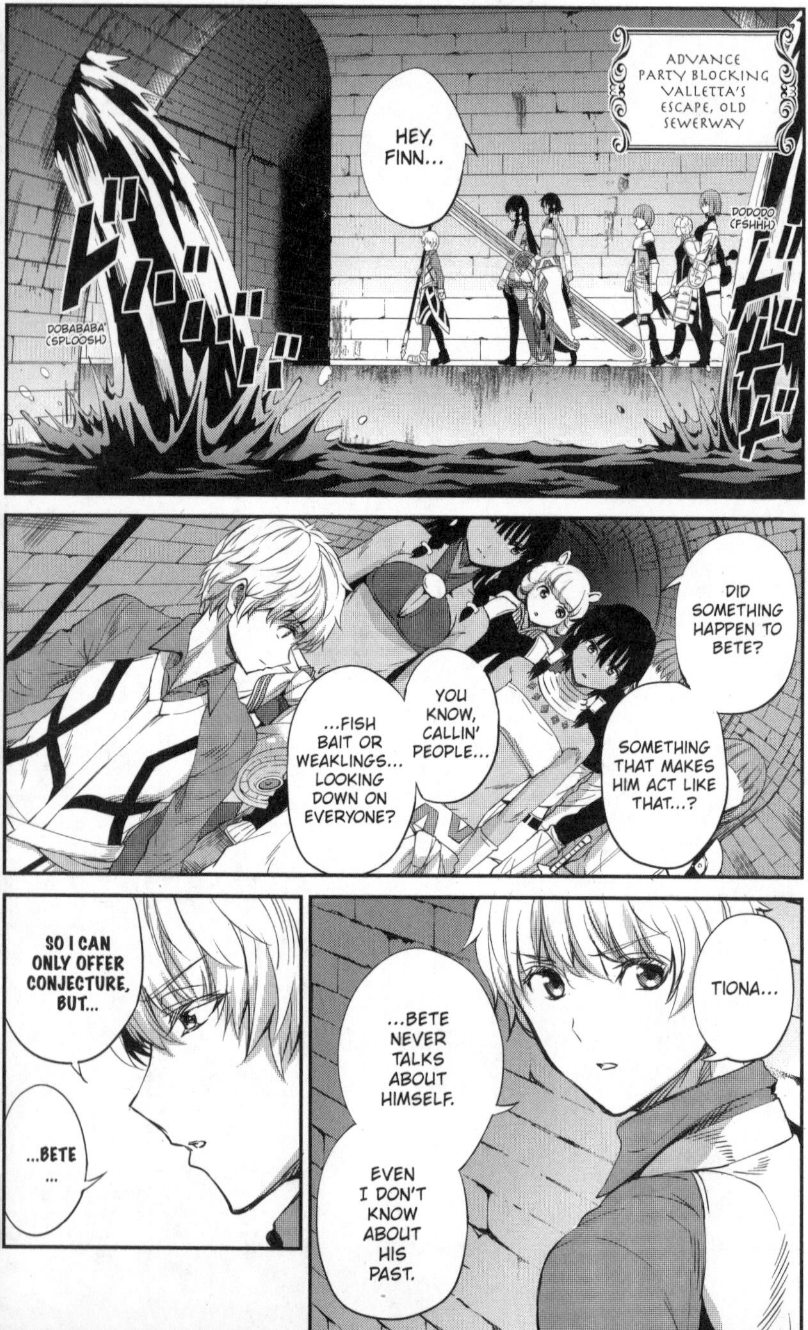
ADVANCE PARTY BLOCKING VALLETTA'S ESCAPE, OLD SEWERWAY
DODODO (FSHHH)
HEY, FINN...
DOBABABA (SPLOOSH)
DID SOMETHING HAPPEN TO BETE?
SOMETHING THAT MAKES HIM ACT LIKE THAT...?
YOU KNOW, CALLIN' PEOPLE...
...FISH BAIT OR WEAKLINGS... LOOKING DOWN ON EVERYONE?
TIONA...
...BETE NEVER TALKS ABOUT HIMSELF.
EVEN I DON'T KNOW ABOUT HIS PAST.
SO I CAN ONLY OFFER CONJECTURE, BUT...
...BETE ...

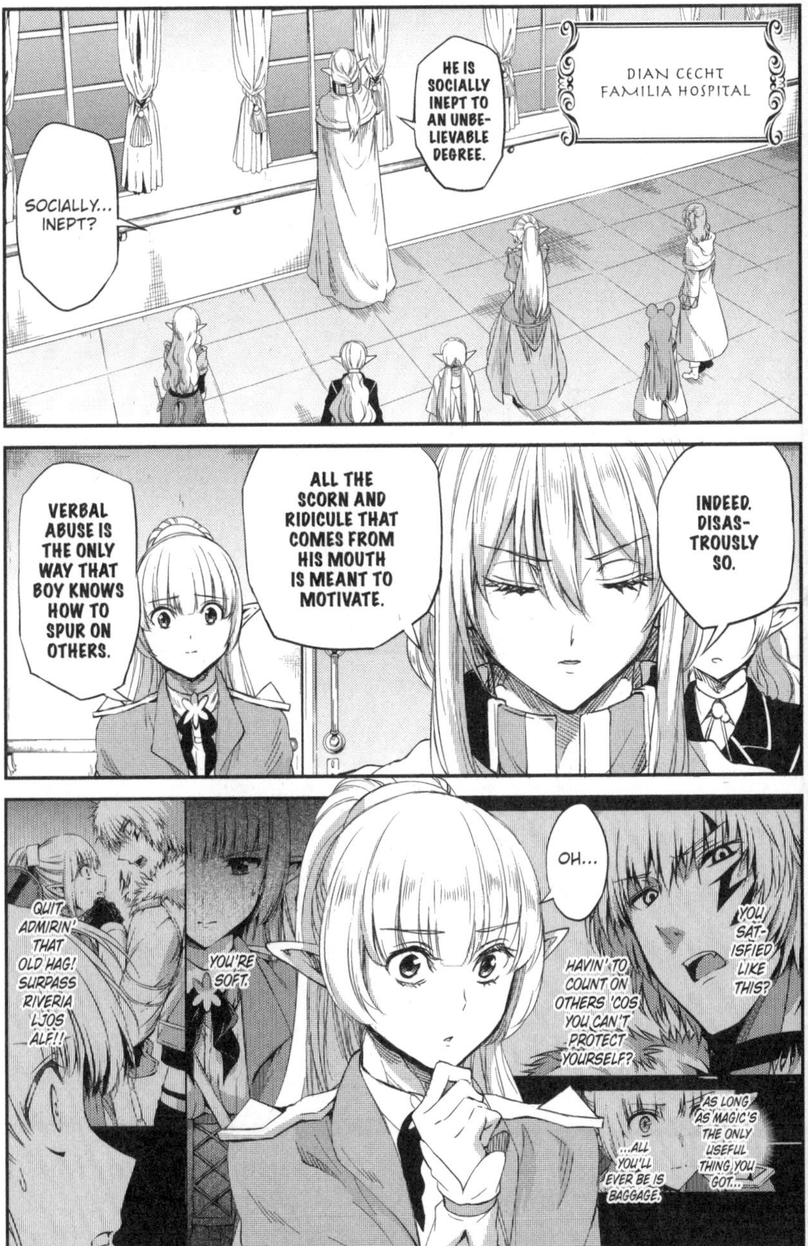
DIAN CECHT FAMILIA HOSPITAL
HE IS SOCIALLY INEPT TO AN UNBELIEVABLE DEGREE.
SOCIALLY... INEPT?
INDEED. DISASTROUSLY SO.
ALL THE SCORN AND RIDICULE THAT COMES FROM HIS MOUTH IS MEANT TO MOTIVATE.
VERBAL ABUSE IS THE ONLY WAY THAT BOY KNOWS HOW TO SPUR ON OTHERS.
OH...
YOU SATISFIED LIKE THIS?
HAVIN' TO COUNT ON OTHERS 'COS YOU CAN'T PROTECT YOURSELF?
AS LONG AS MAGIC'S THE ONLY USEFUL THING YOU GOT...
...ALL YOU'LL EVER BE IS BAGGAGE.
YOU'RE SOFT.
QUIT ADMIRIN' THAT OLD HAG! SURPASS RIVERIA LJOS ALF!!

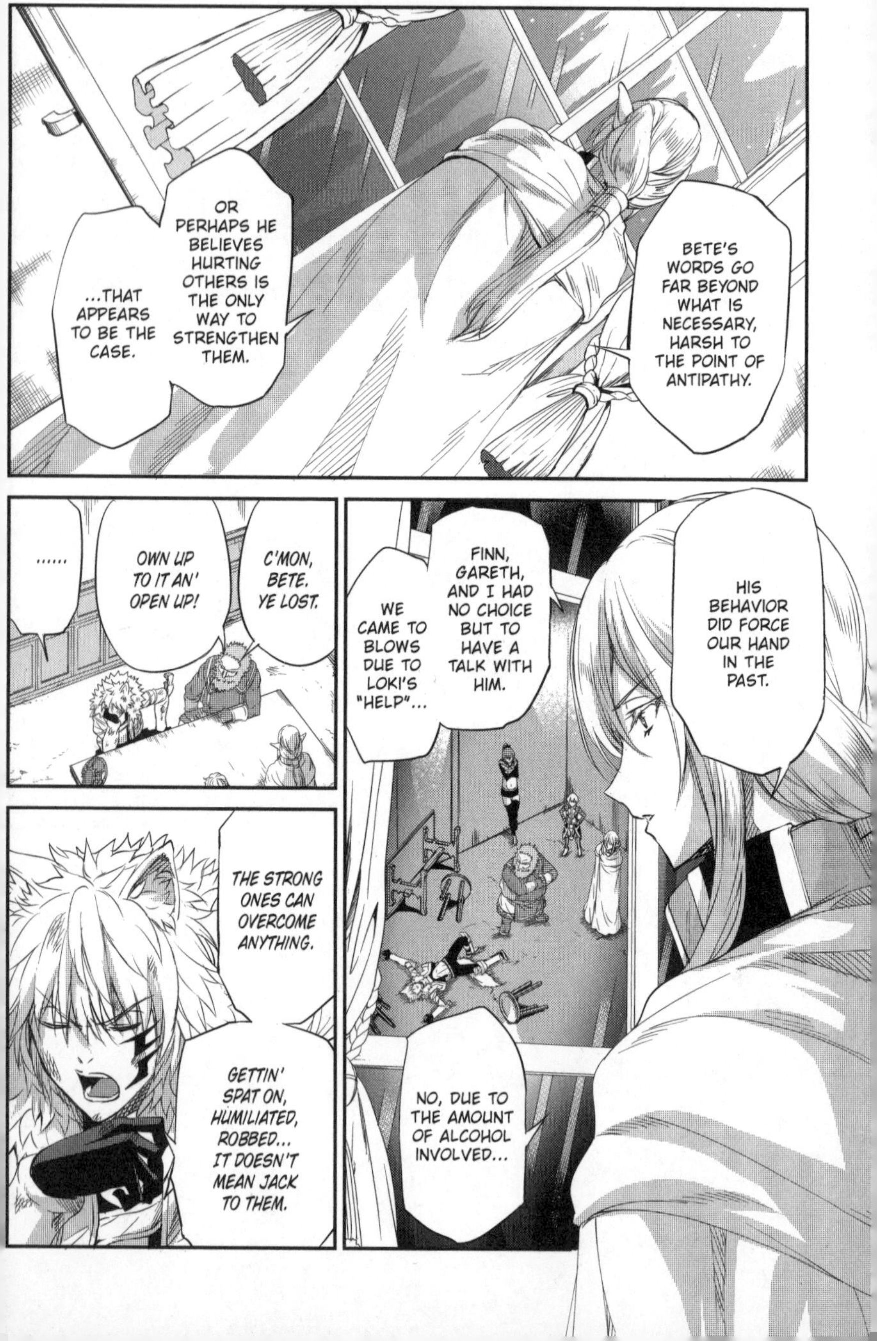
BETE'S WORDS GO FAR BEYOND WHAT IS NECESSARY, HARSH TO THE POINT OF ANTIPATHY.
OR PERHAPS HE BELIEVES HURTING OTHERS IS THE ONLY WAY TO STRENGTHEN THEM.
...THAT APPEARS TO BE THE CASE.
HIS BEHAVIOR DID FORCE OUR HAND IN THE PAST.
FINN, GARETH, AND I HAD NO CHOICE BUT TO HAVE A TALK WITH HIM.
WE CAME TO BLOWS DUE TO LOKI'S "HELP"...
NO, DUE TO THE AMOUNT OF ALCOHOL INVOLVED...
C'MON, BETE. YE LOST.
OWN UP TO IT AN' OPEN UP!
......
THE STRONG ONES CAN OVERCOME ANYTHING.
GETTIN' SPAT ON, HUMILIATED, ROBBED... IT DOESN'T MEAN JACK TO THEM.

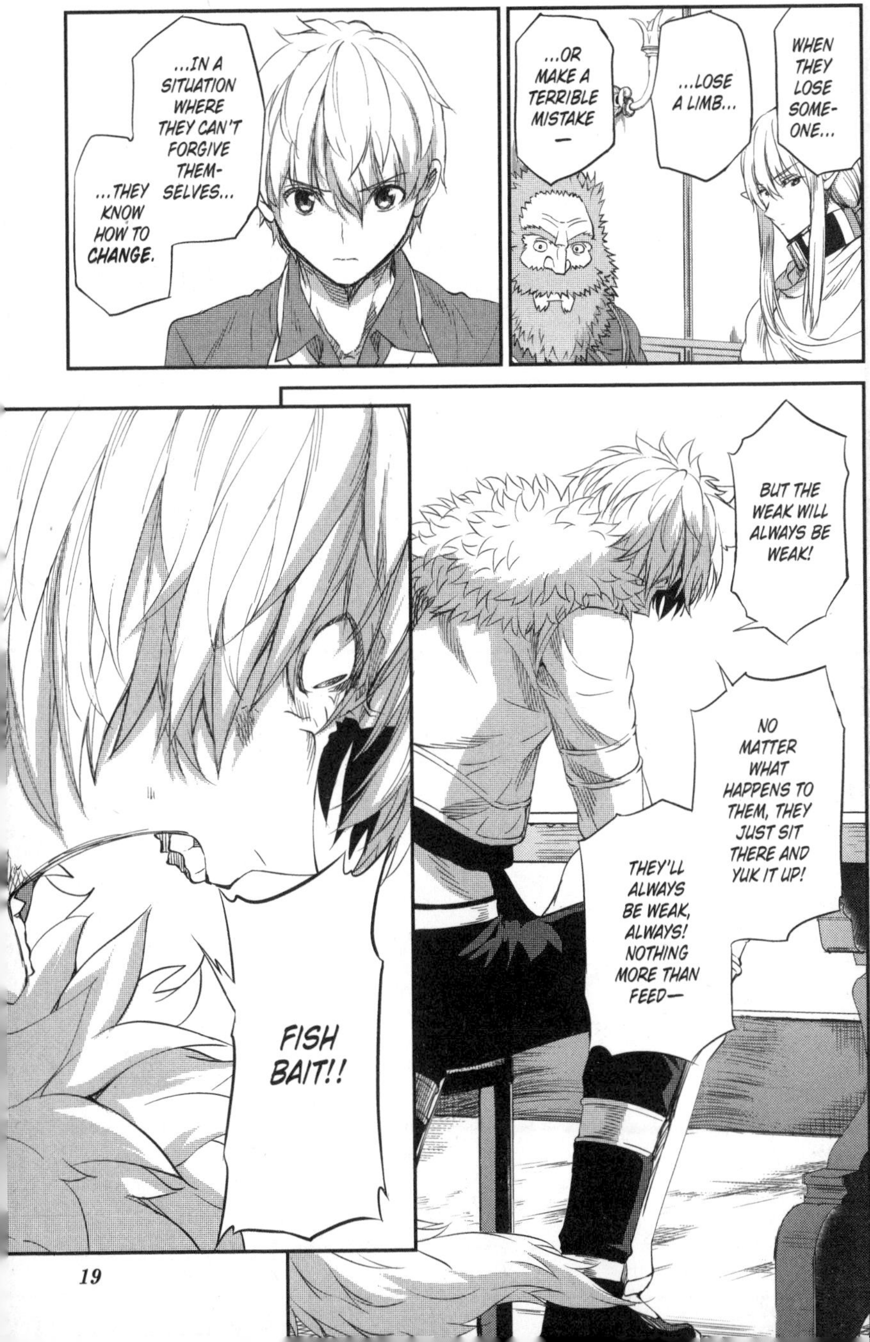
WHEN THEY LOSE SOME-ONE...
...LOSE A LIMB...
...OR MAKE A TERRIBLE MISTAKE —
...IN A SITUATION WHERE THEY CAN'T FORGIVE THEM-SELVES...
...THEY KNOW HOW TO CHANGE.
BUT THE WEAK WILL ALWAYS BE WEAK!
NO MATTER WHAT HAPPENS TO THEM, THEY JUST SIT THERE AND YUK IT UP!
THEY'LL ALWAYS BE WEAK, ALWAYS! NOTHING MORE THAN FEED—
FISH BAIT!!

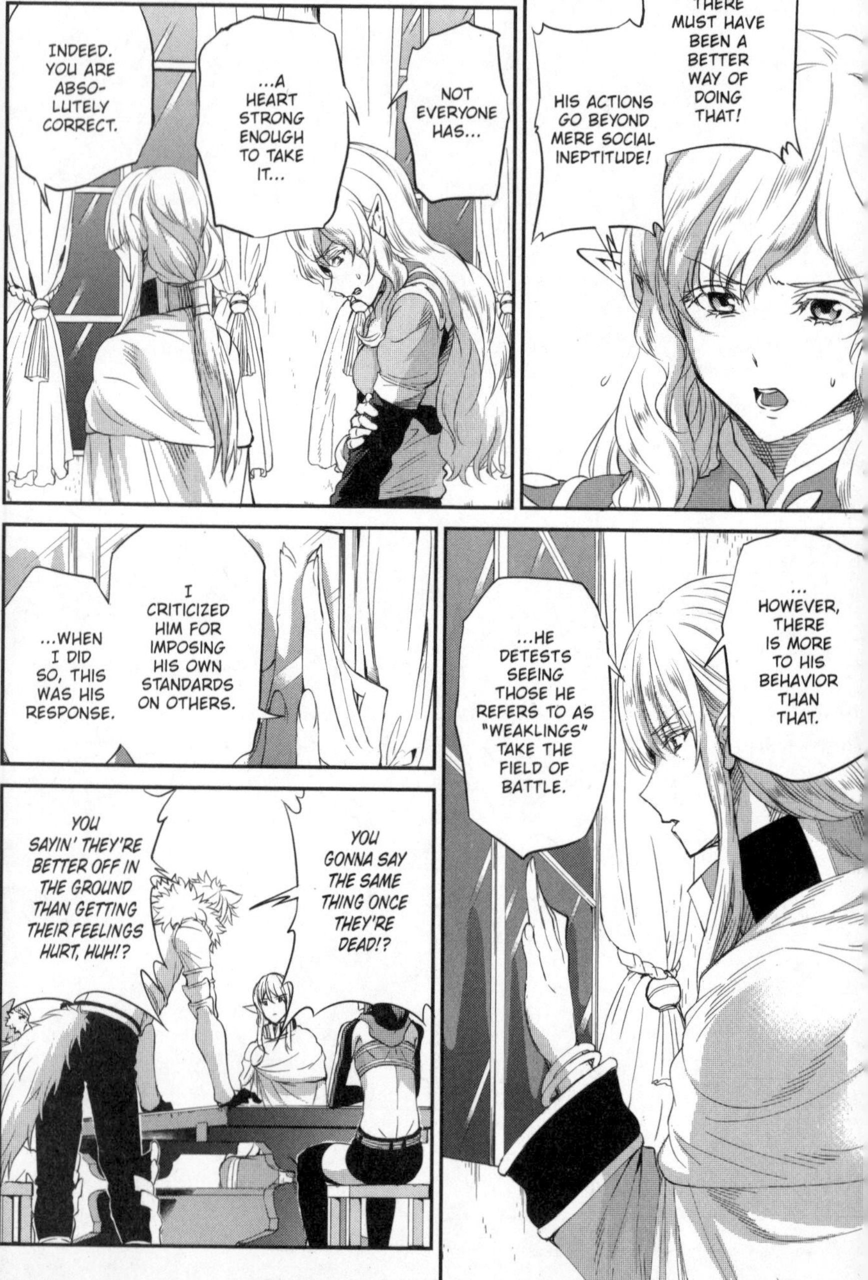
...BUT THERE MUST HAVE BEEN A BETTER WAY OF DOING THAT!
HIS ACTIONS GO BEYOND MERE SOCIAL INEPTITUDE!
NOT EVERYONE HAS...
...A HEART STRONG ENOUGH TO TAKE IT...
INDEED. YOU ARE ABSO-LUTELY CORRECT.
... HOWEVER, THERE IS MORE TO HIS BEHAVIOR THAN THAT.
...HE DETESTS SEEING THOSE HE REFERS TO AS "WEAKLINGS" TAKE THE FIELD OF BATTLE.
I CRITICIZED HIM FOR IMPOSING HIS OWN STANDARDS ON OTHERS.
...WHEN I DID SO, THIS WAS HIS RESPONSE.
YOU GONNA SAY THE SAME THING ONCE THEY'RE DEAD!?
YOU SAYIN' THEY'RE BETTER OFF IN THE GROUND THAN GETTING THEIR FEELINGS HURT, HUH!?

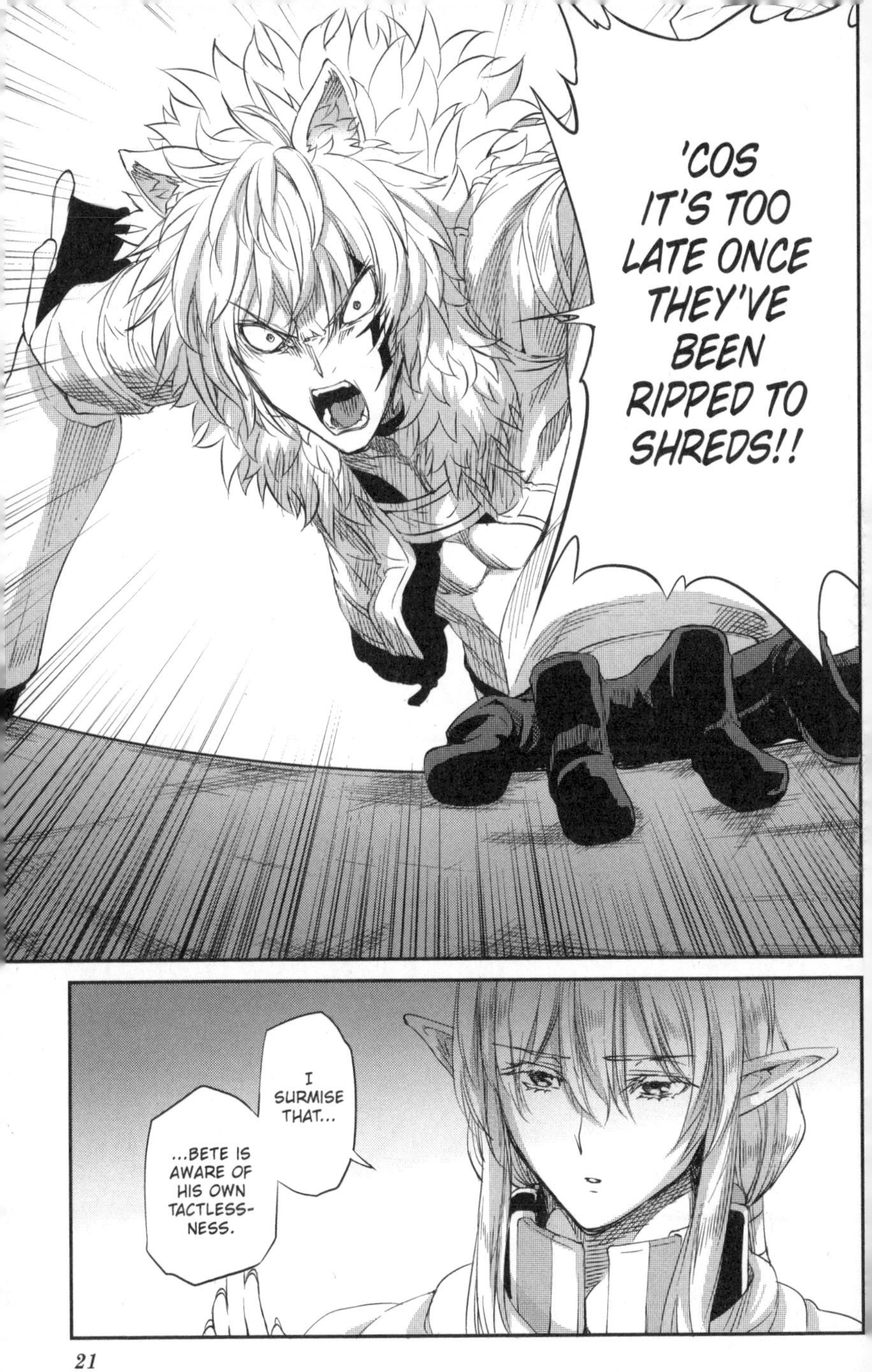
'COS IT'S TOO LATE ONCE THEY'VE BEEN RIPPED TO SHREDS!!
I SURMISE THAT...
...BETE IS AWARE OF HIS OWN TACTLESS-NESS.

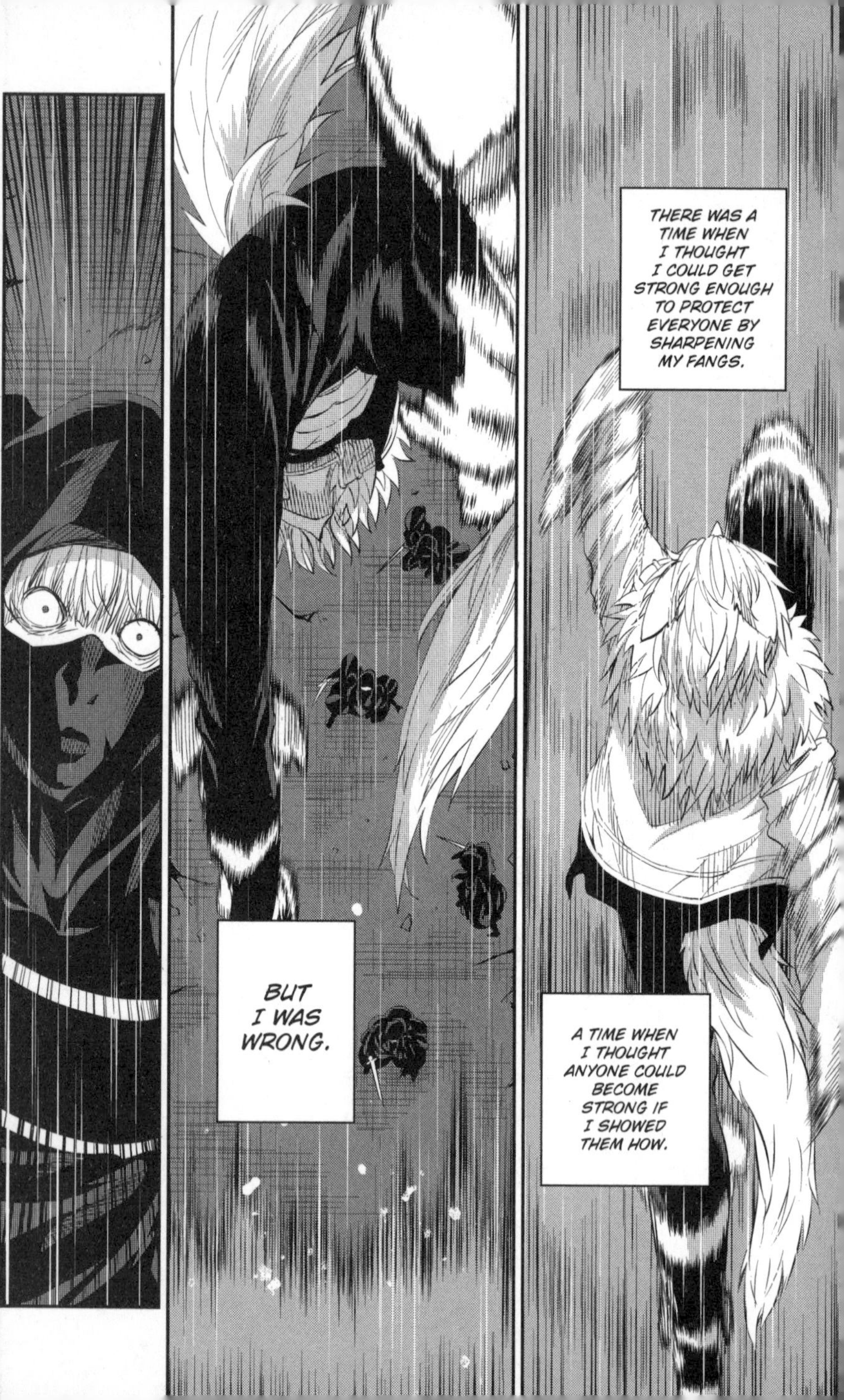
THERE WAS A TIME WHEN I THOUGHT I COULD GET STRONG ENOUGH TO PROTECT EVERYONE BY SHARPENING MY FANGS.
A TIME WHEN I THOUGHT ANYONE COULD BECOME STRONG IF I SHOWED THEM HOW.
BUT I WAS WRONG.

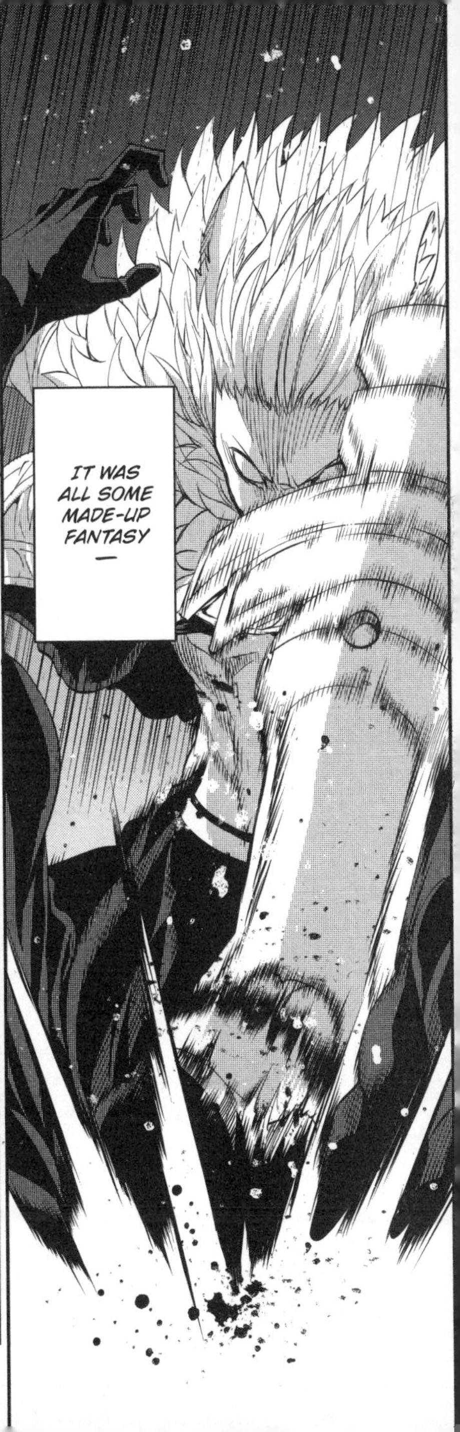
IT WAS ALL SOME MADE-UP FANTASY
—

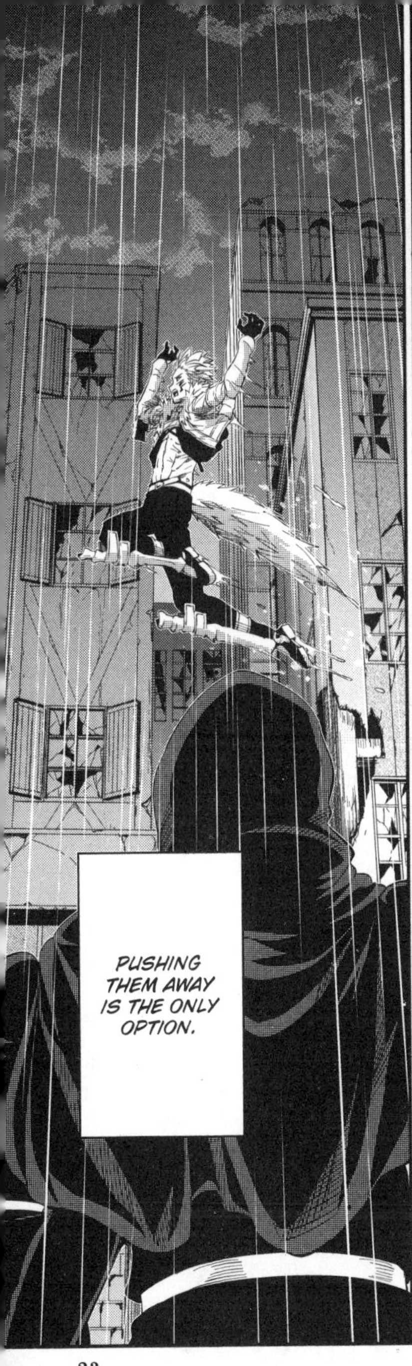
PUSHING THEM AWAY IS THE ONLY OPTION.

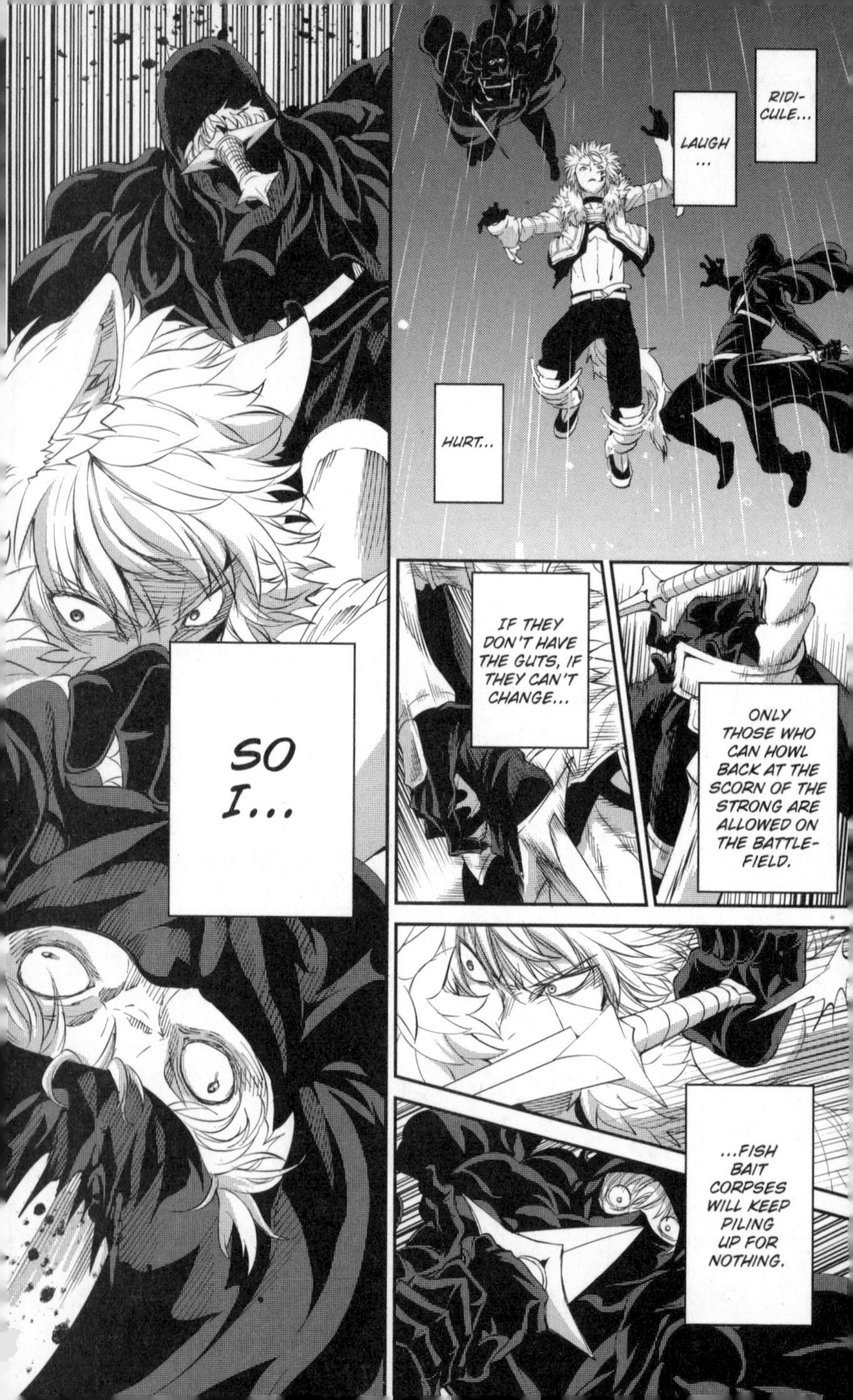
RIDI-CULE...
LAUGH...
HURT...
ONLY THOSE WHO CAN HOWL BACK AT THE SCORN OF THE STRONG ARE ALLOWED ON THE BATTLE-FIELD.
IF THEY DON'T HAVE THE GUTS, IF THEY CAN'T CHANGE...
...FISH BAIT CORPSES WILL KEEP PILING UP FOR NOTHING.
SO I...

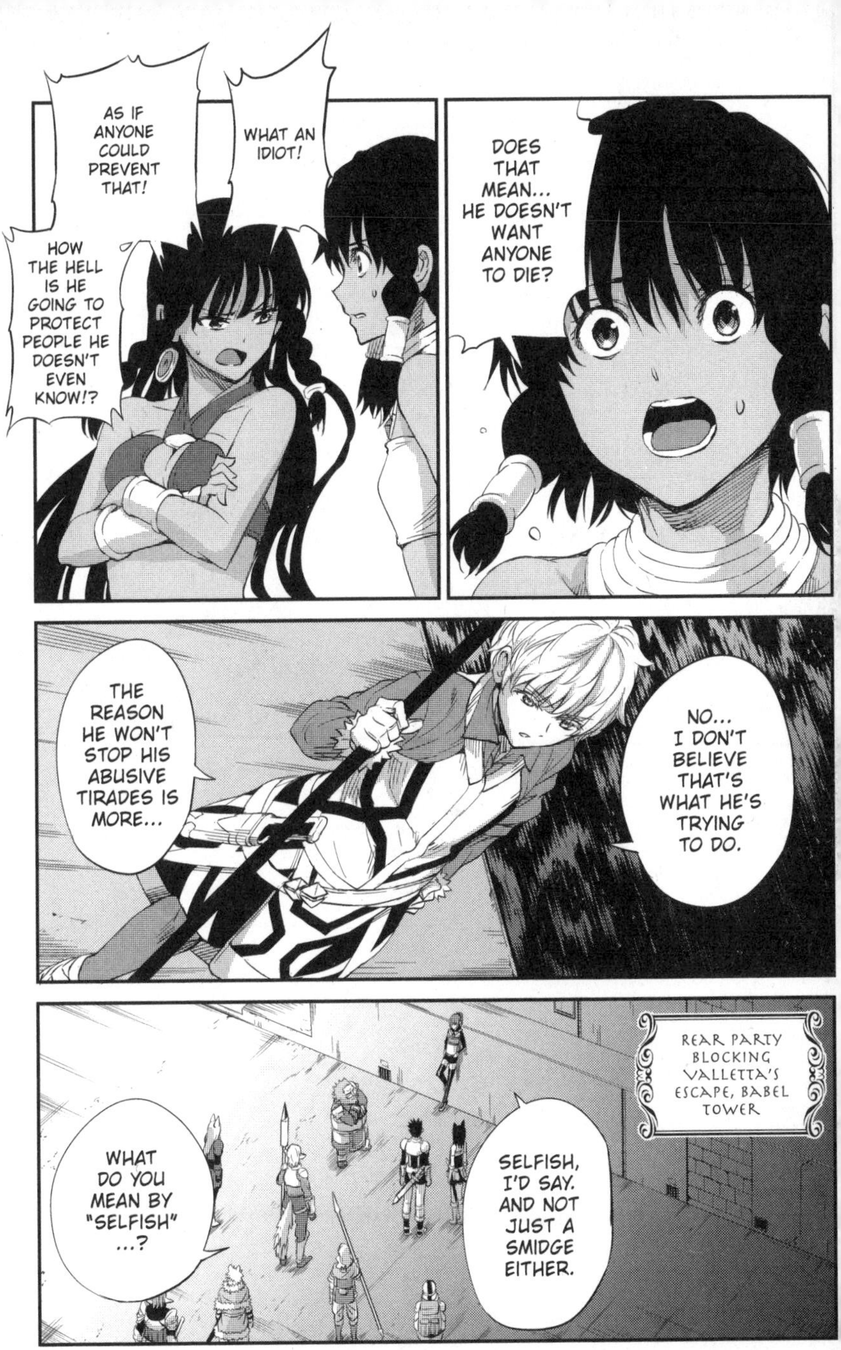
DOES THAT MEAN... HE DOESN'T WANT ANYONE TO DIE?
WHAT AN IDIOT!
AS IF ANYONE COULD PREVENT THAT!
HOW THE HELL IS HE GOING TO PROTECT PEOPLE HE DOESN'T EVEN KNOW!?
NO... I DON'T BELIEVE THAT'S WHAT HE'S TRYING TO DO.
THE REASON HE WON'T STOP HIS ABUSIVE TIRADES IS MORE...
REAR PARTY BLOCKING VALLETTA'S ESCAPE, BABEL TOWER
SELFISH, I'D SAY. AND NOT JUST A SMIDGE EITHER.
WHAT DO YOU MEAN BY "SELFISH" ...?

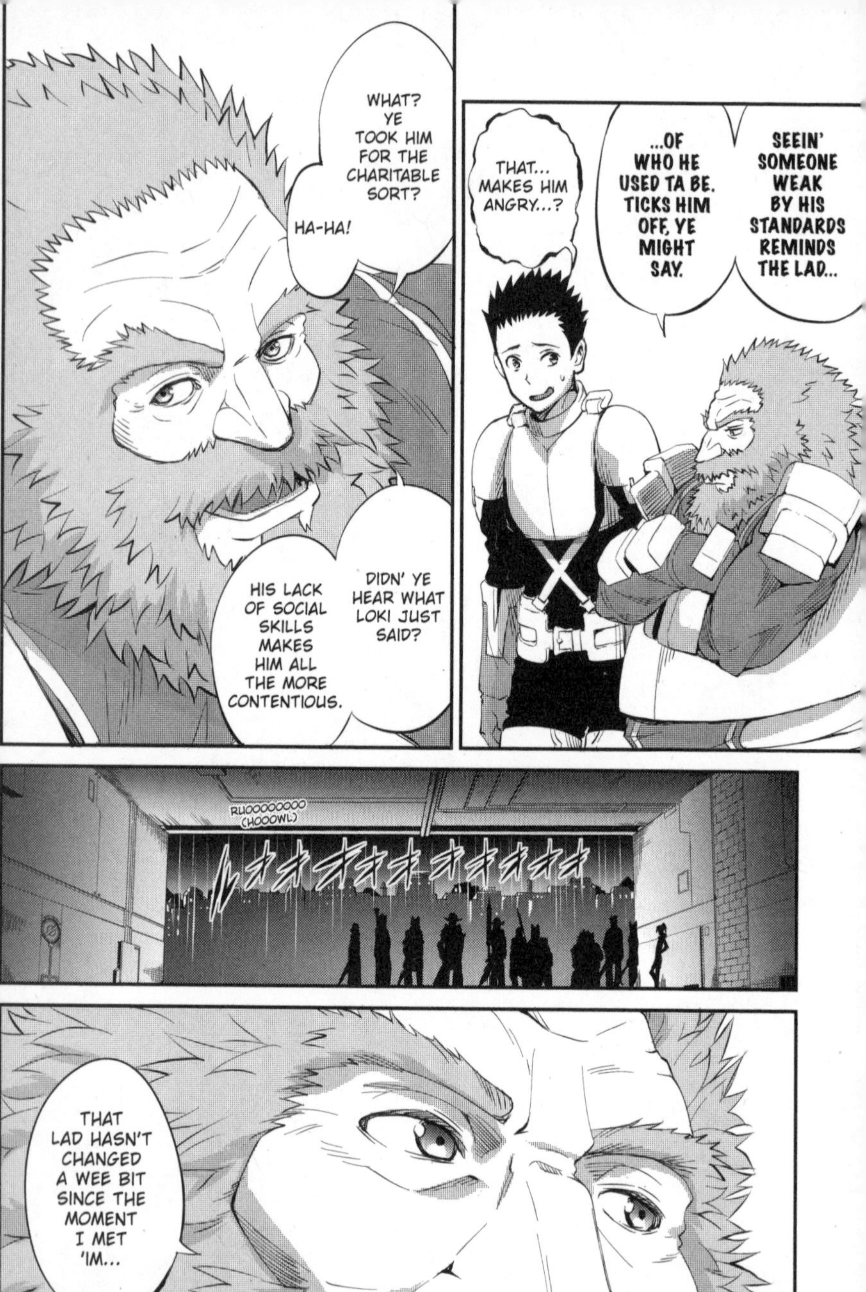

SEEIN' SOMEONE WEAK BY HIS STANDARDS REMINDS THE LAD...
...OF WHO HE USED TA BE. TICKS HIM OFF, YE MIGHT SAY.
THAT... MAKES HIM ANGRY...?
WHAT? YE TOOK HIM FOR THE CHARITABLE SORT?
HA-HA!
DIDN' YE HEAR WHAT LOKI JUST SAID?
HIS LACK OF SOCIAL SKILLS MAKES HIM ALL THE MORE CONTENTIOUS.
RUOOOOOOOO (HOOOWL)
THAT LAD HASN'T CHANGED A WEE BIT SINCE THE MOMENT I MET 'IM...

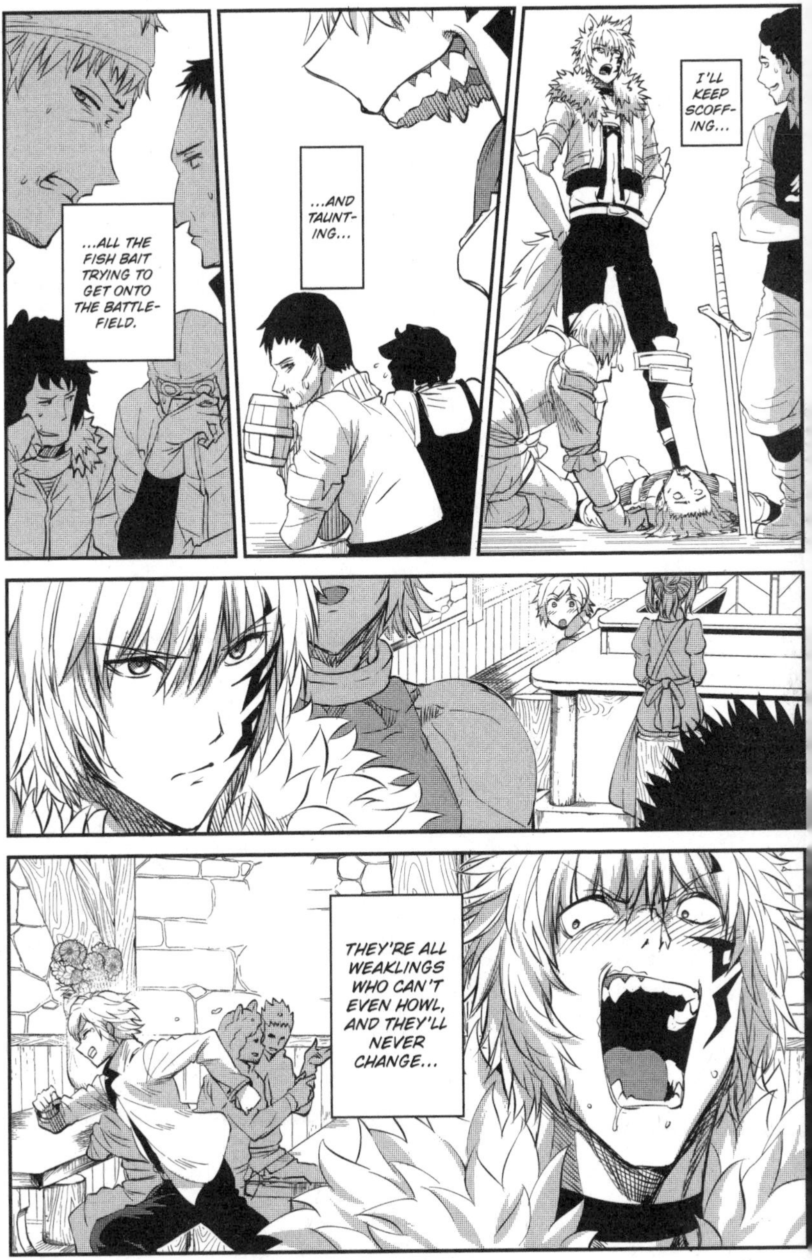

I'LL KEEP SCOFF-ING...
...AND TAUNT-ING...
...ALL THE FISH BAIT TRYING TO GET ONTO THE BATTLE-FIELD.
THEY'RE ALL WEAKLINGS WHO CAN'T EVEN HOWL, AND THEY'LL NEVER CHANGE...

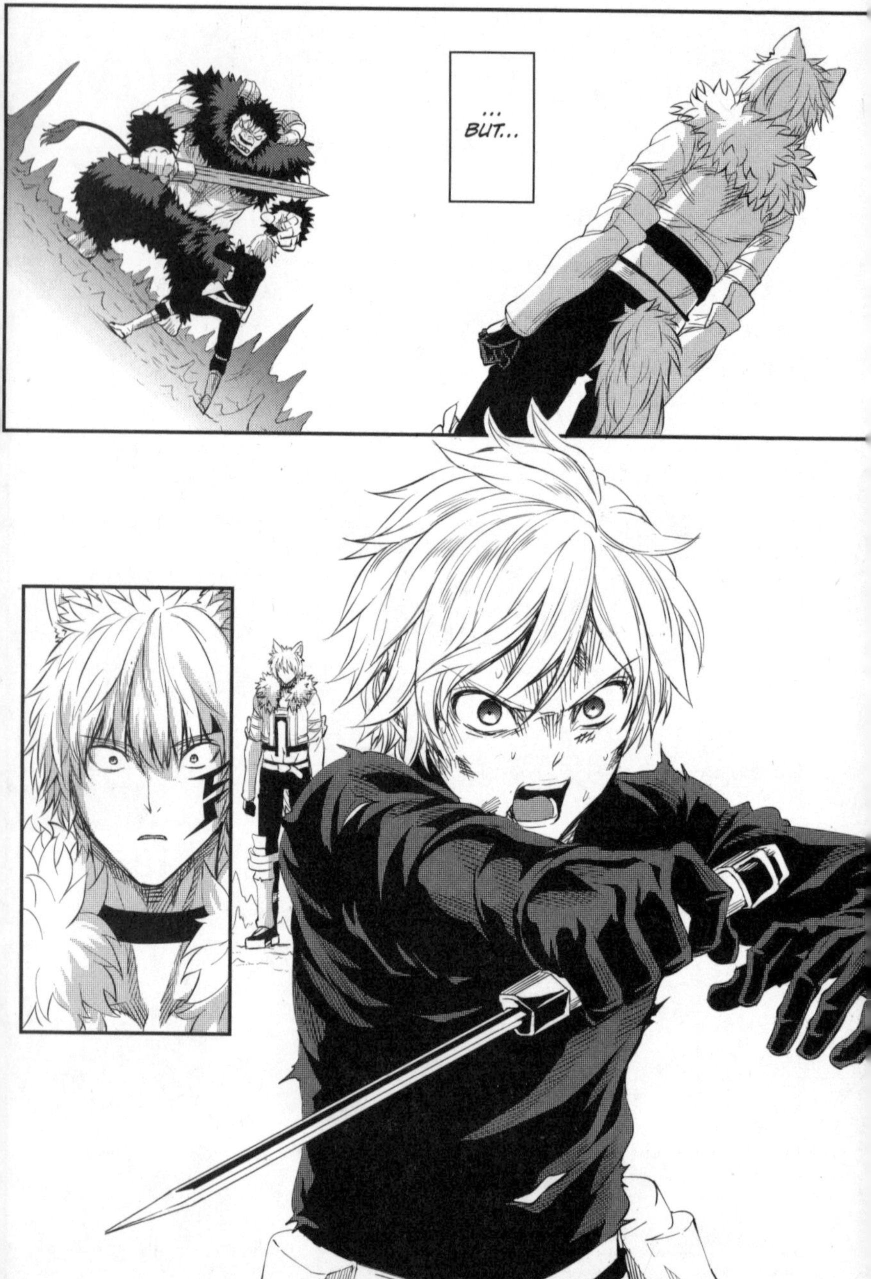
...BUT...

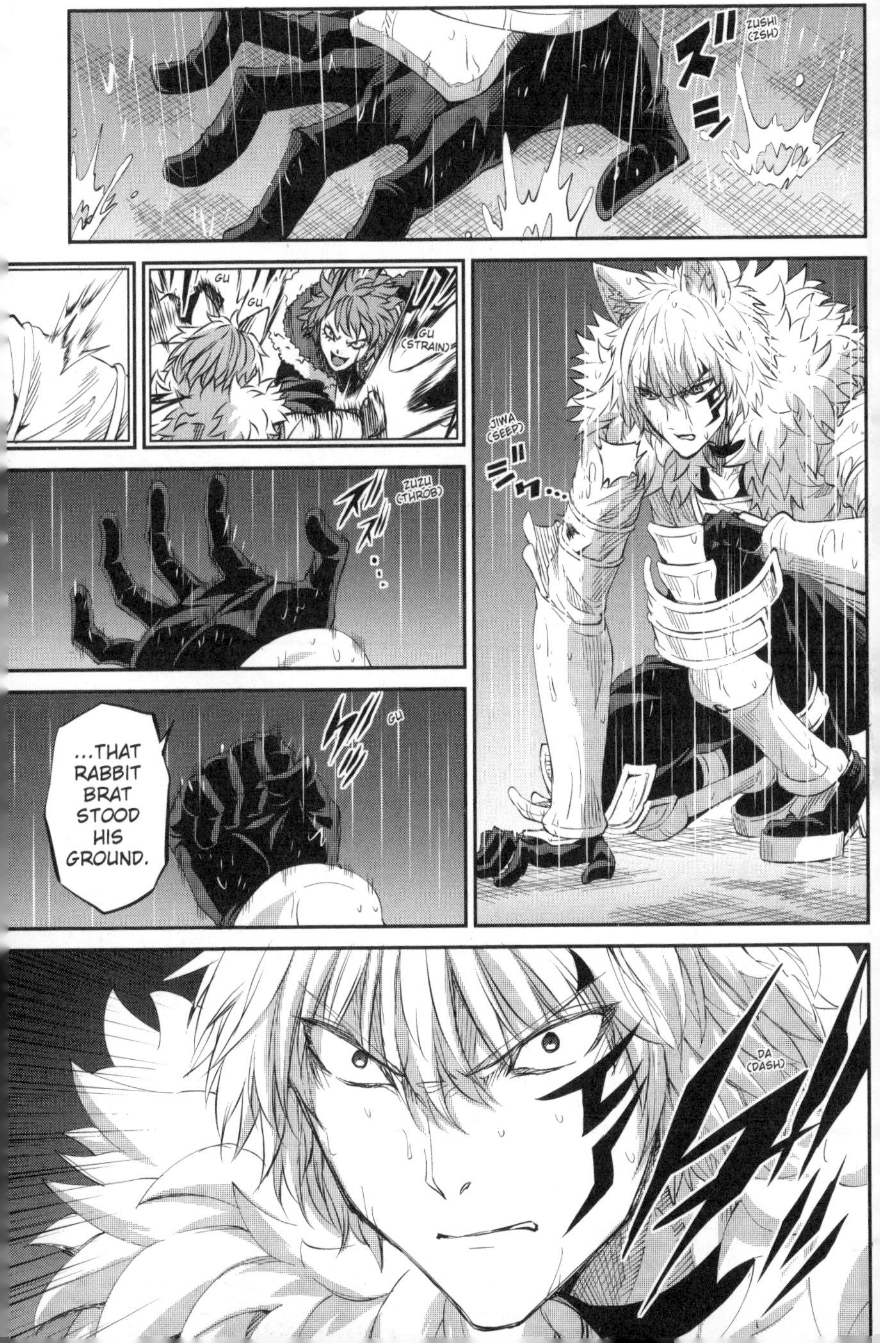
ZUSHI (ZSH)
JIWA (SEEP)
GU
GU
GU (STRAIN)
ZUZU (THROB)
...THAT RABBIT BRAT STOOD HIS GROUND.
GU
DA (DASH)

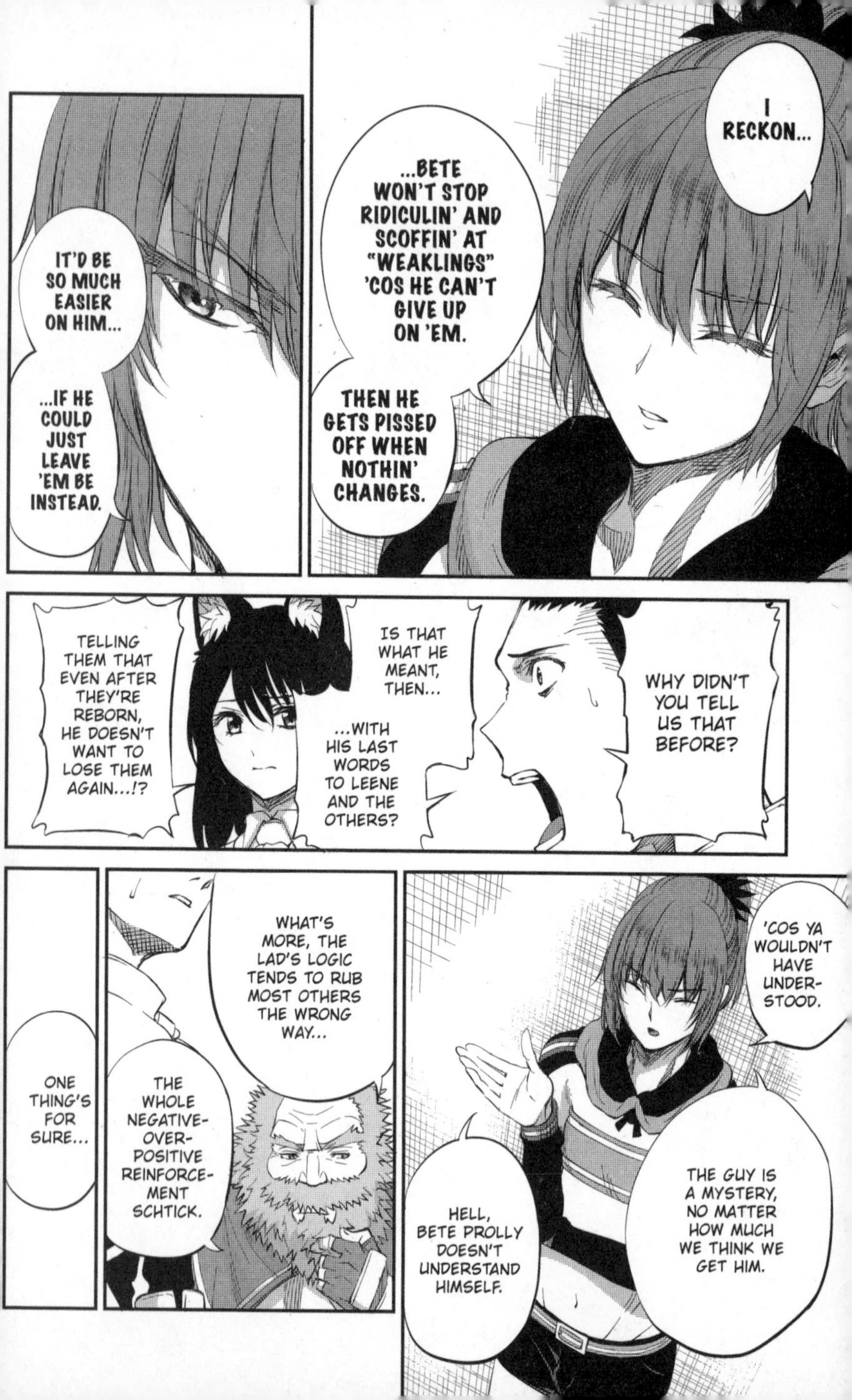
I RECKON...
...BETE WON'T STOP RIDICULIN' AND SCOFFIN' AT "WEAKLINGS" 'COS HE CAN'T GIVE UP ON 'EM.
THEN HE GETS PISSED OFF WHEN NOTHIN' CHANGES.
IT'D BE SO MUCH EASIER ON HIM...
...IF HE COULD JUST LEAVE 'EM BE INSTEAD.
WHY DIDN'T YOU TELL US THAT BEFORE?
IS THAT WHAT HE MEANT, THEN...
...WITH HIS LAST WORDS TO LEENE AND THE OTHERS?
TELLING THEM THAT EVEN AFTER THEY'RE REBORN, HE DOESN'T WANT TO LOSE THEM AGAIN...!?
'COS YA WOULDN'T HAVE UNDER-STOOD.
THE GUY IS A MYSTERY, NO MATTER HOW MUCH WE THINK WE GET HIM.
HELL, BETE PROLLY DOESN'T UNDERSTAND HIMSELF.
WHAT'S MORE, THE LAD'S LOGIC TENDS TO RUB MOST OTHERS THE WRONG WAY...
THE WHOLE NEGATIVE-OVER-POSITIVE REINFORCEMENT-MENT SCHTICK.
ONE THING'S FOR SURE...

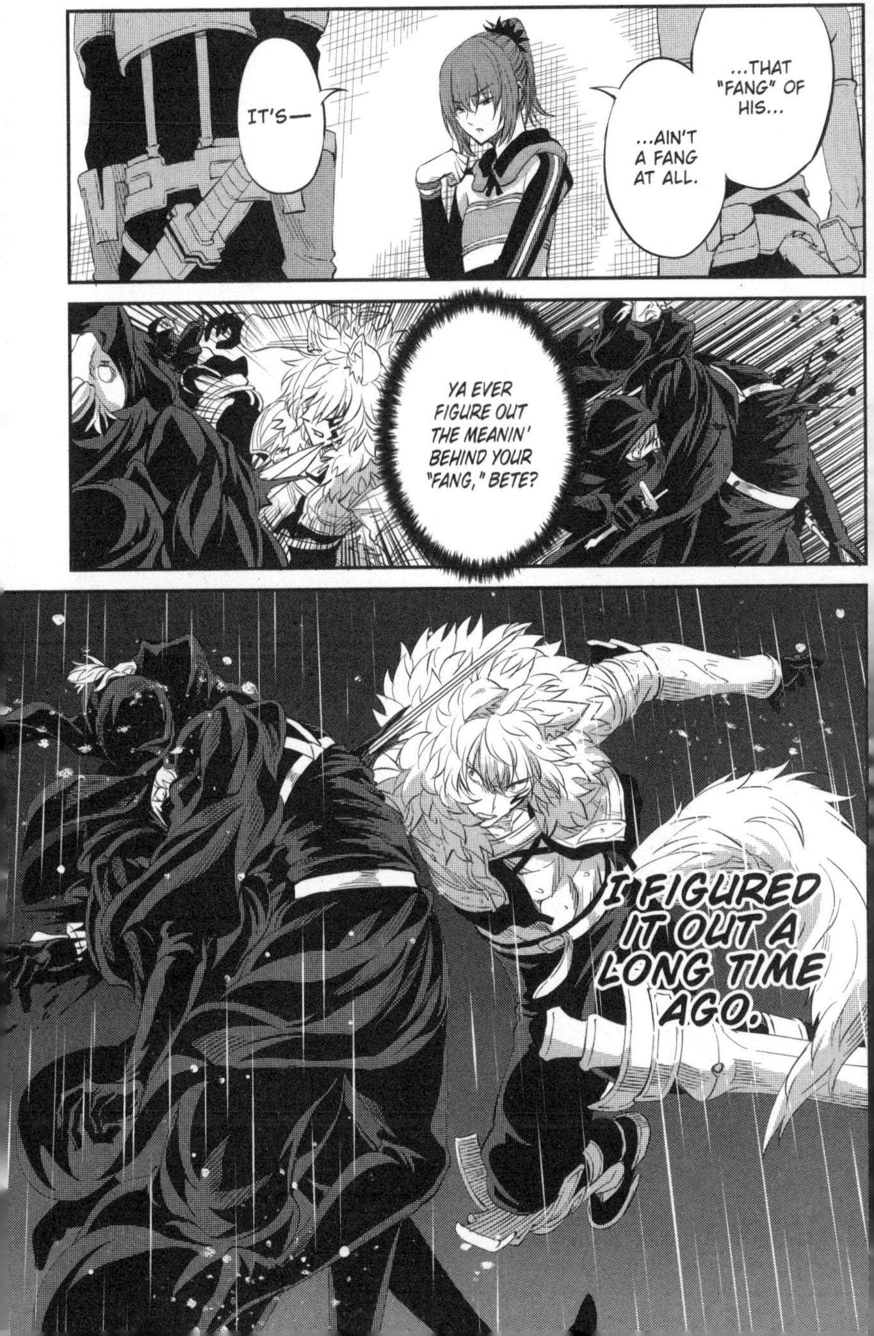
...THAT "FANG" OF HIS...
...AIN'T A FANG AT ALL.
IT'S—
YA EVER FIGURE OUT THE MEANIN' BEHIND YOUR "FANG," BETE?
I FIGURED IT OUT A LONG TIME AGO.

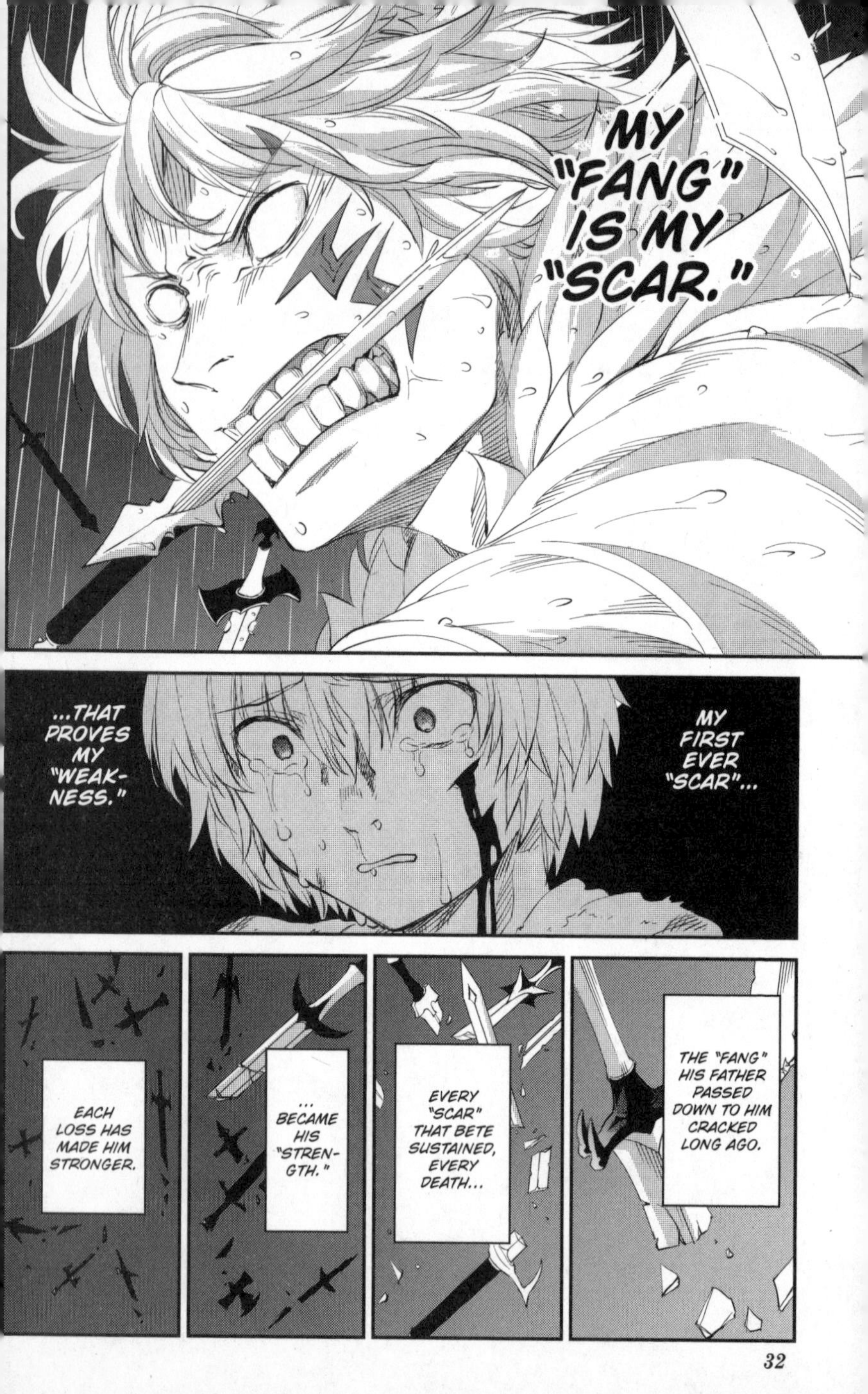
MY "FANG" IS MY "SCAR."
MY FIRST EVER "SCAR"...
...THAT PROVES MY "WEAK-NESS."
THE "FANG" HIS FATHER PASSED DOWN TO HIM CRACKED LONG AGO.
EVERY "SCAR" THAT BETE SUSTAINED, EVERY DEATH...
...BECAME HIS "STREN-GTH."
EACH LOSS HAS MADE HIM STRONGER.

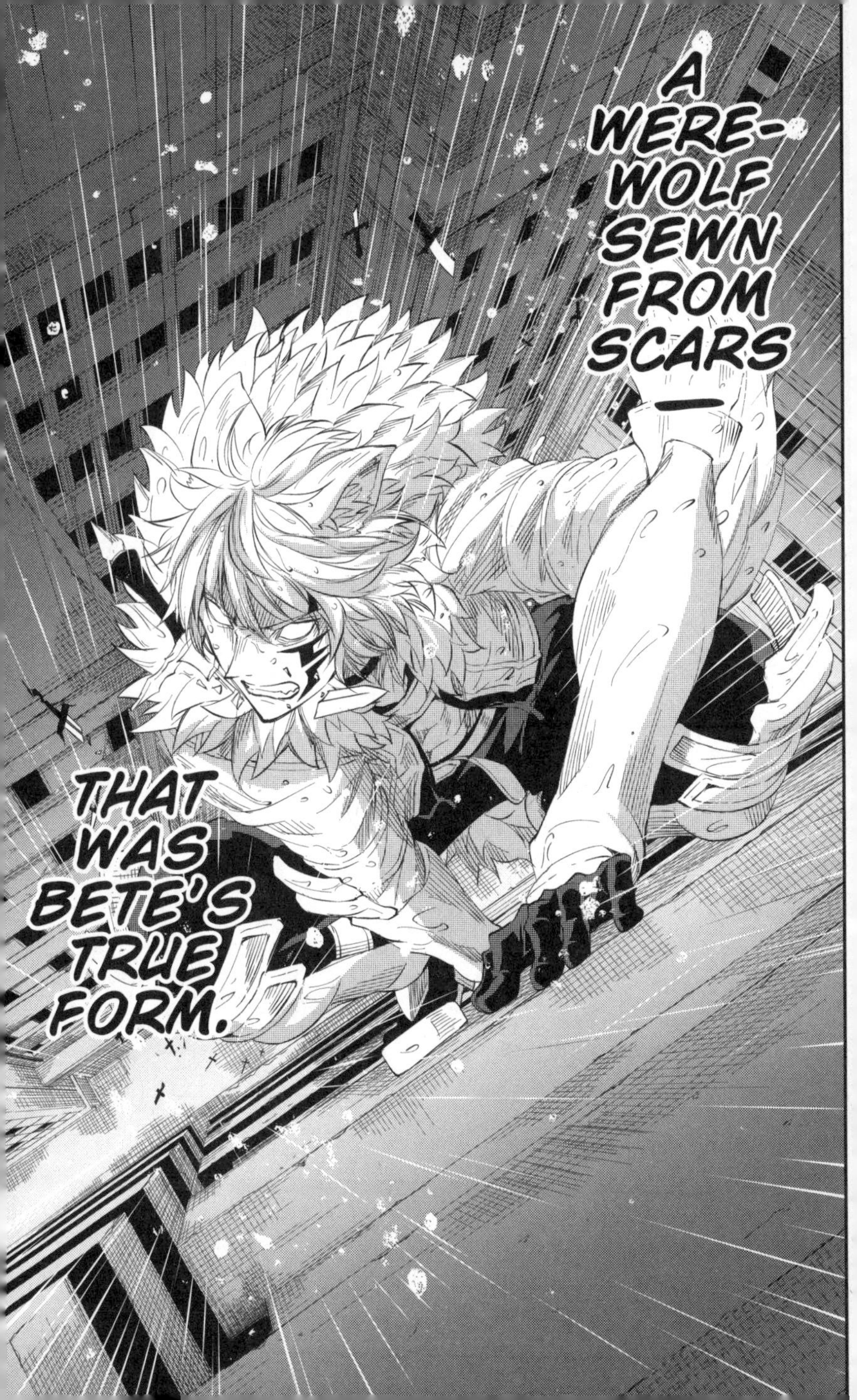
A WERE-WOLF SEWN FROM SCARS—
THAT WAS BETE'S TRUE FORM.

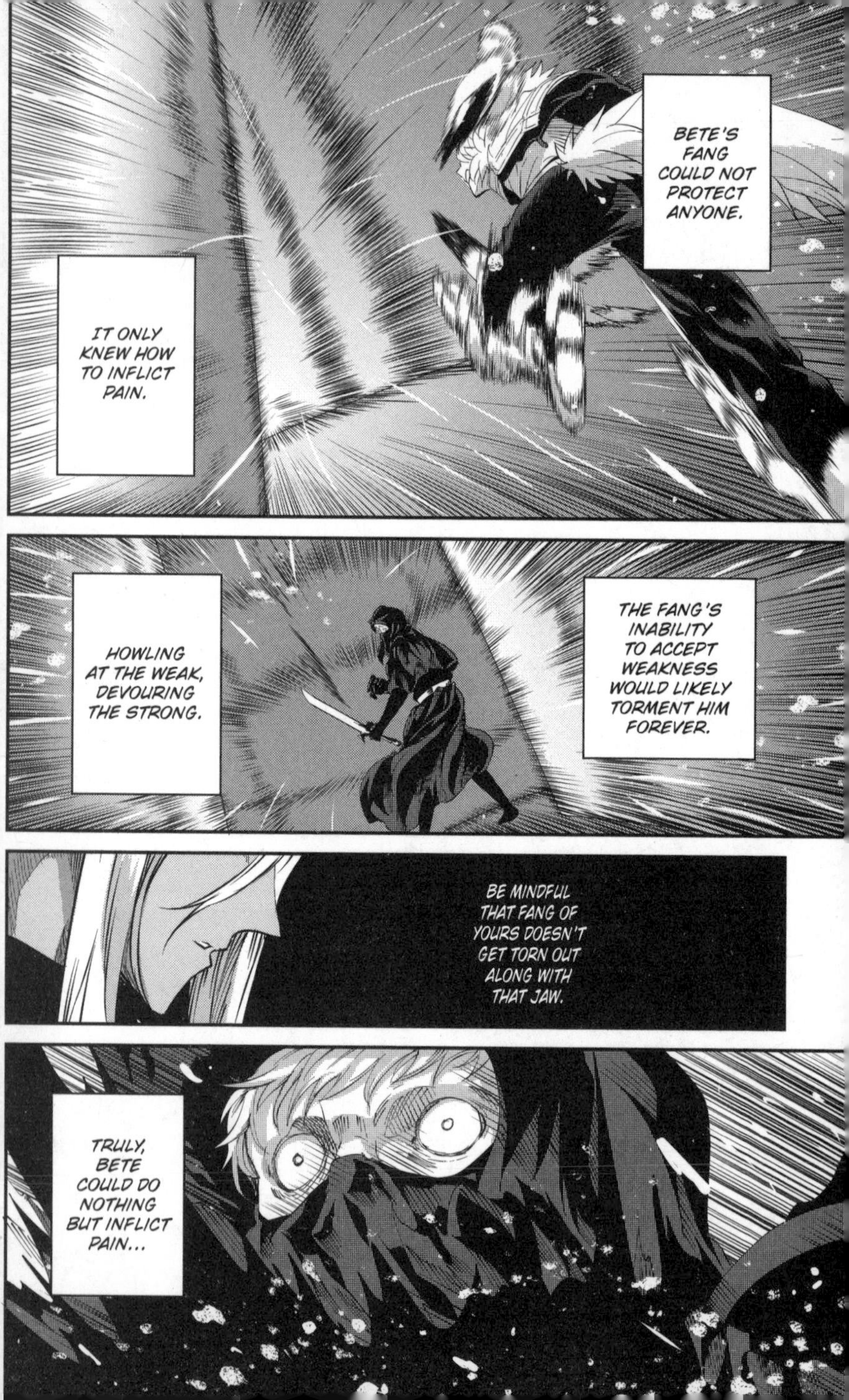
BETE'S FANG COULD NOT PROTECT ANYONE.
IT ONLY KNEW HOW TO INFLICT PAIN.
THE FANG'S INABILITY TO ACCEPT WEAKNESS WOULD LIKELY TORMENT HIM FOREVER.
HOWLING AT THE WEAK, DEVOURING THE STRONG.
BE MINDFUL THAT FANG OF YOURS DOESN'T GET TORN OUT ALONG WITH THAT JAW.
TRULY, BETE COULD DO NOTHING BUT INFLICT PAIN...

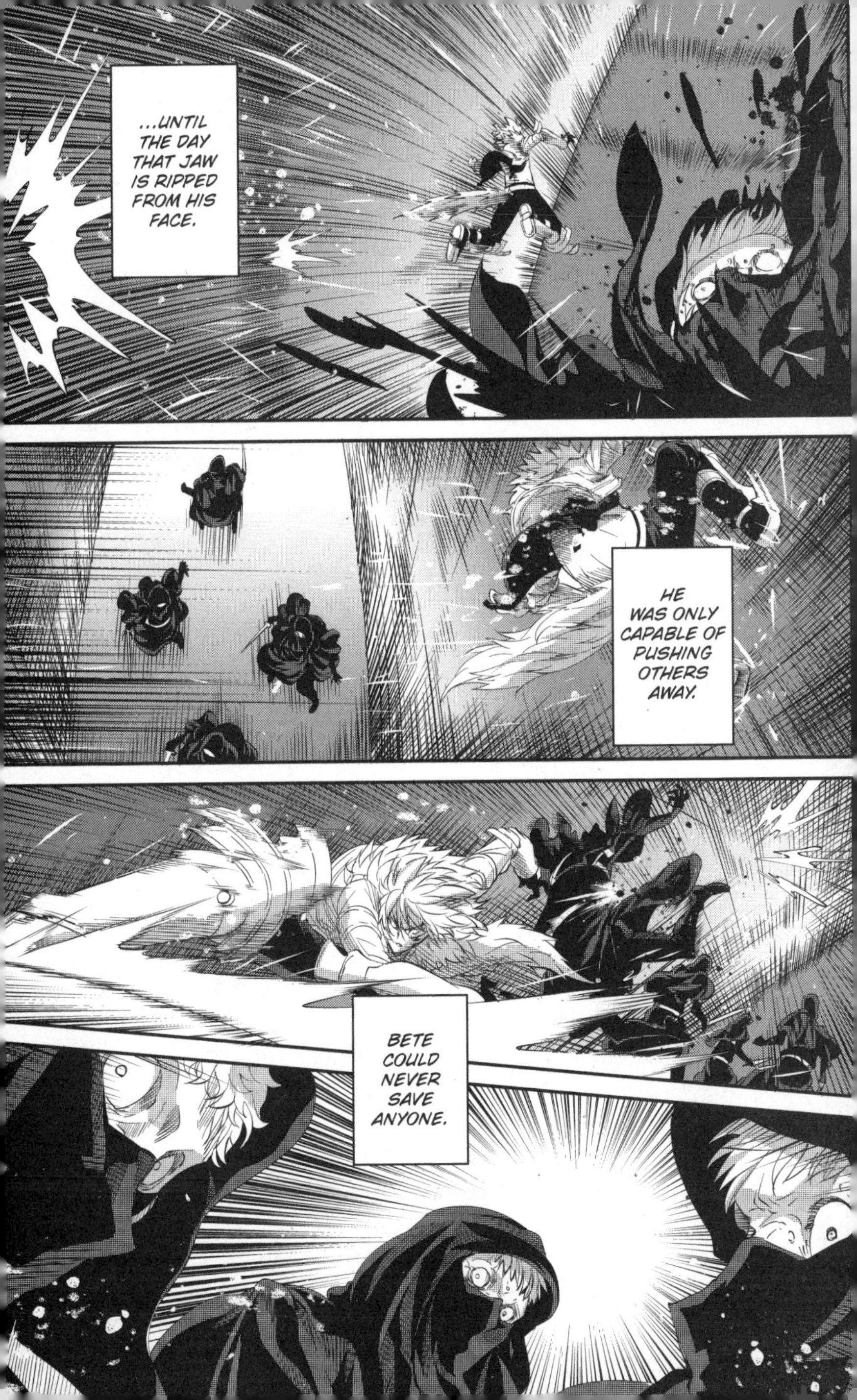
...UNTIL THE DAY THAT JAW IS RIPPED FROM HIS FACE.
HE WAS ONLY CAPABLE OF PUSHING OTHERS AWAY.
BETE COULD NEVER SAVE ANYONE.

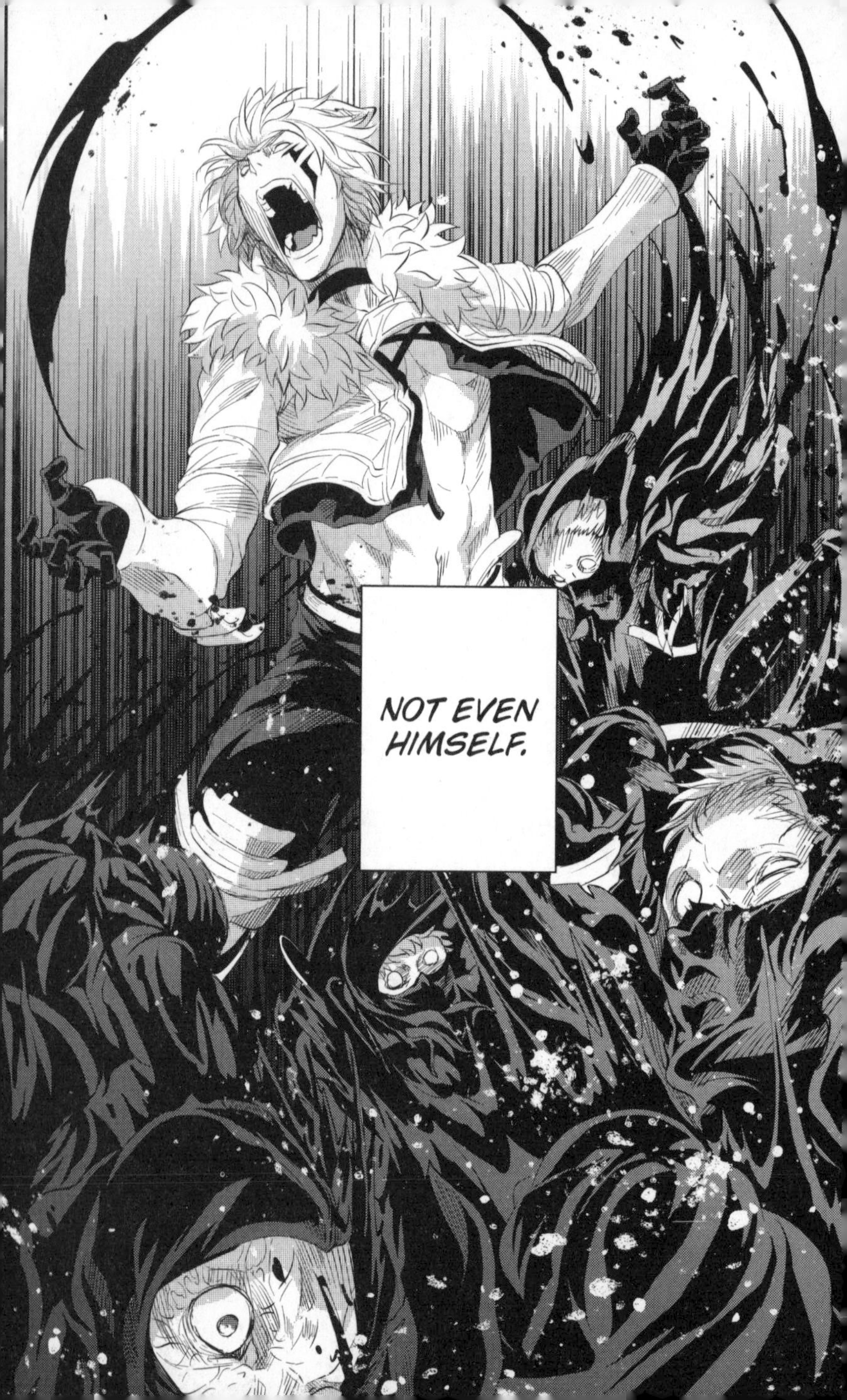
NOT EVEN HIMSELF.

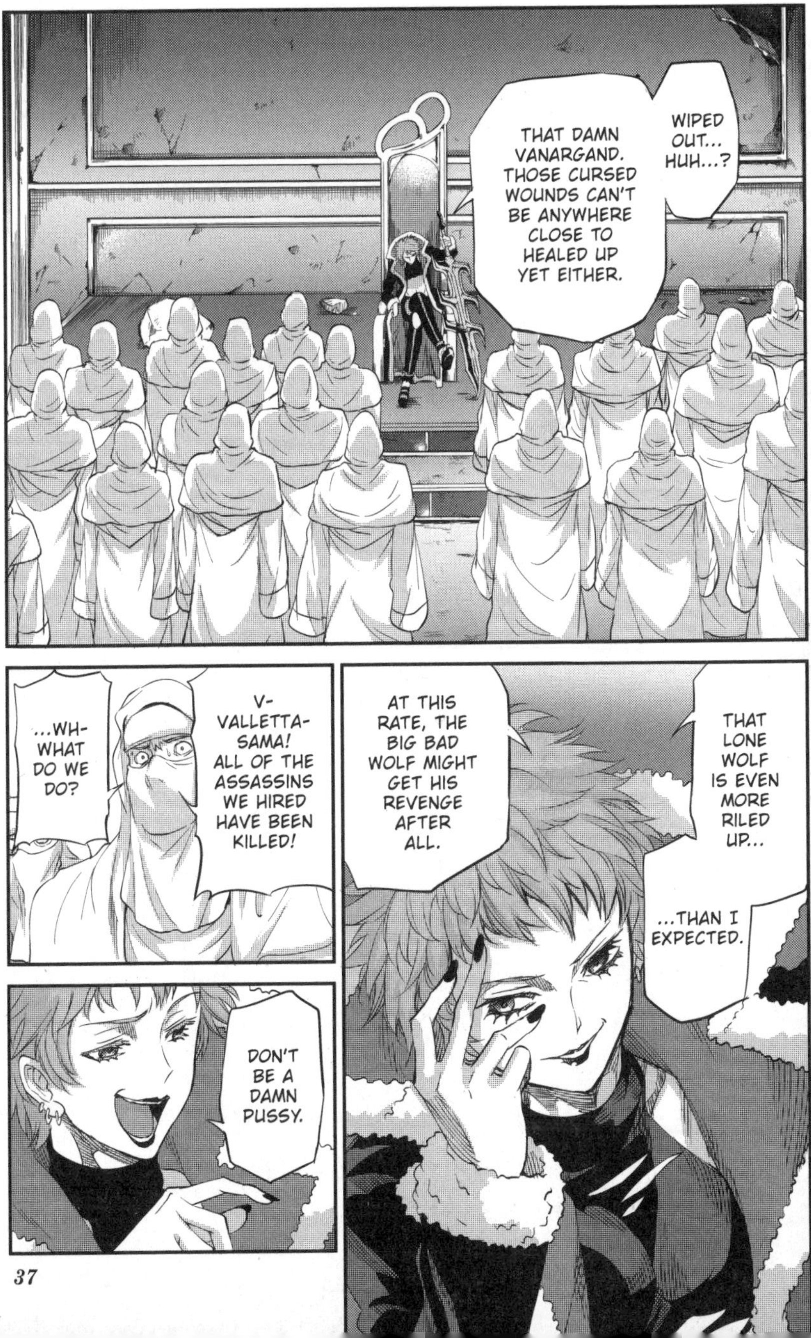
WIPED OUT... HUH...?
THAT DAMN VANARGAND. THOSE CURSED WOUNDS CAN'T BE ANYWHERE CLOSE TO HEALED UP YET EITHER.
THAT LONE WOLF IS EVEN MORE RILED UP...
...THAN I EXPECTED.
AT THIS RATE, THE BIG BAD WOLF MIGHT GET HIS REVENGE AFTER ALL.
V-VALLETTA-SAMA! ALL OF THE ASSASSINS WE HIRED HAVE BEEN KILLED!
...WH-WHAT DO WE DO?
DON'T BE A DAMN PUSSY.

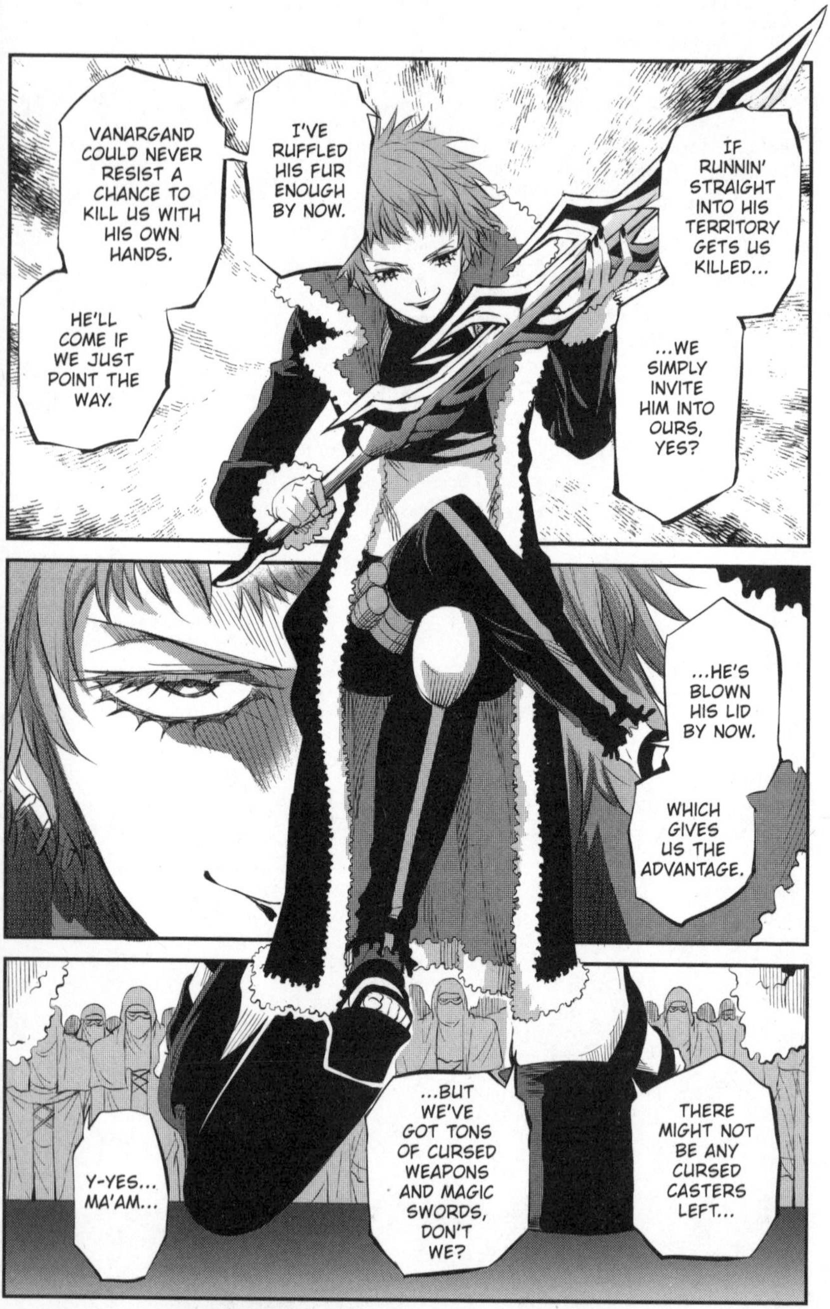
IF RUNNIN' STRAIGHT INTO HIS TERRITORY GETS US KILLED...
...WE SIMPLY INVITE HIM INTO OURS, YES?
I'VE RUFFLED HIS FUR ENOUGH BY NOW.
VANARGAND COULD NEVER RESIST A CHANCE TO KILL US WITH HIS OWN HANDS.
HE'LL COME IF WE JUST POINT THE WAY.
...HE'S BLOWN HIS LID BY NOW.
WHICH GIVES US THE ADVANTAGE.
THERE MIGHT NOT BE ANY CURSED CASTERS LEFT...
...BUT WE'VE GOT TONS OF CURSED WEAPONS AND MAGIC SWORDS, DON'T WE?
Y-YES... MA'AM...

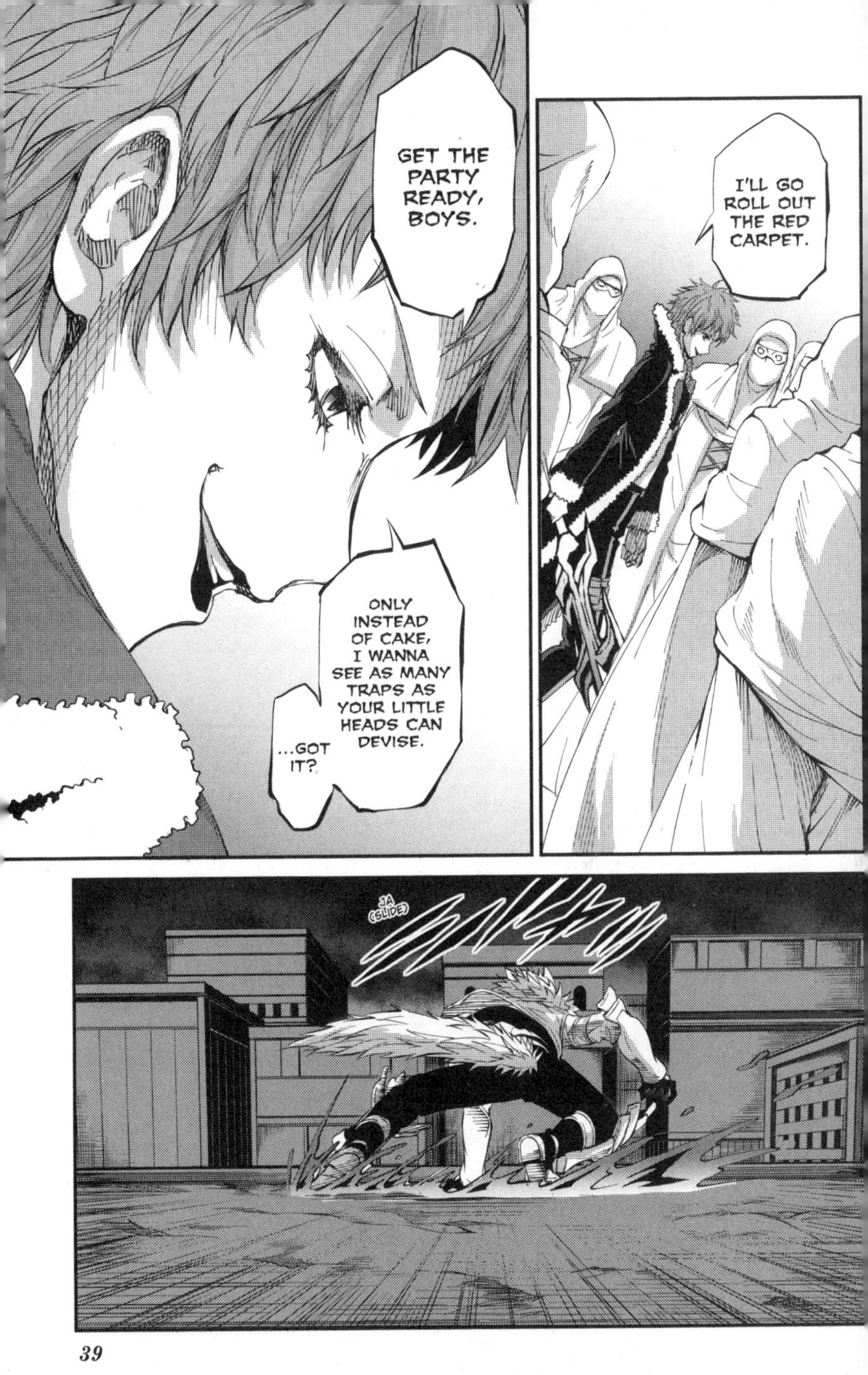
I'LL GO ROLL OUT THE RED CARPET.
GET THE PARTY READY, BOYS.
ONLY INSTEAD OF CAKE, I WANNA SEE AS MANY TRAPS AS YOUR LITTLE HEADS CAN DEVISE.
...GOT IT?
JA (SLIDE)

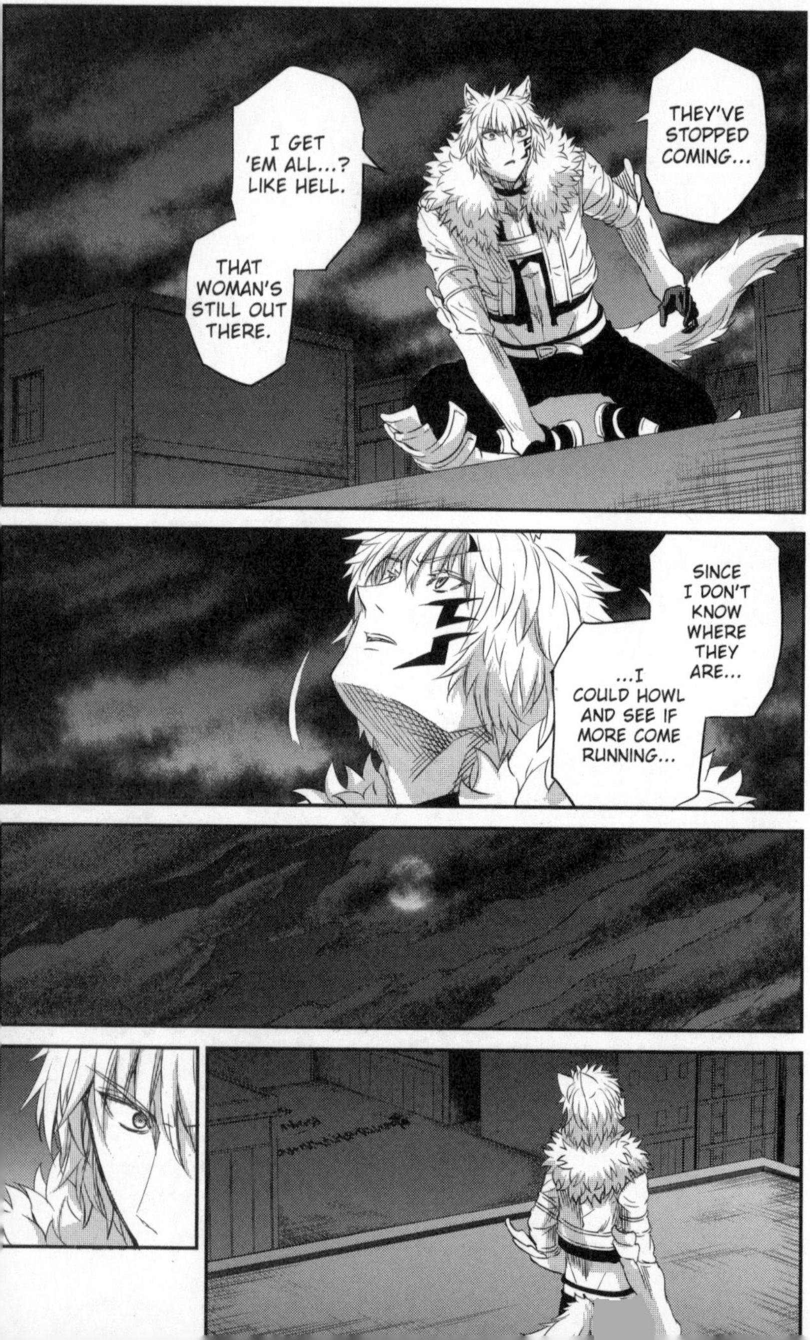
THEY'VE STOPPED COMING...
I GET 'EM ALL...? LIKE HELL.
THAT WOMAN'S STILL OUT THERE.
SINCE I DON'T KNOW WHERE THEY ARE...
...I COULD HOWL AND SEE IF MORE COME RUNNING...

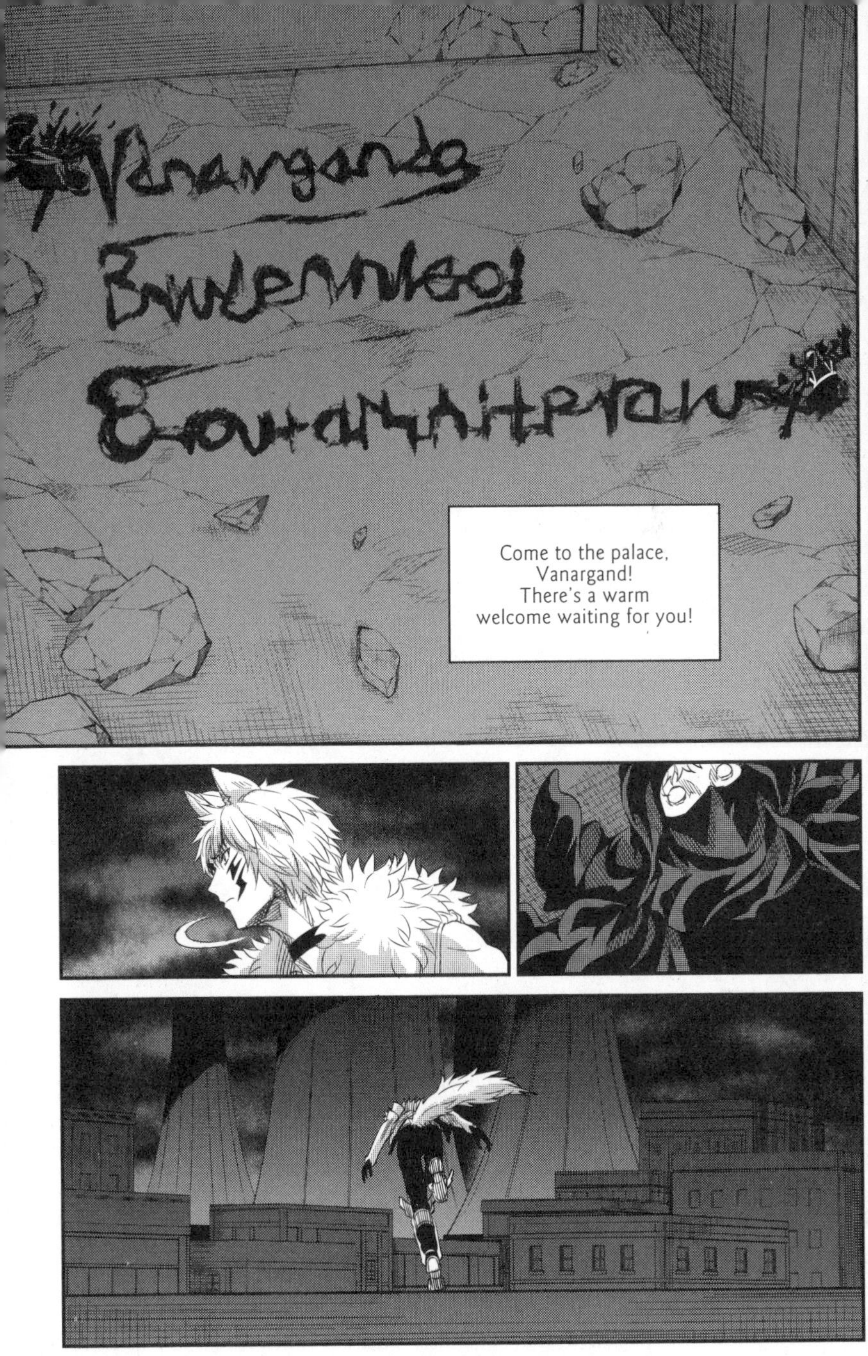
Come to the palace, Vanargand! There's a warm welcome waiting for you!

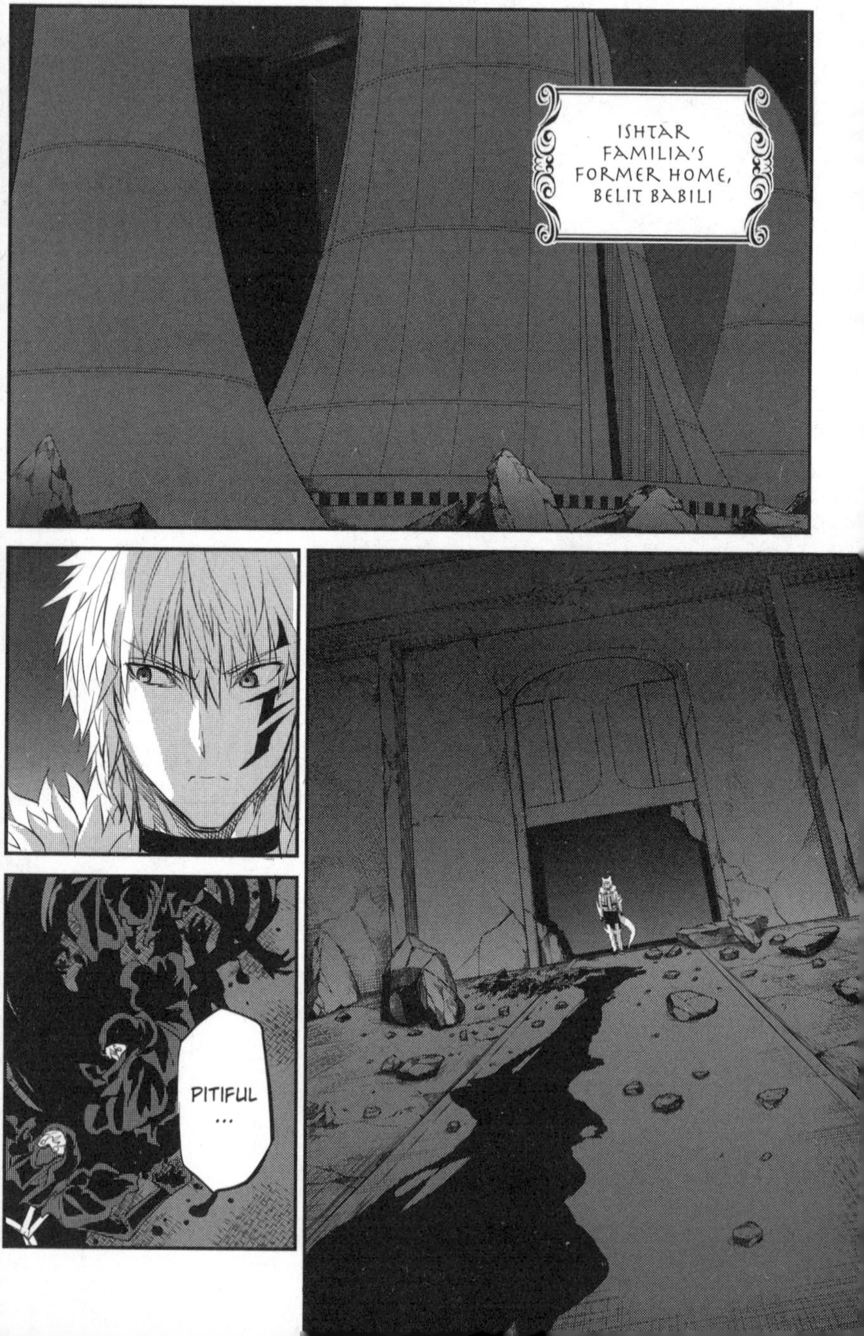
ISHTAR FAMILIA'S FORMER HOME, BELIT BABILI
PITIFUL ...

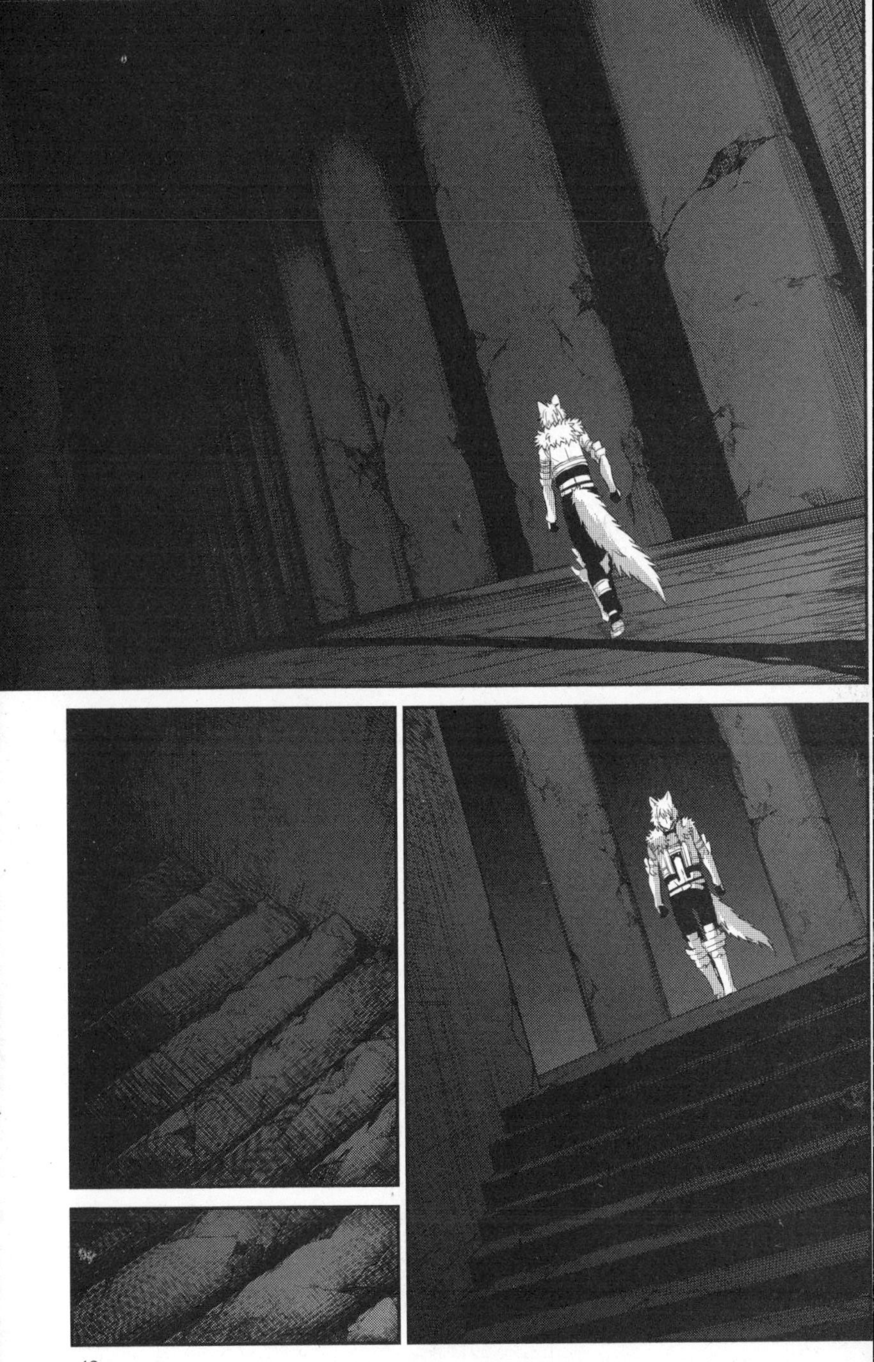

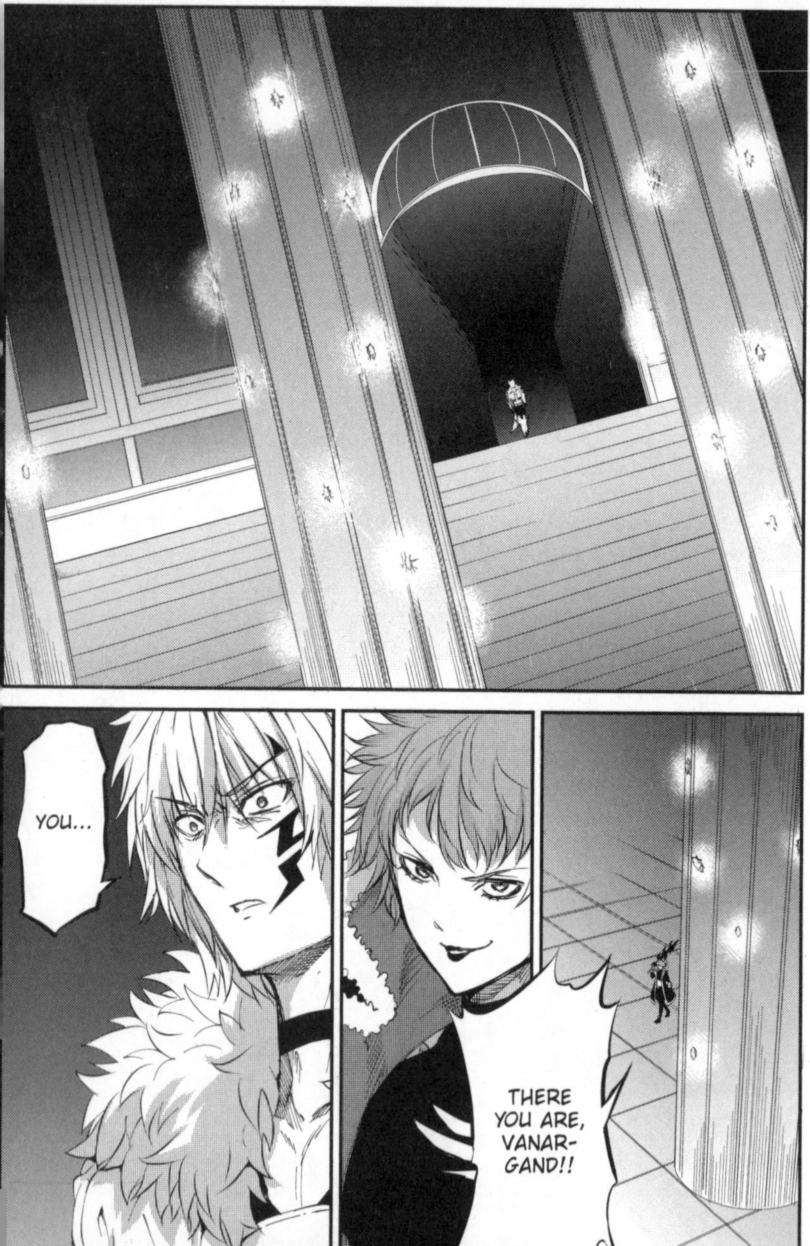
THERE YOU ARE, VANARGAND!!
YOU...

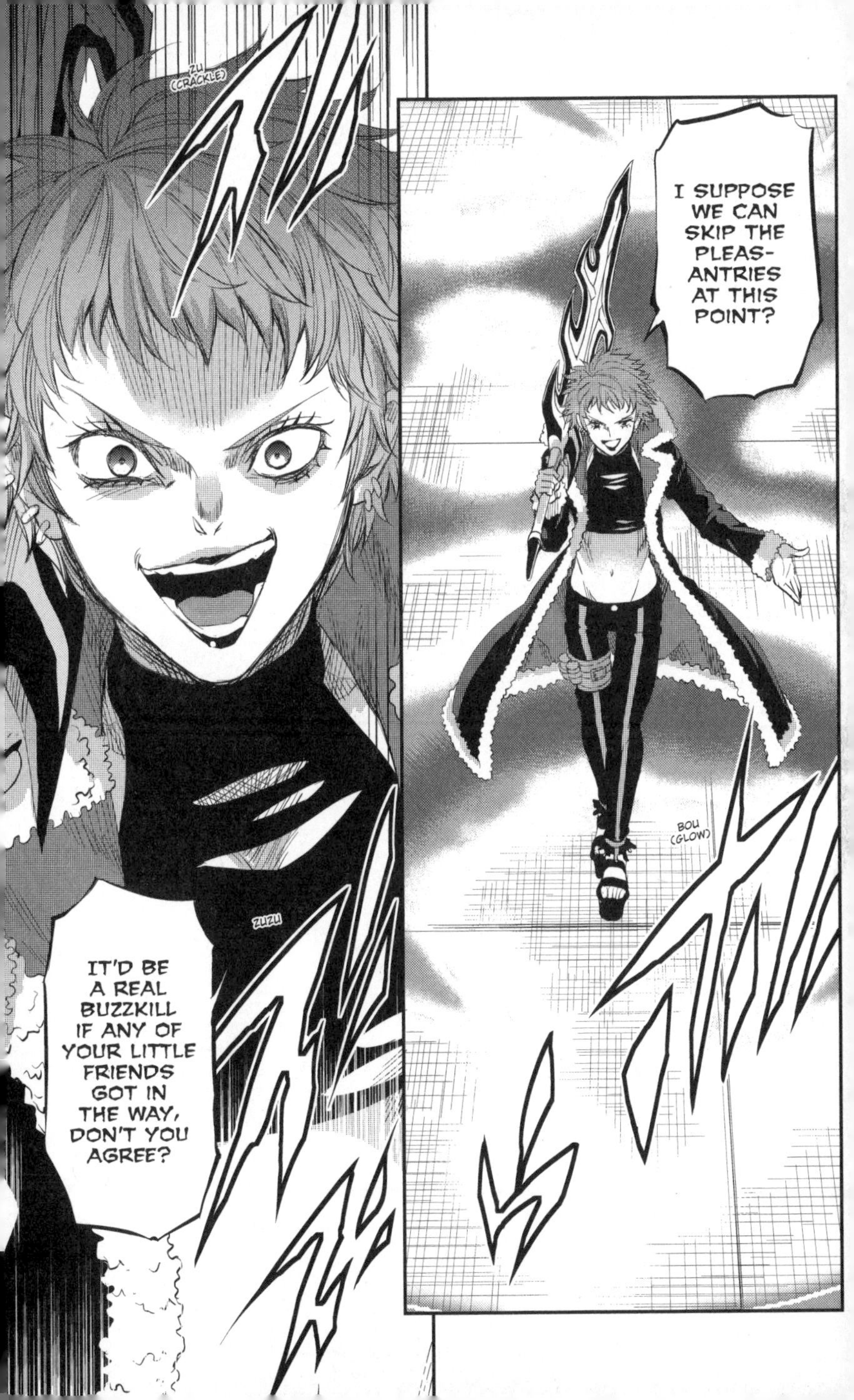
I SUPPOSE WE CAN SKIP THE PLEAS-ANTRIES AT THIS POINT?
BOU (GLOW)
ZU (CRACKLE)
ZUZU
IT'D BE A REAL BUZZKILL IF ANY OF YOUR LITTLE FRIENDS GOT IN THE WAY, DON'T YOU AGREE?

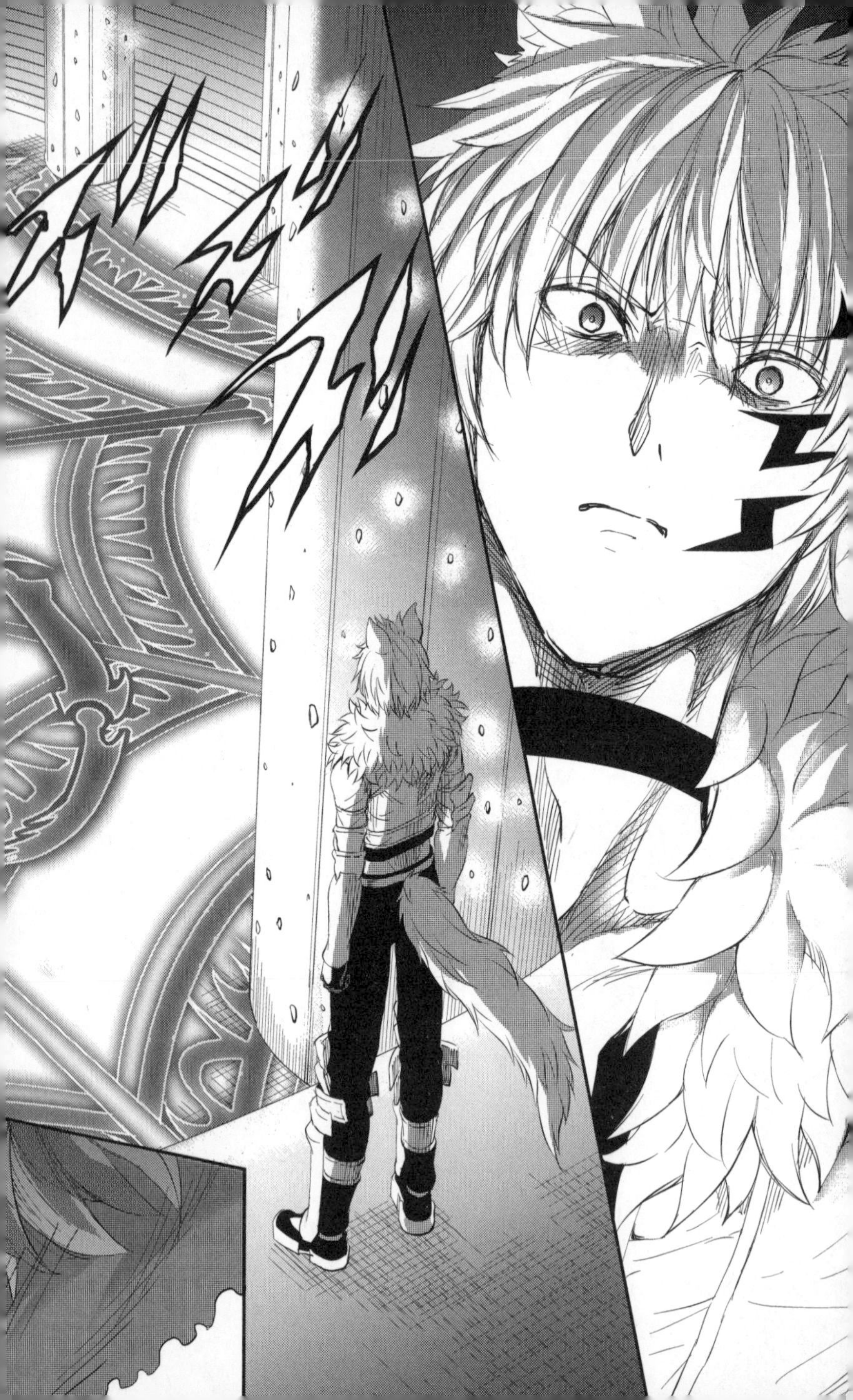

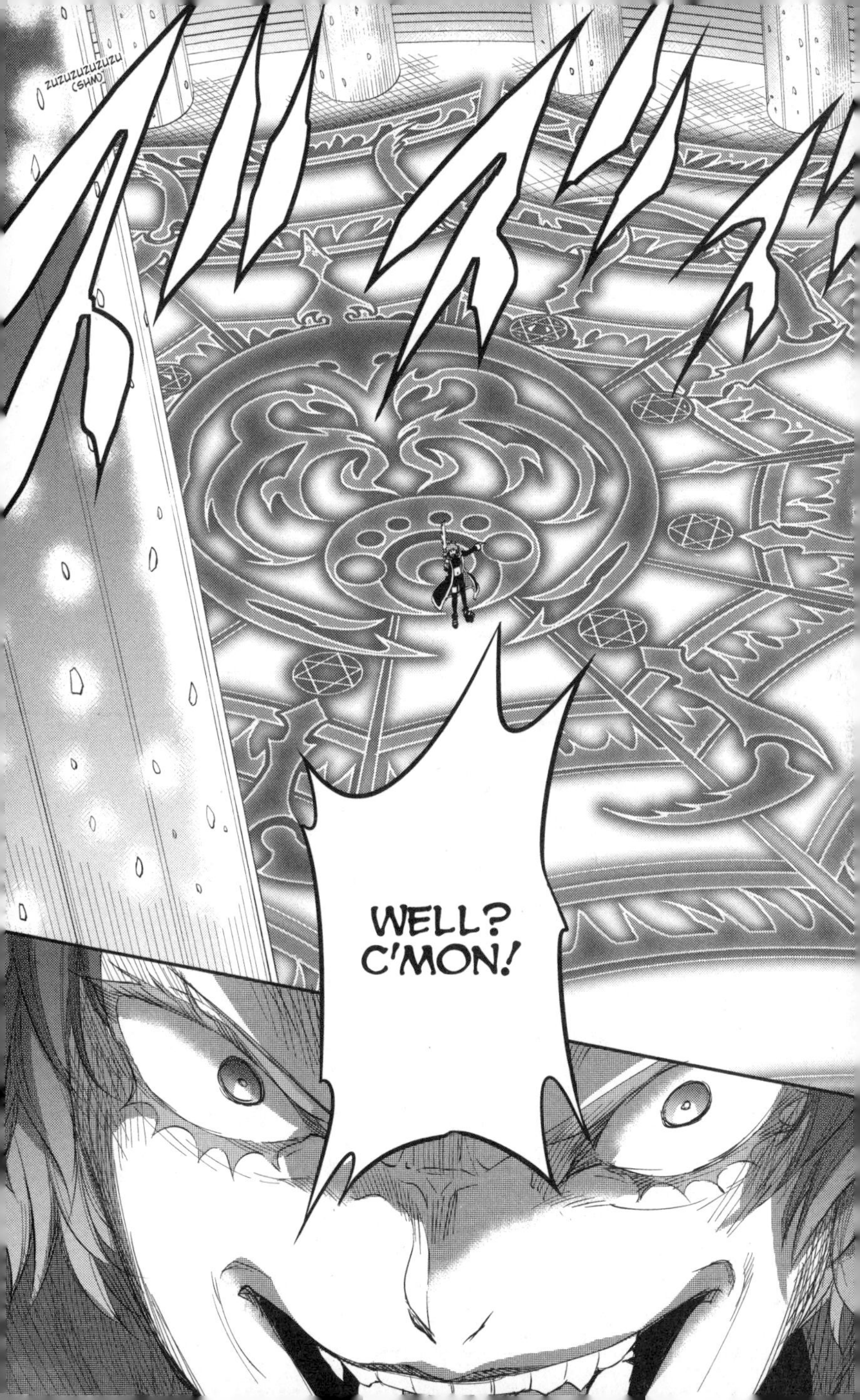
ZUZUZUZUZUZU (SHN)
WELL? C'MON!

Is it Wrong to Try to Pick Up Girls in a Dungeon? On the Side

Sword Oratoria

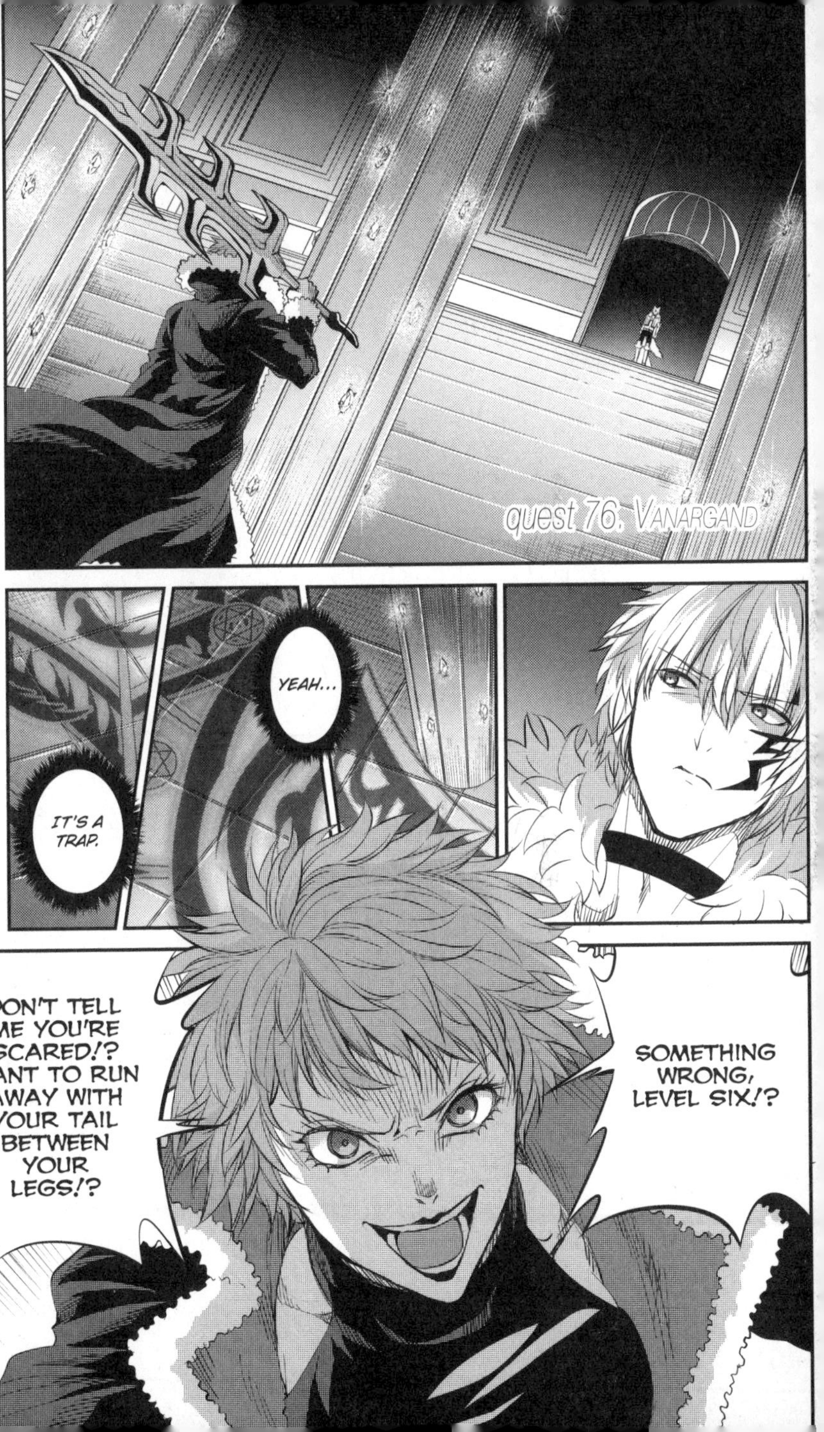
quest 76. VANARGAND
YEAH...
IT'S A TRAP.
SOMETHING WRONG, LEVEL SIX!?
DON'T TELL ME YOU'RE SCARED!? WANT TO RUN AWAY WITH YOUR TAIL BETWEEN YOUR LEGS!?

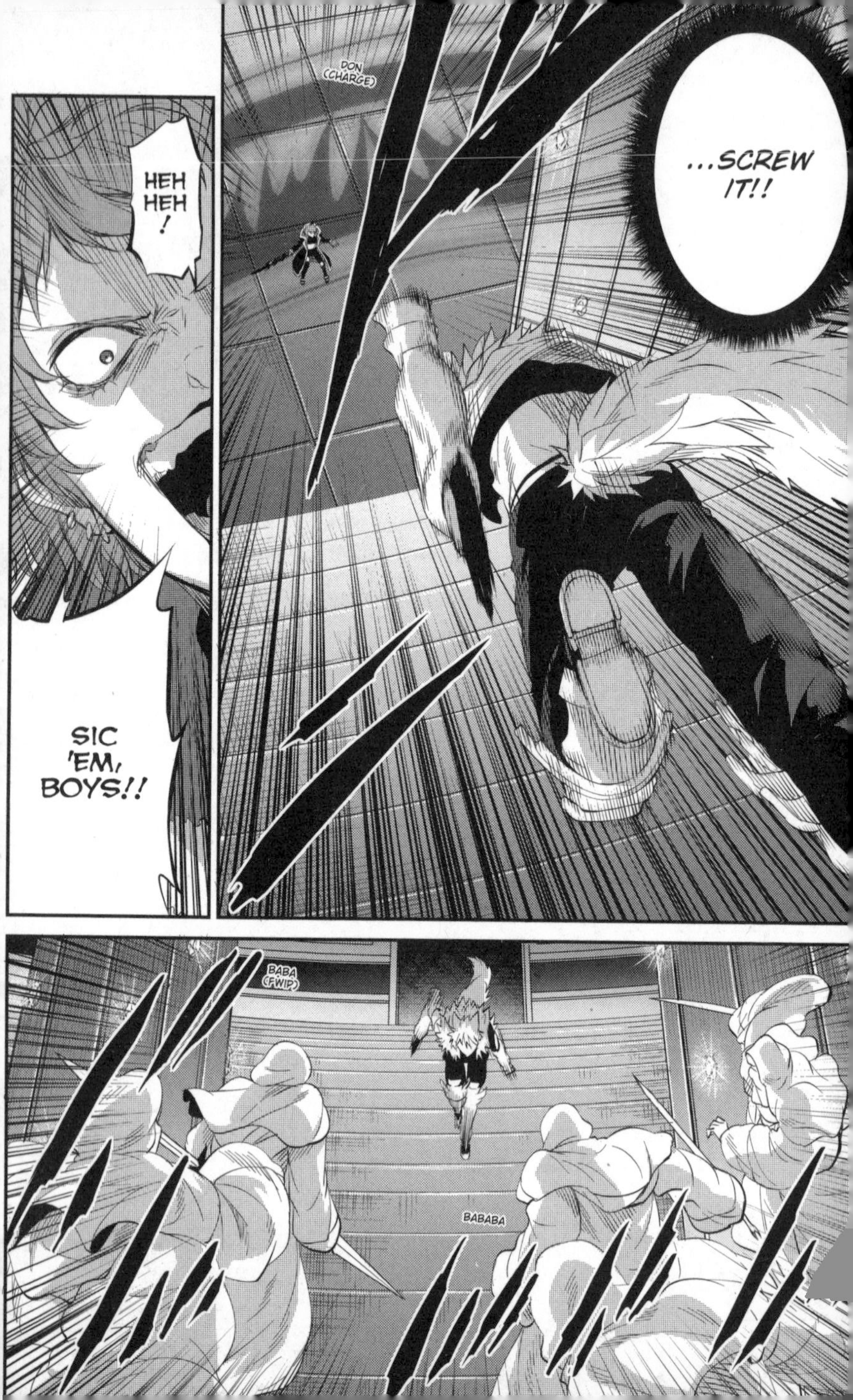
DON (CHARGE)
...SCREW IT!!
HEH HEH!
SIC 'EM, BOYS!!
BABA (FWIP)
BABABA

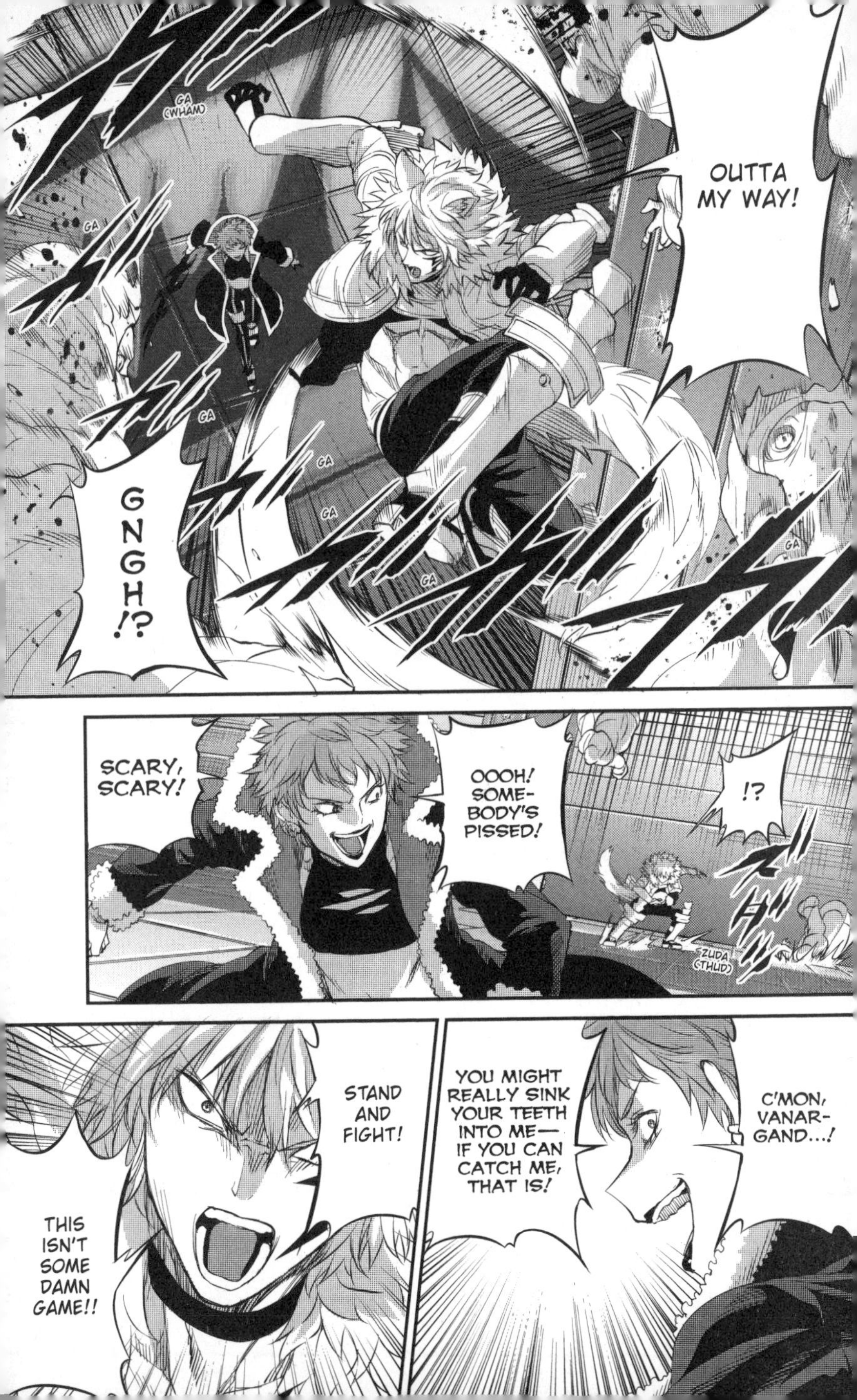
OUTTA MY WAY!
GA (WHAM)
GA
GA
GA
GA
GA
GA
GNGH!?
!?
ZUDA (THUD)
OOOH! SOME-BODY'S PISSED!
SCARY, SCARY!
C'MON, VANAR-GAND...!
YOU MIGHT REALLY SINK YOUR TEETH INTO ME—IF YOU CAN CATCH ME, THAT IS!
STAND AND FIGHT!
THIS ISN'T SOME DAMN GAME!!

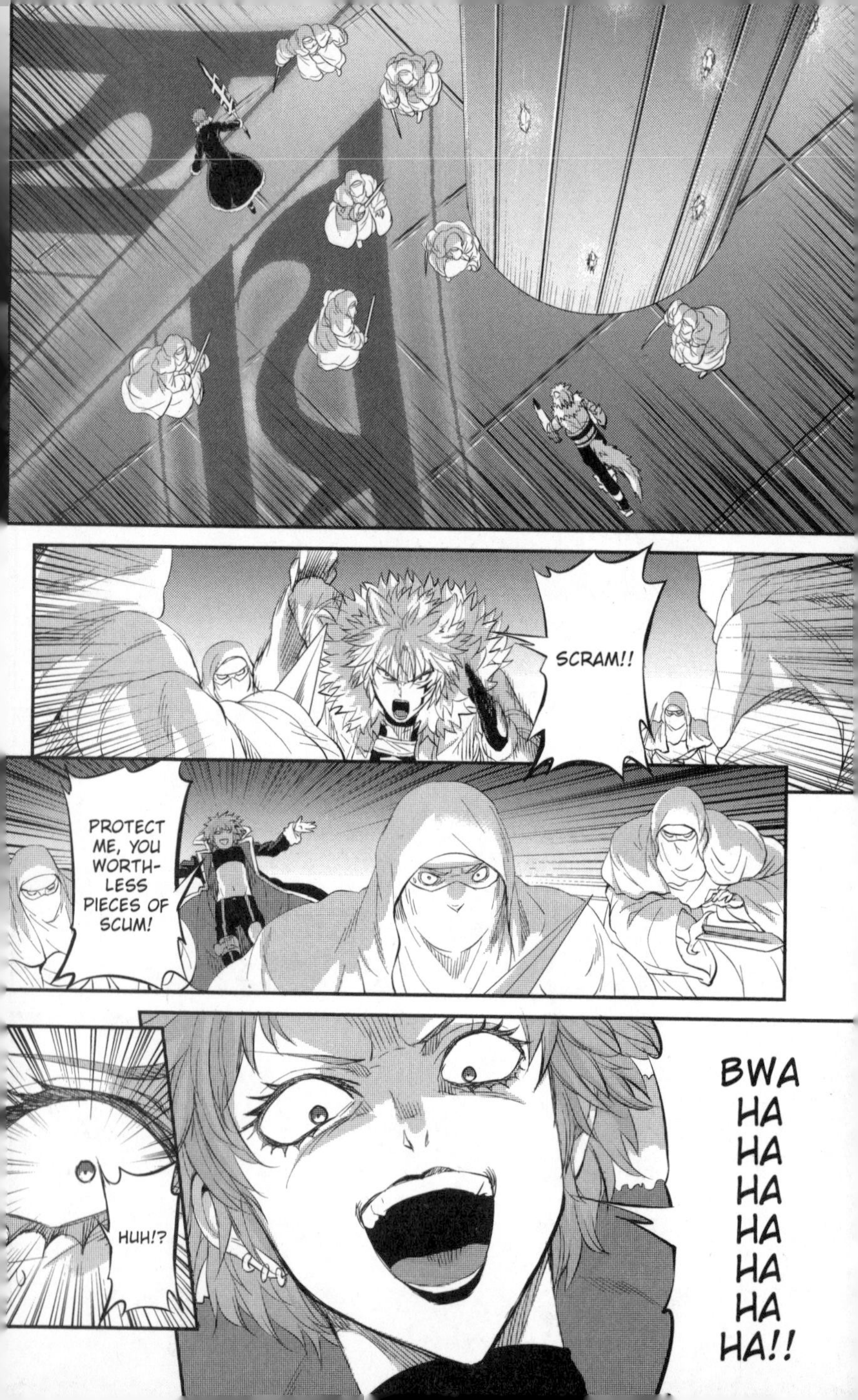
SCRAM!!
PROTECT ME, YOU WORTH-LESS PIECES OF SCUM!
BWA HA HA HA HA HA HA HA HA!!
HUH!?

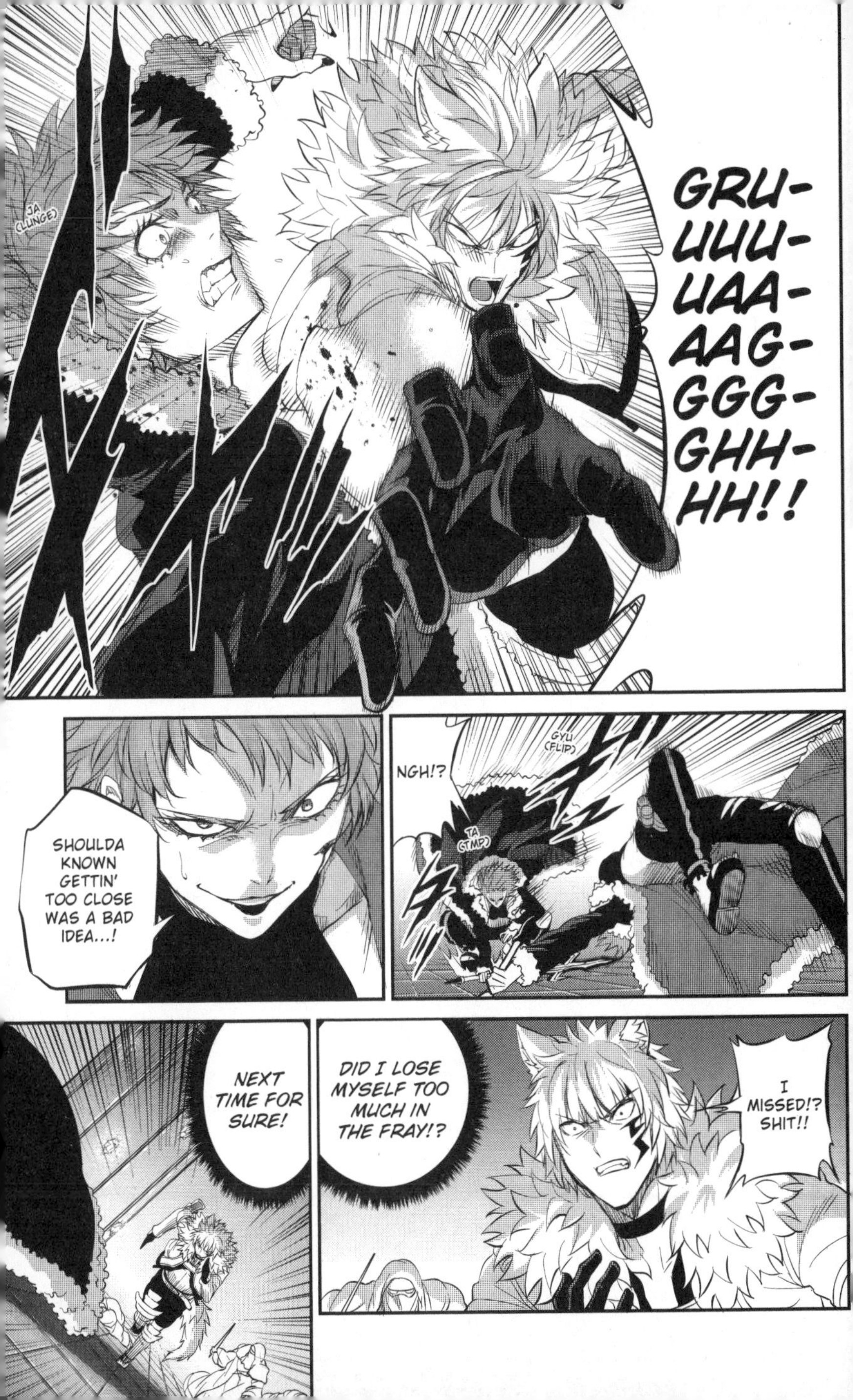
GRU-UUU-UAA-AAG-GGG-GHH-HH!!
JA (LUNGE)
GYU (FLIP)
NGH!?
TA (TMP)
SHOULDA KNOWN GETTIN' TOO CLOSE WAS A BAD IDEA...!
I MISSED!? SHIT!!
DID I LOSE MYSELF TOO MUCH IN THE FRAY!?
NEXT TIME FOR SURE!

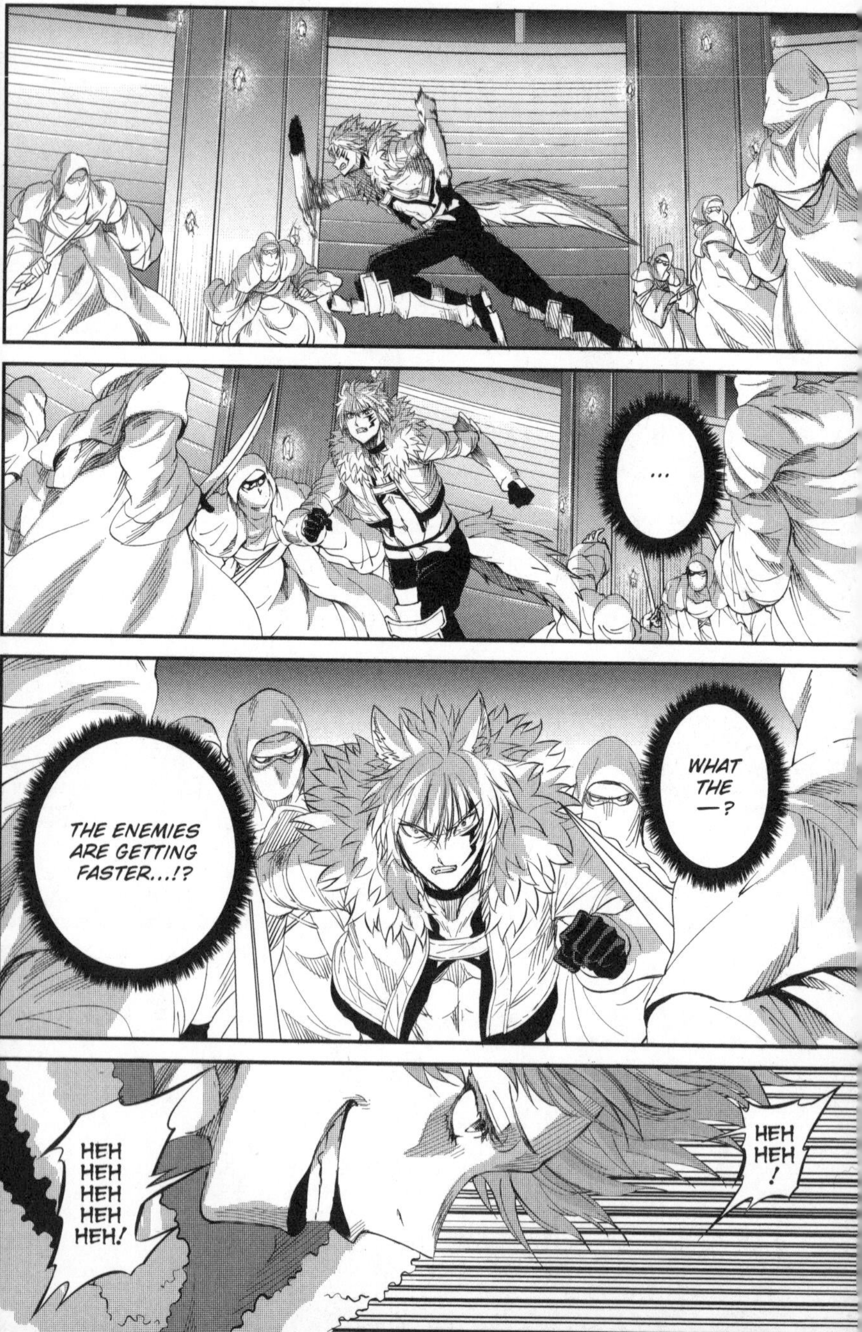
...
WHAT THE—?
THE ENEMIES ARE GETTING FASTER...!?
HEH HEH!
HEH HEH HEH HEH HEH!

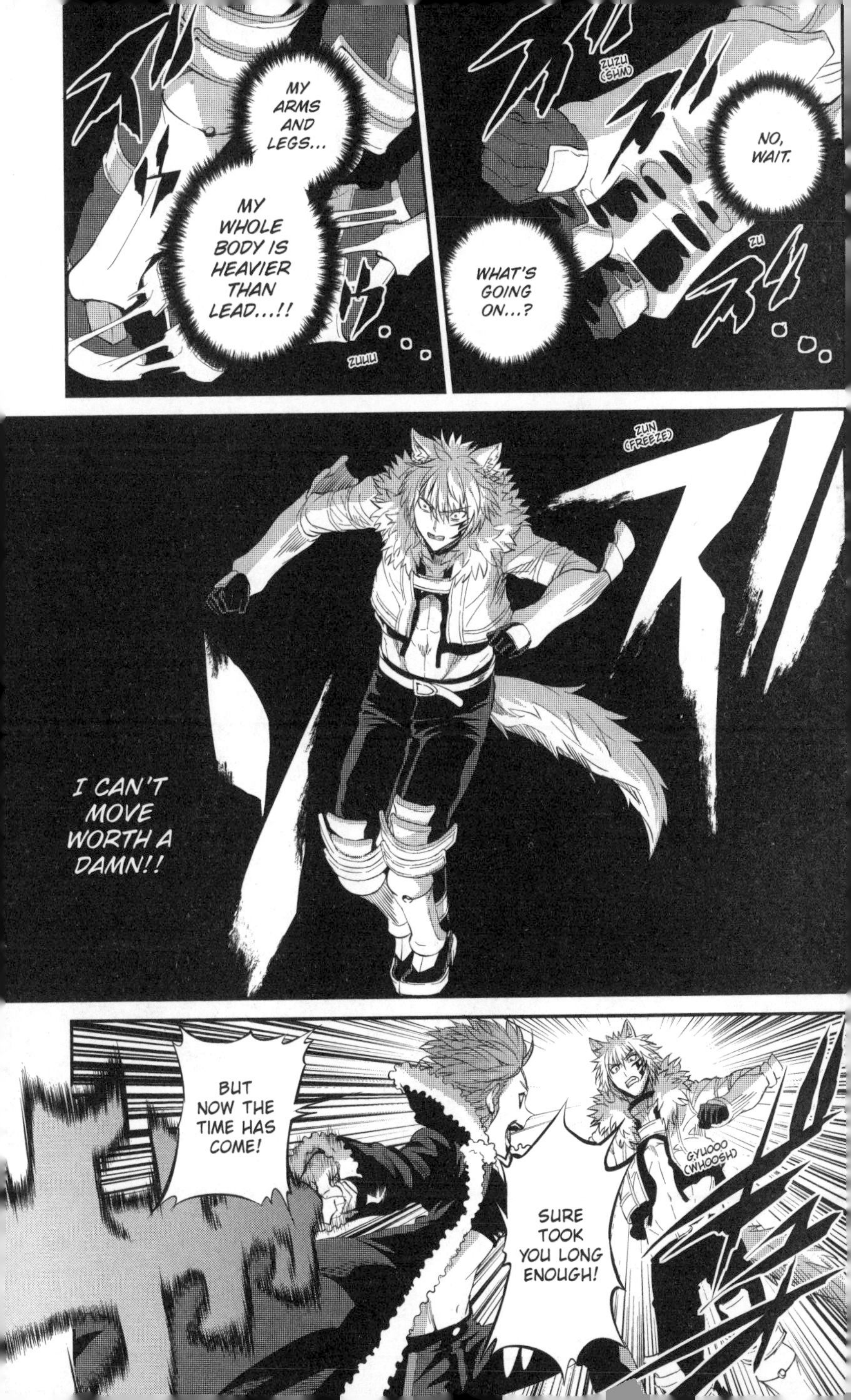
ZUZU (SHM)
NO, WAIT.
WHAT'S GOING ON...?
ZU
MY ARMS AND LEGS...
MY WHOLE BODY IS HEAVIER THAN LEAD...!!
ZUUU
ZUN (FREEZE)
I CAN'T MOVE WORTH A DAMN!!
GYUOOO (WHOOSH)
BUT NOW THE TIME HAS COME!
SURE TOOK YOU LONG ENOUGH!

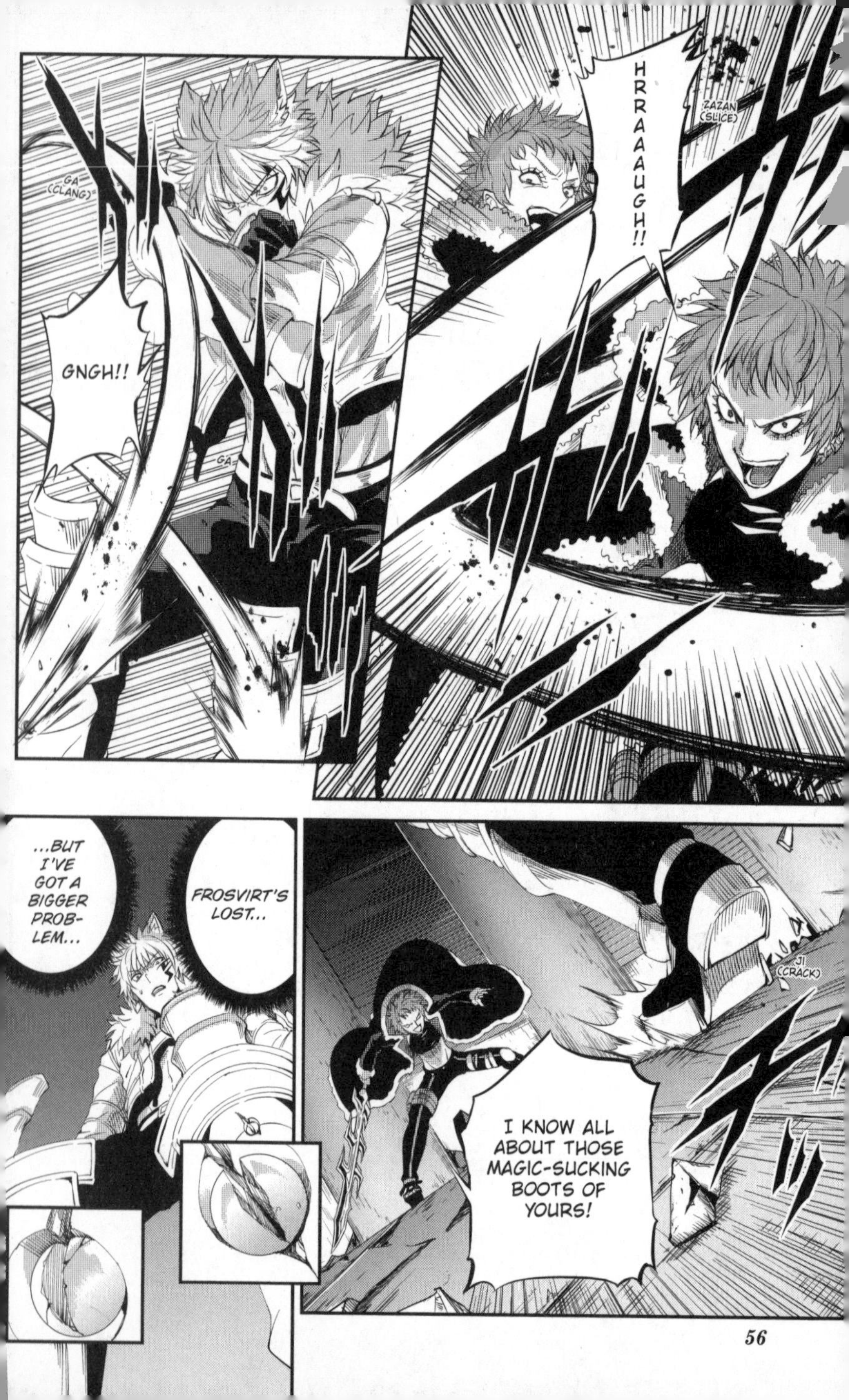
HRRAAAUGH!!
ZAZAN (SLICE)
GA (CLANG)
GNGH!!
GA
JI (CRACK)
I KNOW ALL ABOUT THOSE MAGIC-SUCKING BOOTS OF YOURS!
FROSVIRT'S LOST...
...BUT I'VE GOT A BIGGER PROB-LEM...

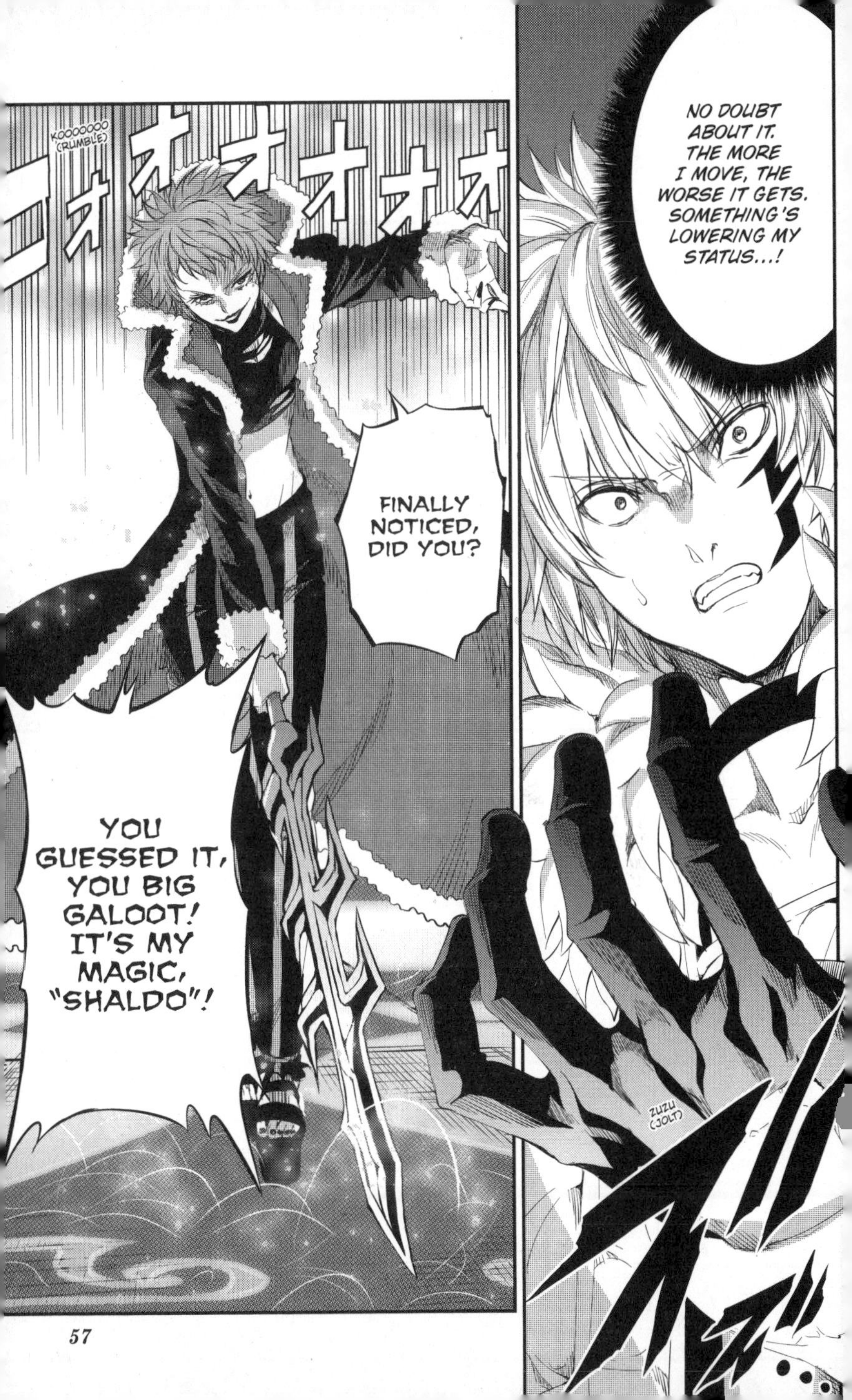
NO DOUBT ABOUT IT. THE MORE I MOVE, THE WORSE IT GETS. SOMETHING'S LOWERING MY STATUS...!
ZUZU (JOLT)
KOOOOOOO (RUMBLE)
FINALLY NOTICED, DID YOU?
YOU GUESSED IT, YOU BIG GALOOT! IT'S MY MAGIC, "SHALDO"!

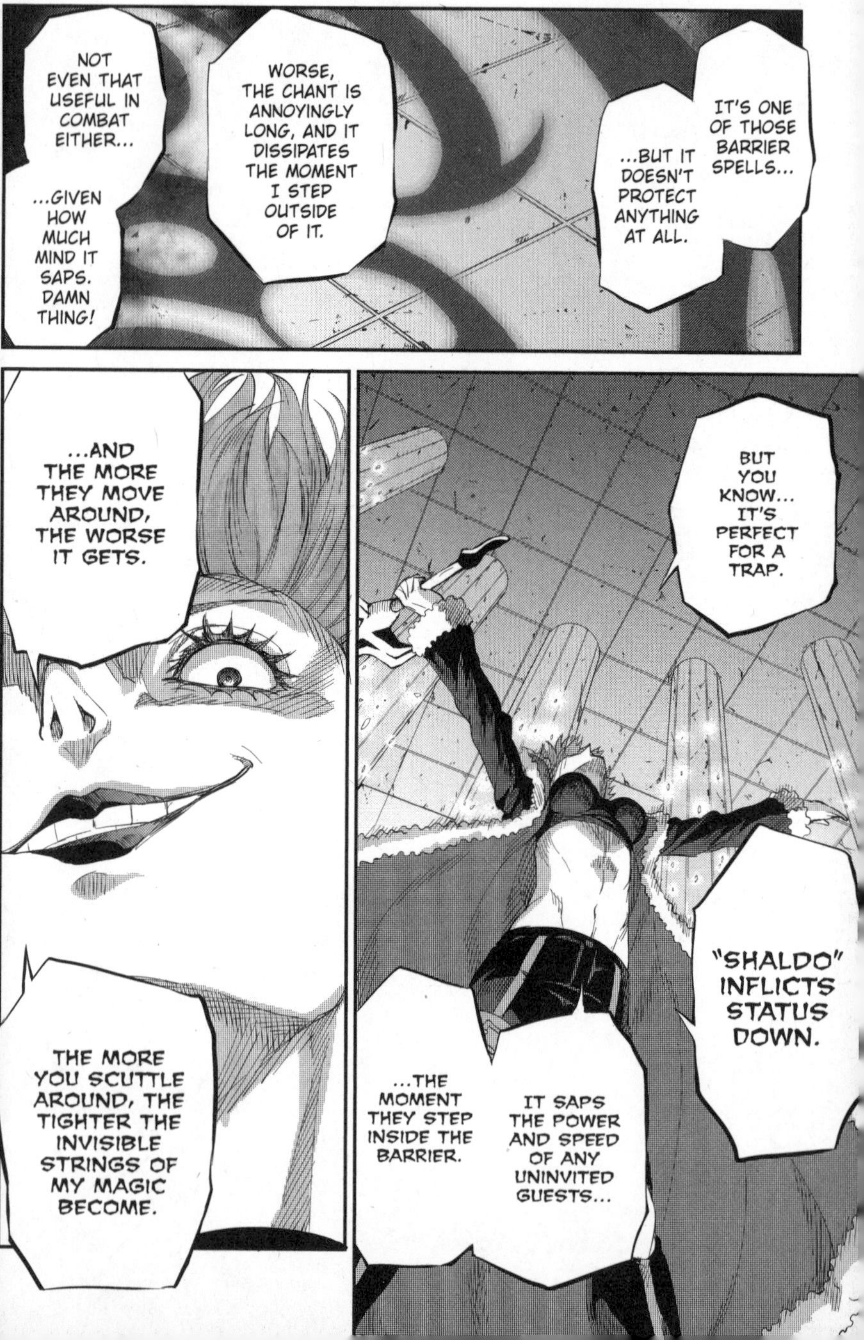
IT'S ONE OF THOSE BARRIER SPELLS...
...BUT IT DOESN'T PROTECT ANYTHING AT ALL.
WORSE, THE CHANT IS ANNOYINGLY LONG, AND IT DISSIPATES THE MOMENT I STEP OUTSIDE OF IT.
NOT EVEN THAT USEFUL IN COMBAT EITHER...
...GIVEN HOW MUCH MIND IT SAPS. DAMN THING!
BUT YOU KNOW... IT'S PERFECT FOR A TRAP.
"SHALDO" INFLICTS STATUS DOWN.
IT SAPS THE POWER AND SPEED OF ANY UNINVITED GUESTS...
...THE MOMENT THEY STEP INSIDE THE BARRIER.
...AND THE MORE THEY MOVE AROUND, THE WORSE IT GETS.
THE MORE YOU SCUTTLE AROUND, THE TIGHTER THE INVISIBLE STRINGS OF MY MAGIC BECOME.

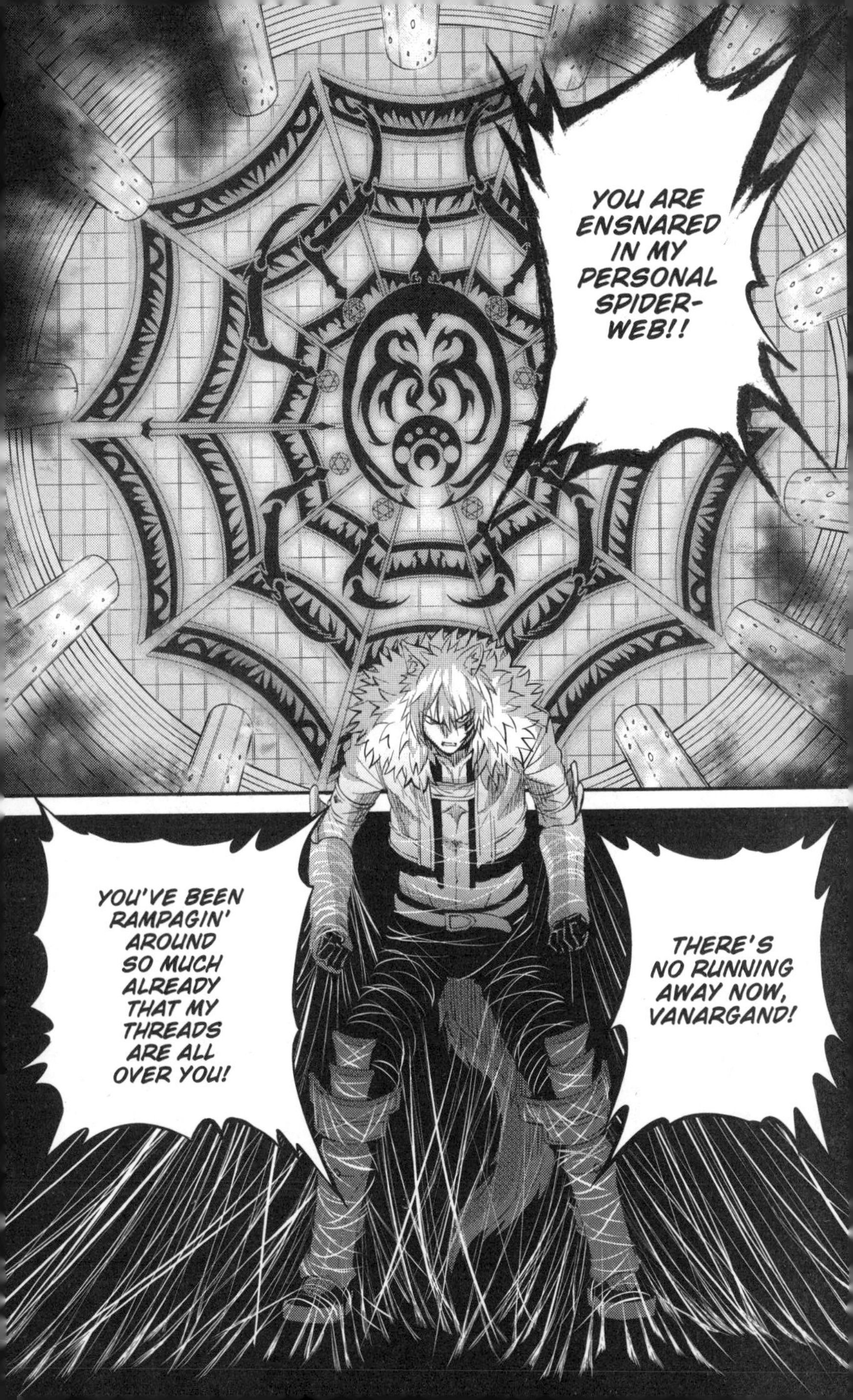
YOU ARE ENSNARED IN MY PERSONAL SPIDER-WEB!!
THERE'S NO RUNNING AWAY NOW, VANARGAND!
YOU'VE BEEN RAMPAGIN' AROUND SO MUCH ALREADY THAT MY THREADS ARE ALL OVER YOU!

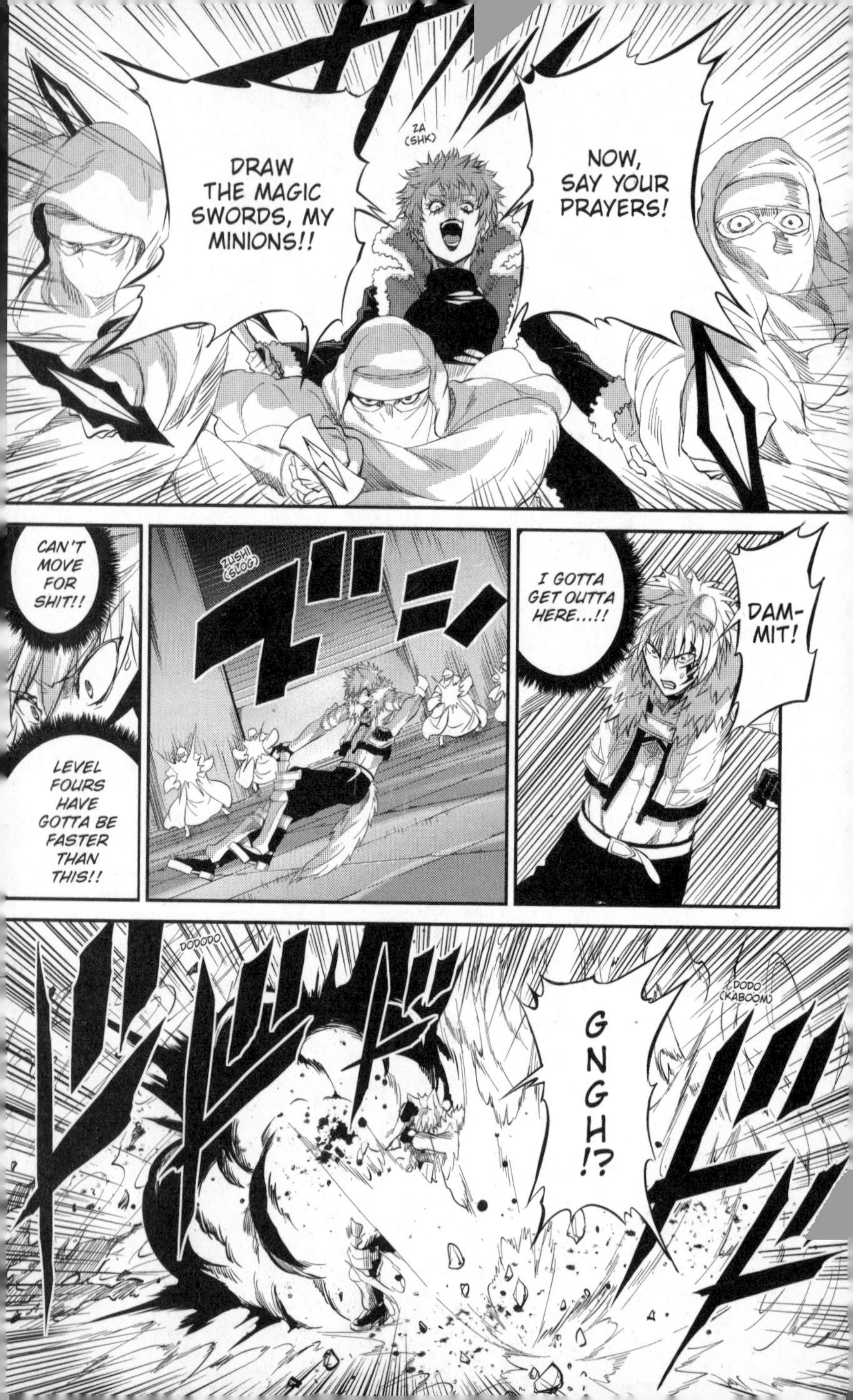
ZA (SHK)
NOW, SAY YOUR PRAYERS!
DRAW THE MAGIC SWORDS, MY MINIONS!!
DAM-MIT!
I GOTTA GET OUTTA HERE...!!
ZUSHI (SLOG)
CAN'T MOVE FOR SHIT!!
LEVEL FOURS HAVE GOTTA BE FASTER THAN THIS!!
DODO (KABOOM)
GNGH!?
DODODO

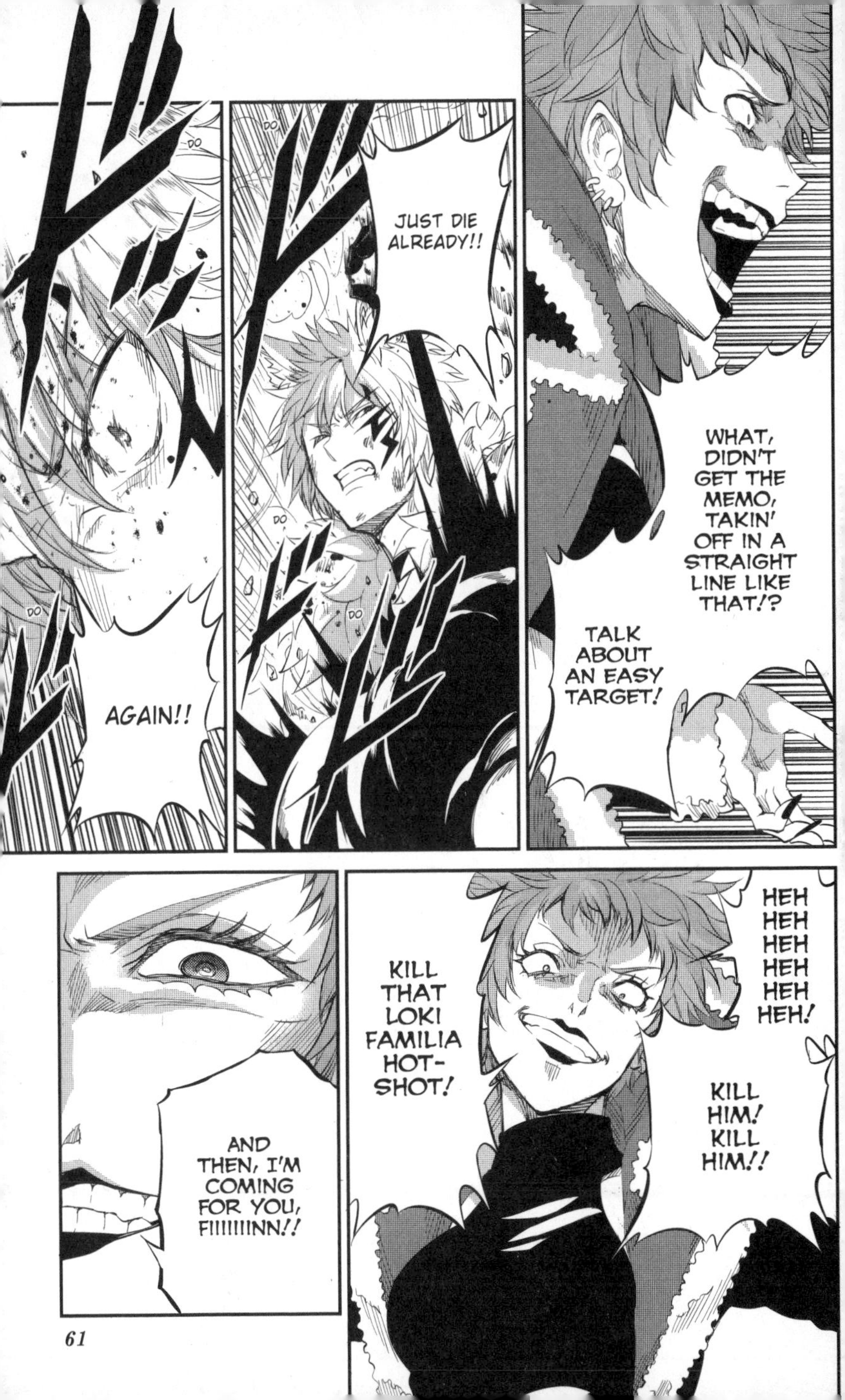
WHAT, DIDN'T GET THE MEMO, TAKIN' OFF IN A STRAIGHT LINE LIKE THAT!?
TALK ABOUT AN EASY TARGET!
DO
JUST DIE ALREADY!!
DO
DO
DO
AGAIN!!
DO
HEH HEH HEH HEH HEH HEH!
KILL THAT LOKI FAMILIA HOT-SHOT!
KILL HIM! KILL HIM!!
AND THEN, I'M COMING FOR YOU, FIIIIIIINN!!

Vängärgänd
Rudennetieri
E01

VANARGAND...
COME TO
THE PALACE.

THIS
IS...

...OH
NO!

THAT
CAME
FROM
UNDER-
GROUND!?

ZUZU
(SHAKE)

...!?

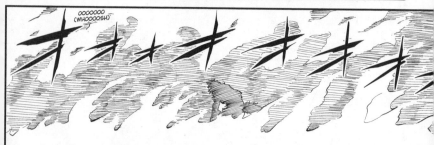

OOOOOOO —
(WHOOOOSH)

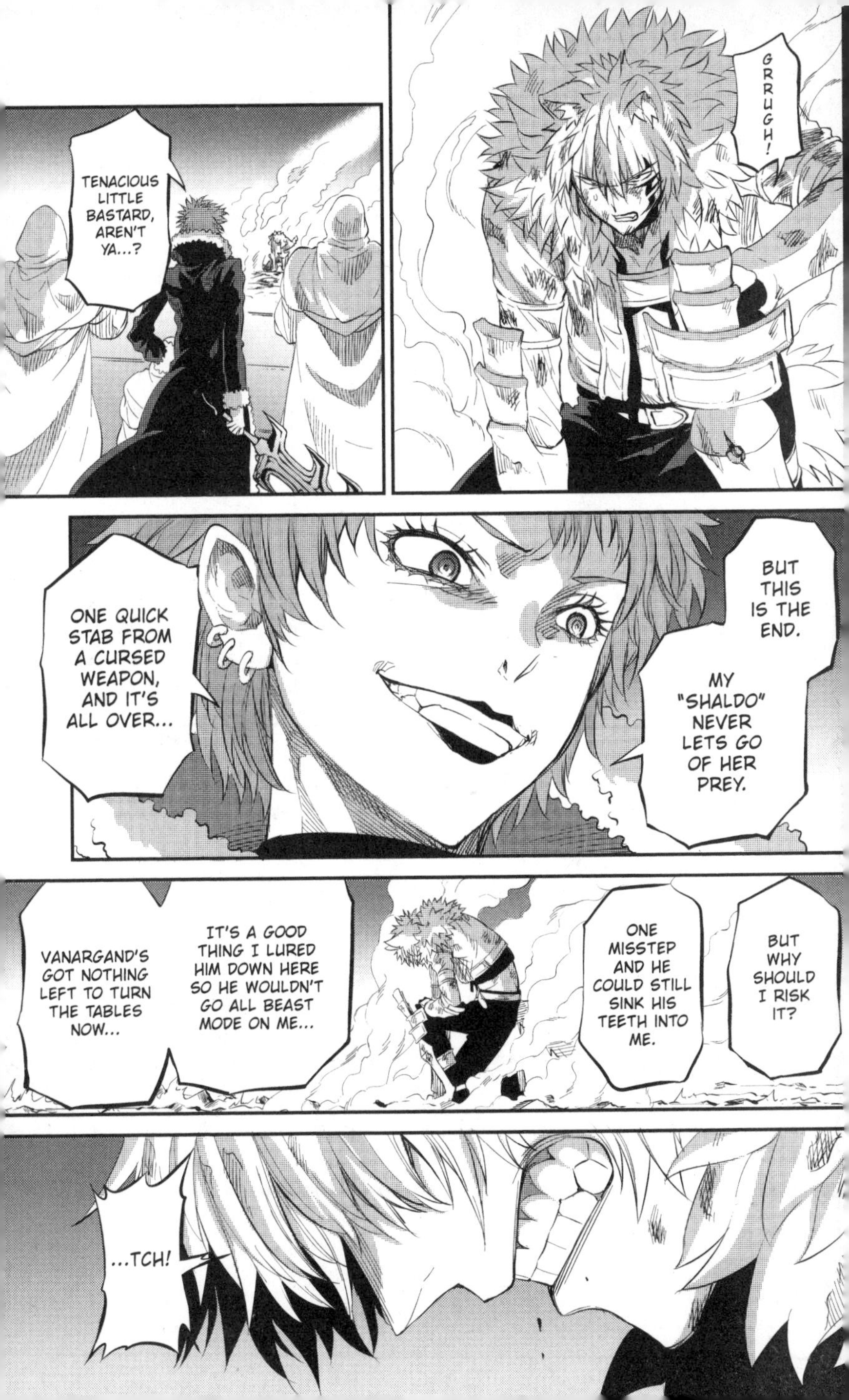
GRRUGH!
TENACIOUS LITTLE BASTARD, AREN'T YA...?
BUT THIS IS THE END.
MY "SHALDO" NEVER LETS GO OF HER PREY.
ONE QUICK STAB FROM A CURSED WEAPON, AND IT'S ALL OVER...
BUT WHY SHOULD I RISK IT?
ONE MISSTEP AND HE COULD STILL SINK HIS TEETH INTO ME.
IT'S A GOOD THING I LURED HIM DOWN HERE SO HE WOULDN'T GO ALL BEAST MODE ON ME...
VANARGAND'S GOT NOTHING LEFT TO TURN THE TABLES NOW...
...TCH!

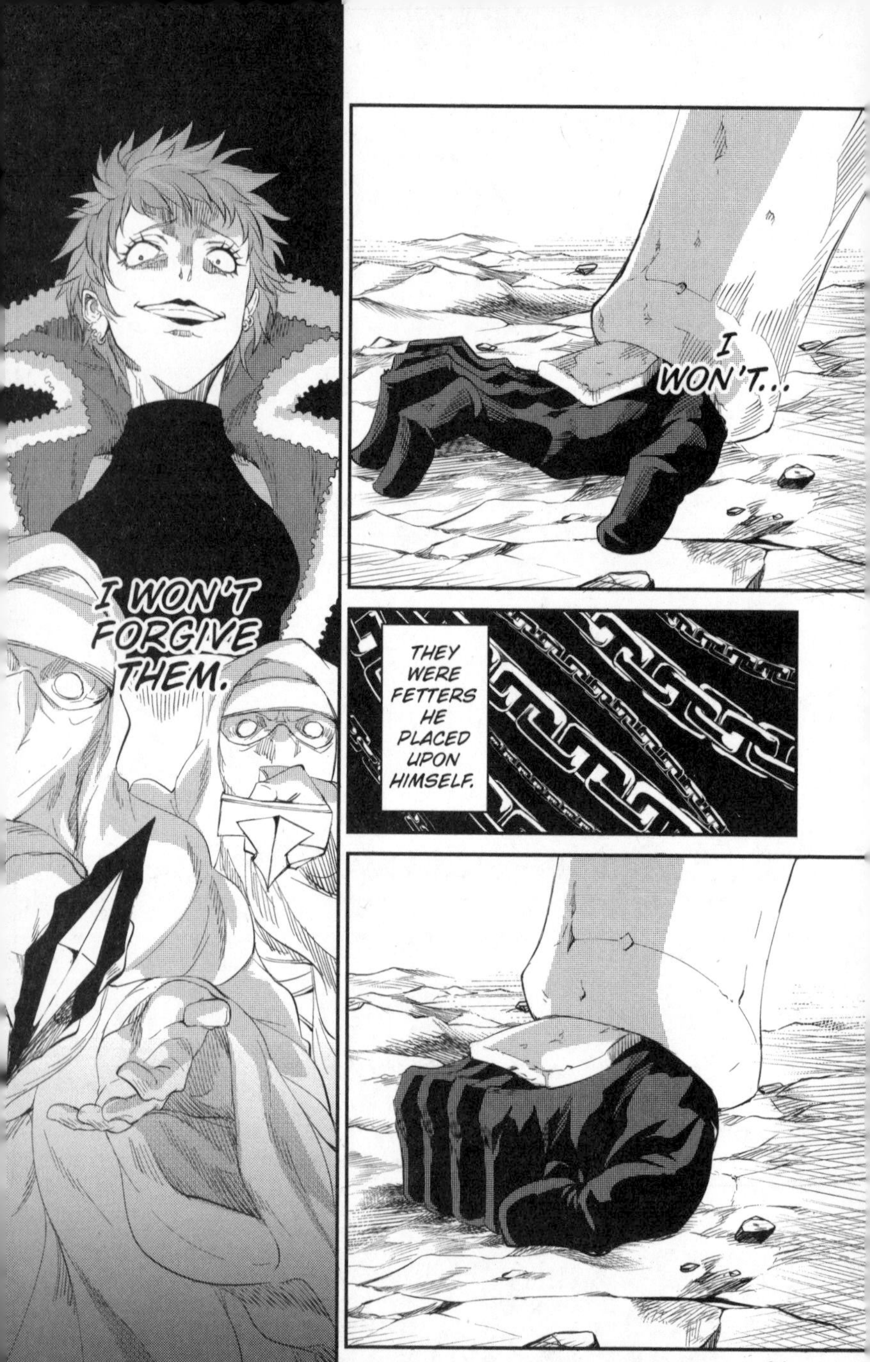
I WON'T...
THEY WERE FETTERS HE PLACED UPON HIMSELF.
I WON'T FORGIVE THEM.

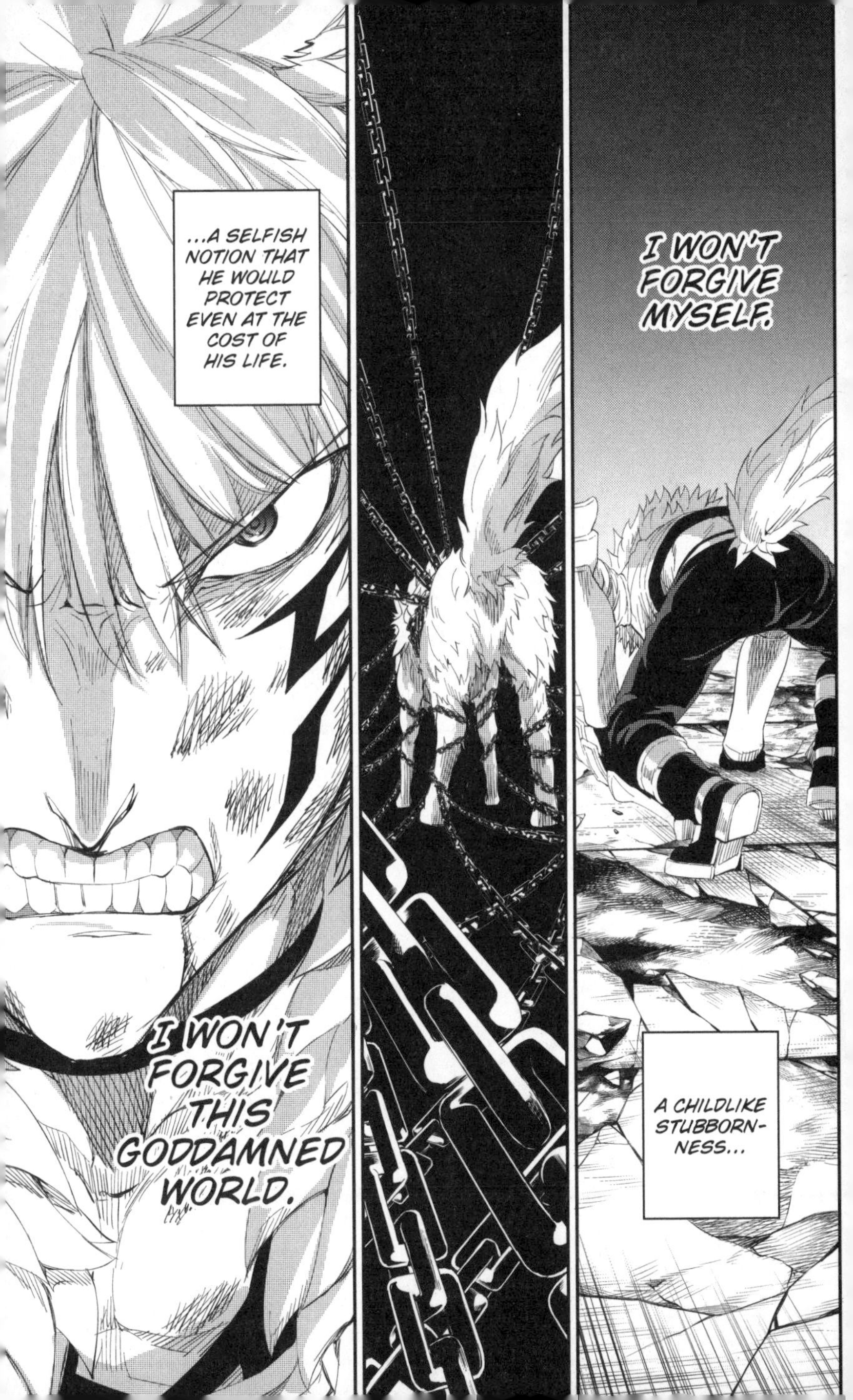
I WON'T FORGIVE MYSELF.
A CHILDLIKE STUBBORN-NESS...
...A SELFISH NOTION THAT HE WOULD PROTECT EVEN AT THE COST OF HIS LIFE.
I WON'T FORGIVE THIS GODDAMNED WORLD.

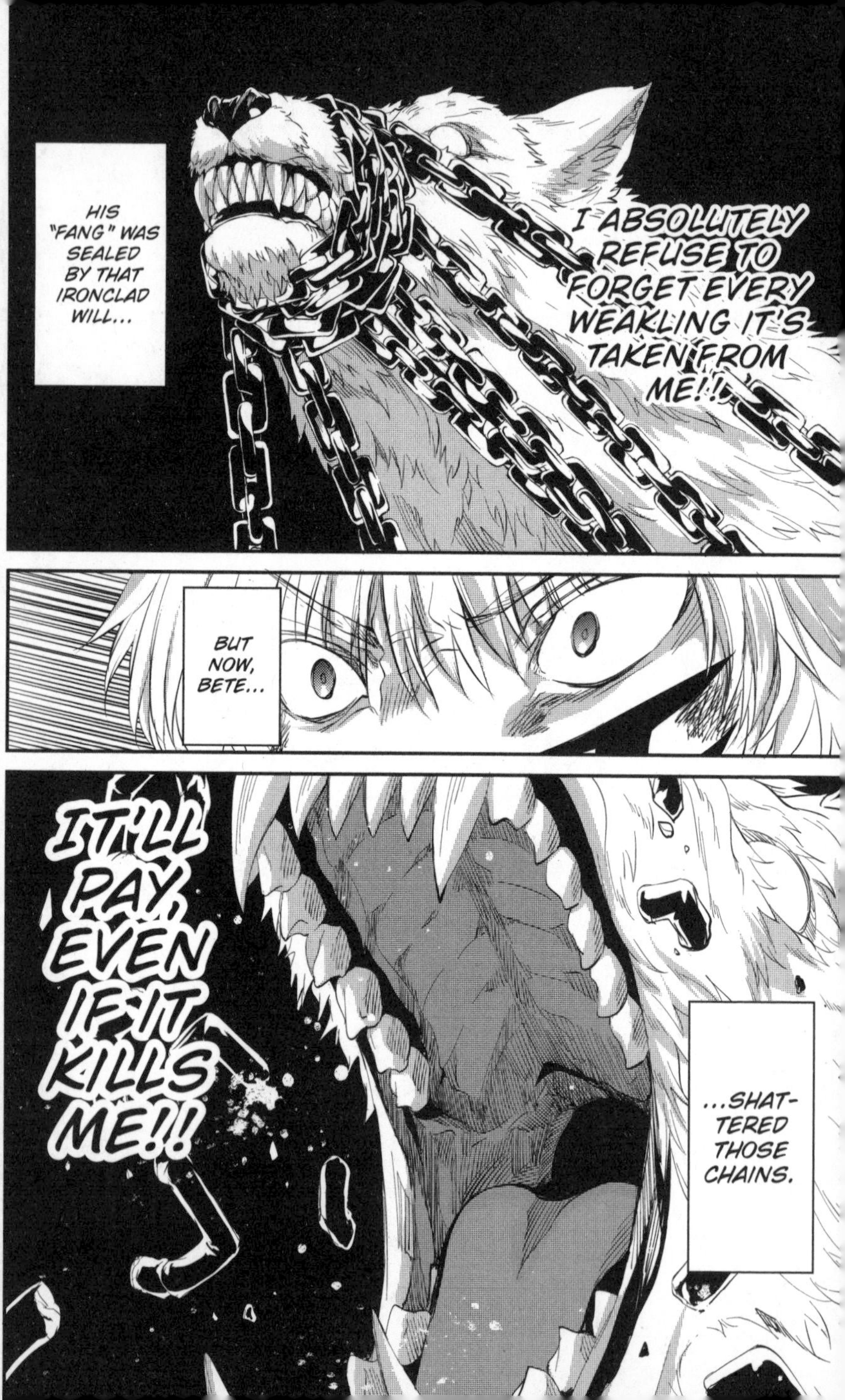
I ABSOLUTELY REFUSE TO FORGET EVERY WEAKLING IT'S TAKEN FROM ME!!
HIS "FANG" WAS SEALED BY THAT IRONCLAD WILL...
BUT NOW, BETE...
...SHAT-TERED THOSE CHAINS.
IT'LL PAY, EVEN IF IT KILLS ME!!

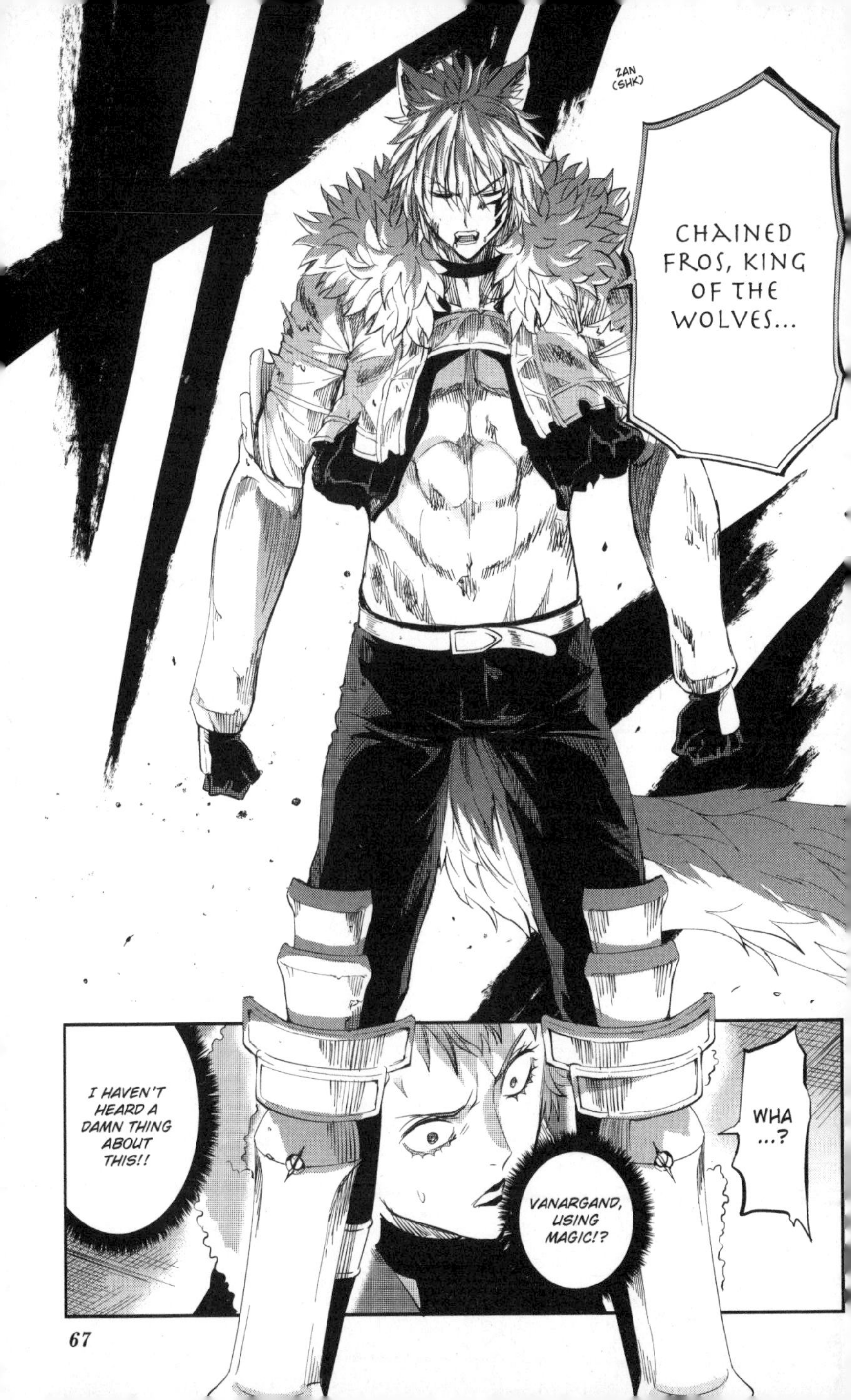
ZAN (SHK)
CHAINED FROS, KING OF THE WOLVES...
WHA ...?
VANARGAND, USING MAGIC!?
I HAVEN'T HEARD A DAMN THING ABOUT THIS!!

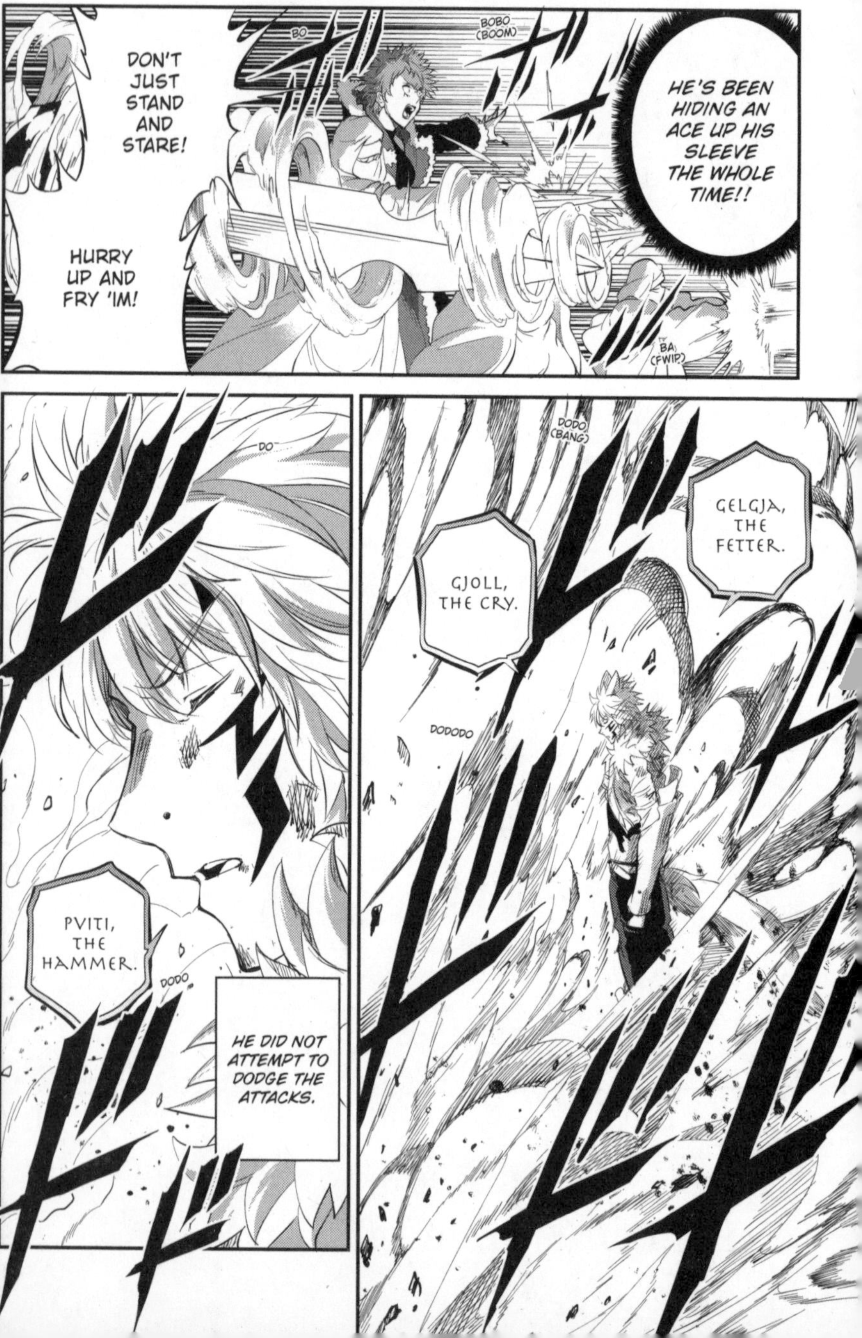

HE'S BEEN HIDING AN ACE UP HIS SLEEVE THE WHOLE TIME!!
BOBO (BOOM)
BO
DON'T JUST STAND AND STARE!
HURRY UP AND FRY 'IM!
BA (FWIP)
DODO (BANG)
GELGJA, THE FETTER.
GJOLL, THE CRY.
DODODO
DO
PVITI, THE HAMMER.
DODO
HE DID NOT ATTEMPT TO DODGE THE ATTACKS.

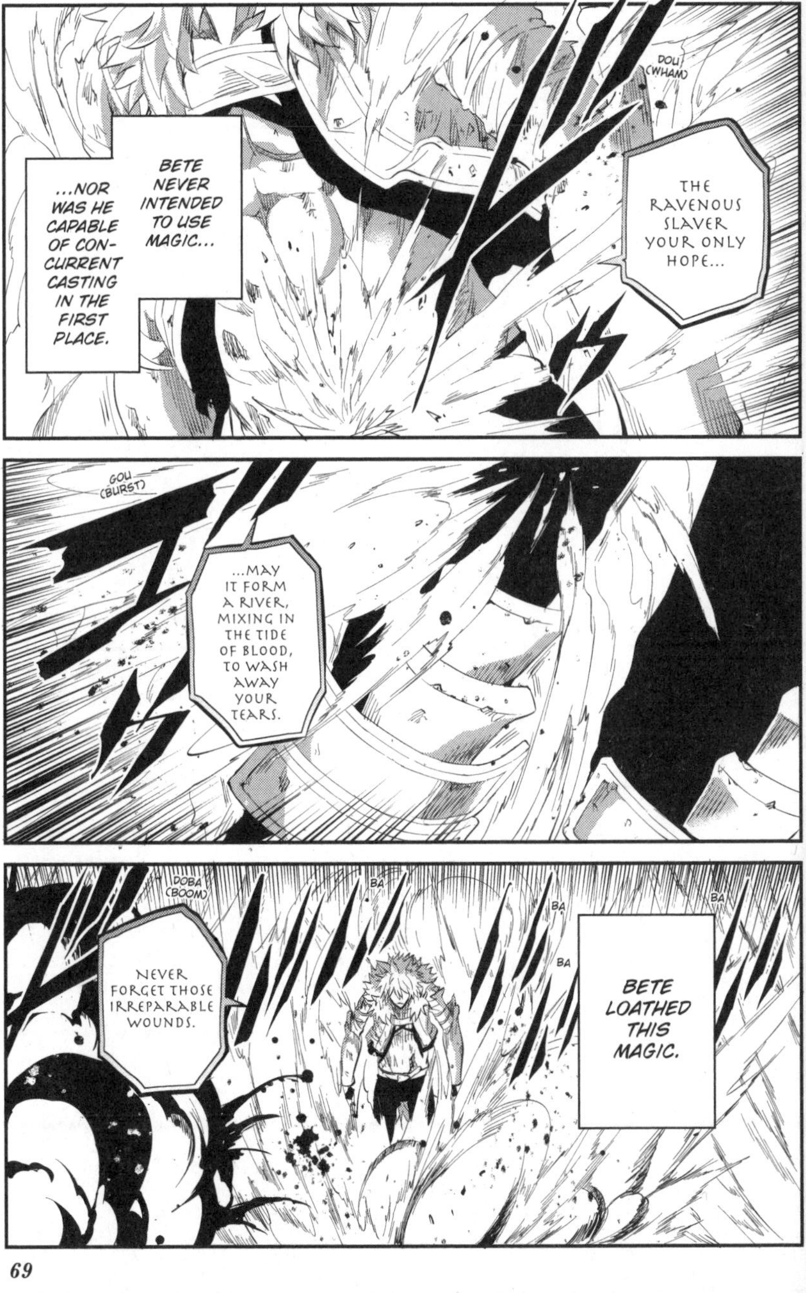
DOU (WHAM)
THE RAVENOUS SLAVER YOUR ONLY HOPE...
BETE NEVER INTENDED TO USE MAGIC...
...NOR WAS HE CAPABLE OF CON-CURRENT CASTING IN THE FIRST PLACE.
GOU (BURST)
...MAY IT FORM A RIVER, MIXING IN THE TIDE OF BLOOD, TO WASH AWAY YOUR TEARS.
BA
BA
BA
BA
BETE LOATHED THIS MAGIC.
DOBA (BOOM)
NEVER FORGET THOSE IRREPARABLE WOUNDS.

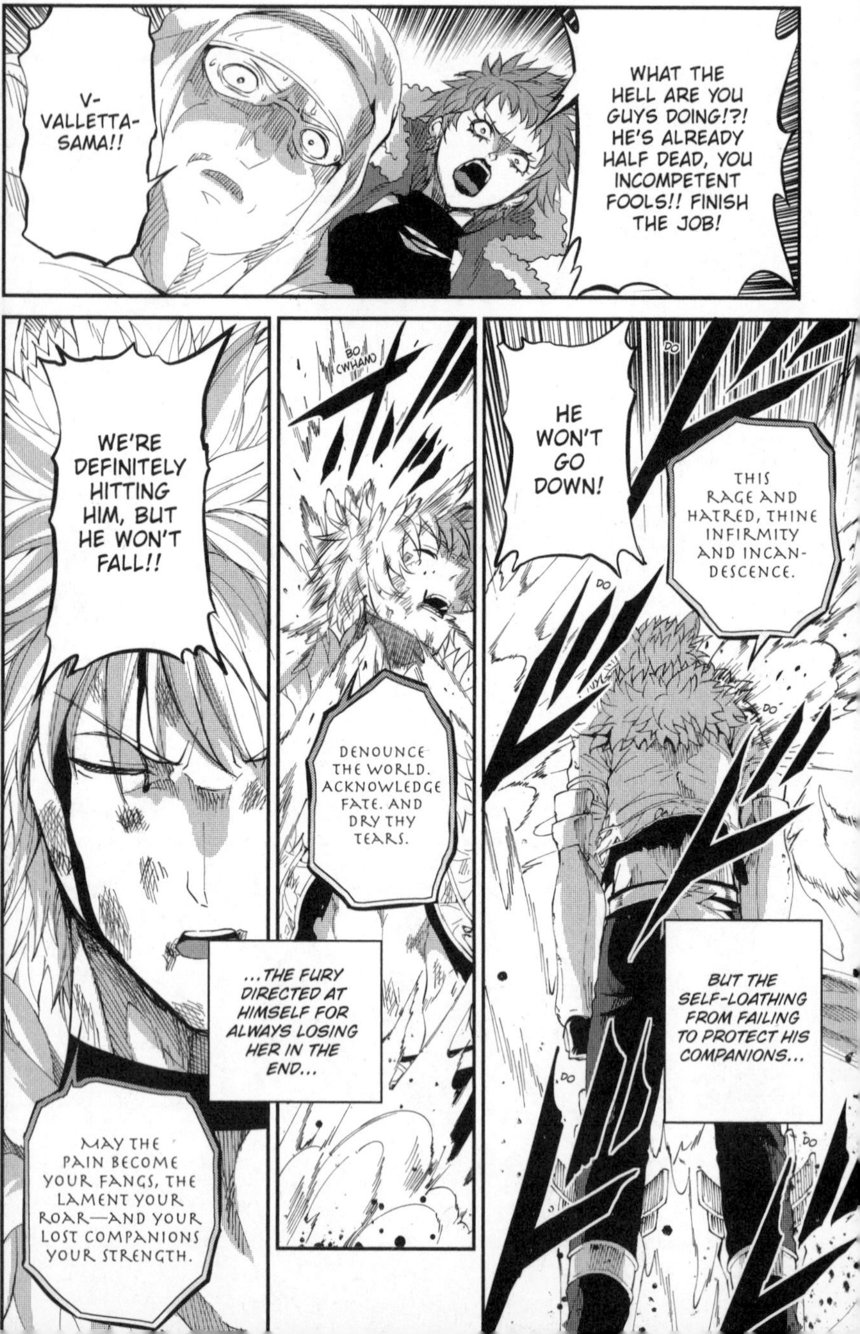
WHAT THE HELL ARE YOU GUYS DOING!?! HE'S ALREADY HALF DEAD, YOU INCOMPETENT FOOLS!! FINISH THE JOB!
V-VALLETTA-SAMA!!
DO
HE WON'T GO DOWN!
THIS RAGE AND HATRED, THINE INFIRMITY AND INCANDESCENCE.
DO
DO
BUT THE SELF-LOATHING FROM FAILING TO PROTECT HIS COMPANIONS...
DO
DO
BO CWHAM
DENOUNCE THE WORLD. ACKNOWLEDGE FATE. AND DRY THY TEARS.
...THE FURY DIRECTED AT HIMSELF FOR ALWAYS LOSING HER IN THE END...
WE'RE DEFINITELY HITTING HIM, BUT HE WON'T FALL!!
MAY THE PAIN BECOME YOUR FANGS, THE LAMENT YOUR ROAR—AND YOUR LOST COMPANIONS YOUR STRENGTH.

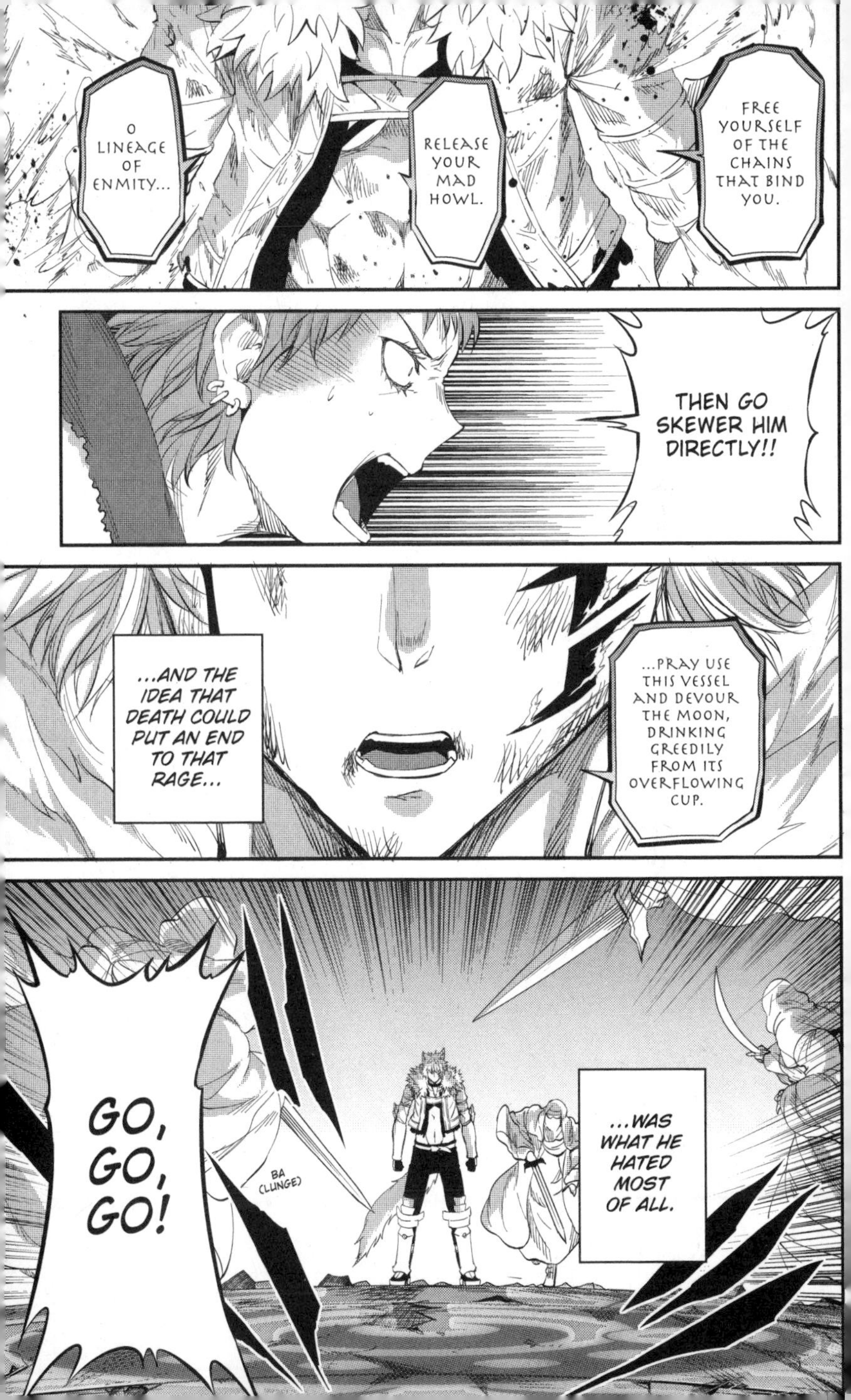
FREE YOURSELF OF THE CHAINS THAT BIND YOU.
RELEASE YOUR MAD HOWL.
O LINEAGE OF ENMITY...
THEN GO SKEWER HIM DIRECTLY!!
...PRAY USE THIS VESSEL AND DEVOUR THE MOON, DRINKING GREEDILY FROM ITS OVERFLOWING CUP.
...AND THE IDEA THAT DEATH COULD PUT AN END TO THAT RAGE...
...WAS WHAT HE HATED MOST OF ALL.
BA (LUNGE)
GO, GO, GO!

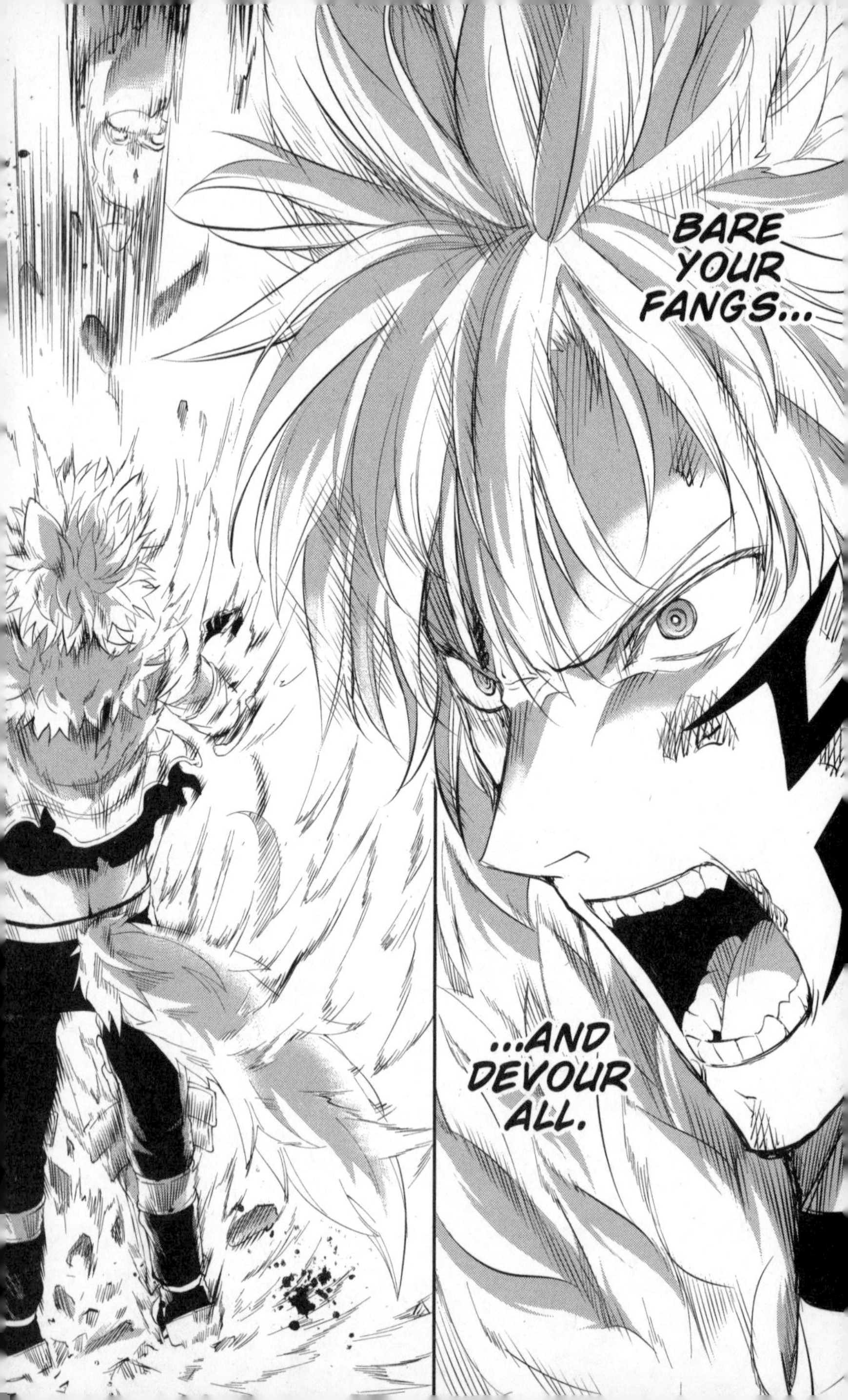
BARE YOUR FANGS...
...AND DEVOUR ALL.

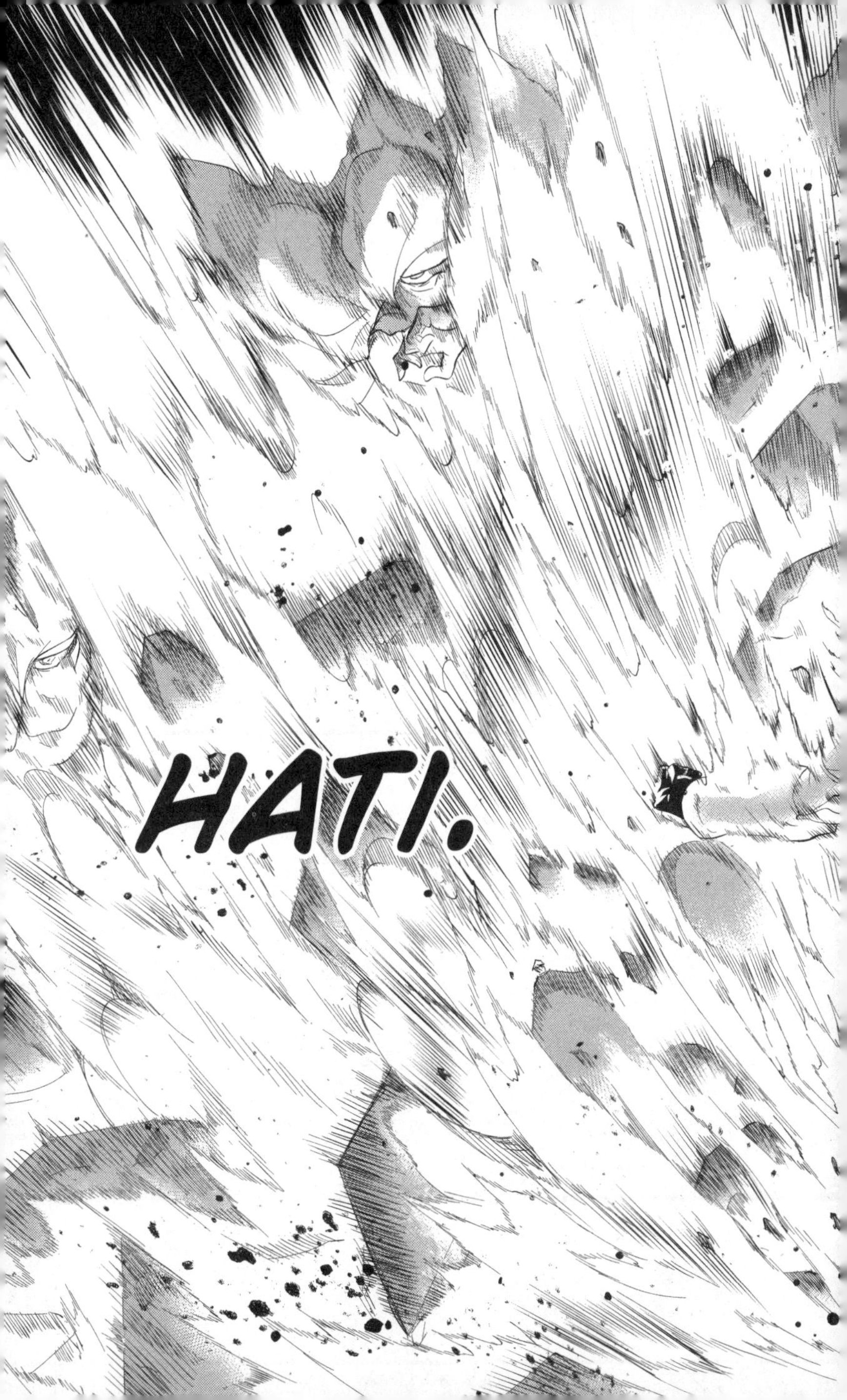
HATI.

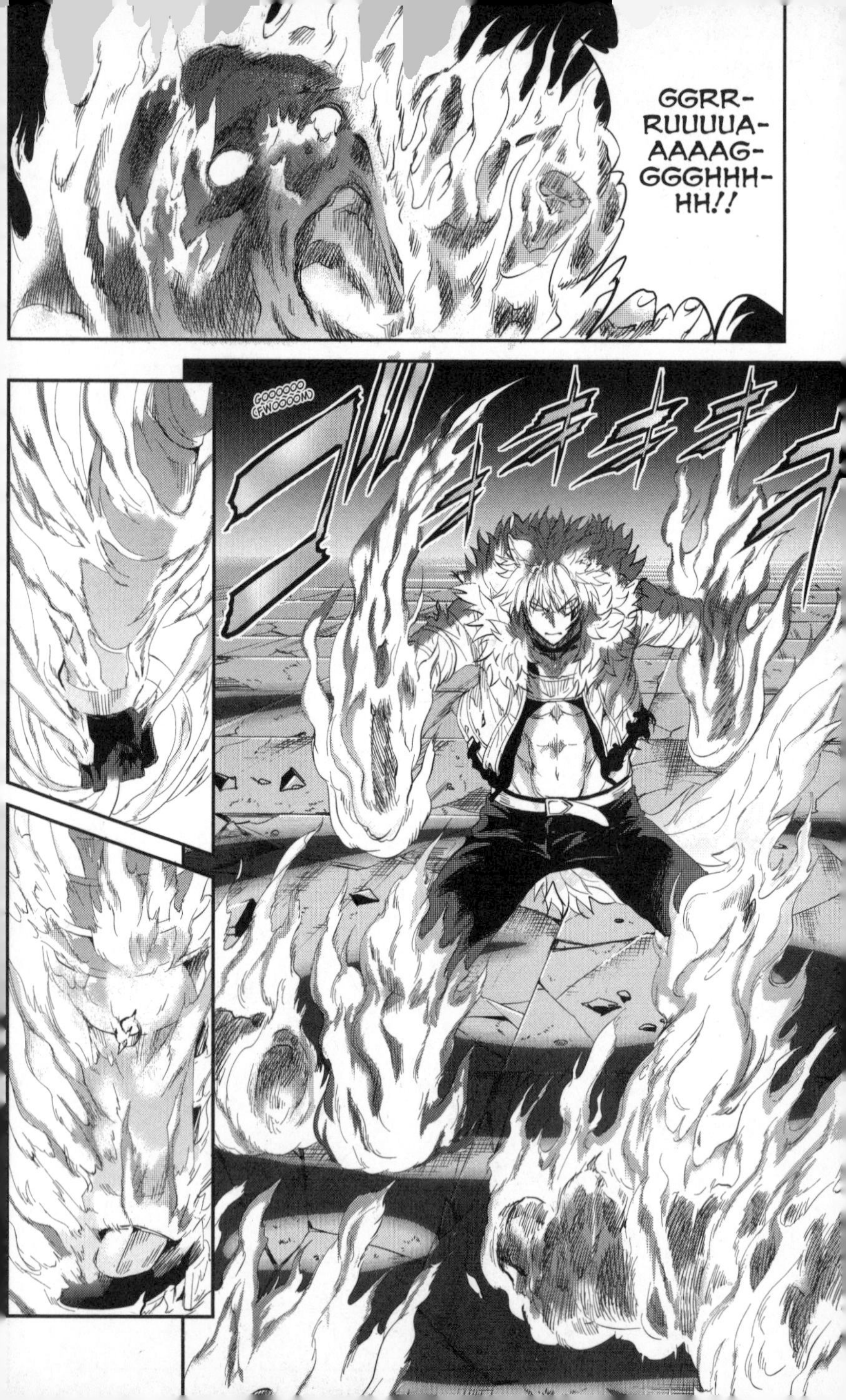
GGRR-RUUUUA-AAAAG-GGGHHH-HH!!
GOOOOOO (FWOOOOM)
ゴォォォォォ

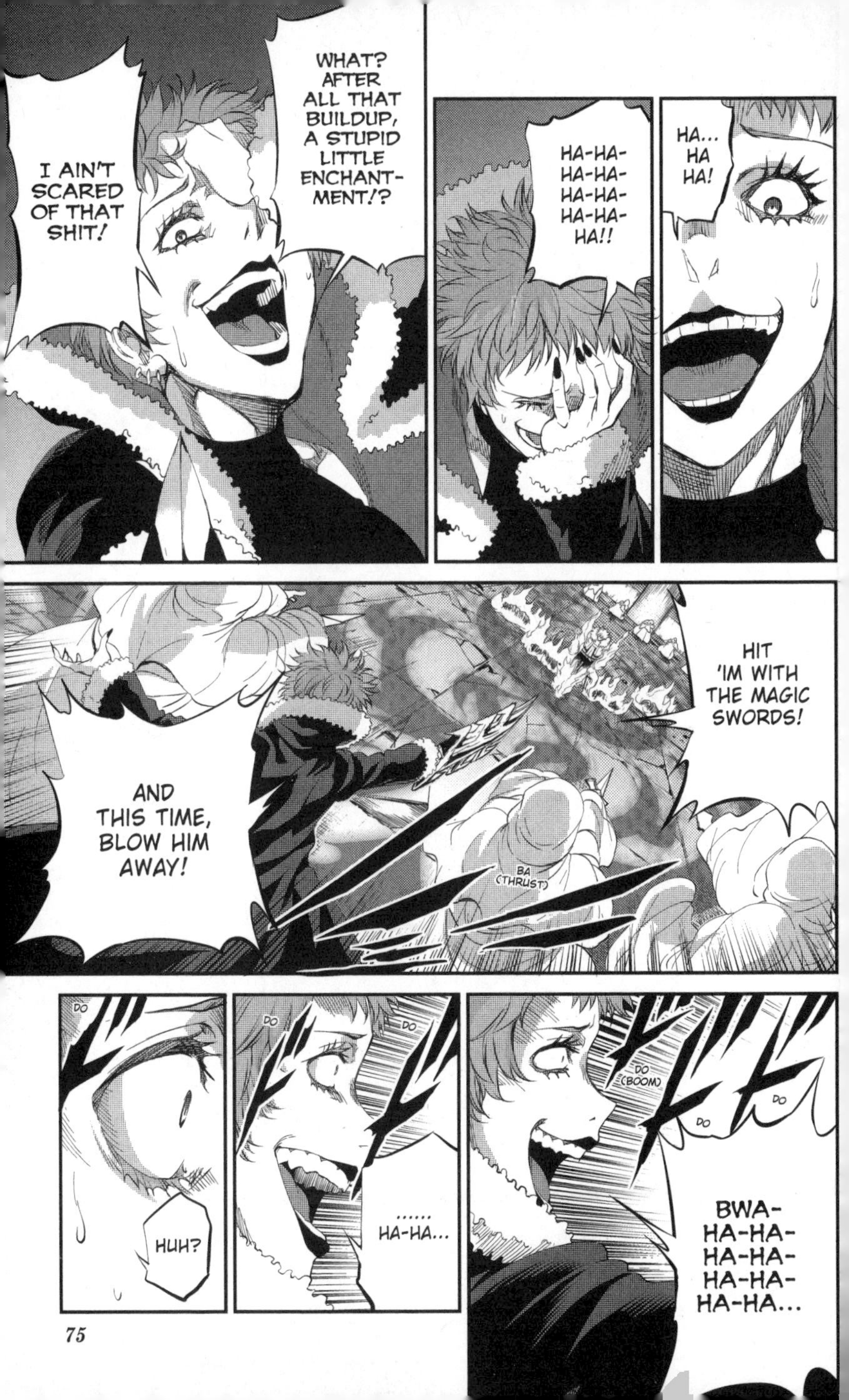
HA... HA HA!
HA-HA-HA-HA-HA-HA-HA-HA-HA!!
WHAT? AFTER ALL THAT BUILDUP, A STUPID LITTLE ENCHANTMENT!?
I AIN'T SCARED OF THAT SHIT!
HIT 'IM WITH THE MAGIC SWORDS!
BA (THRUST)
AND THIS TIME, BLOW HIM AWAY!
DO (BOOM)
DO
DO
BWA-HA-HA-HA-HA-HA-HA-HA-HA...
DO
DO
...... HA-HA...
DO
HUH?

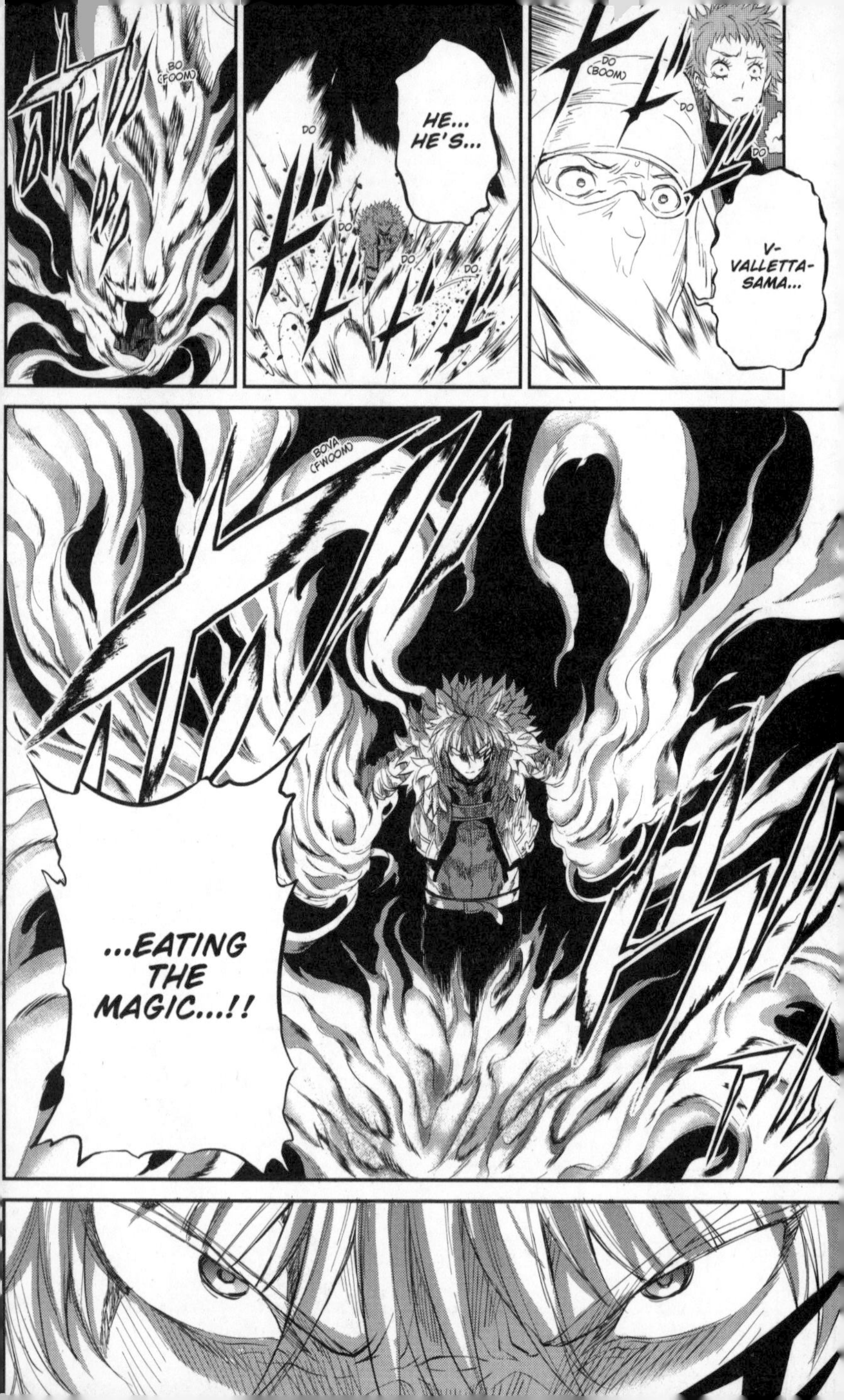
DO (BOOM)
DO
DO
V- VALLETTA-SAMA...
HE... HE'S...
DO
DO
DO
DO
BO (FOOM)
BOVA (FWOOM)
...EATING THE MAGIC...!!

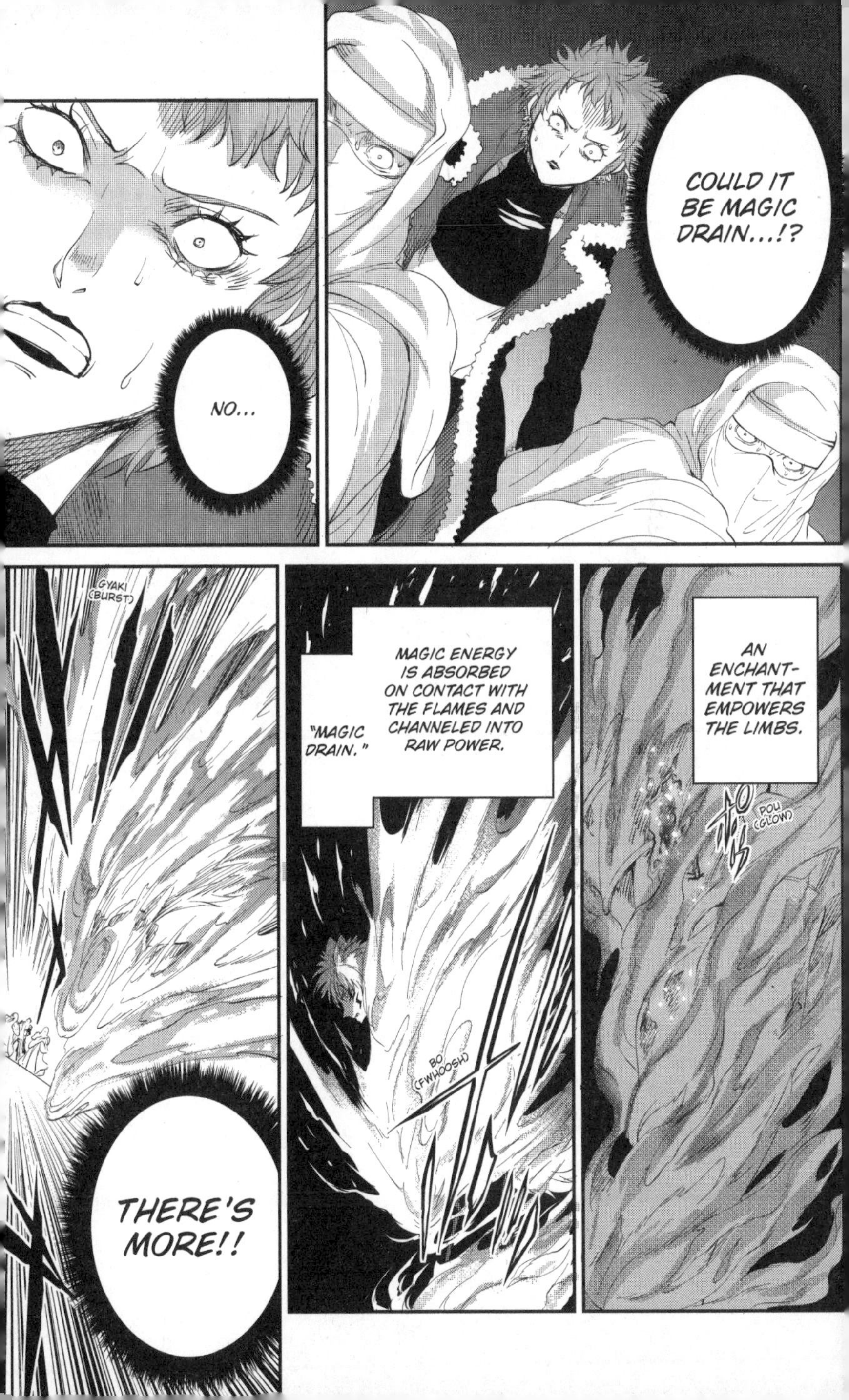
COULD IT BE MAGIC DRAIN...!?
NO...
AN ENCHANT-MENT THAT EMPOWERS THE LIMBS.
POU (GLOW)
MAGIC ENERGY IS ABSORBED ON CONTACT WITH THE FLAMES AND CHANNELED INTO RAW POWER.
"MAGIC DRAIN."
BO (FWHOOSH)
GYAKI (BURST)
THERE'S MORE!!

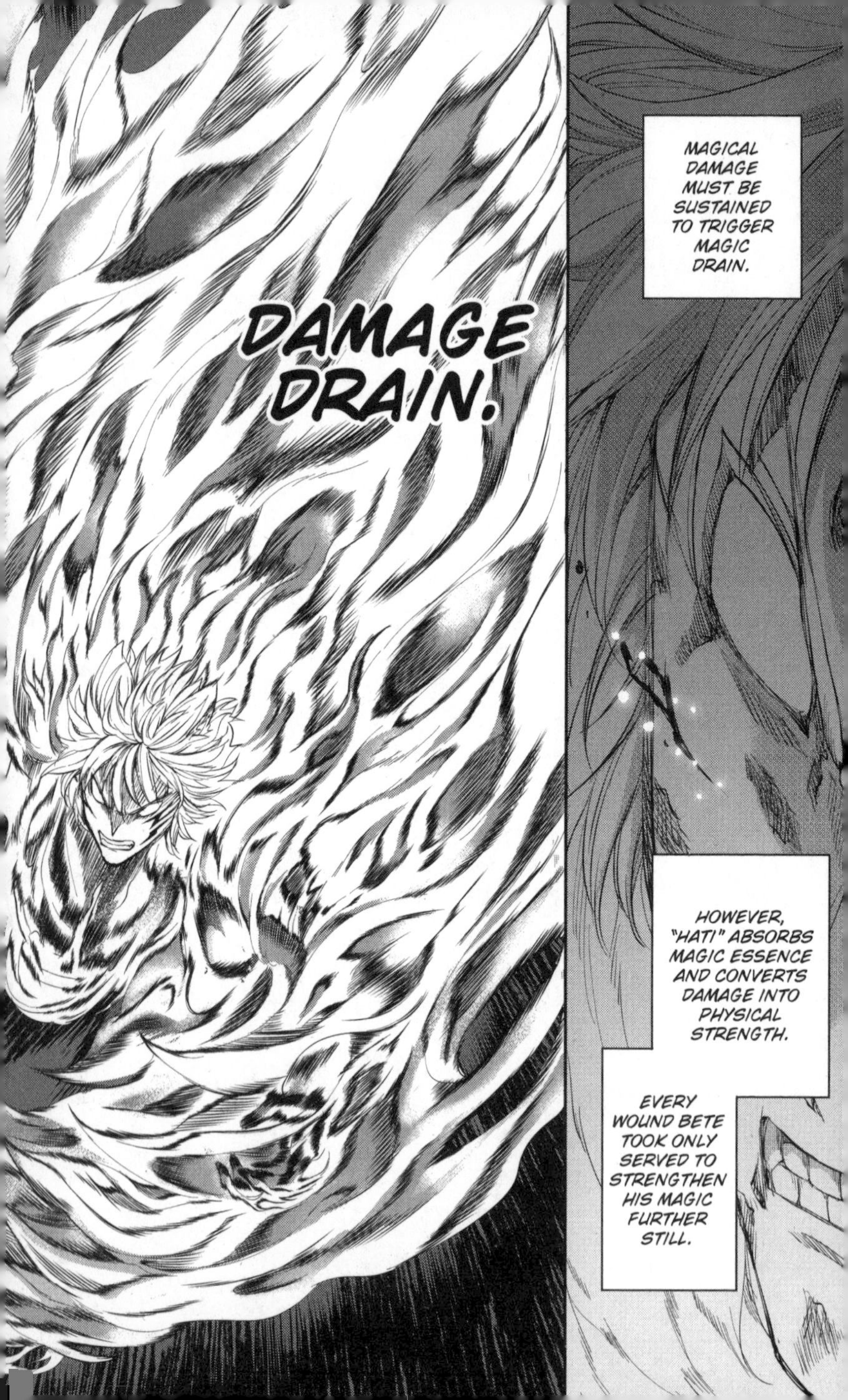
MAGICAL DAMAGE MUST BE SUSTAINED TO TRIGGER MAGIC DRAIN.
HOWEVER, "HATI" ABSORBS MAGIC ESSENCE AND CONVERTS DAMAGE INTO PHYSICAL STRENGTH.
EVERY WOUND BETE TOOK ONLY SERVED TO STRENGTHEN HIS MAGIC FURTHER STILL.
DAMAGE DRAIN.

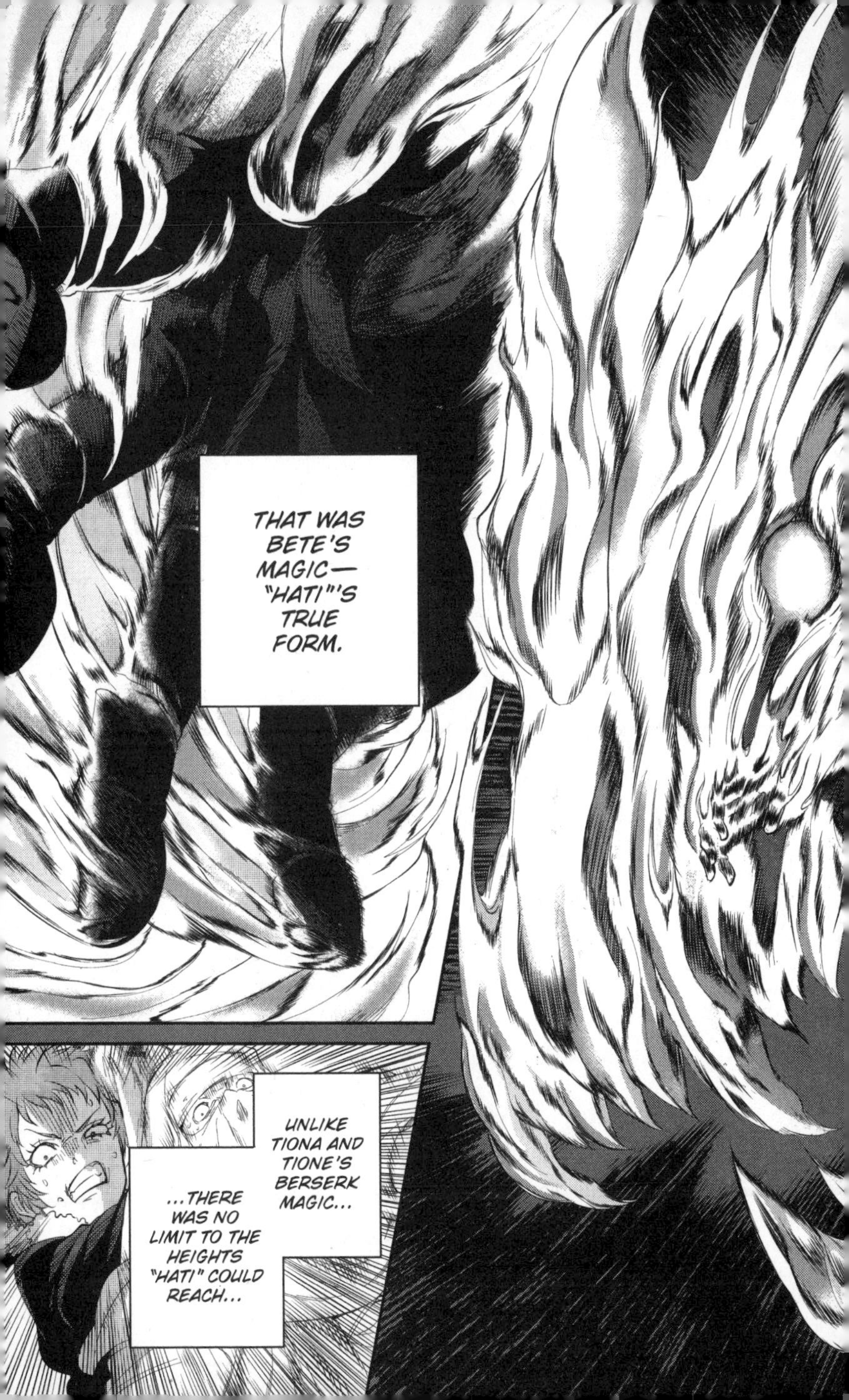
THAT WAS BETE'S MAGIC—"HATI"'S TRUE FORM.
UNLIKE TIONA AND TIONE'S BERSERK MAGIC...
...THERE WAS NO LIMIT TO THE HEIGHTS "HATI" COULD REACH...

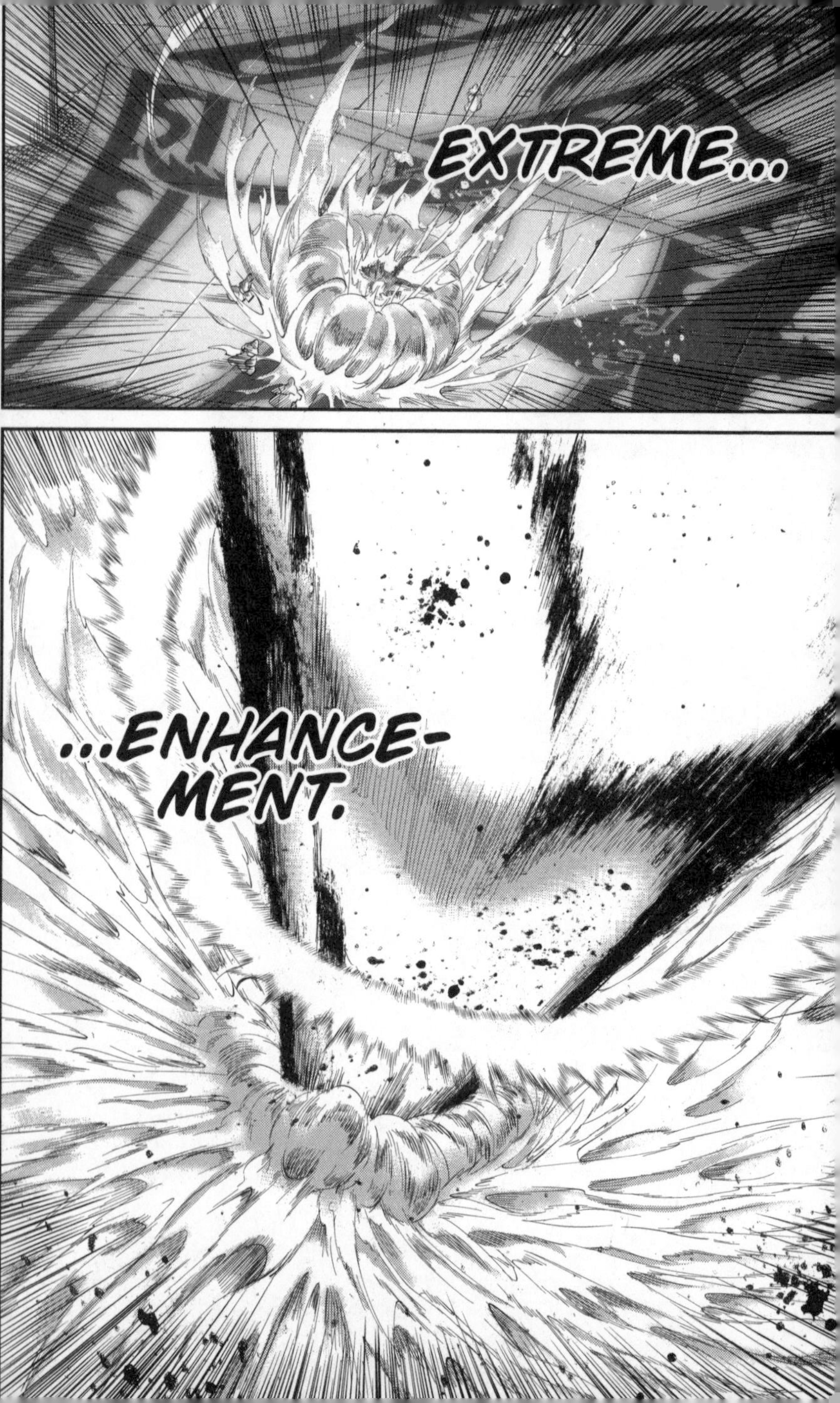
EXTREME...
...ENHANCE-MENT.

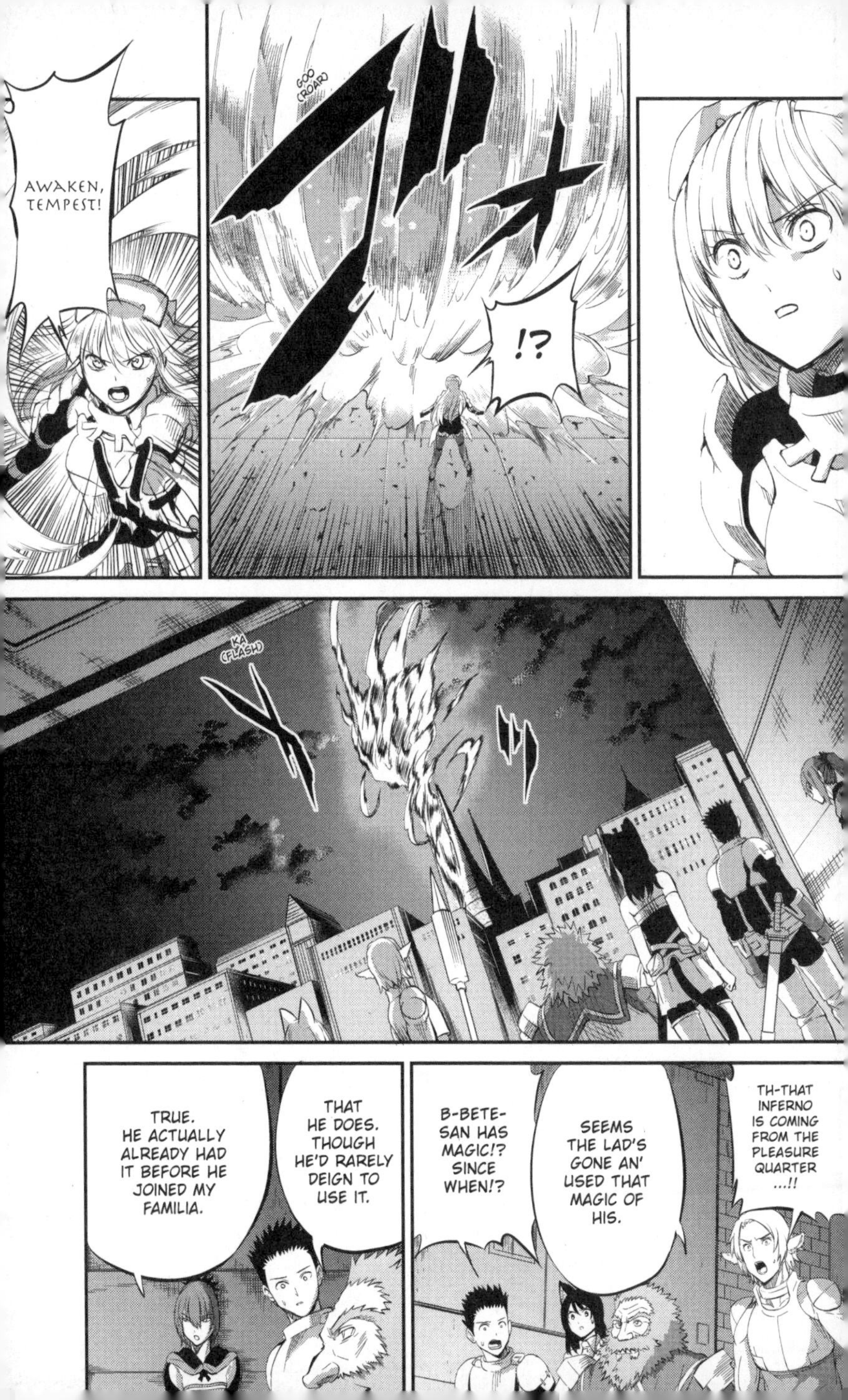
GOO (ROAR)
!?
AWAKEN, TEMPEST!
KA (FLASH)
TH-THAT INFERNO IS COMING FROM THE PLEASURE QUARTER ...!!
SEEMS THE LAD'S GONE AN' USED THAT MAGIC OF HIS.
B-BETE-SAN HAS MAGIC!? SINCE WHEN!?
THAT HE DOES. THOUGH HE'D RARELY DEIGN TO USE IT.
TRUE. HE ACTUALLY ALREADY HAD IT BEFORE HE JOINED MY FAMILIA.

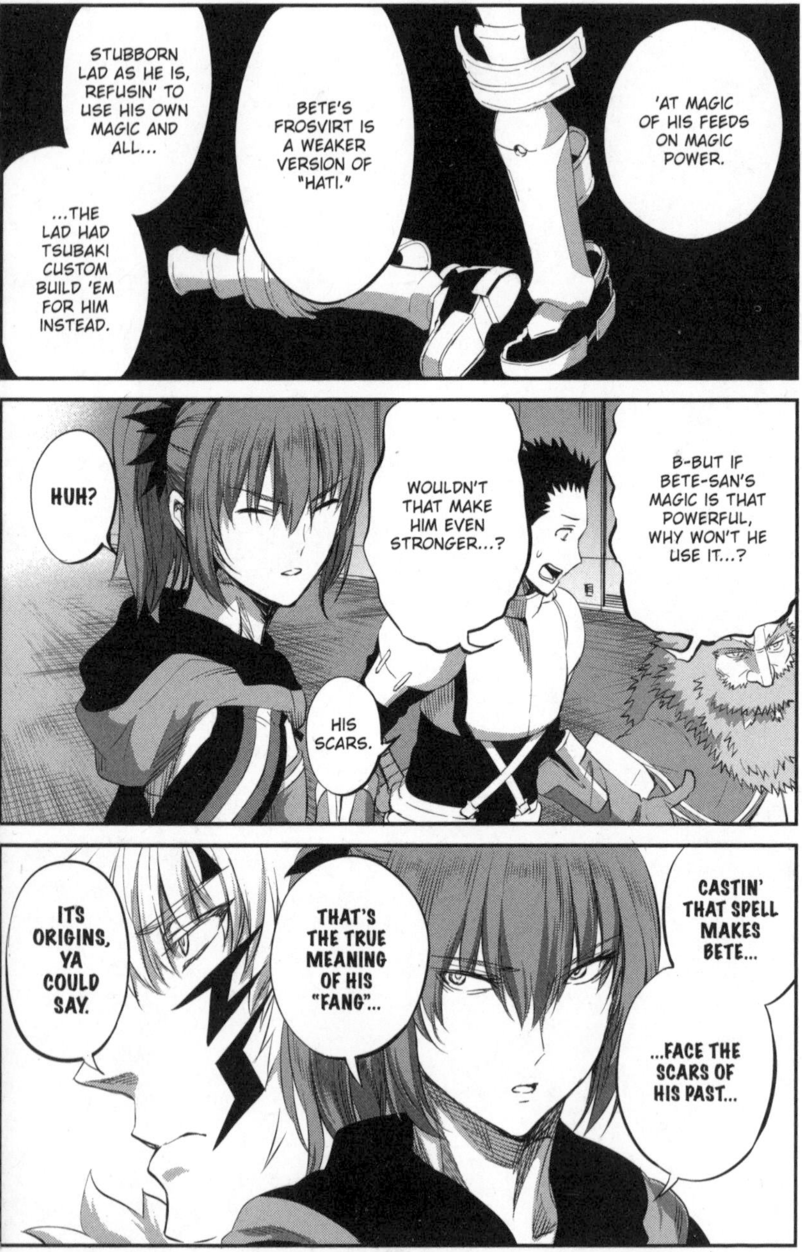
'AT MAGIC OF HIS FEEDS ON MAGIC POWER.
BETE'S FROSVIRT IS A WEAKER VERSION OF "HATI."
STUBBORN LAD AS HE IS, REFUSIN' TO USE HIS OWN MAGIC AND ALL...
...THE LAD HAD TSUBAKI CUSTOM BUILD 'EM FOR HIM INSTEAD.
B-BUT IF BETE-SAN'S MAGIC IS THAT POWERFUL, WHY WON'T HE USE IT...?
WOULDN'T THAT MAKE HIM EVEN STRONGER...?
HUH?
HIS SCARS.
CASTIN' THAT SPELL MAKES BETE...
...FACE THE SCARS OF HIS PAST...
THAT'S THE TRUE MEANING OF HIS "FANG"...
ITS ORIGINS, YA COULD SAY.

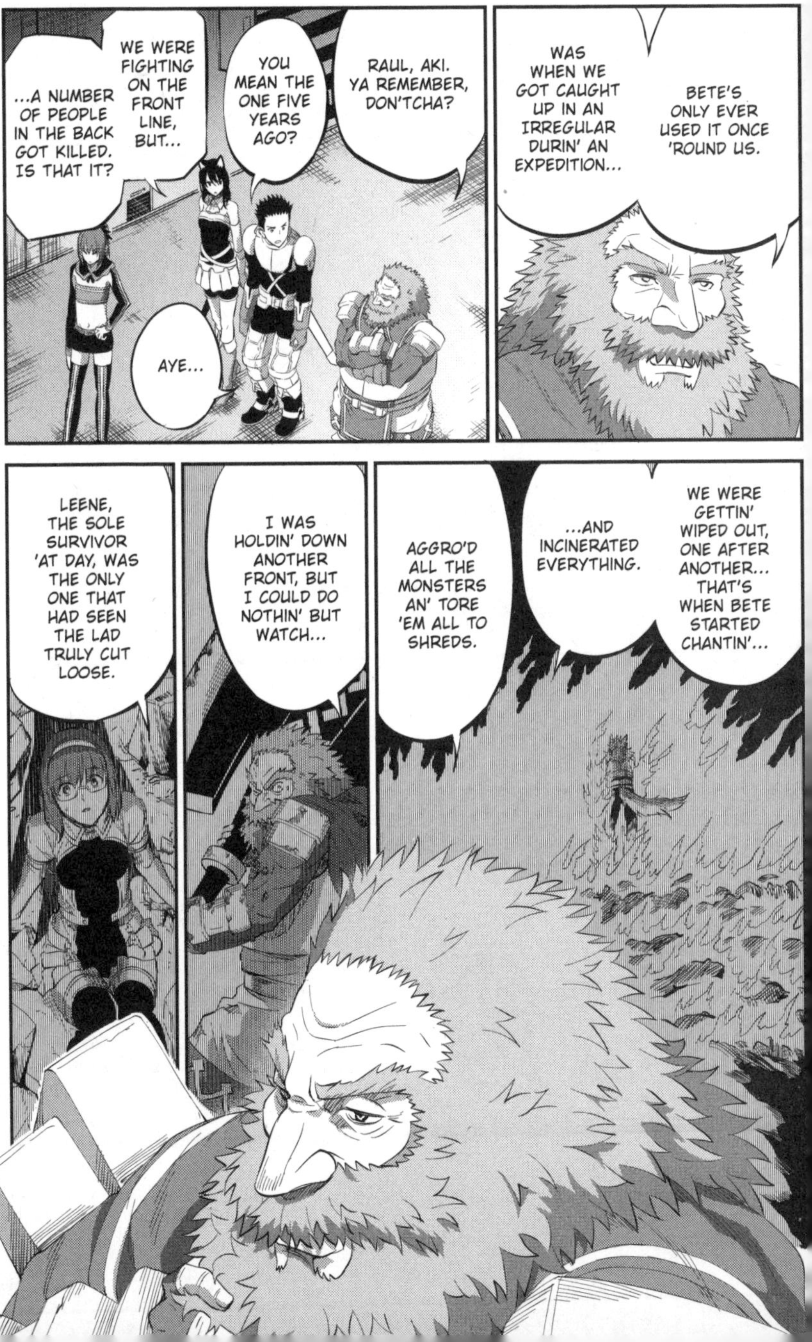
BETE'S ONLY EVER USED IT ONCE 'ROUND US.
WAS WHEN WE GOT CAUGHT UP IN AN IRREGULAR DURIN' AN EXPEDITION...
RAUL, AKI. YA REMEMBER, DON'TCHA?
YOU MEAN THE ONE FIVE YEARS AGO?
WE WERE FIGHTING ON THE FRONT LINE, BUT...
...A NUMBER OF PEOPLE IN THE BACK GOT KILLED. IS THAT IT?
AYE...
WE WERE GETTIN' WIPED OUT, ONE AFTER ANOTHER... THAT'S WHEN BETE STARTED CHANTIN'...
...AND INCINERATED EVERYTHING.
AGGRO'D ALL THE MONSTERS AN' TORE 'EM ALL TO SHREDS.
I WAS HOLDIN' DOWN ANOTHER FRONT, BUT I COULD DO NOTHIN' BUT WATCH...
LEENE, THE SOLE SURVIVOR 'AT DAY, WAS THE ONLY ONE THAT HAD SEEN THE LAD TRULY CUT LOOSE.

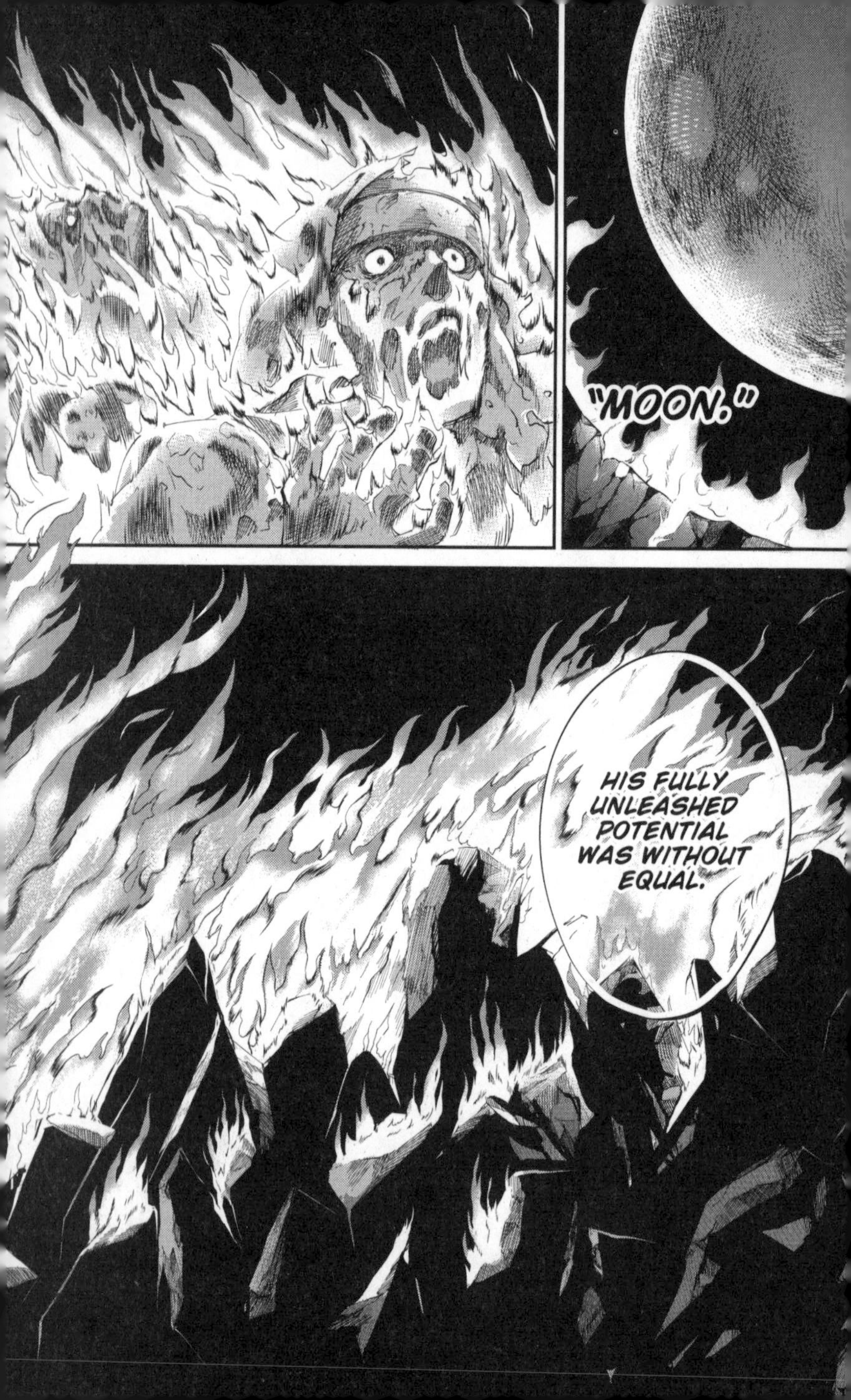
"MOON."
HIS FULLY UNLEASHED POTENTIAL WAS WITHOUT EQUAL.

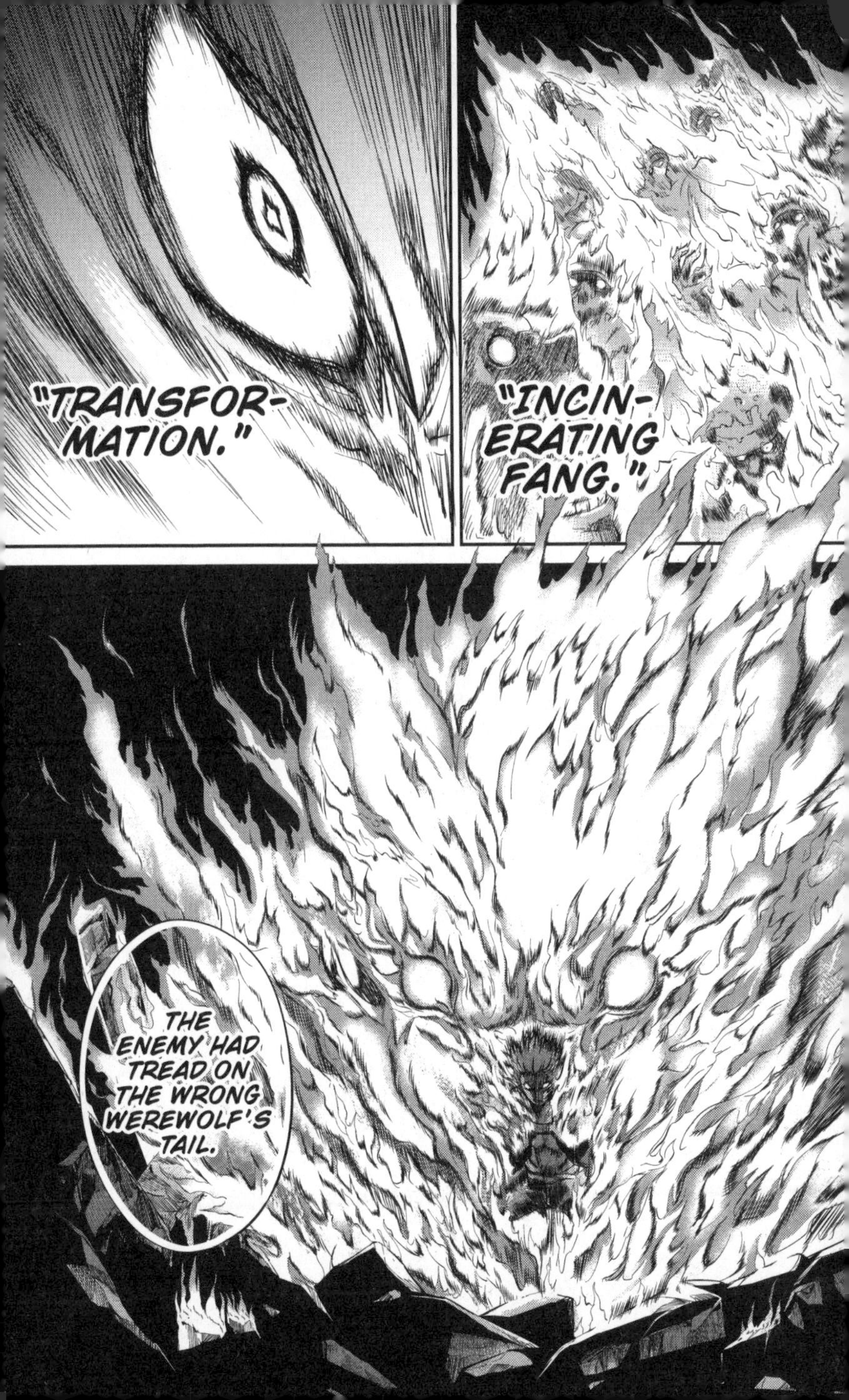
"INCIN-ERATING FANG."
"TRANSFOR-MATION."
THE ENEMY HAD TREAD ON THE WRONG WEREWOLF'S TAIL.

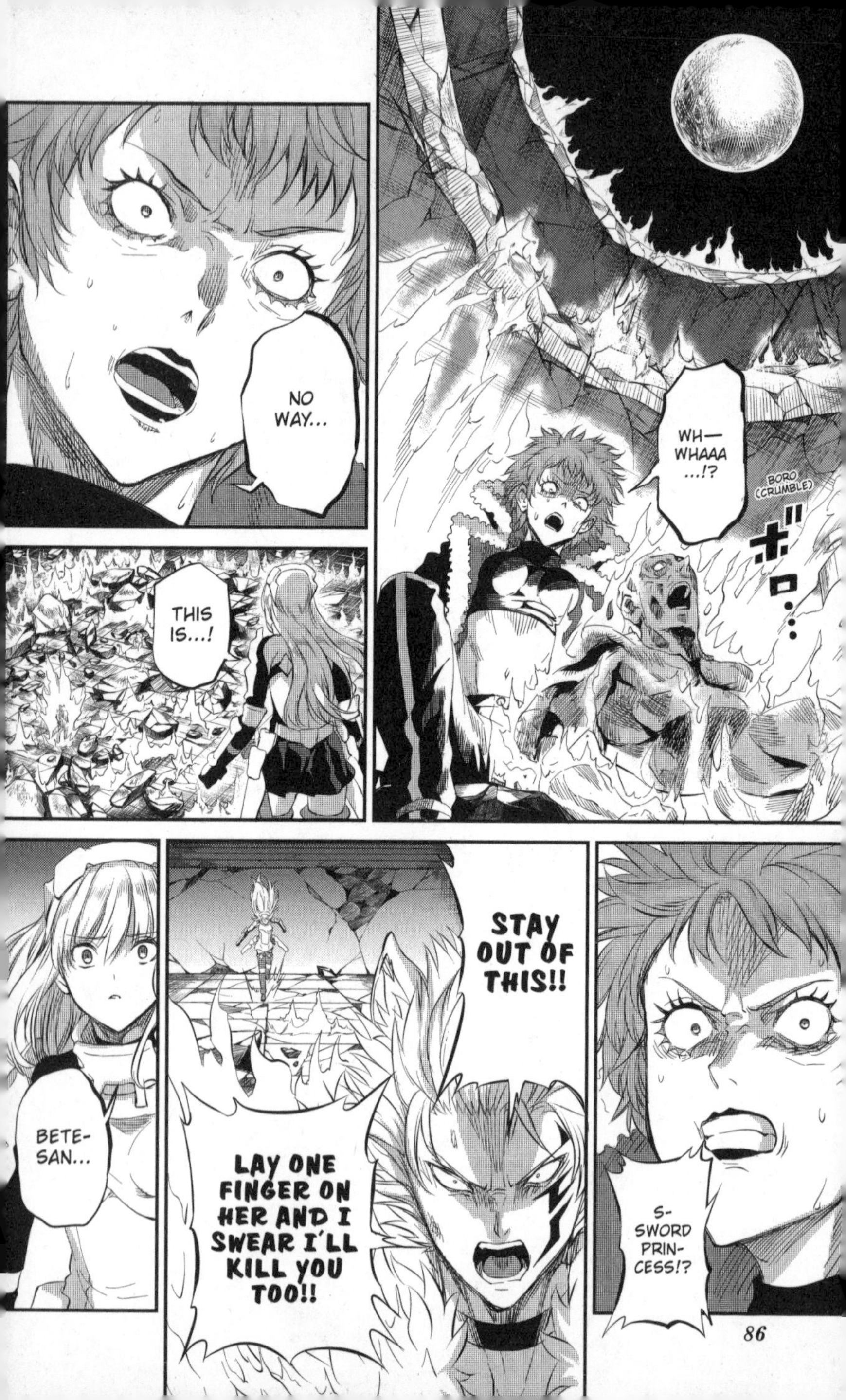
WH— WHAAA ...!?
BORO (CRUMBLE)
NO WAY...
THIS IS...!
S-SWORD PRINCESS!?
STAY OUT OF THIS!!
LAY ONE FINGER ON HER AND I SWEAR I'LL KILL YOU TOO!!
BETE-SAN...

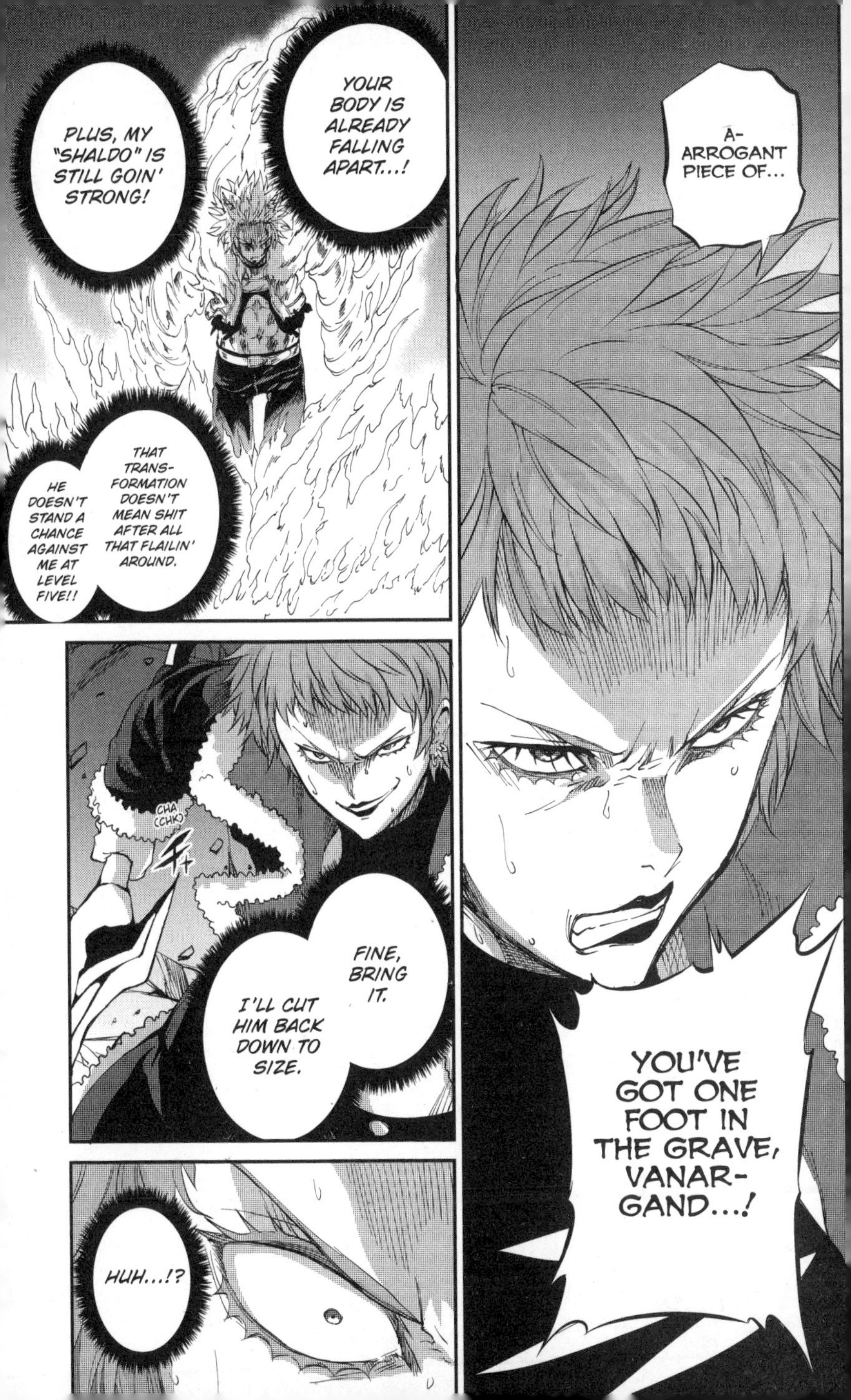
A- ARROGANT PIECE OF...
YOU'VE GOT ONE FOOT IN THE GRAVE, VANAR-GAND...!
YOUR BODY IS ALREADY FALLING APART...!
PLUS, MY "SHALDO" IS STILL GOIN' STRONG!
THAT TRANS-FORMATION DOESN'T MEAN SHIT AFTER ALL THAT FLAILIN' AROUND.
HE DOESN'T STAND A CHANCE AGAINST ME AT LEVEL FIVE!!
CHA (CHK)
FINE, BRING IT.
I'LL CUT HIM BACK DOWN TO SIZE.
HUH...!?

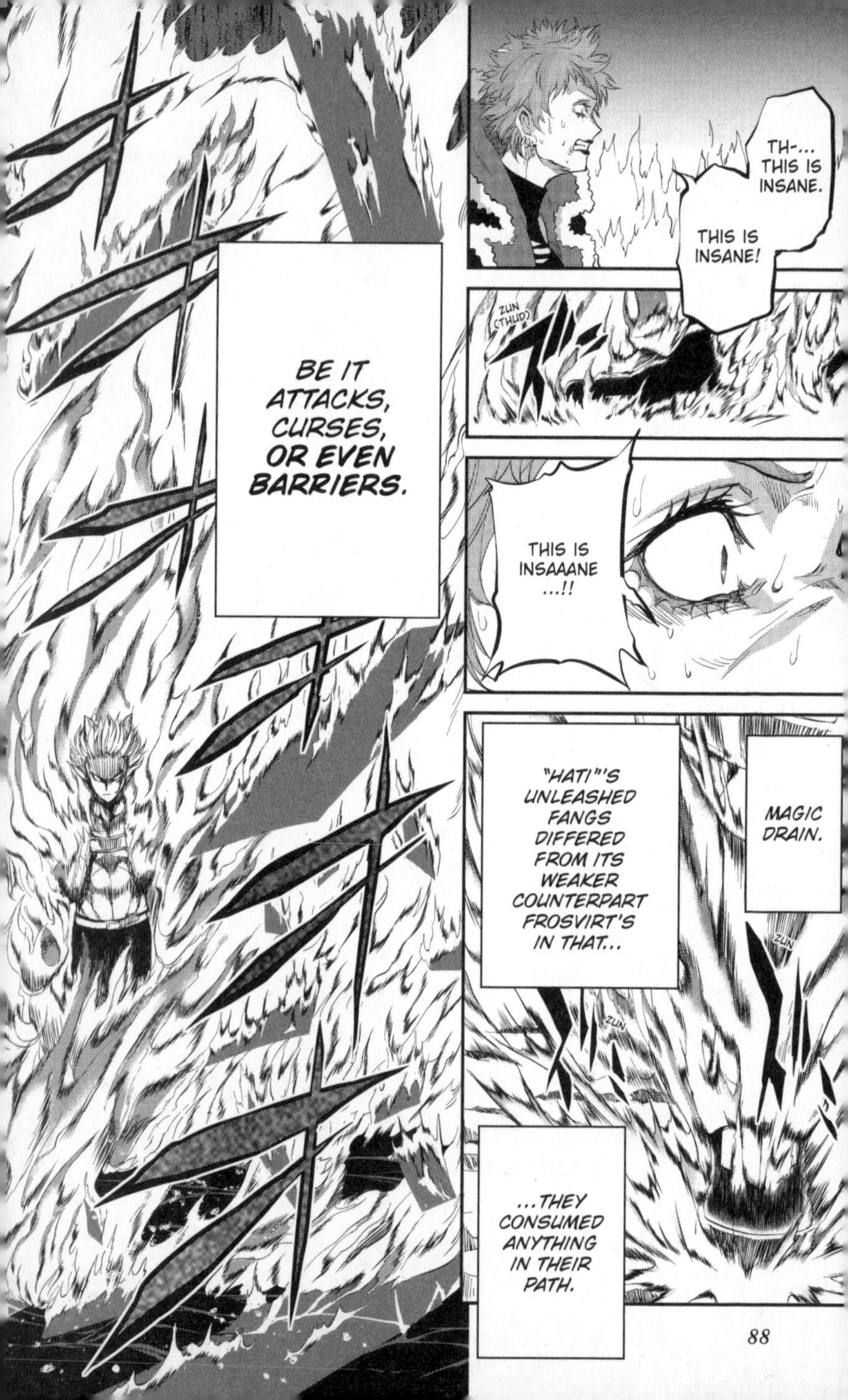
TH-... THIS IS INSANE.
THIS IS INSANE!
ZUN (THUD)
THIS IS INSAAANE ...!!
MAGIC DRAIN.
"HATI"'S UNLEASHED FANGS DIFFERED FROM ITS WEAKER COUNTERPART FROSVIRT'S IN THAT...
ZUN
ZUN
...THEY CONSUMED ANYTHING IN THEIR PATH.
BE IT ATTACKS, CURSES, OR EVEN BARRIERS.

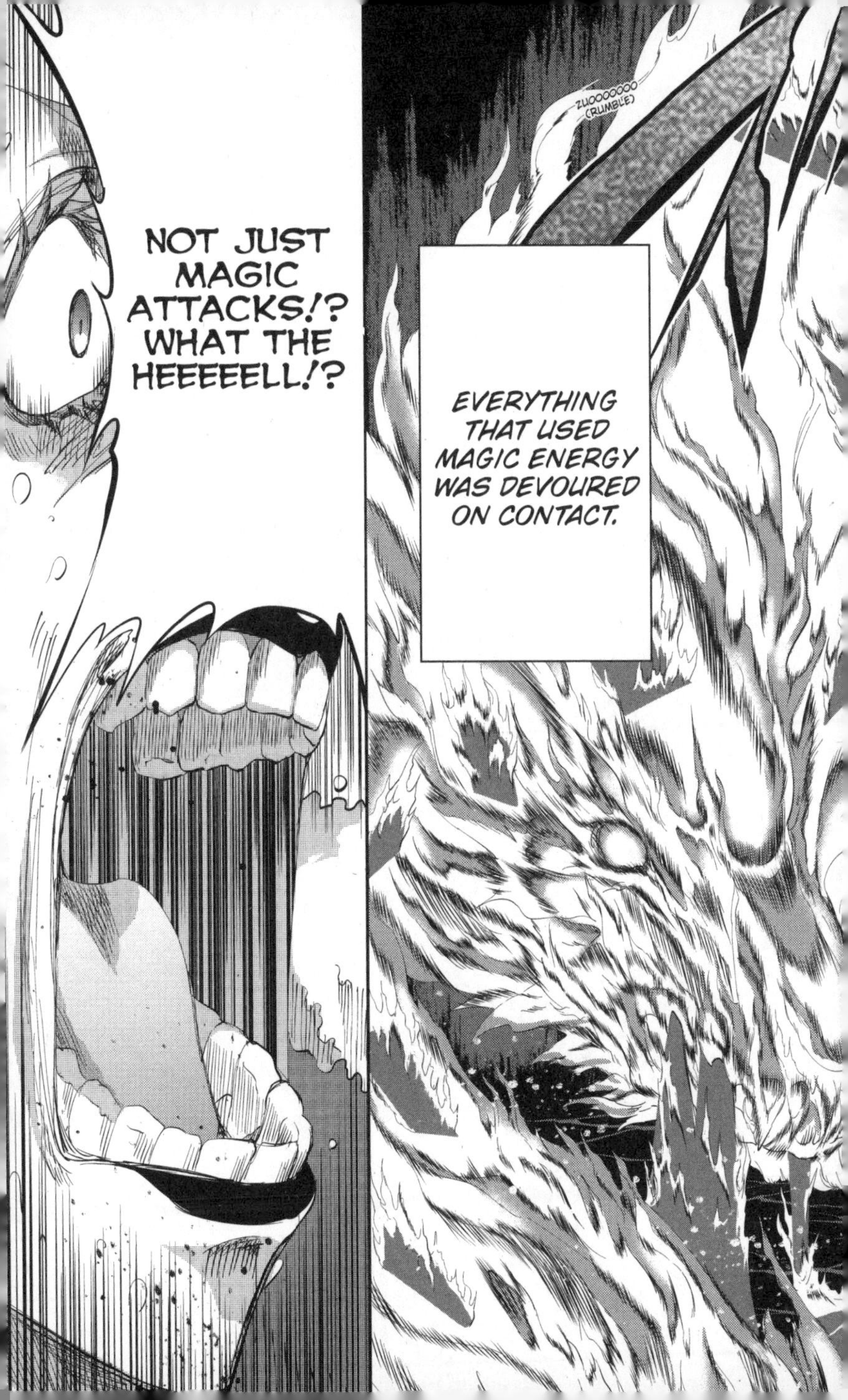
ZUOOOOOOO (RUMBLE)
EVERYTHING THAT USED MAGIC ENERGY WAS DEVOURED ON CONTACT.
NOT JUST MAGIC ATTACKS!? WHAT THE HEEEEELL!?

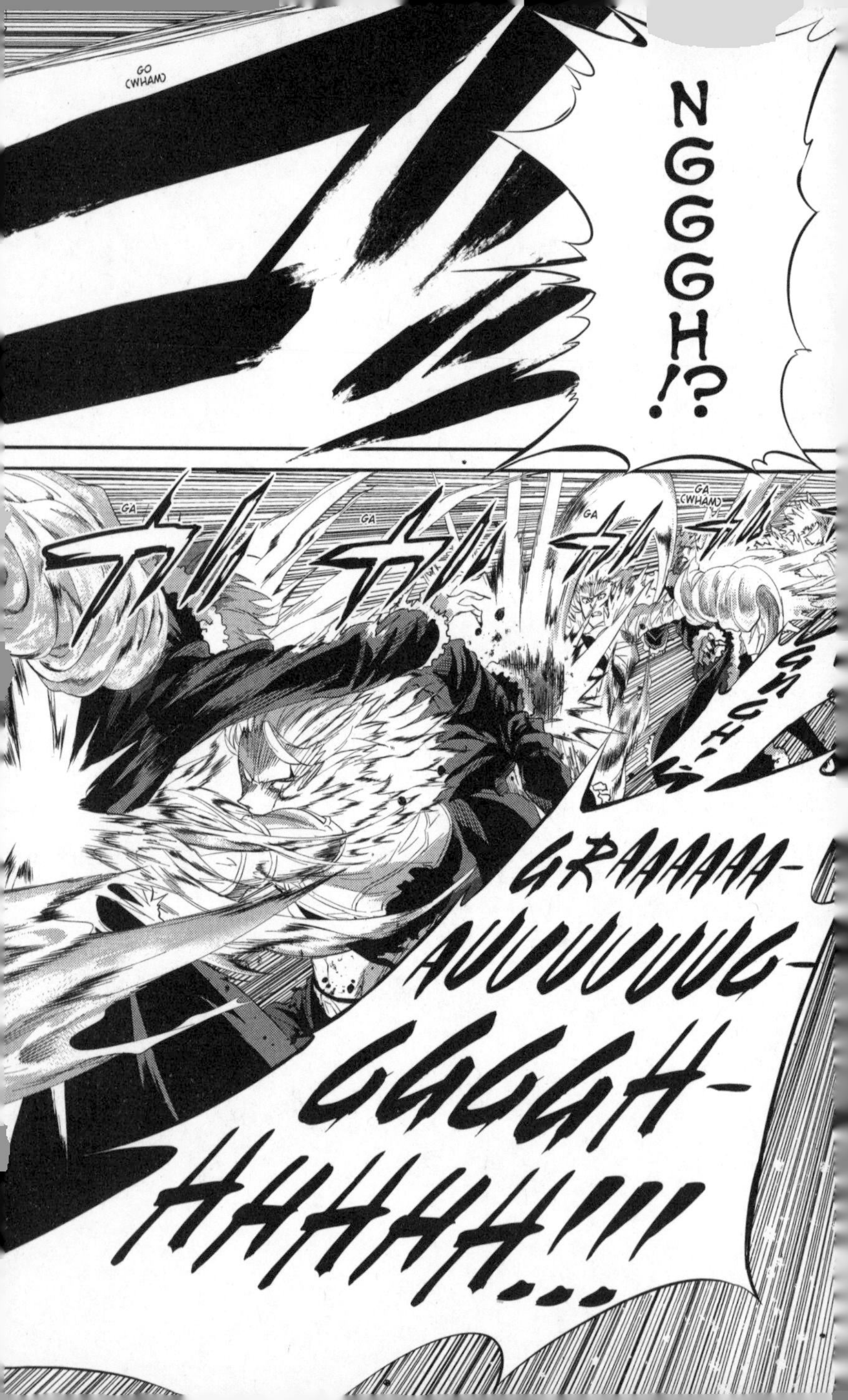
NGGGH!?
GO (WHAM)
NGNGH-!?
GA (WHAM)
GA
GA
GA
GRAAAAAA-AUUUUUUG-GGGGH-HHHHH!!!...

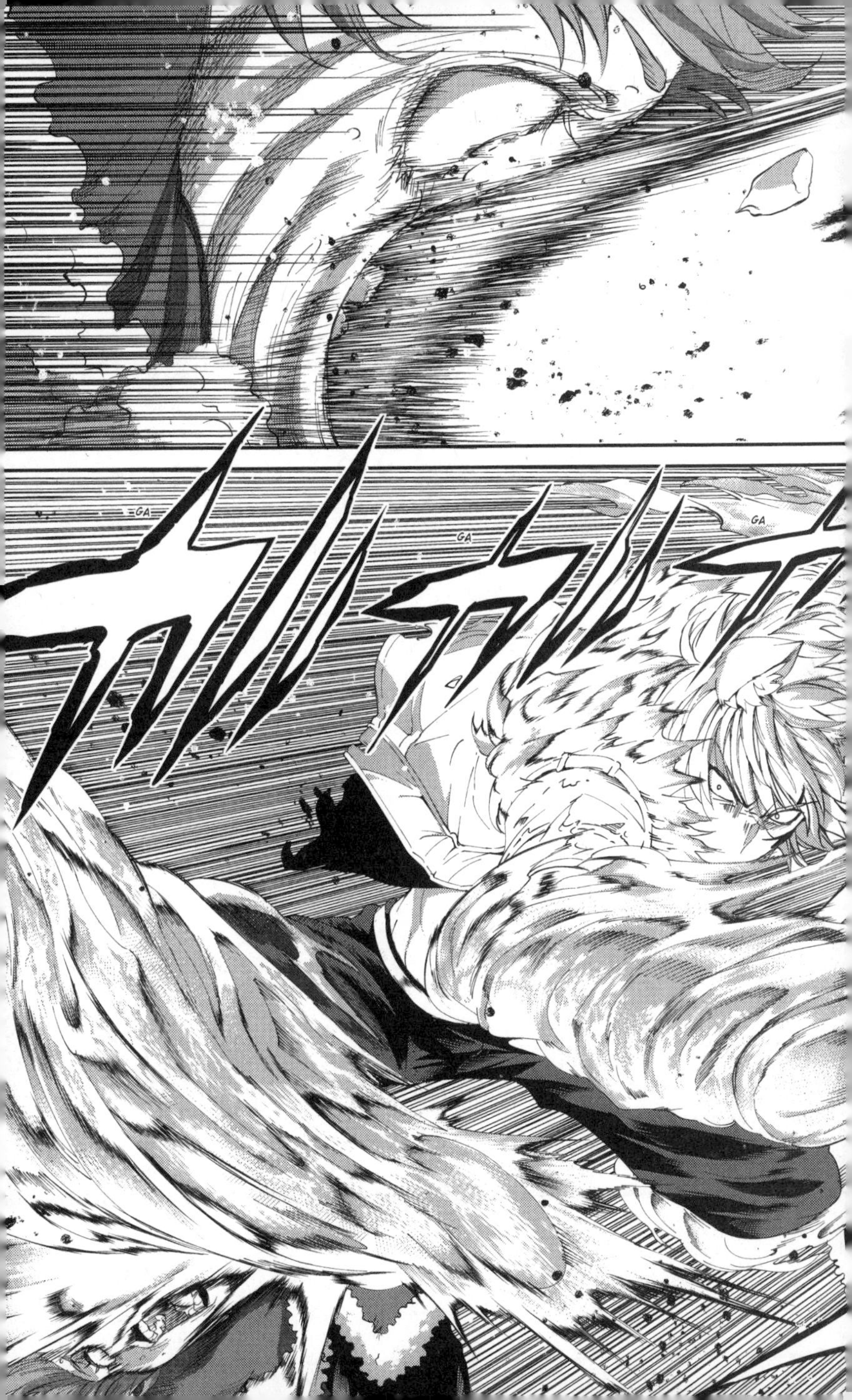
GA
GA
GA

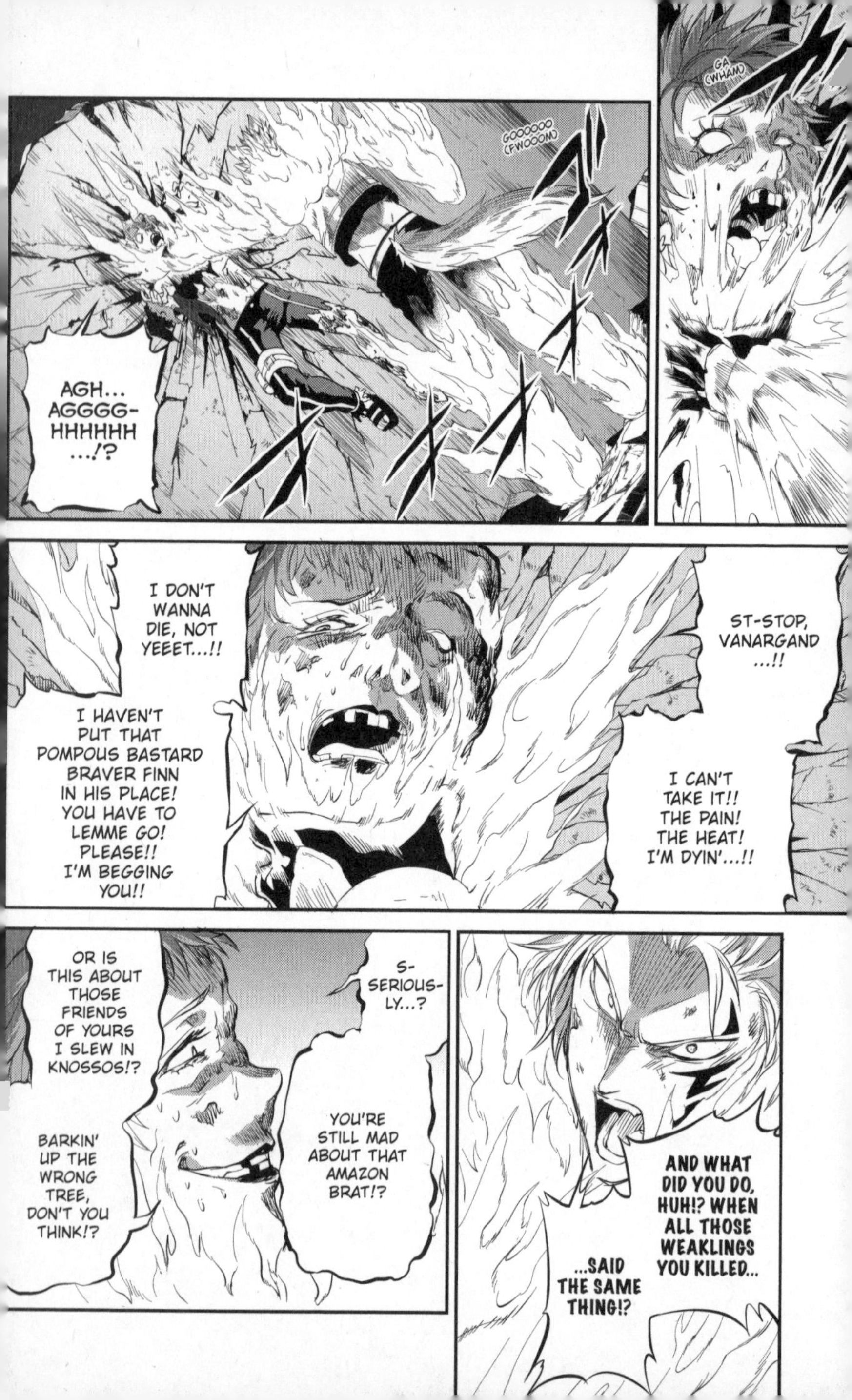
GA (WHAM)
GOOOOOO (FWOOOM)
AGH... AGGGG-HHHHHH ...!?
ST-STOP, VANARGAND ...!!
I CAN'T TAKE IT!! THE PAIN! THE HEAT! I'M DYIN'...!!
I DON'T WANNA DIE, NOT YEEET...!!
I HAVEN'T PUT THAT POMPOUS BASTARD BRAVER FINN IN HIS PLACE! YOU HAVE TO LEMME GO! PLEASE!! I'M BEGGING YOU!!
AND WHAT DID YOU DO, HUH!? WHEN ALL THOSE WEAKLINGS YOU KILLED...
...SAID THE SAME THING!?
S-SERIOUS-LY...?
OR IS THIS ABOUT THOSE FRIENDS OF YOURS I SLEW IN KNOSSOS!?
YOU'RE STILL MAD ABOUT THAT AMAZON BRAT!?
BARKIN' UP THE WRONG TREE, DON'T YOU THINK!?

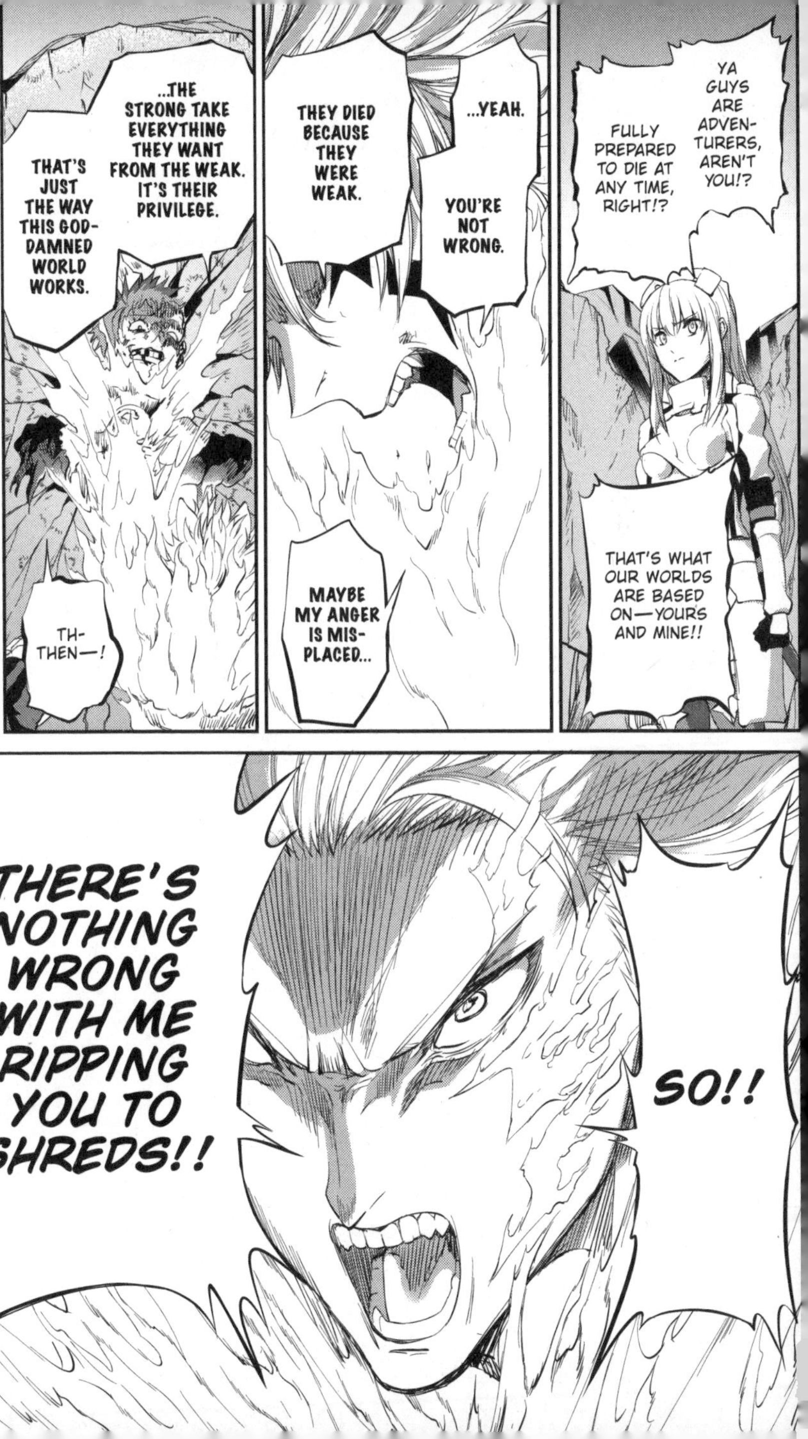
YA GUYS ARE ADVENTURERS, AREN'T YOU!?
FULLY PREPARED TO DIE AT ANY TIME, RIGHT!?
THAT'S WHAT OUR WORLDS ARE BASED ON—YOURS AND MINE!!
...YEAH.
YOU'RE NOT WRONG.
THEY DIED BECAUSE THEY WERE WEAK.
MAYBE MY ANGER IS MISPLACED...
...THE STRONG TAKE EVERYTHING THEY WANT FROM THE WEAK. IT'S THEIR PRIVILEGE.
THAT'S JUST THE WAY THIS GOD-DAMNED WORLD WORKS.
TH-THEN—!
SO!!
THERE'S NOTHING WRONG WITH ME RIPPING YOU TO SHREDS!!

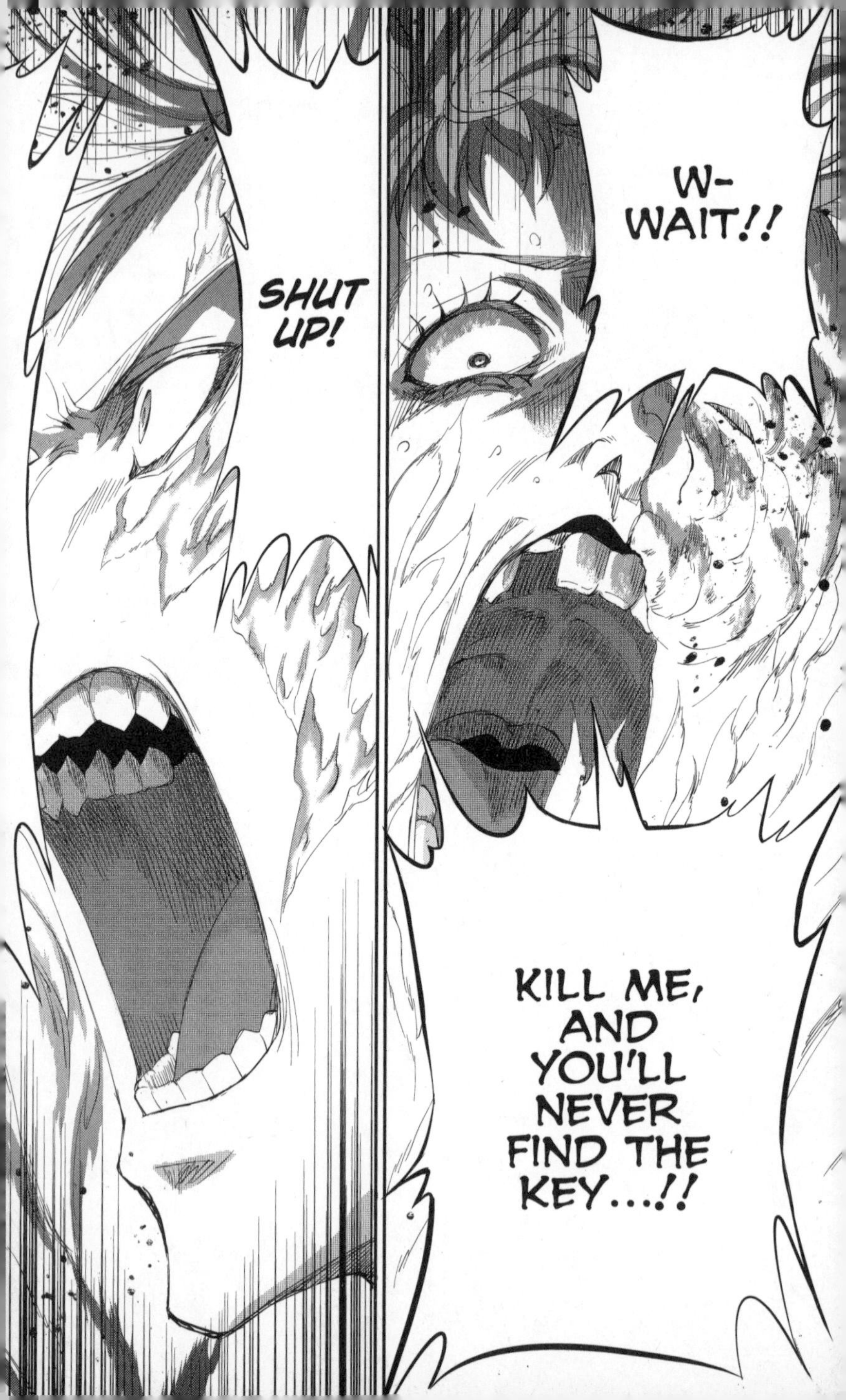
W-WAIT!!
KILL ME, AND YOU'LL NEVER FIND THE KEY...!!
SHUT UP!

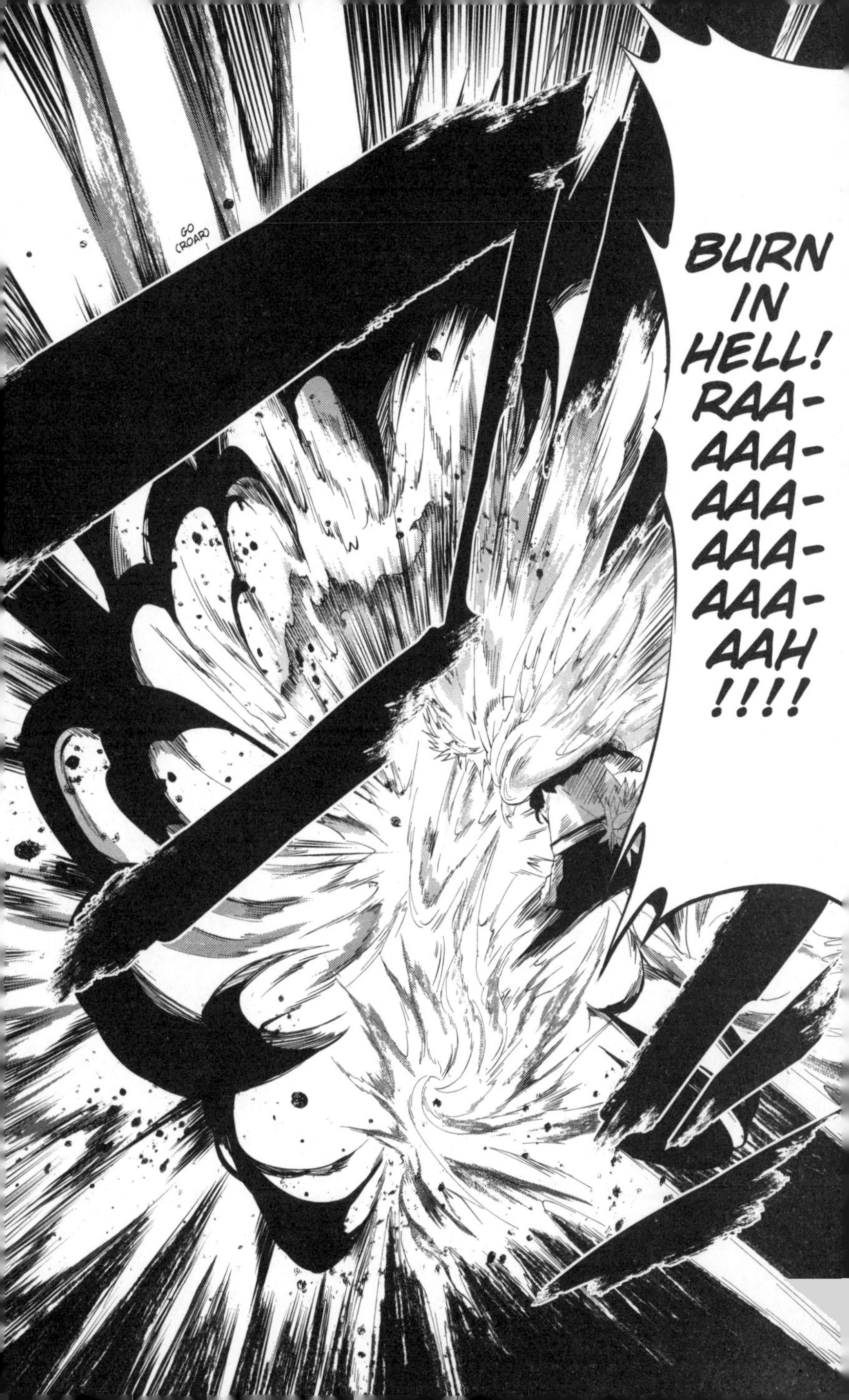
BURN IN HELL! RAA-AAA-AAA-AAA-AAA-AAH!!!!
GO
(ROAR)

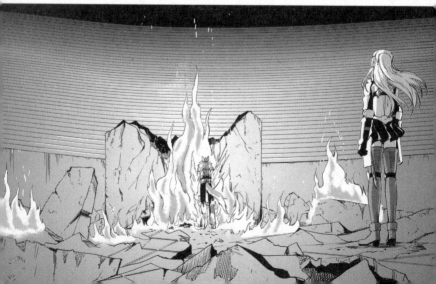

Is it WRONG to TRY to PICK UP GIRLS IN A DUNGEON? ON THE SIDE

Sword Oratoria

quest 77. Forget-Me-Not

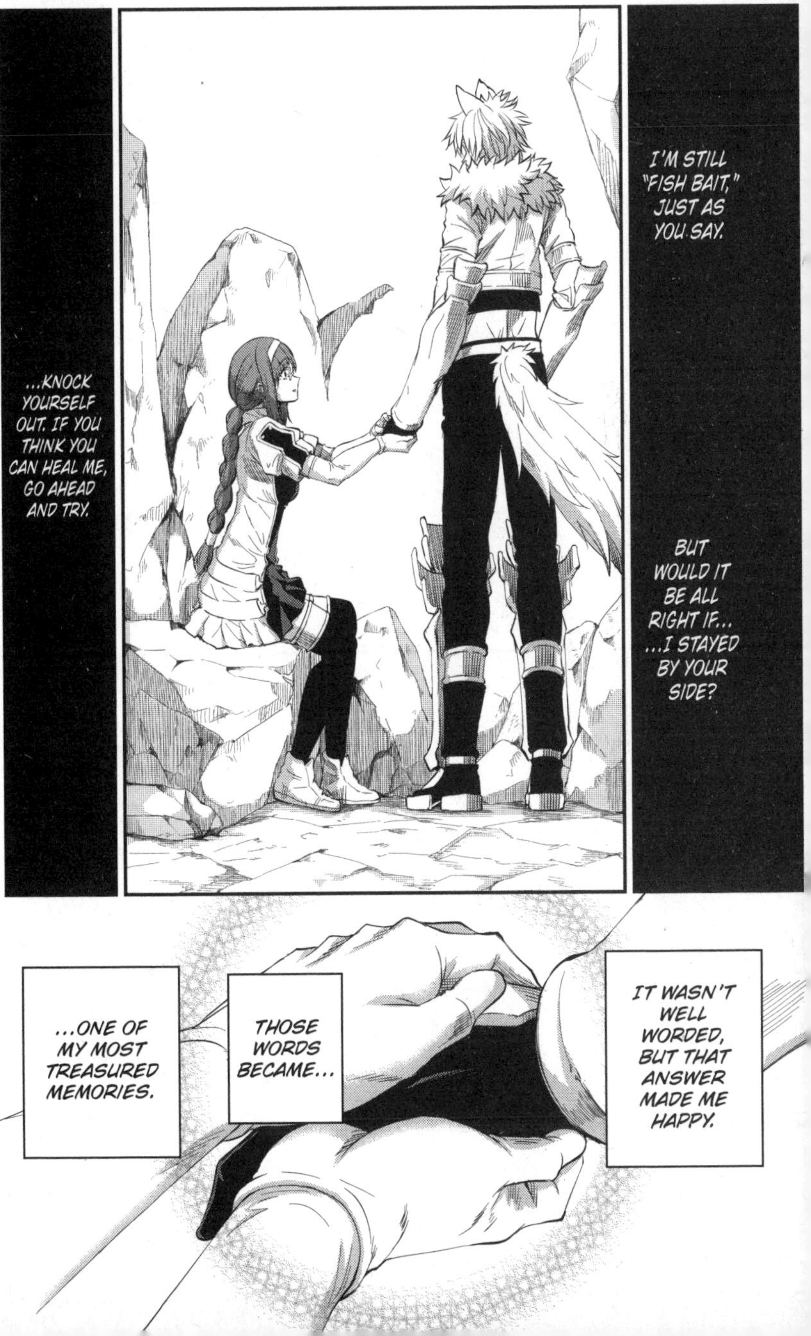
I'M STILL "FISH BAIT," JUST AS YOU SAY.
BUT WOULD IT BE ALL RIGHT IF... ...I STAYED BY YOUR SIDE?
...KNOCK YOURSELF OUT. IF YOU THINK YOU CAN HEAL ME, GO AHEAD AND TRY.
IT WASN'T WELL WORDED, BUT THAT ANSWER MADE ME HAPPY.
THOSE WORDS BECAME...
...ONE OF MY MOST TREASURED MEMORIES.

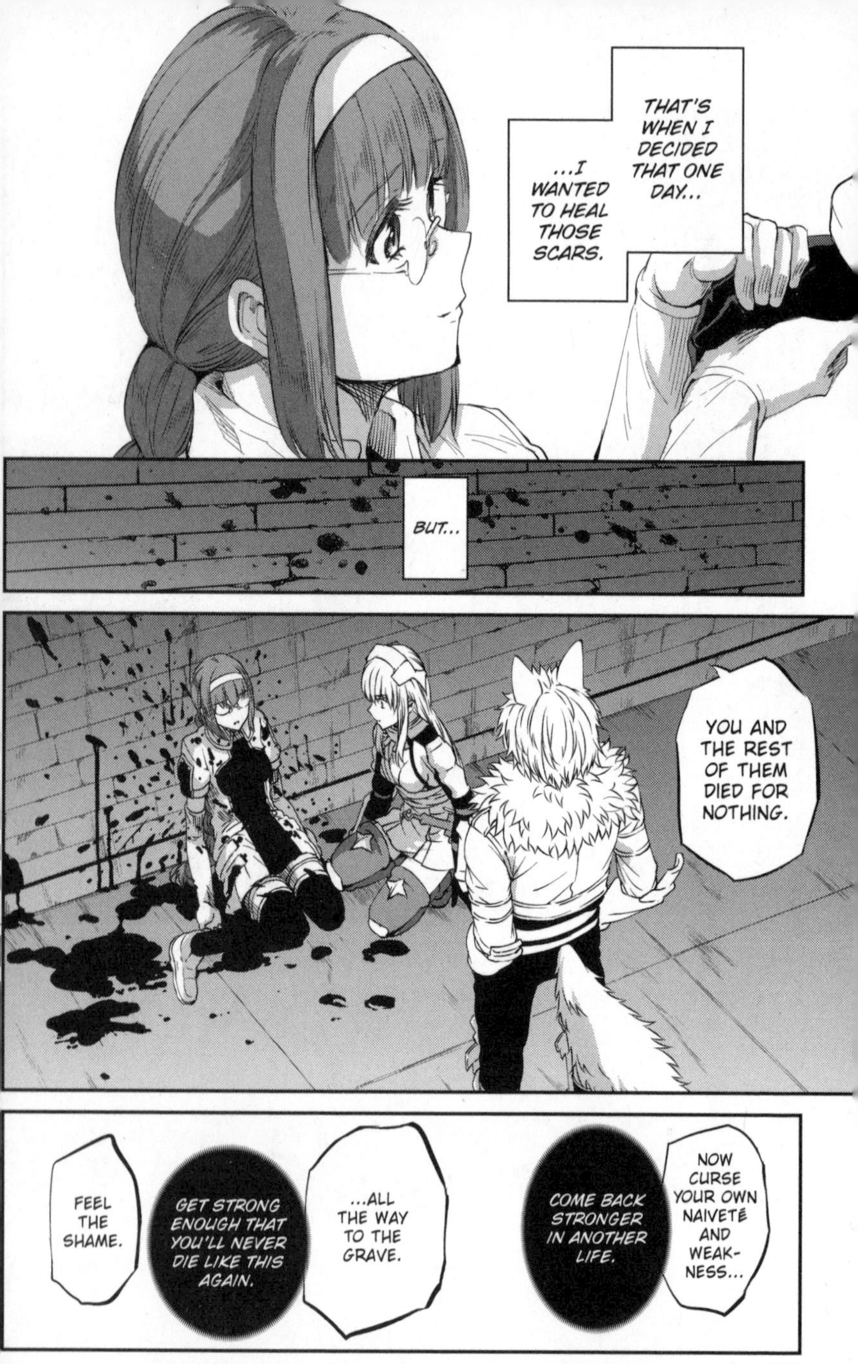
THAT'S WHEN I DECIDED THAT ONE DAY...
...I WANTED TO HEAL THOSE SCARS.
BUT...
YOU AND THE REST OF THEM DIED FOR NOTHING.
NOW CURSE YOUR OWN NAIVETÉ AND WEAKNESS...
COME BACK STRONGER IN ANOTHER LIFE.
...ALL THE WAY TO THE GRAVE.
GET STRONG ENOUGH THAT YOU'LL NEVER DIE LIKE THIS AGAIN.
FEEL THE SHAME.

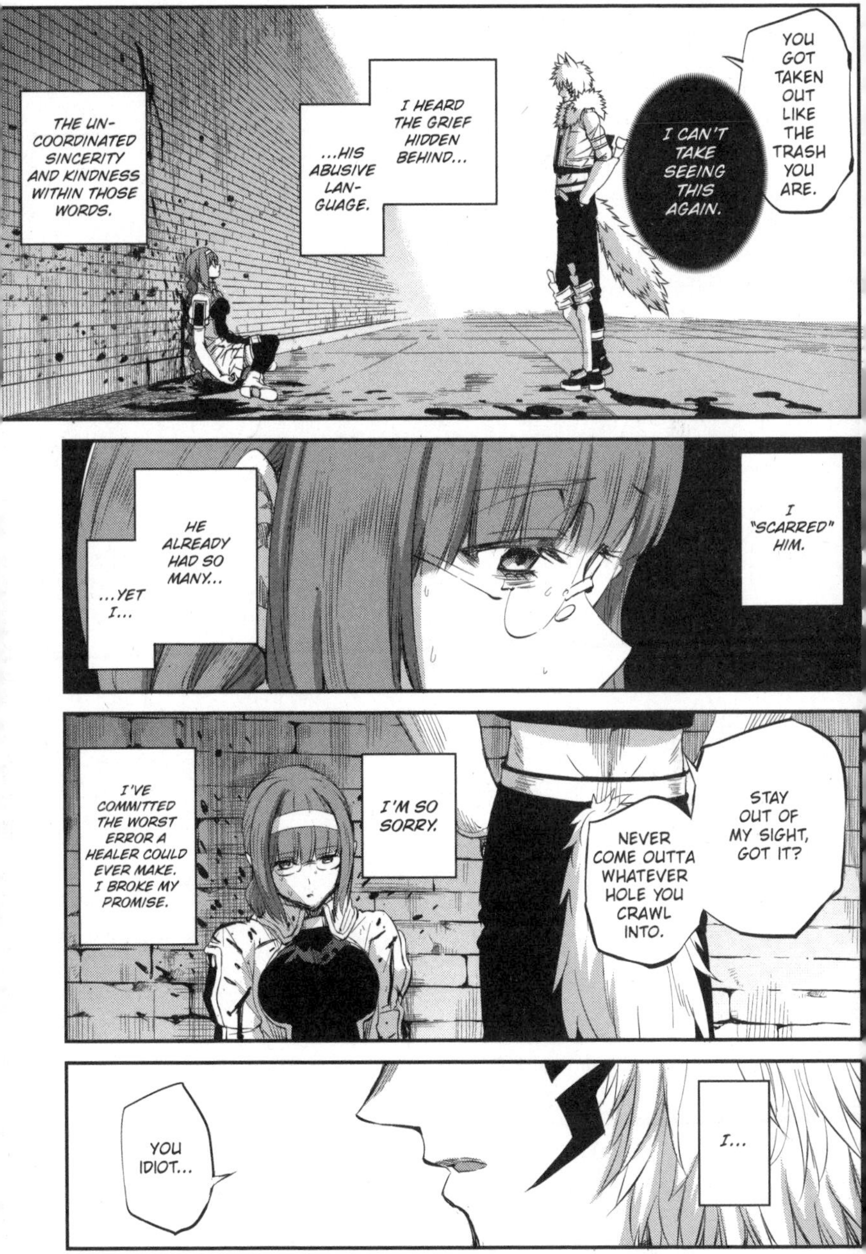
YOU GOT TAKEN OUT LIKE THE TRASH YOU ARE.
I CAN'T TAKE SEEING THIS AGAIN.
I HEARD THE GRIEF HIDDEN BEHIND...
...HIS ABUSIVE LAN-GUAGE.
THE UN-COORDINATED SINCERITY AND KINDNESS WITHIN THOSE WORDS.
I "SCARRED" HIM.
HE ALREADY HAD SO MANY...
...YET I...
STAY OUT OF MY SIGHT, GOT IT?
NEVER COME OUTTA WHATEVER HOLE YOU CRAWL INTO.
I'M SO SORRY.
I'VE COMMITTED THE WORST ERROR A HEALER COULD EVER MAKE. I BROKE MY PROMISE.
I...
YOU IDIOT...

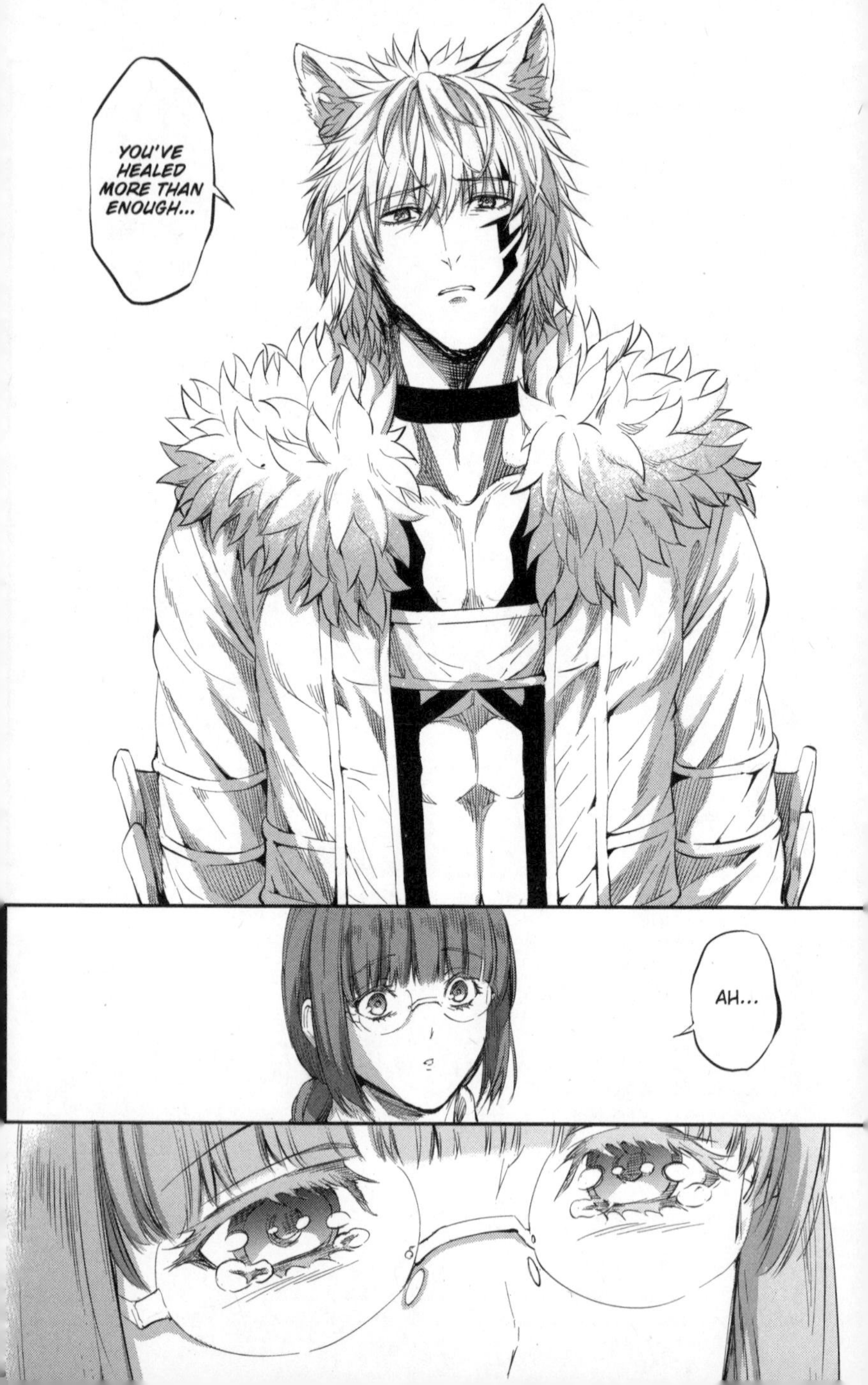
YOU'VE HEALED MORE THAN ENOUGH...
AH...

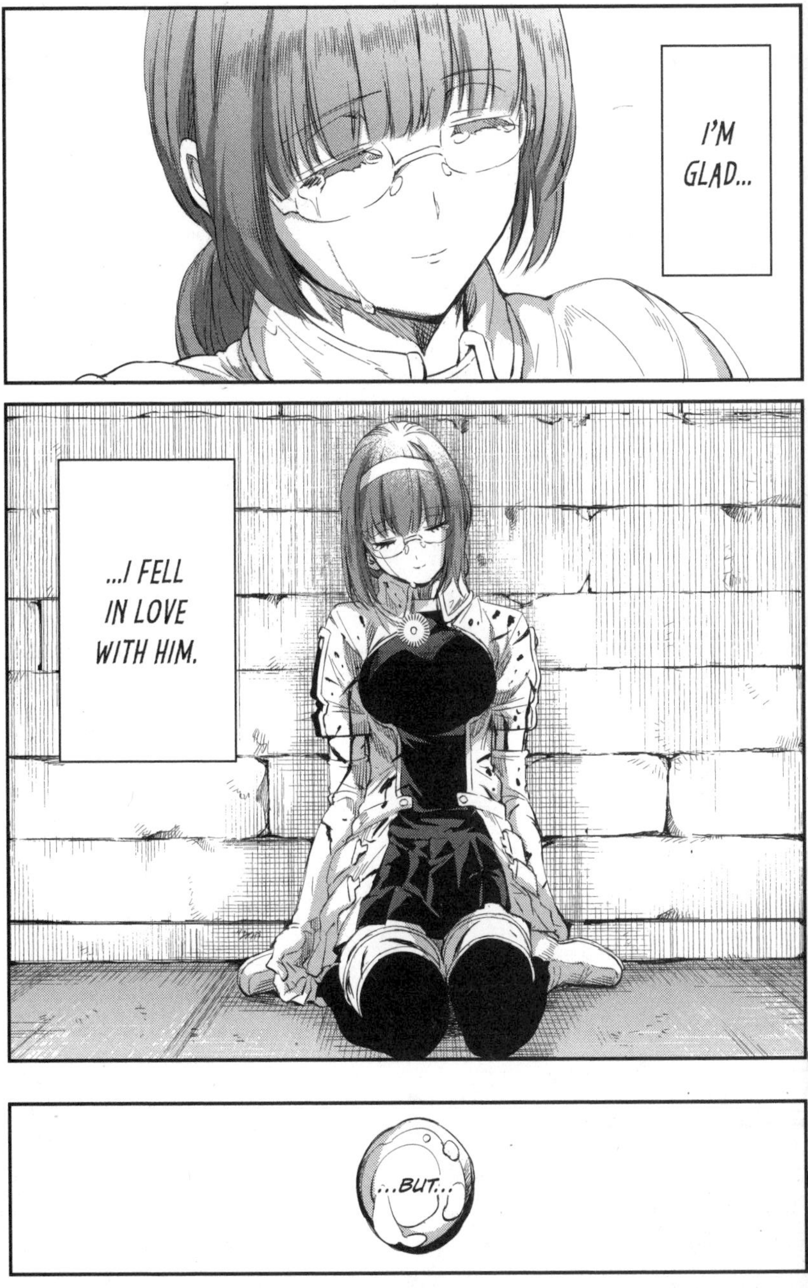
I'M GLAD...
...I FELL IN LOVE WITH HIM.
...BUT...

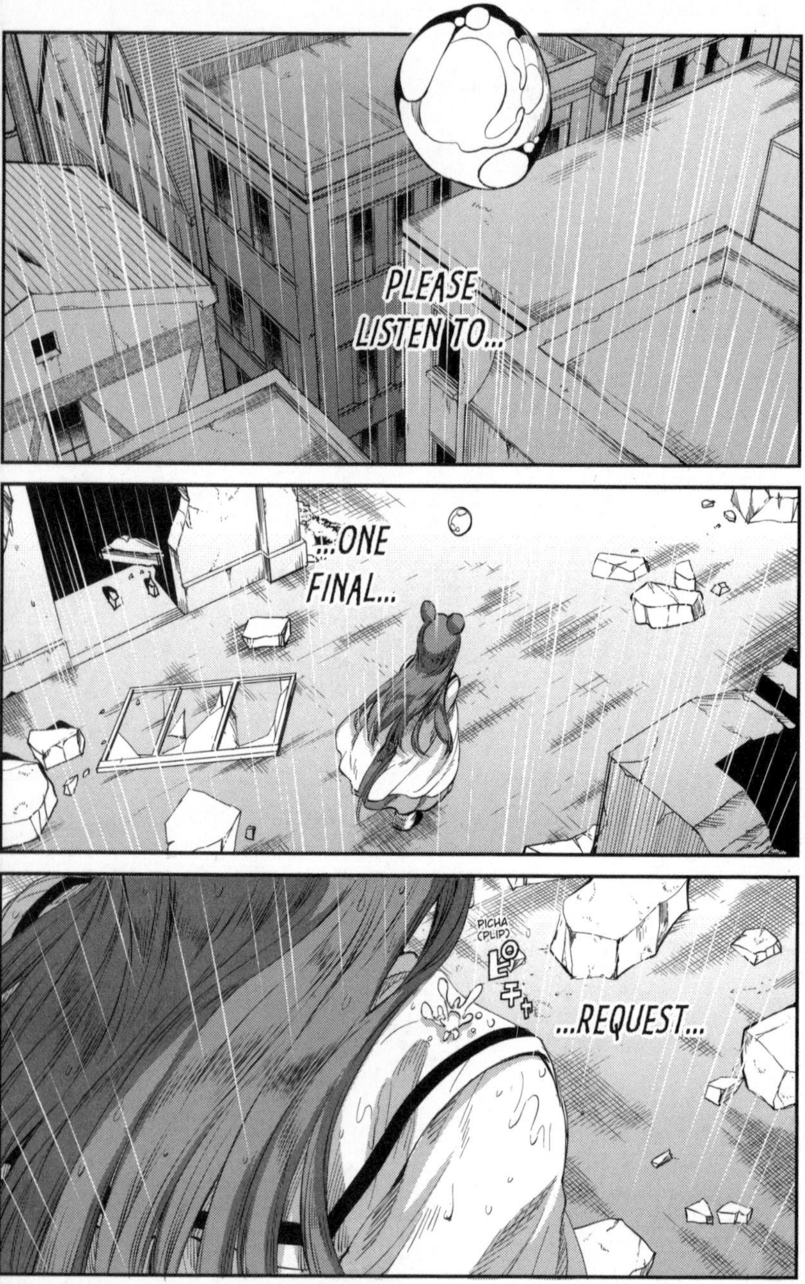
PLEASE LISTEN TO...
...ONE FINAL...
PICHA (PLIP)
ピチャ
...REQUEST...

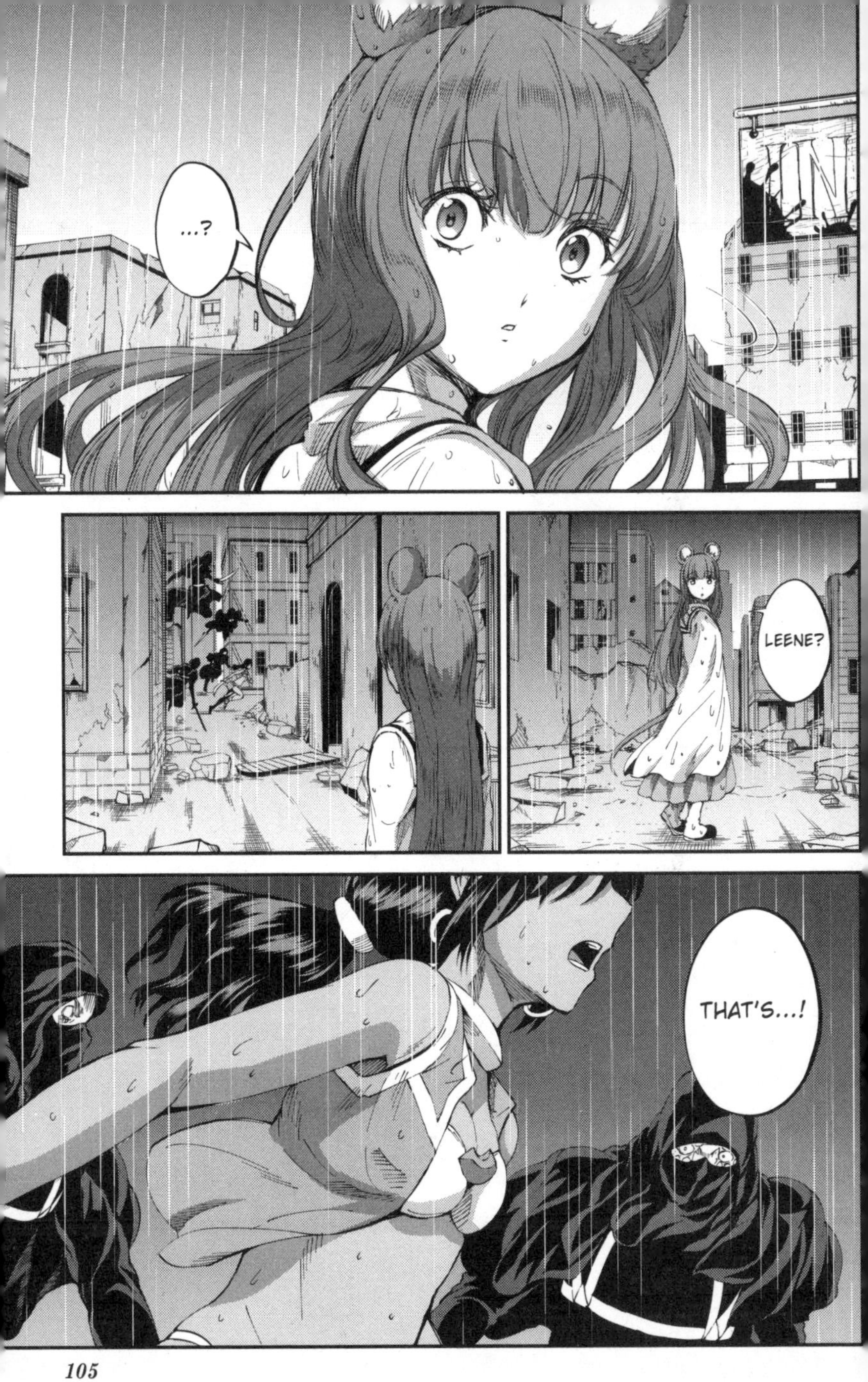
...?
LEENE?
THAT'S...!

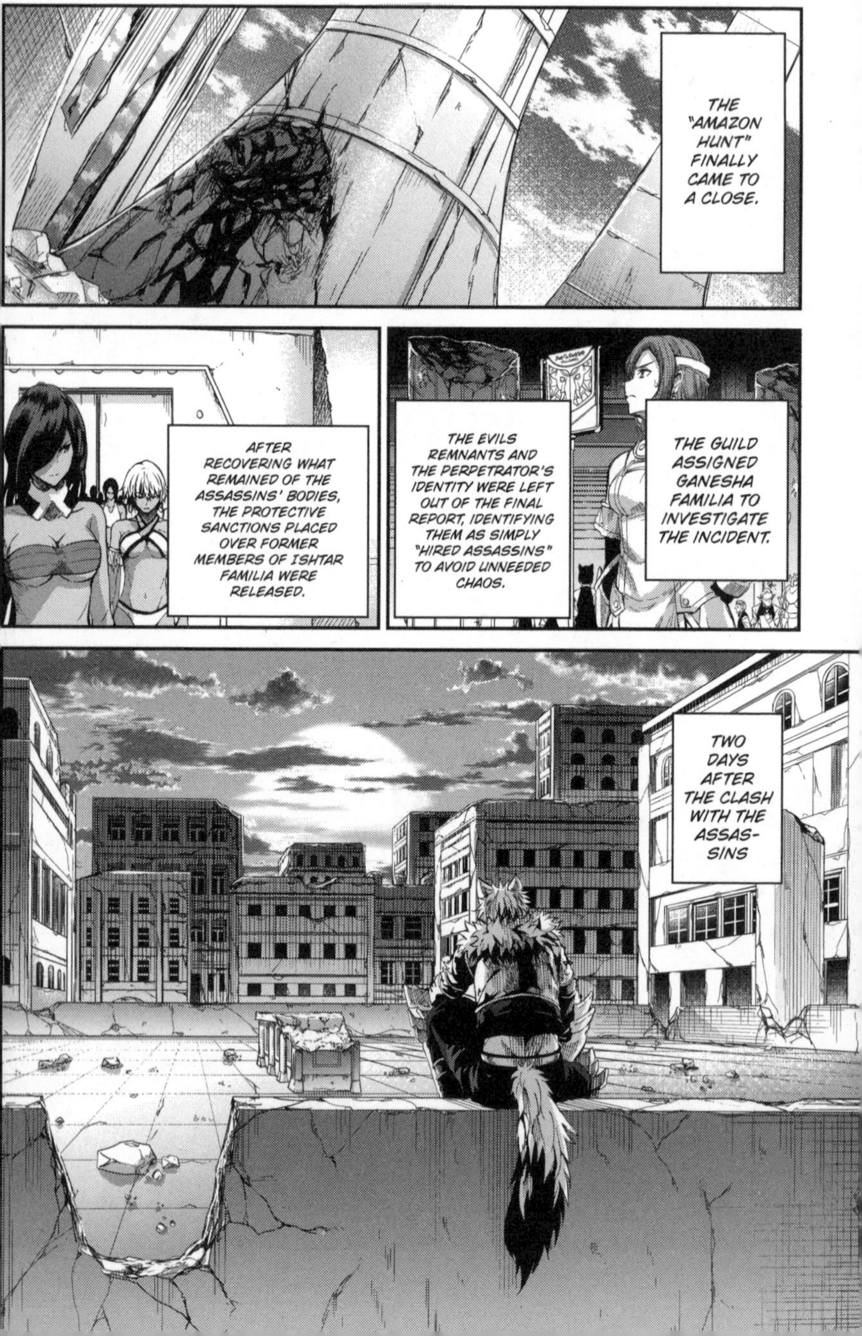
THE "AMAZON HUNT" FINALLY CAME TO A CLOSE.
THE GUILD ASSIGNED GANESHA FAMILIA TO INVESTIGATE THE INCIDENT.
THE EVILS REMNANTS AND THE PERPETRATOR'S IDENTITY WERE LEFT OUT OF THE FINAL REPORT, IDENTIFYING THEM AS SIMPLY "HIRED ASSASSINS" TO AVOID UNNEEDED CHAOS.
AFTER RECOVERING WHAT REMAINED OF THE ASSASSINS' BODIES, THE PROTECTIVE SANCTIONS PLACED OVER FORMER MEMBERS OF ISHTAR FAMILIA WERE RELEASED.
TWO DAYS AFTER THE CLASH WITH THE ASSAS-SINS

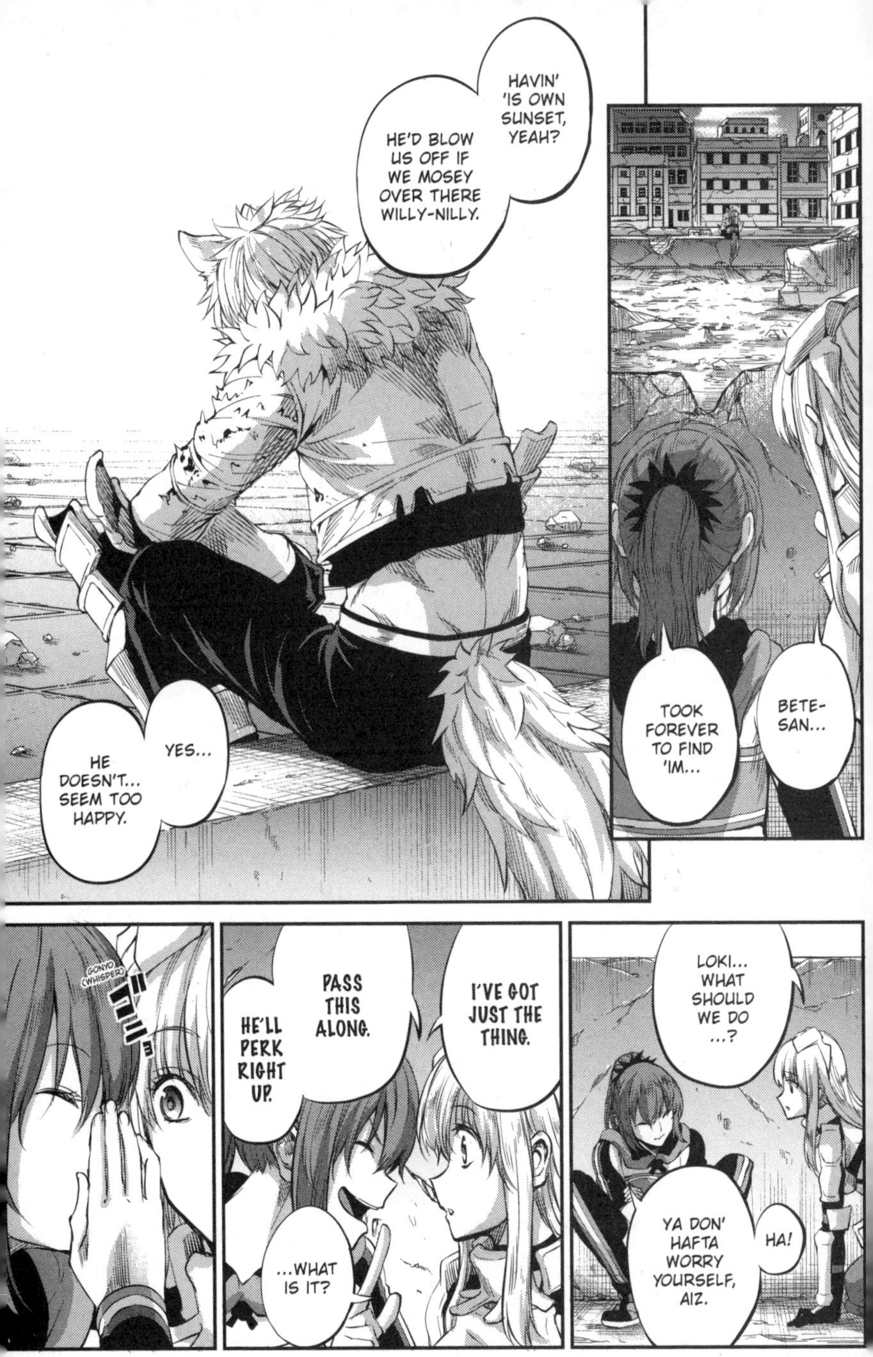
BETE-SAN...
TOOK FOREVER TO FIND 'IM...
HAVIN' 'IS OWN SUNSET, YEAH?
HE'D BLOW US OFF IF WE MOSEY OVER THERE WILLY-NILLY.
YES...
HE DOESN'T... SEEM TOO HAPPY.
LOKI... WHAT SHOULD WE DO ...?
HA!
YA DON' HAFTA WORRY YOURSELF, AIZ.
I'VE GOT JUST THE THING.
PASS THIS ALONG.
HE'LL PERK RIGHT UP.
...WHAT IS IT?
GONYO (WHISPER)

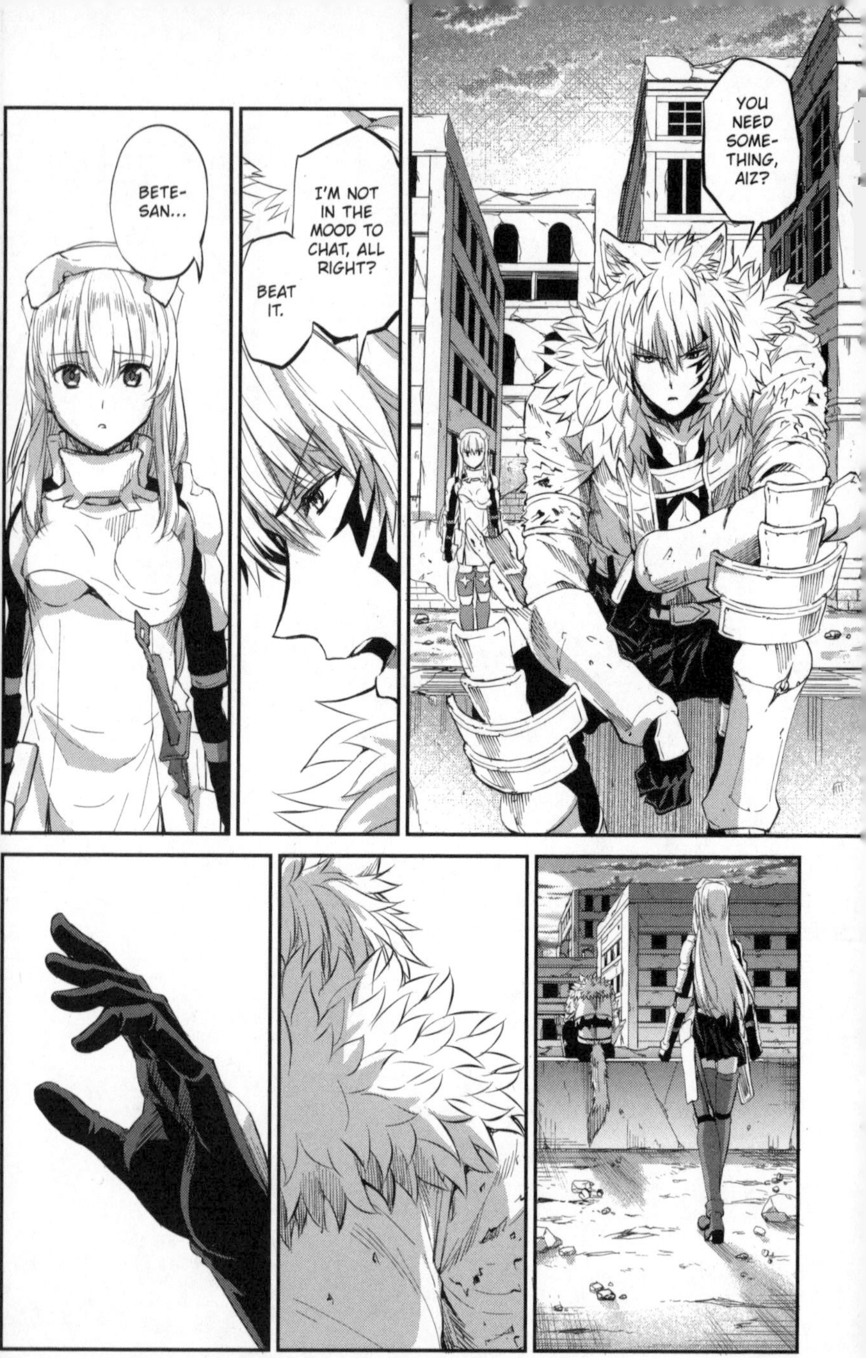
YOU NEED SOME-THING, AIZ?
I'M NOT IN THE MOOD TO CHAT, ALL RIGHT?
BEAT IT.
BETE-SAN...

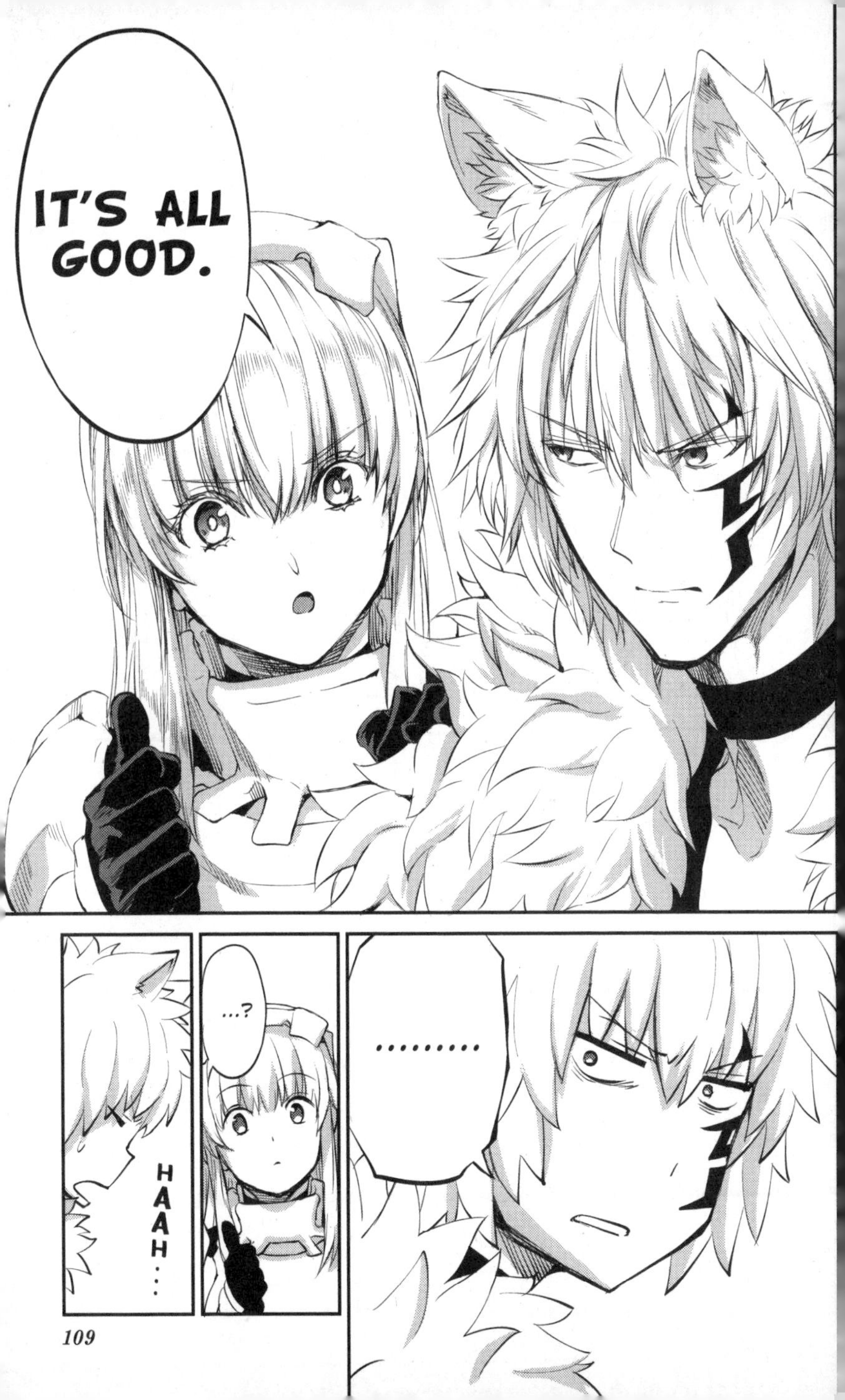
IT'S ALL GOOD.
....
...?
HAAAH...

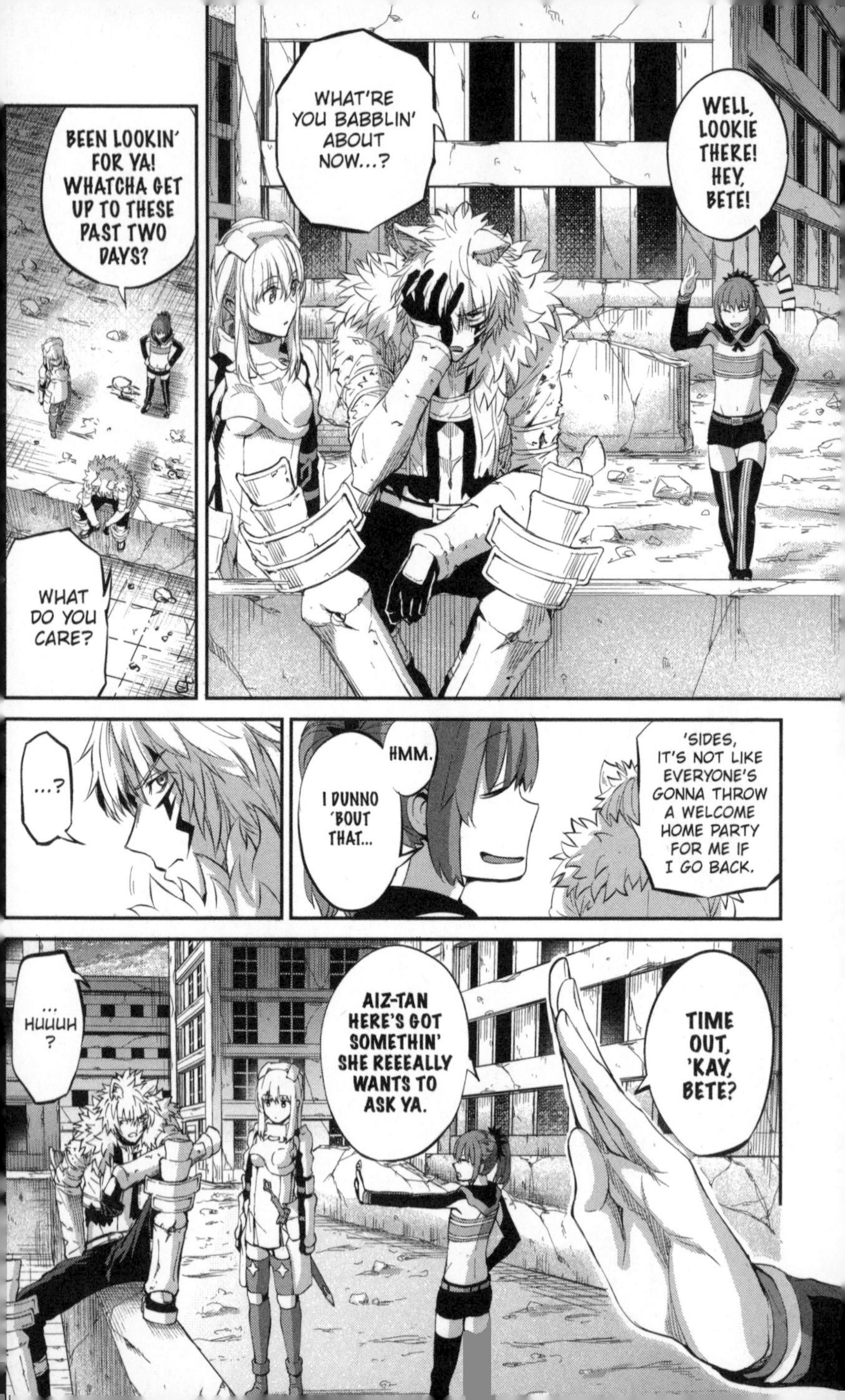
WELL, LOOKIE THERE! HEY, BETE!
WHAT'RE YOU BABBLIN' ABOUT NOW...?
BEEN LOOKIN' FOR YA! WHATCHA GET UP TO THESE PAST TWO DAYS?
WHAT DO YOU CARE?
'SIDES, IT'S NOT LIKE EVERYONE'S GONNA THROW A WELCOME HOME PARTY FOR ME IF I GO BACK.
HMM.
I DUNNO 'BOUT THAT...
...?
TIME OUT, 'KAY, BETE?
AIZ-TAN HERE'S GOT SOMETHIN' SHE REEEALLY WANTS TO ASK YA.
... HUUUH?

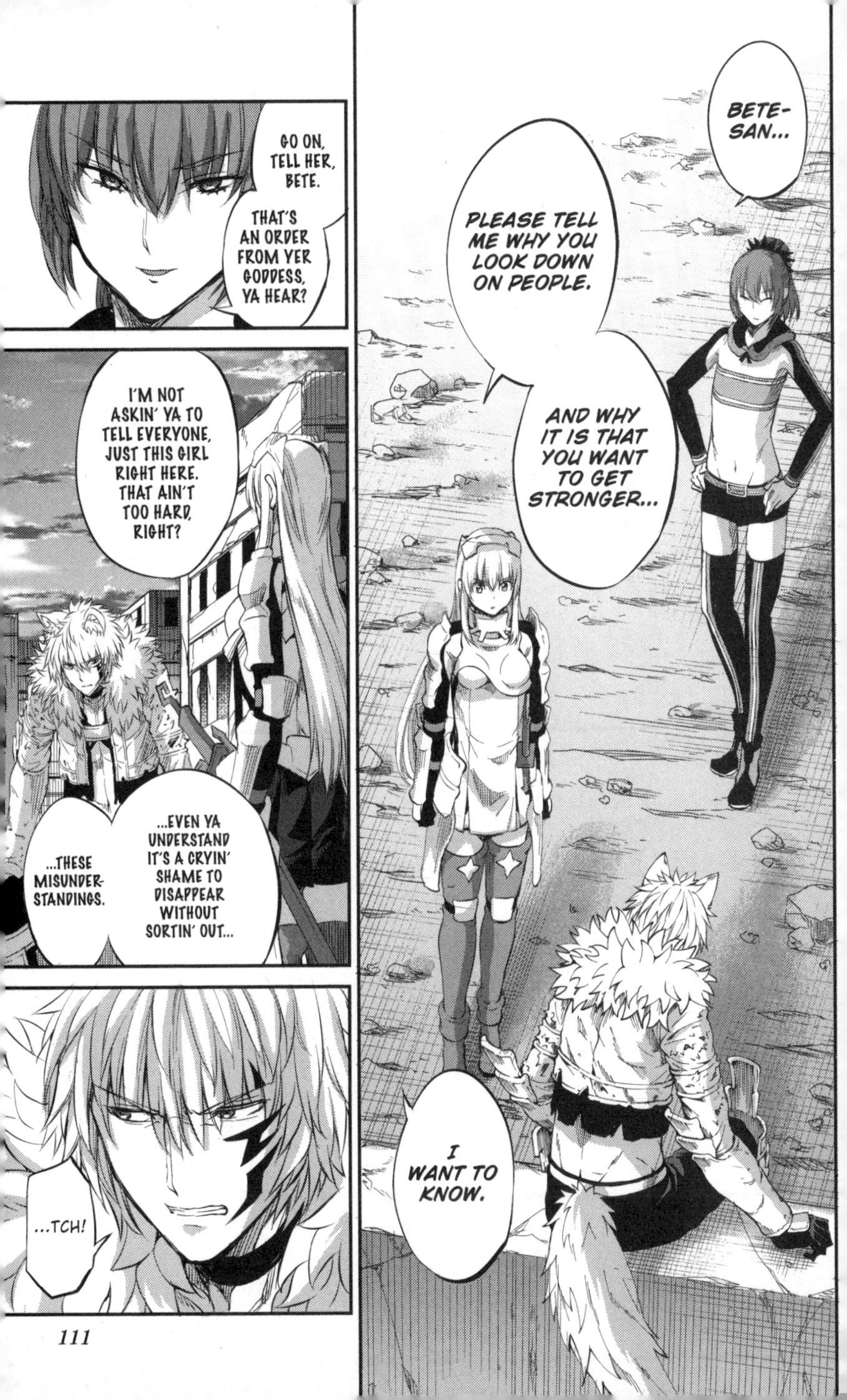
BETE-SAN...
PLEASE TELL ME WHY YOU LOOK DOWN ON PEOPLE.
AND WHY IT IS THAT YOU WANT TO GET STRONGER...
I WANT TO KNOW.
GO ON, TELL HER, BETE.
THAT'S AN ORDER FROM YER GODDESS, YA HEAR?
I'M NOT ASKIN' YA TO TELL EVERYONE, JUST THIS GIRL RIGHT HERE. THAT AIN'T TOO HARD, RIGHT?
...EVEN YA UNDERSTAND IT'S A CRYIN' SHAME TO DISAPPEAR WITHOUT SORTIN' OUT...
...THESE MISUNDER-STANDINGS.
...TCH!

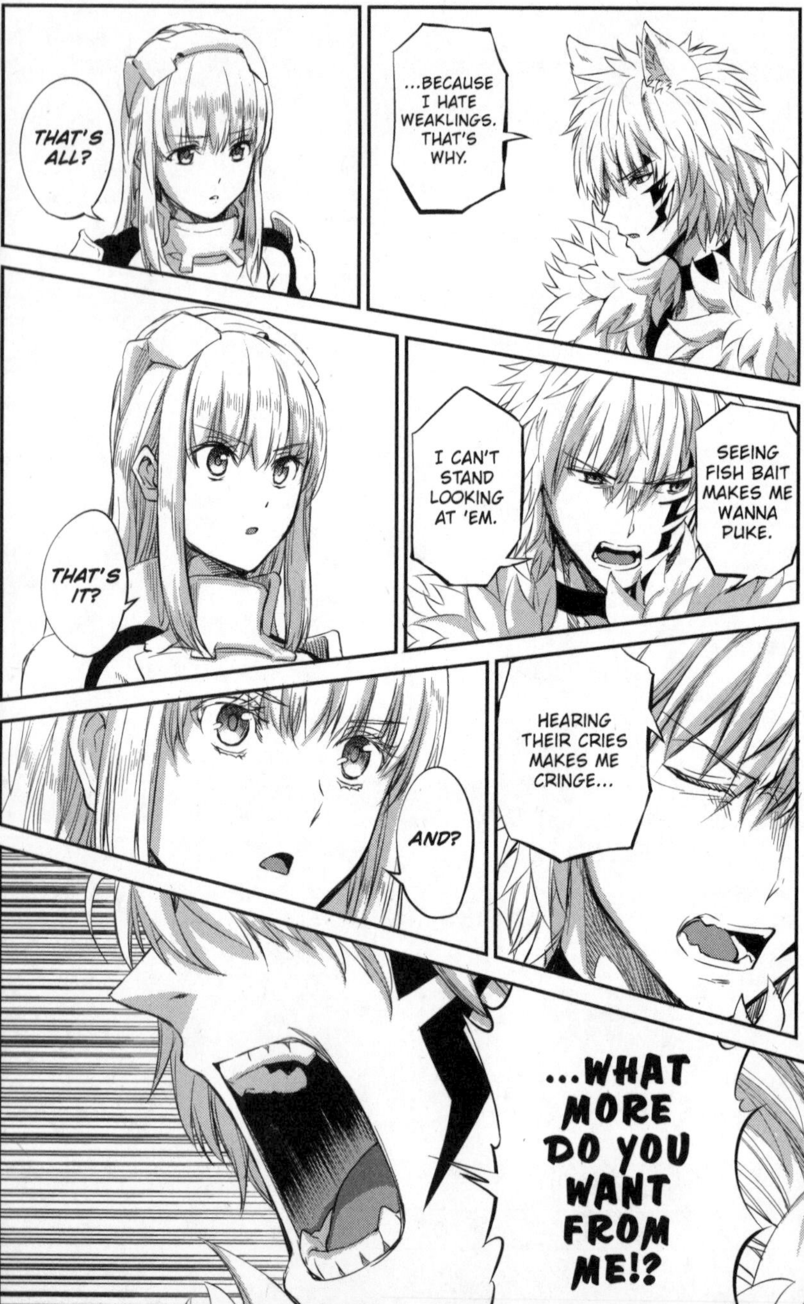
...BECAUSE I HATE WEAKLINGS. THAT'S WHY.
THAT'S ALL?
SEEING FISH BAIT MAKES ME WANNA PUKE.
I CAN'T STAND LOOKING AT 'EM.
THAT'S IT?
HEARING THEIR CRIES MAKES ME CRINGE...
AND?
...WHAT MORE DO YOU WANT FROM ME!?

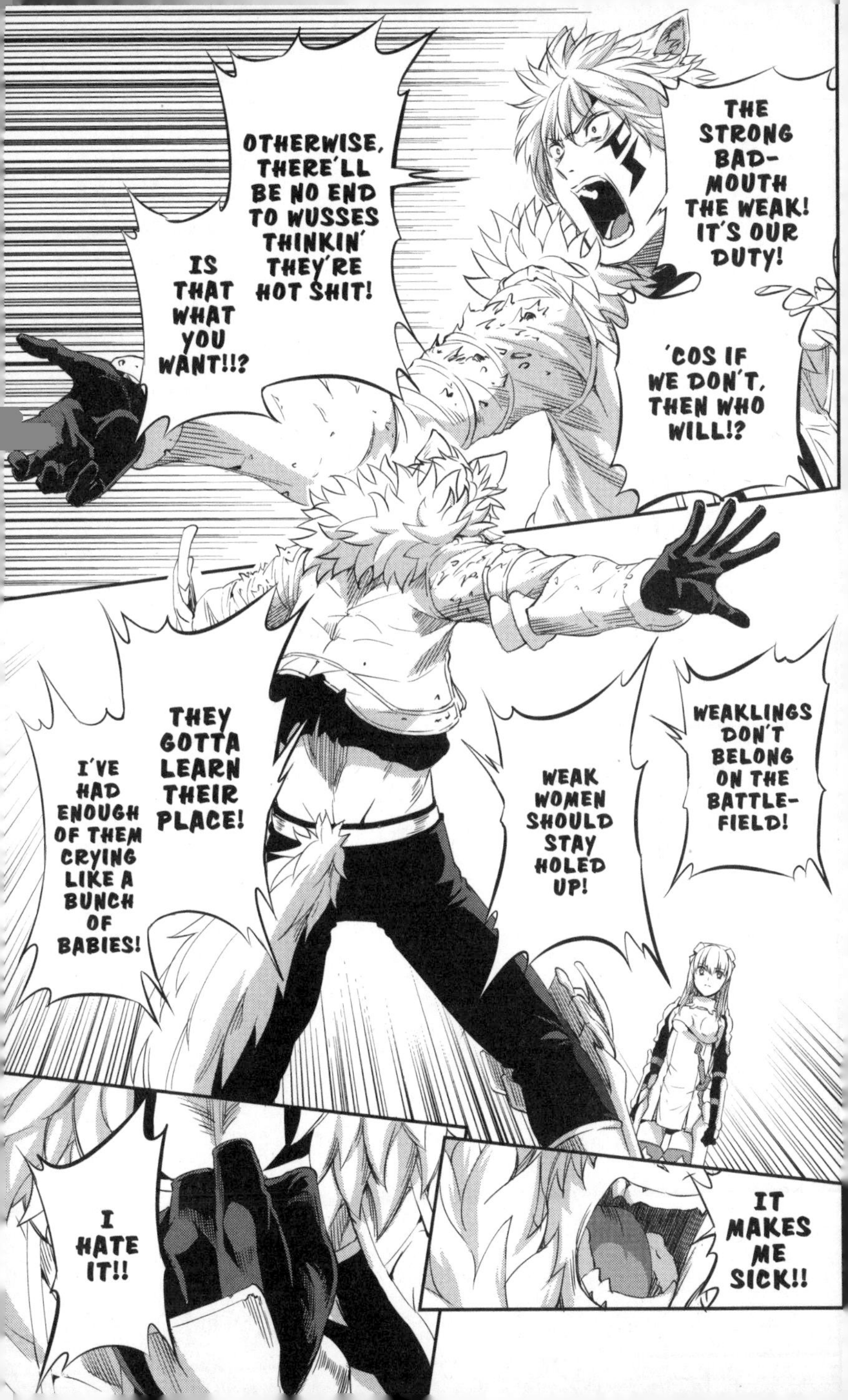
THE STRONG BAD-MOUTH THE WEAK! IT'S OUR DUTY!
'COS IF WE DON'T, THEN WHO WILL!?
OTHERWISE, THERE'LL BE NO END TO WUSSES THINKIN' THEY'RE HOT SHIT!
IS THAT WHAT YOU WANT!!?
WEAKLINGS DON'T BELONG ON THE BATTLE-FIELD!
WEAK WOMEN SHOULD STAY HOLED UP!
THEY GOTTA LEARN THEIR PLACE!
I'VE HAD ENOUGH OF THEM CRYING LIKE A BUNCH OF BABIES!
IT MAKES ME SICK!!
I HATE IT!!

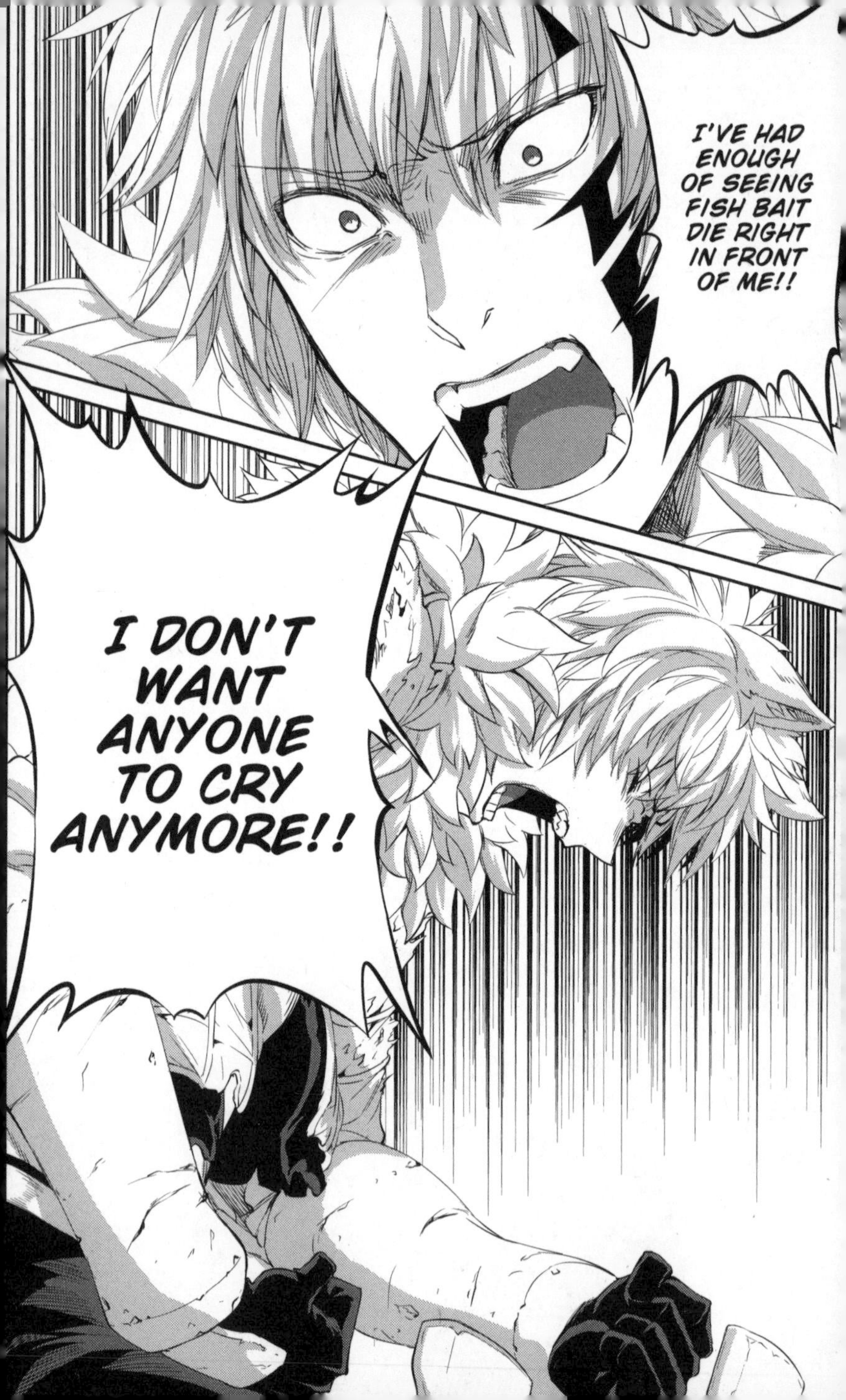
I'VE HAD ENOUGH OF SEEING FISH BAIT DIE RIGHT IN FRONT OF ME!!
I DON'T WANT ANYONE TO CRY ANYMORE!!

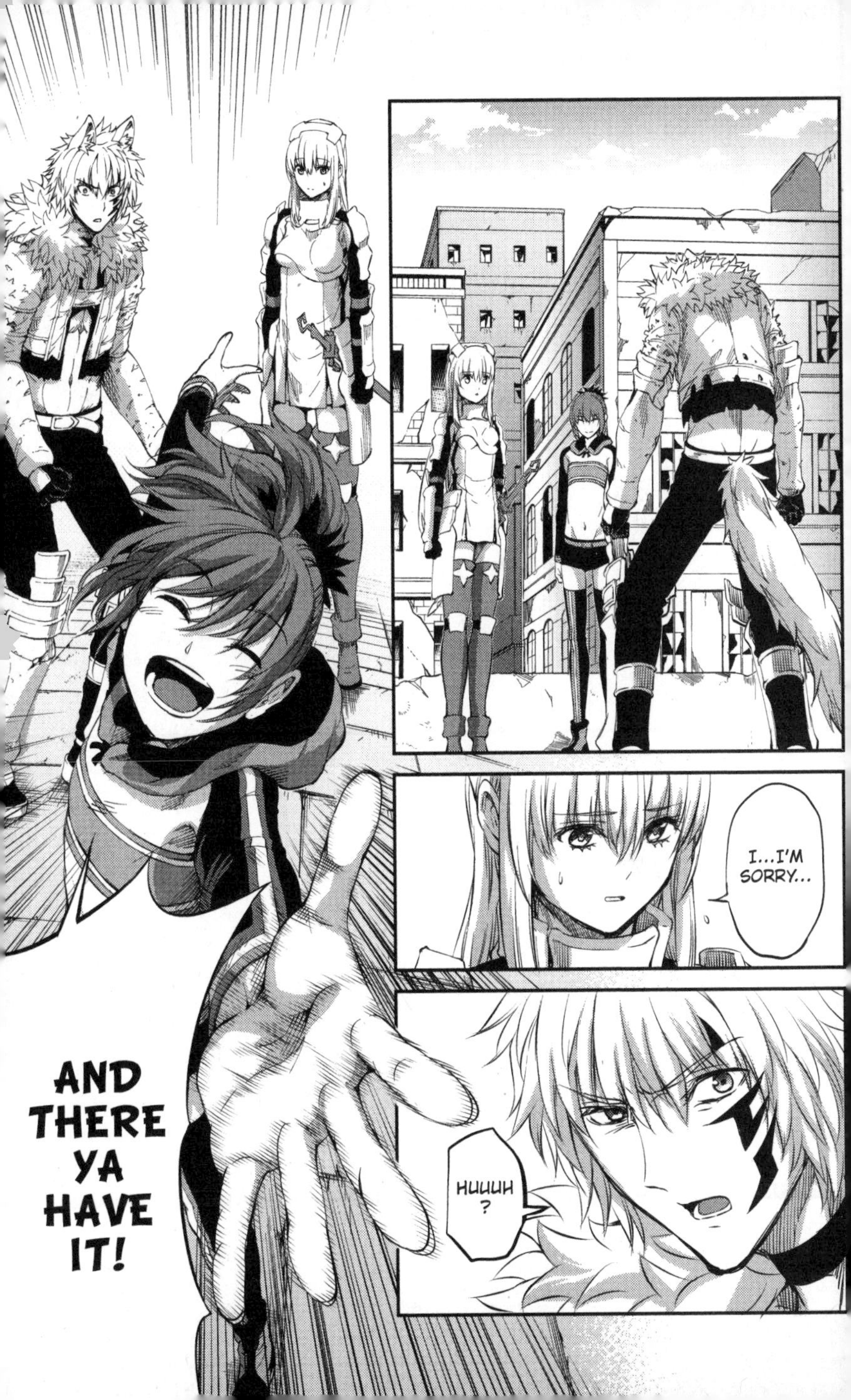
I...I'M SORRY...
HUUUH?
AND THERE YA HAVE IT!

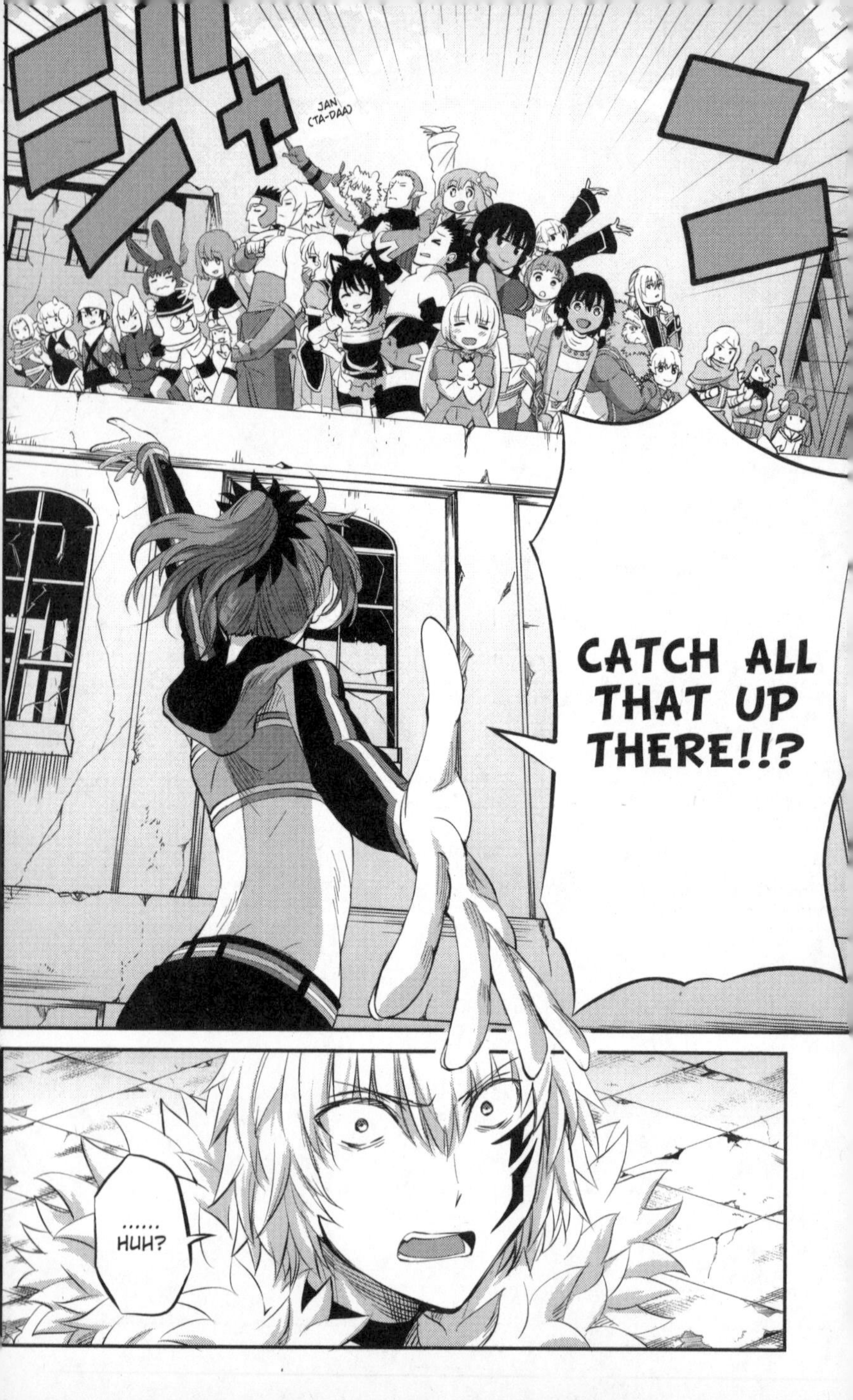
JAN (TA-DAA)
CATCH ALL THAT UP THERE!!?
...... HUH?

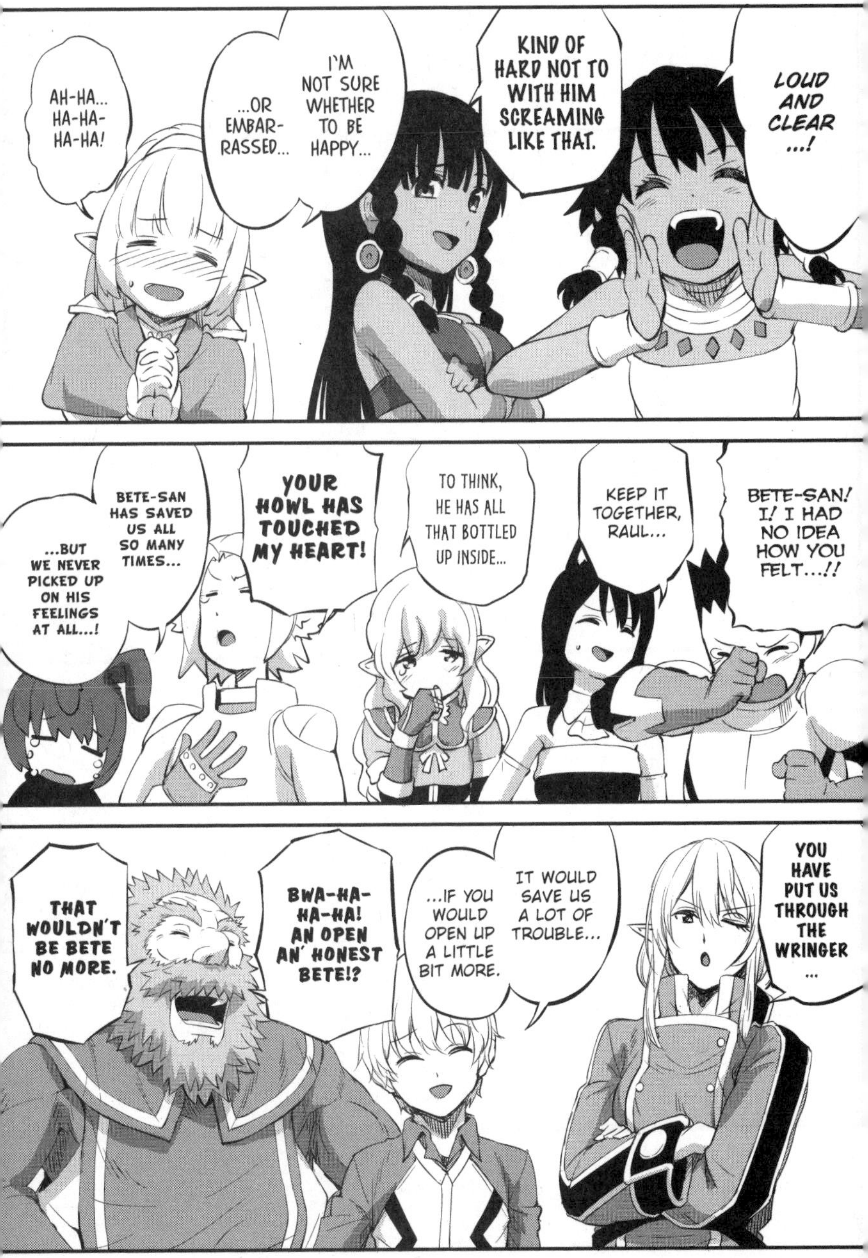
LOUD AND CLEAR ...!
KIND OF HARD NOT TO WITH HIM SCREAMING LIKE THAT.
I'M NOT SURE WHETHER TO BE HAPPY...
...OR EMBARRASSED...
AH-HA... HA-HA-HA-HA!
BETE-SAN! I! I HAD NO IDEA HOW YOU FELT...!!
KEEP IT TOGETHER, RAUL...
TO THINK, HE HAS ALL THAT BOTTLED UP INSIDE...
YOUR HOWL HAS TOUCHED MY HEART!
BETE-SAN HAS SAVED US ALL SO MANY TIMES...
...BUT WE NEVER PICKED UP ON HIS FEELINGS AT ALL...!
YOU HAVE PUT US THROUGH THE WRINGER...
IT WOULD SAVE US A LOT OF TROUBLE...
...IF YOU WOULD OPEN UP A LITTLE BIT MORE.
BWA-HA-HA-HA! AN OPEN AN' HONEST BETE!?
THAT WOULDN'T BE BETE NO MORE.

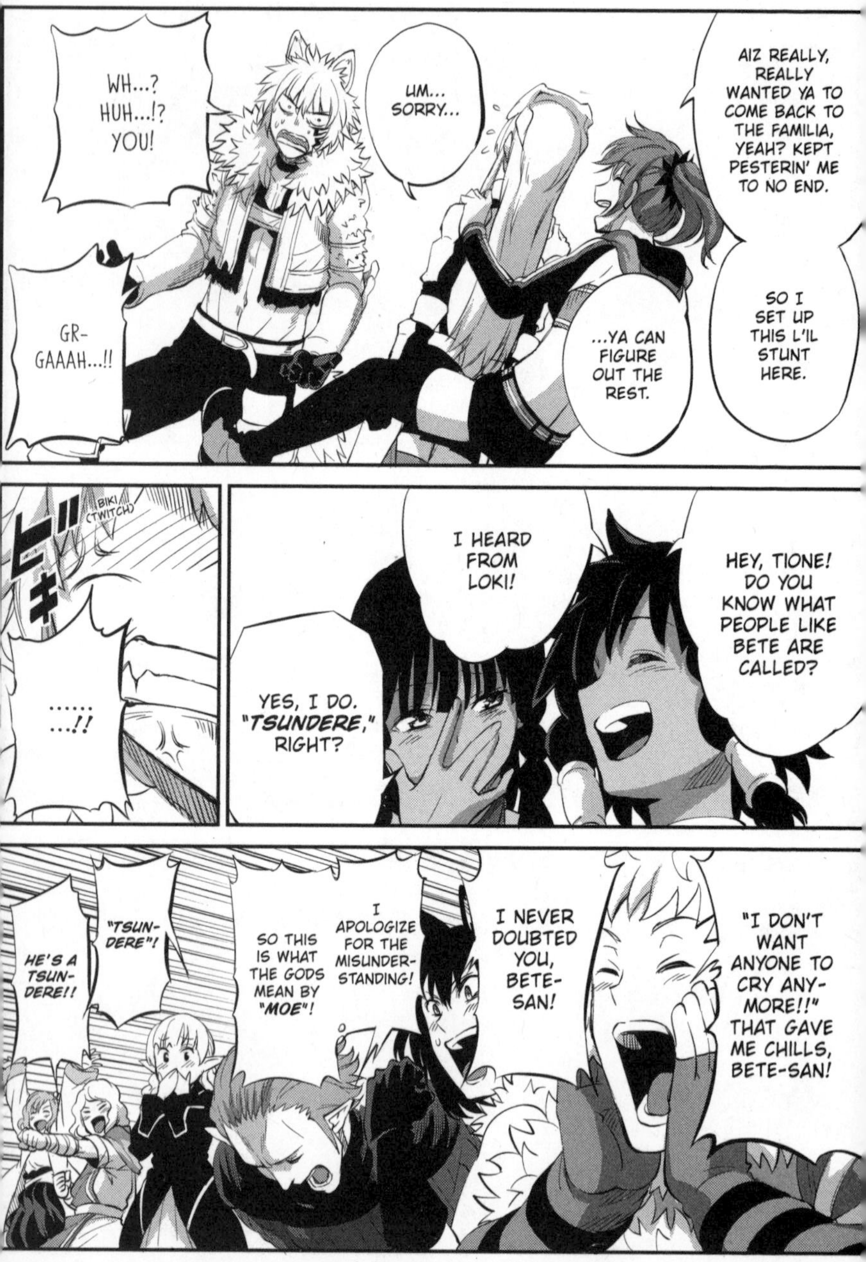
AIZ REALLY, REALLY WANTED YA TO COME BACK TO THE FAMILIA, YEAH? KEPT PESTERIN' ME TO NO END.
SO I SET UP THIS L'IL STUNT HERE.
UM... SORRY...
...YA CAN FIGURE OUT THE REST.
WH...? HUH...!? YOU!
GR-GAAAH...!!
HEY, TIONE! DO YOU KNOW WHAT PEOPLE LIKE BETE ARE CALLED?
I HEARD FROM LOKI!
YES, I DO. "TSUNDERE," RIGHT?
BIKI (TWITCH)
....!!
"I DON'T WANT ANYONE TO CRY ANYMORE!!" THAT GAVE ME CHILLS, BETE-SAN!
I NEVER DOUBTED YOU, BETE-SAN!
I APOLOGIZE FOR THE MISUNDERSTANDING!
SO THIS IS WHAT THE GODS MEAN BY "MOE"!
"TSUNDERE"!
HE'S A TSUNDERE!!

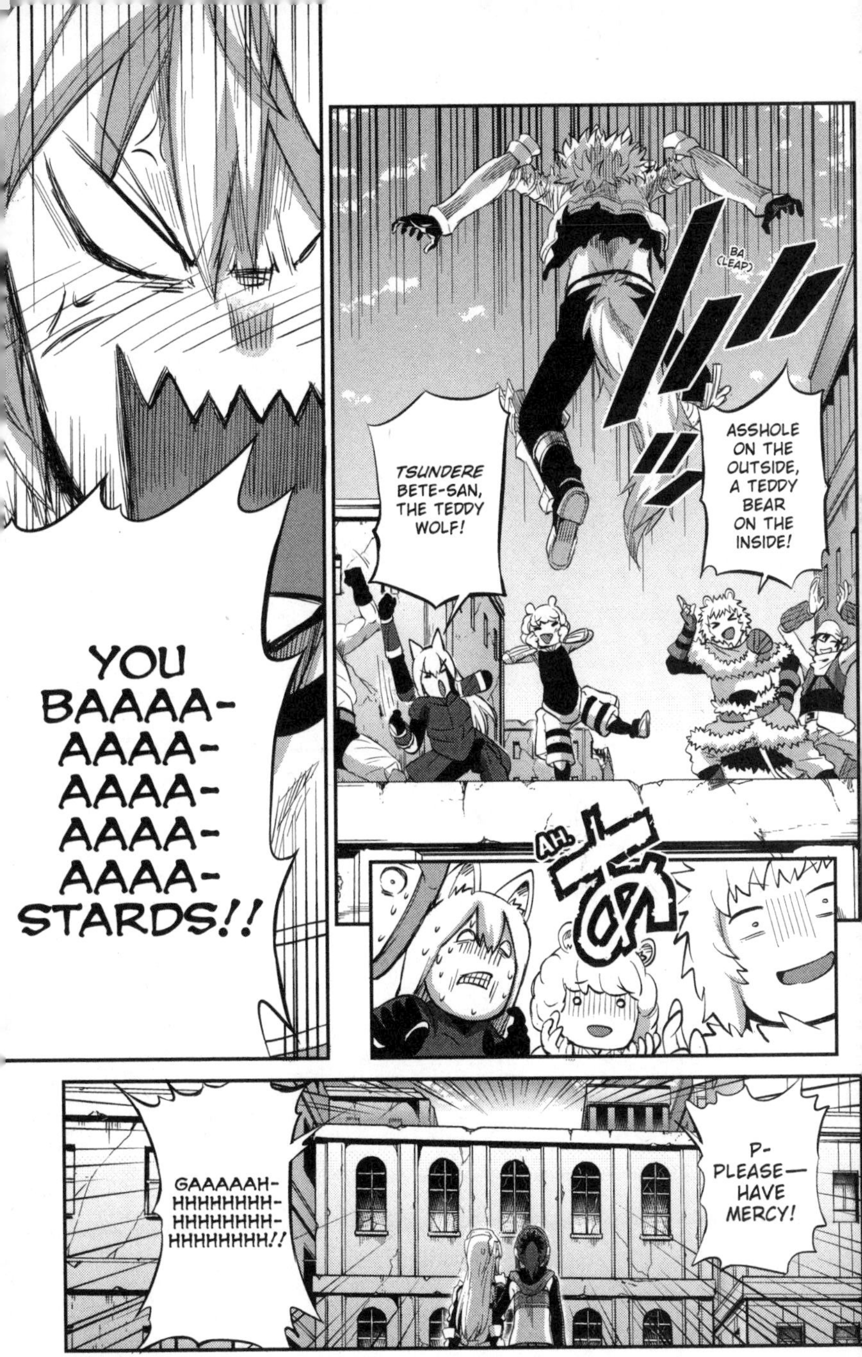
BA (LEAP)
ASSHOLE ON THE OUTSIDE, A TEDDY BEAR ON THE INSIDE!
TSUNDERE BETE-SAN, THE TEDDY WOLF!
AH.
YOU BAAAA-AAAA-AAAA-AAAA-AAAA-STARDS!!
P-PLEASE—HAVE MERCY!
GAAAAAH-HHHHHHHH-HHHHHHHH-HHHHHHHH!!

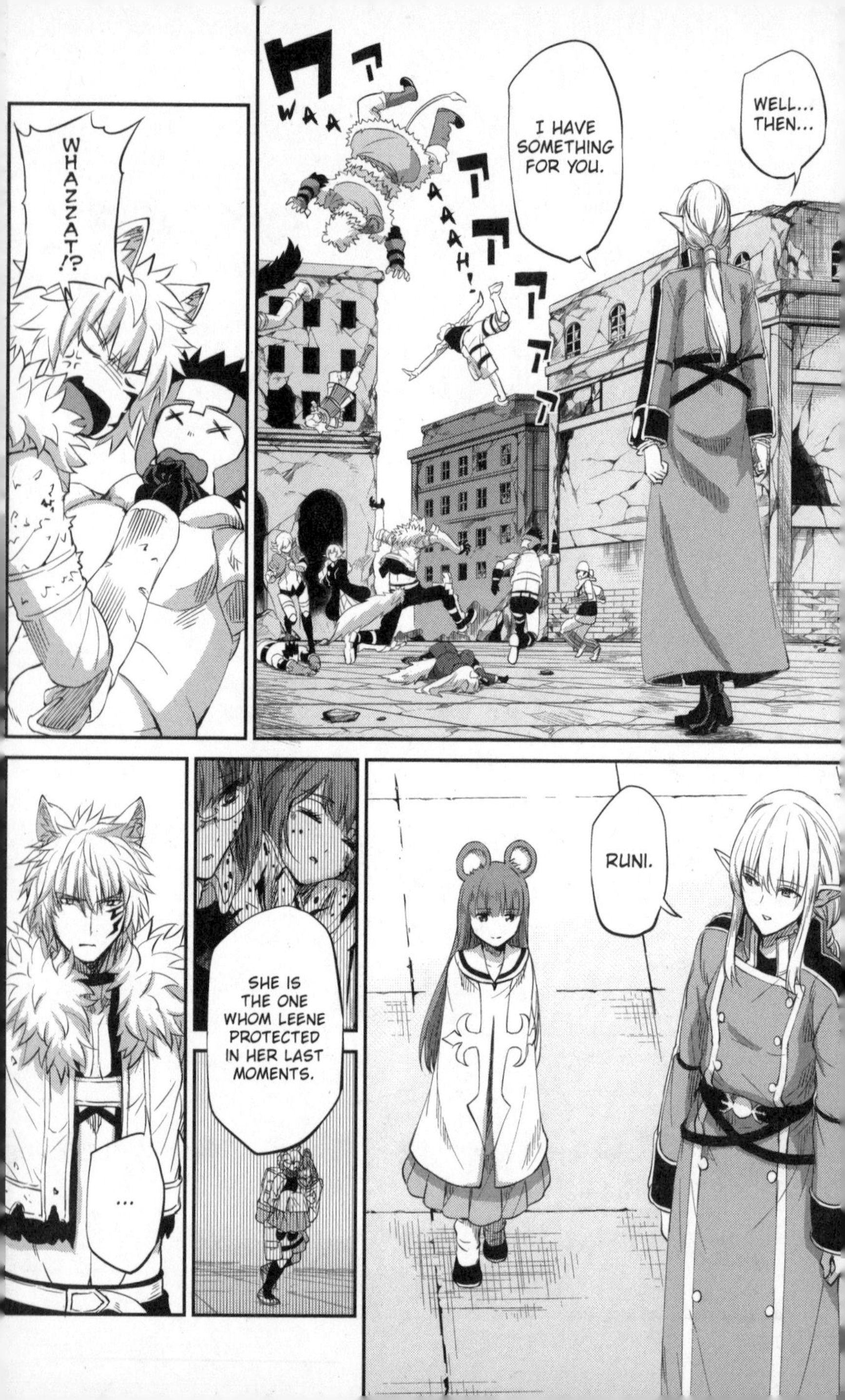
WELL... THEN...
I HAVE SOMETHING FOR YOU.
WAA
AAAH!
WHAZZAT!?
RUNI.
SHE IS THE ONE WHOM LEENE PROTECTED IN HER LAST MOMENTS.
...

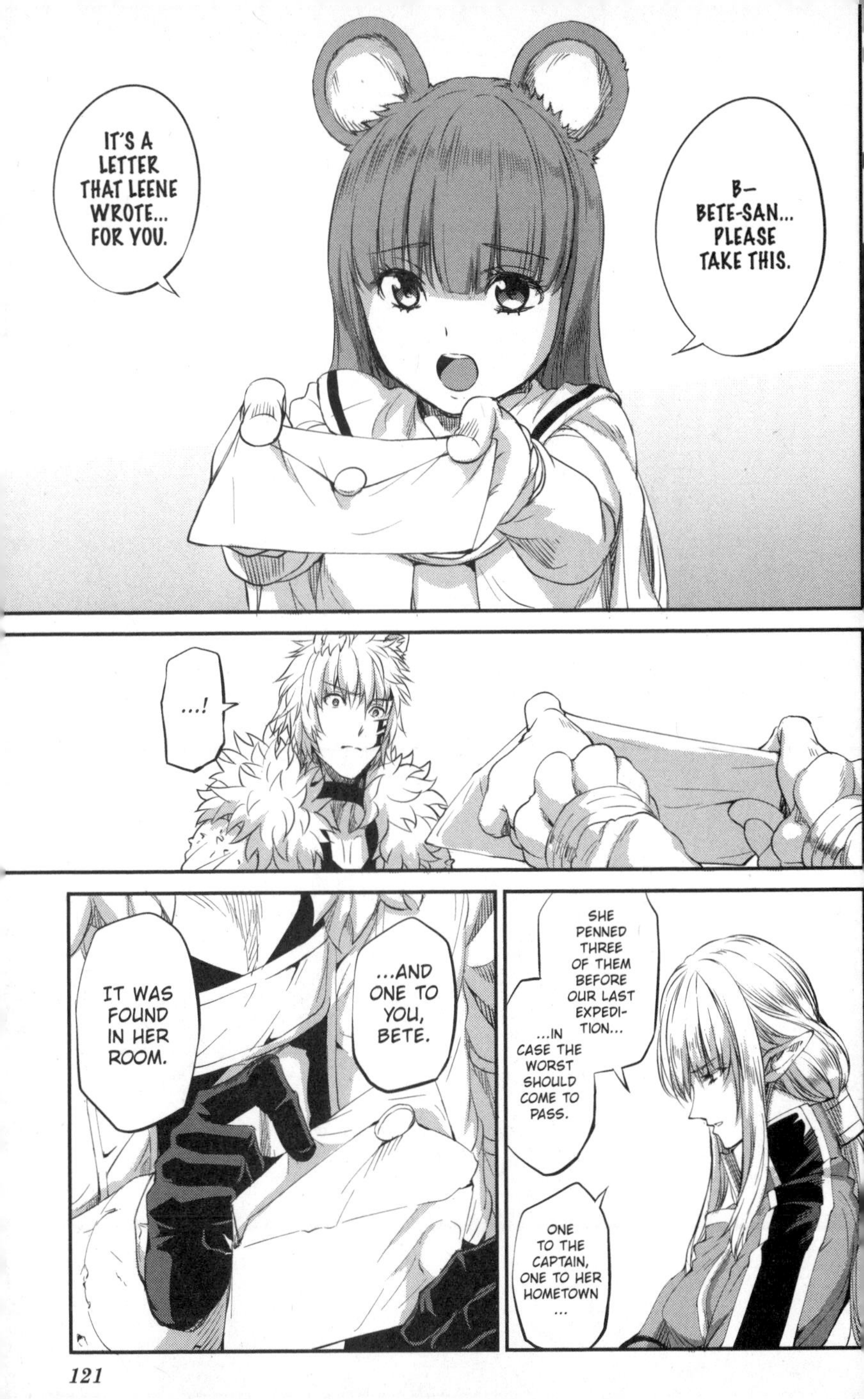
B— BETE-SAN... PLEASE TAKE THIS.
IT'S A LETTER THAT LEENE WROTE... FOR YOU.
...!
SHE PENNED THREE OF THEM BEFORE OUR LAST EXPEDITION...
...IN CASE THE WORST SHOULD COME TO PASS.
ONE TO THE CAPTAIN, ONE TO HER HOMETOWN...
...AND ONE TO YOU, BETE.
IT WAS FOUND IN HER ROOM.

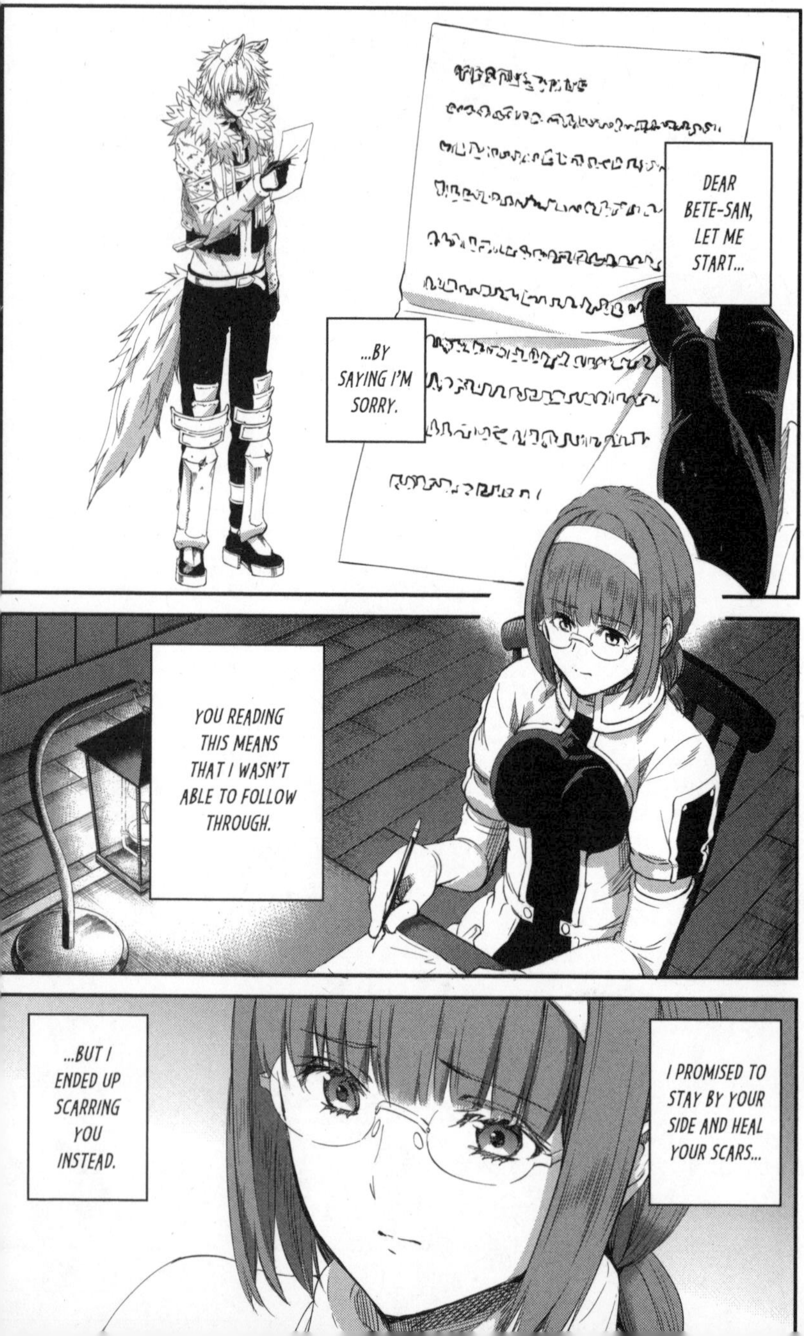
DEAR BETE-SAN, LET ME START...
...BY SAYING I'M SORRY.
YOU READING THIS MEANS THAT I WASN'T ABLE TO FOLLOW THROUGH.
I PROMISED TO STAY BY YOUR SIDE AND HEAL YOUR SCARS...
...BUT I ENDED UP SCARRING YOU INSTEAD.

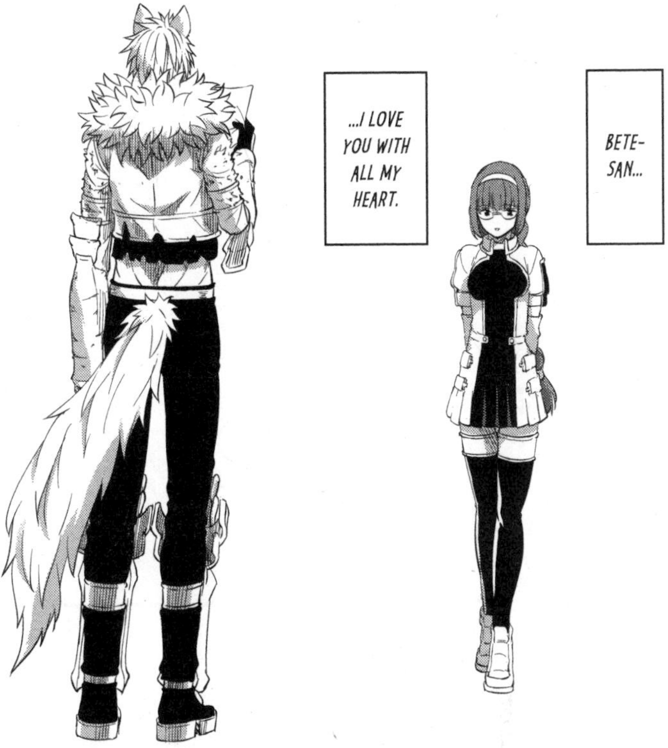
BETE-SAN...
...I LOVE YOU WITH ALL MY HEART.
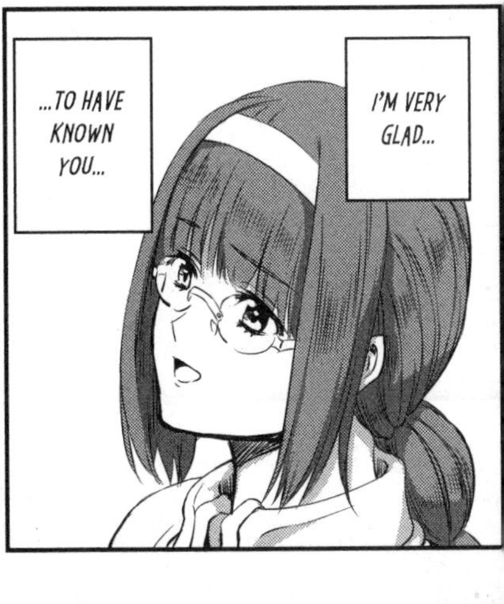
I'M VERY GLAD...
...TO HAVE KNOWN YOU...
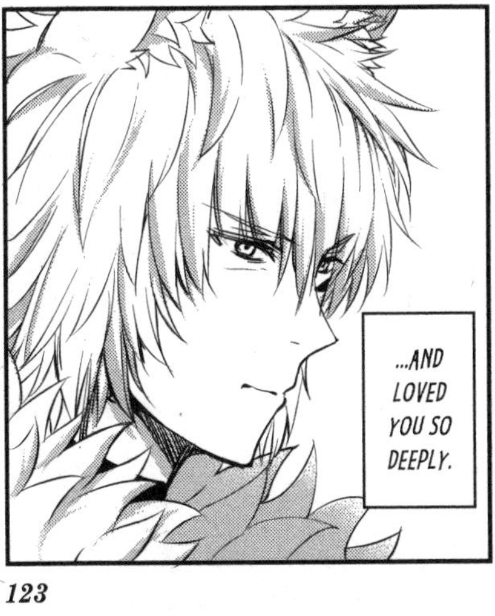
...AND LOVED YOU SO DEEPLY.

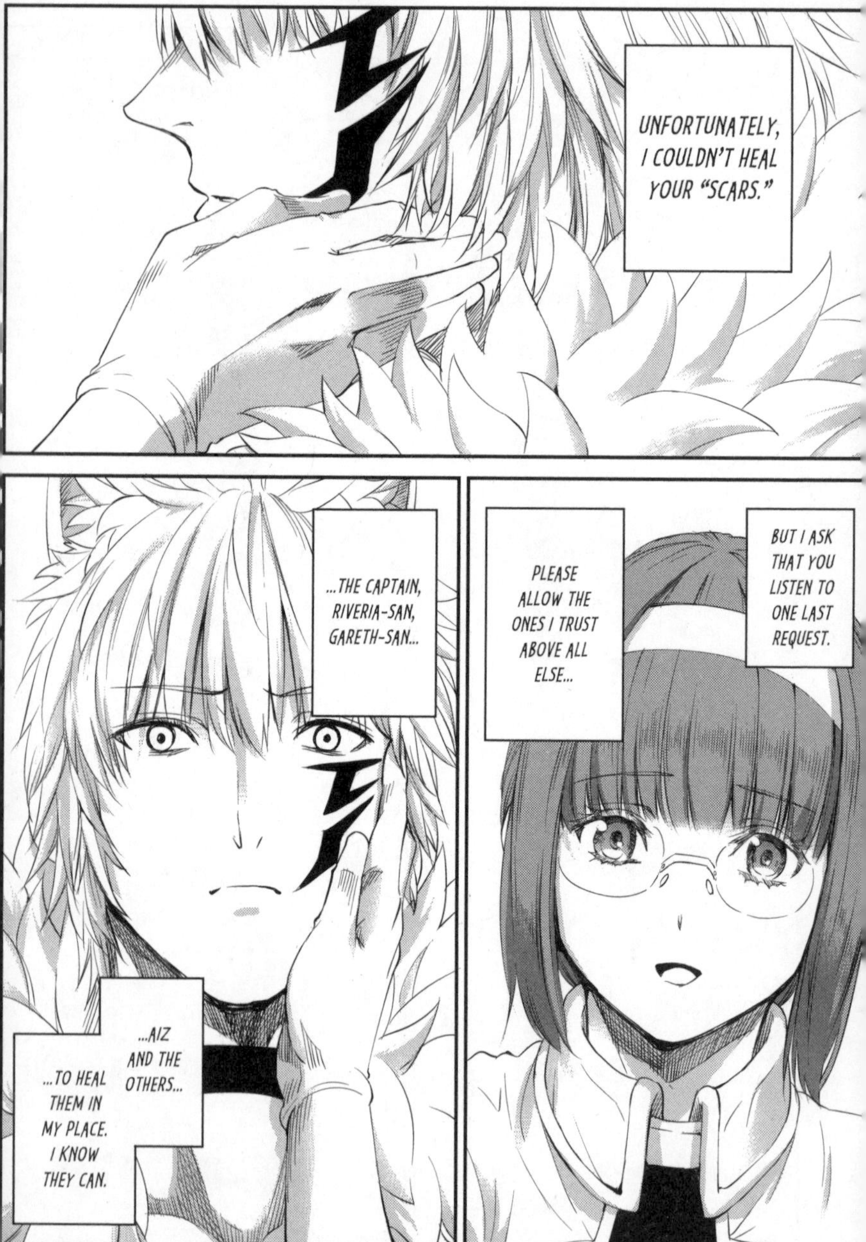
UNFORTUNATELY, I COULDN'T HEAL YOUR "SCARS."
BUT I ASK THAT YOU LISTEN TO ONE LAST REQUEST.
PLEASE ALLOW THE ONES I TRUST ABOVE ALL ELSE...
...THE CAPTAIN, RIVERIA-SAN, GARETH-SAN...
...AIZ AND THE OTHERS...
...TO HEAL THEM IN MY PLACE. I KNOW THEY CAN.

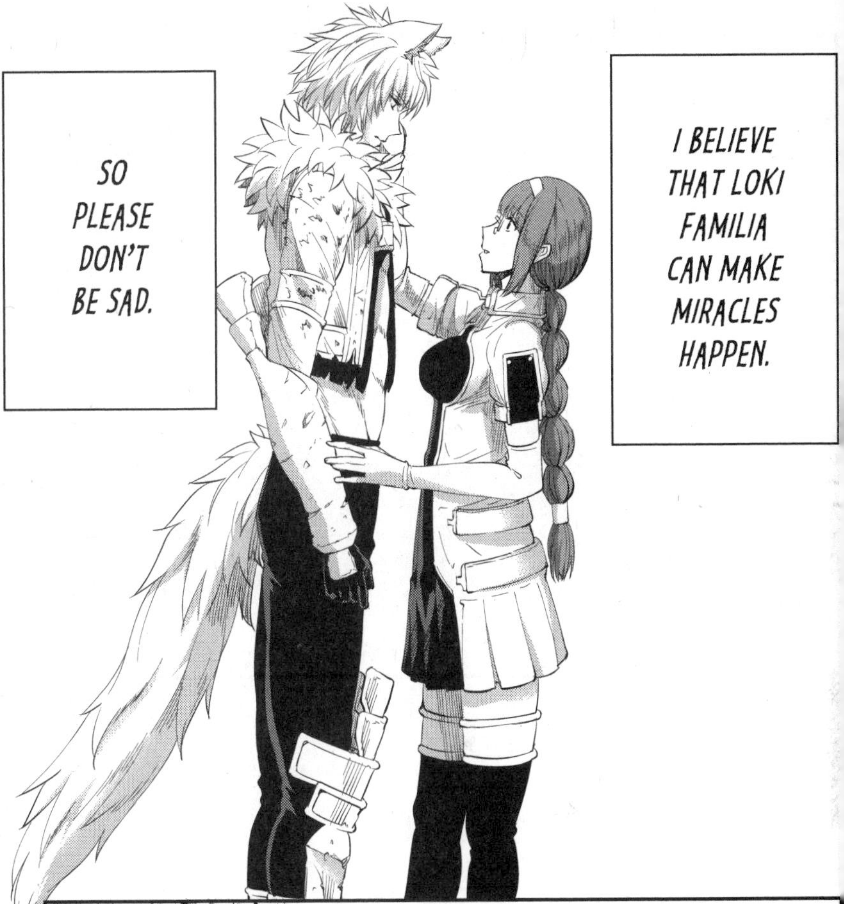
I BELIEVE THAT LOKI FAMILIA CAN MAKE MIRACLES HAPPEN.
SO PLEASE DON'T BE SAD.

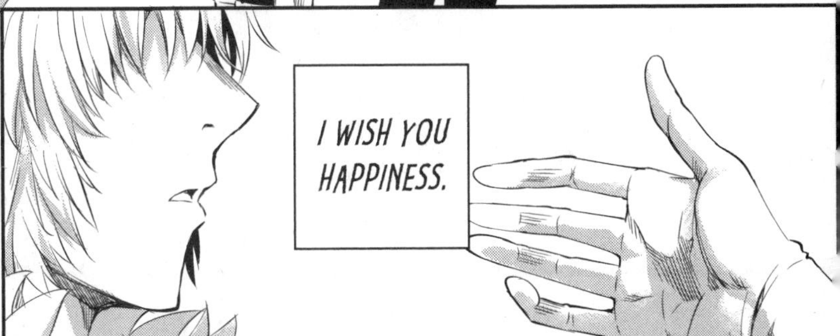
I WISH YOU HAPPINESS.

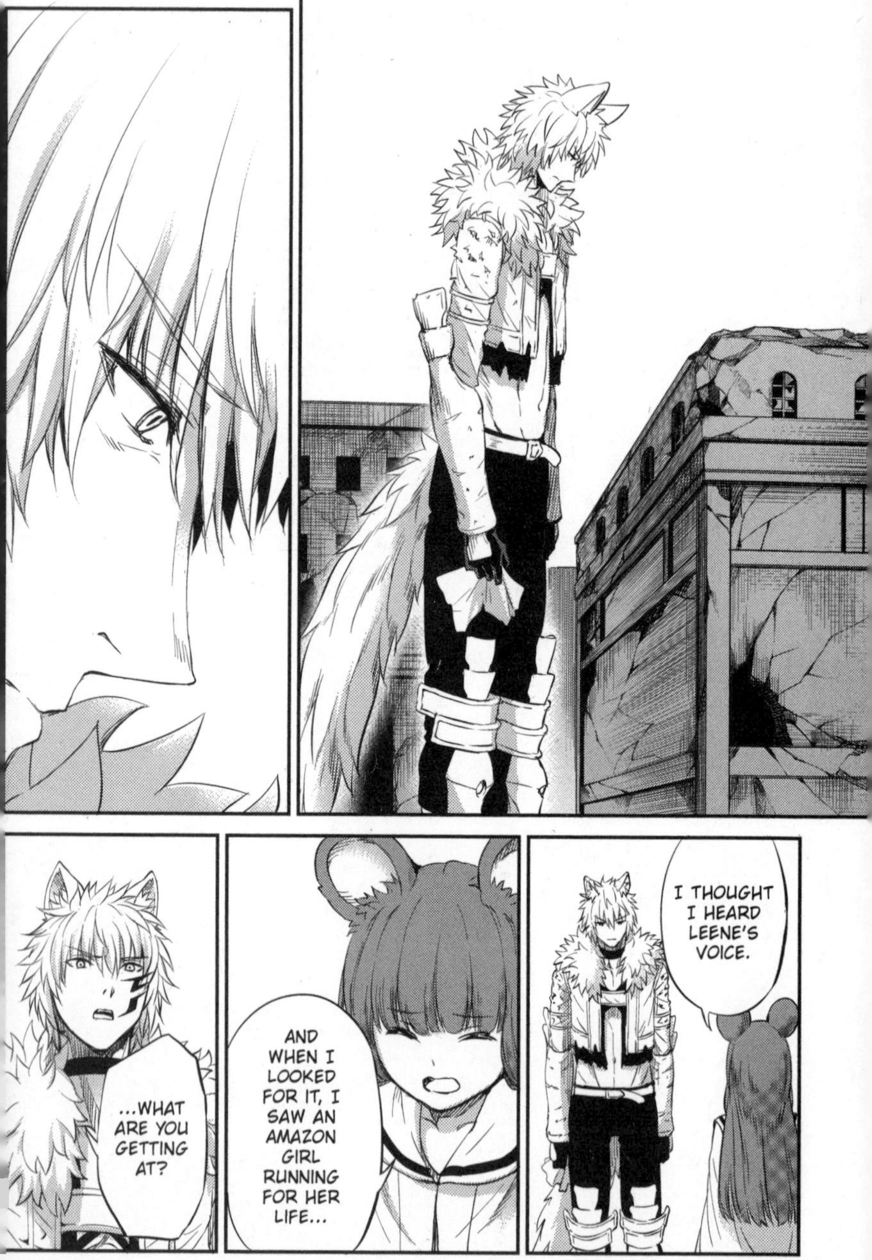
I THOUGHT I HEARD LEENE'S VOICE.
AND WHEN I LOOKED FOR IT, I SAW AN AMAZON GIRL RUNNING FOR HER LIFE...
...WHAT ARE YOU GETTING AT?

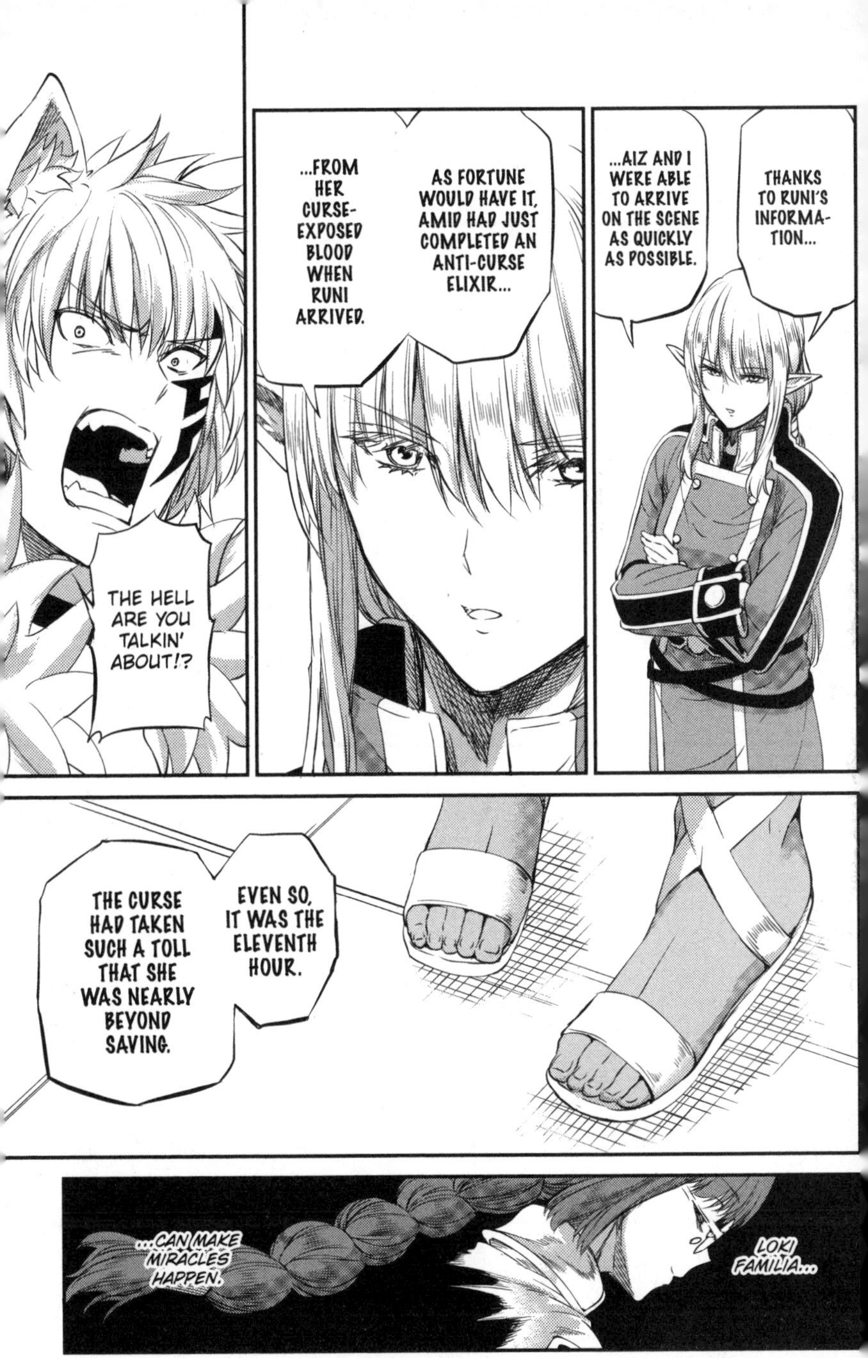
THANKS TO RUNI'S INFORMATION...
...AIZ AND I WERE ABLE TO ARRIVE ON THE SCENE AS QUICKLY AS POSSIBLE.
AS FORTUNE WOULD HAVE IT, AMID HAD JUST COMPLETED AN ANTI-CURSE ELIXIR...
...FROM HER CURSE-EXPOSED BLOOD WHEN RUNI ARRIVED.
THE HELL ARE YOU TALKIN' ABOUT!?
EVEN SO, IT WAS THE ELEVENTH HOUR.
THE CURSE HAD TAKEN SUCH A TOLL THAT SHE WAS NEARLY BEYOND SAVING.
LOKI FAMILIA...
...CAN MAKE MIRACLES HAPPEN.

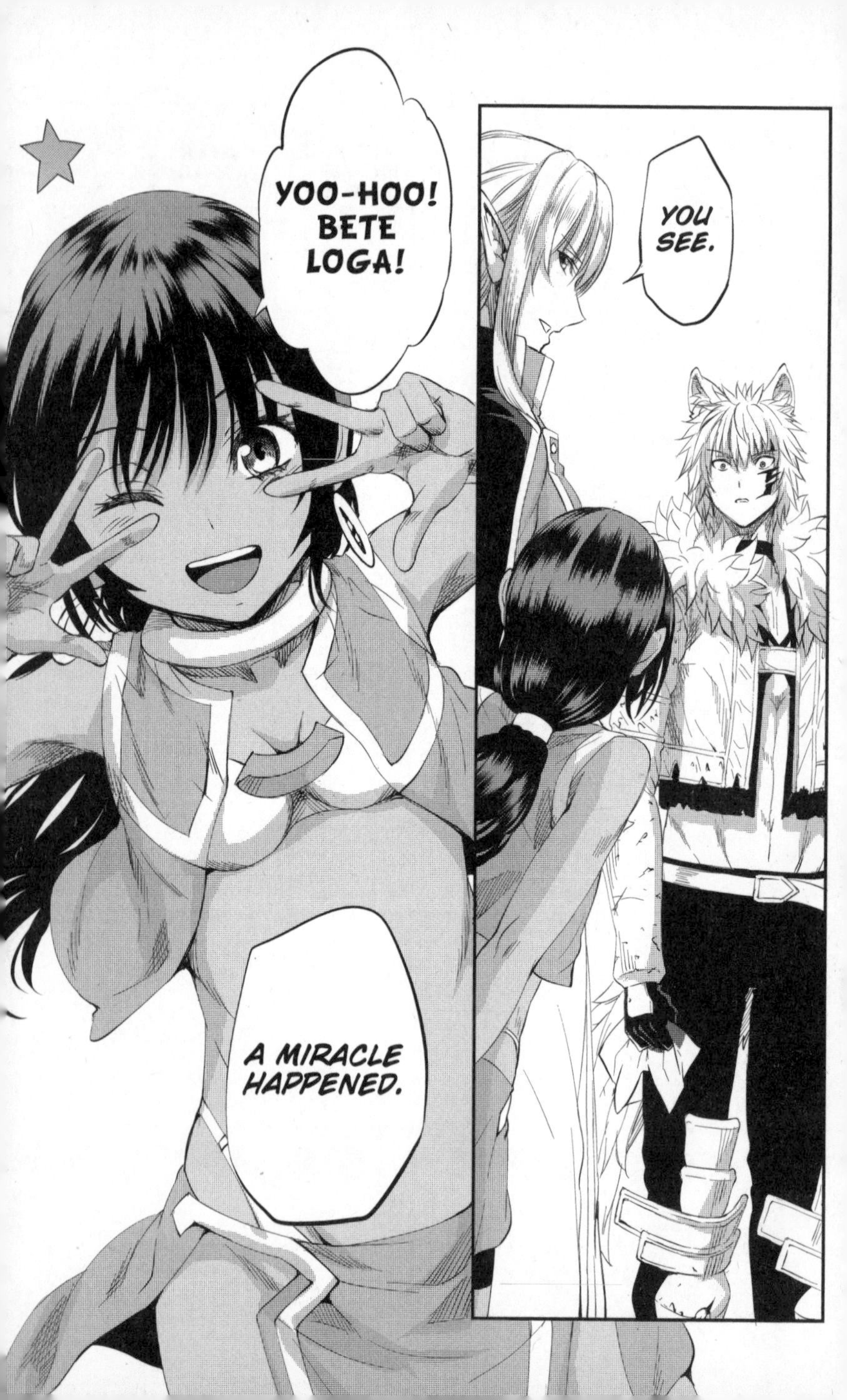
YOU SEE.
YOO-HOO! BETE LOGA!
A MIRACLE HAPPENED.

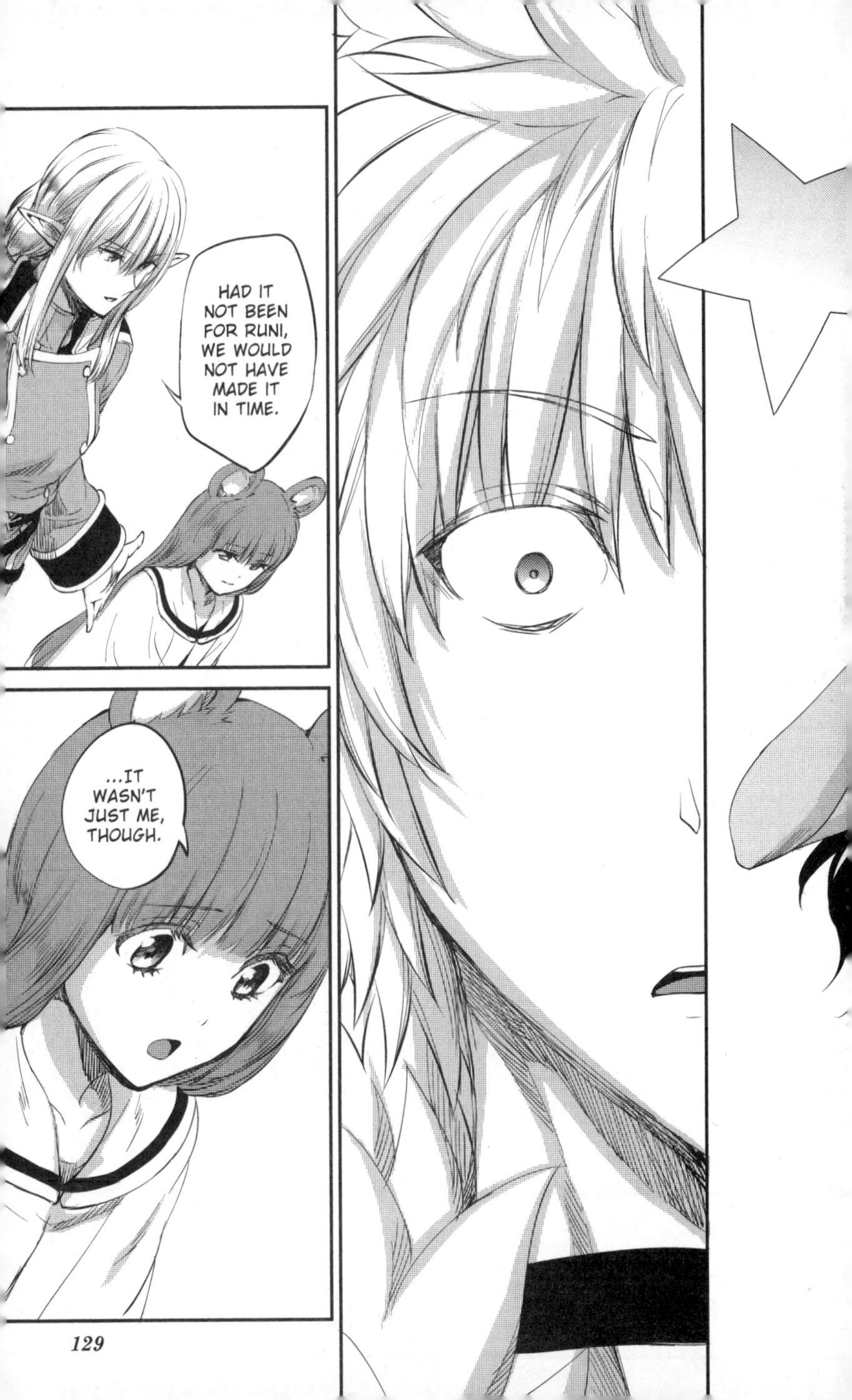
HAD IT NOT BEEN FOR RUNI, WE WOULD NOT HAVE MADE IT IN TIME.
...IT WASN'T JUST ME, THOUGH.

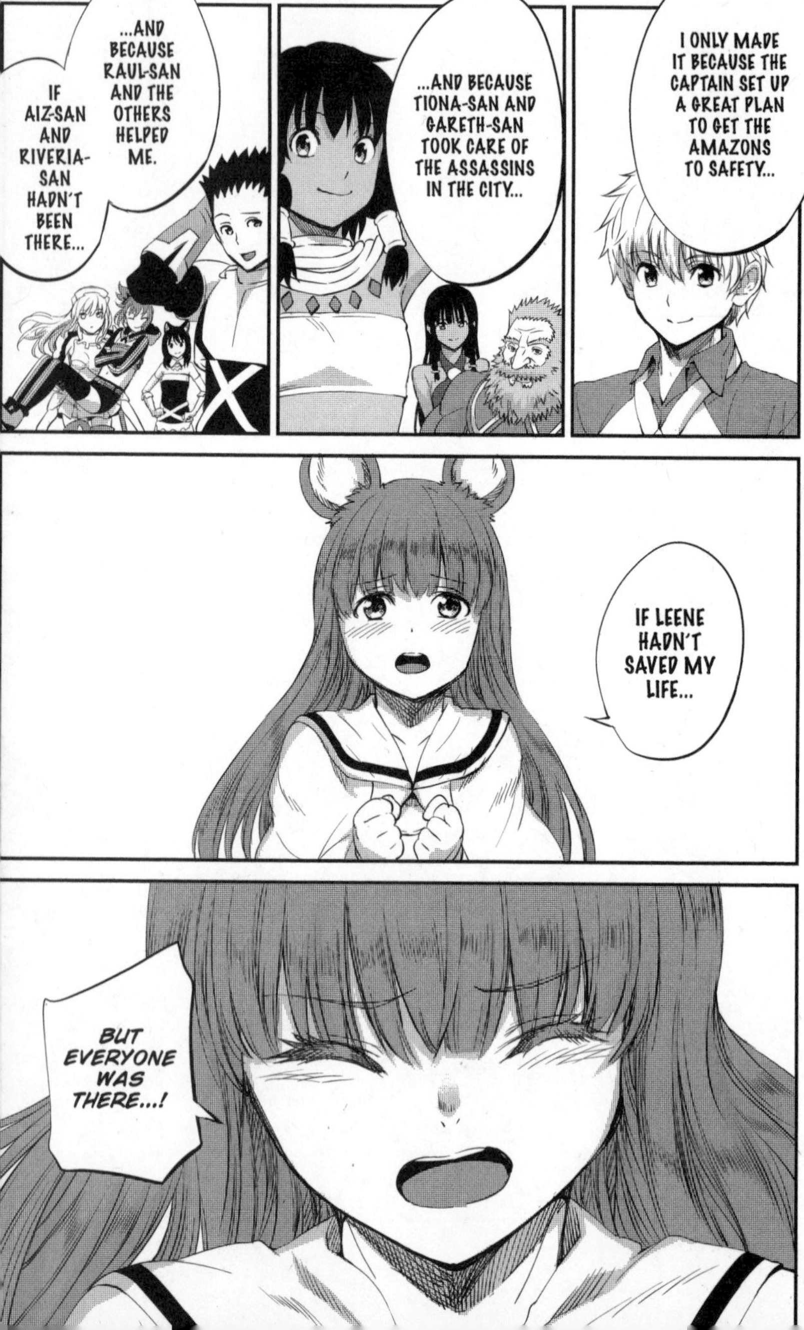
I ONLY MADE IT BECAUSE THE CAPTAIN SET UP A GREAT PLAN TO GET THE AMAZONS TO SAFETY...
...AND BECAUSE TIONA-SAN AND GARETH-SAN TOOK CARE OF THE ASSASSINS IN THE CITY...
...AND BECAUSE RAUL-SAN AND THE OTHERS HELPED ME.
IF AIZ-SAN AND RIVERIA-SAN HADN'T BEEN THERE...
IF LEENE HADN'T SAVED MY LIFE...
BUT EVERYONE WAS THERE...!

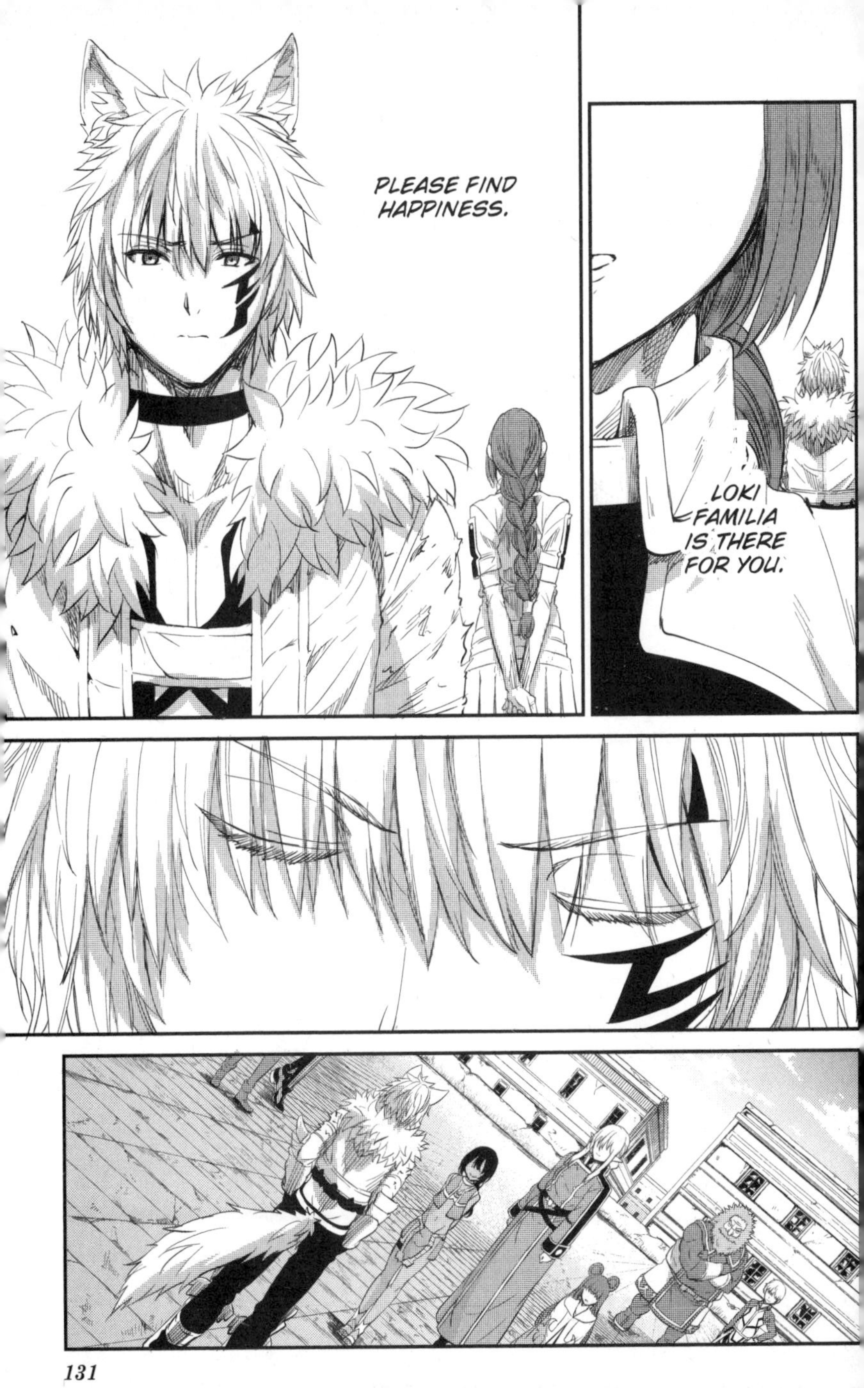
LOKI FAMILIA IS THERE FOR YOU.
PLEASE FIND HAPPINESS.

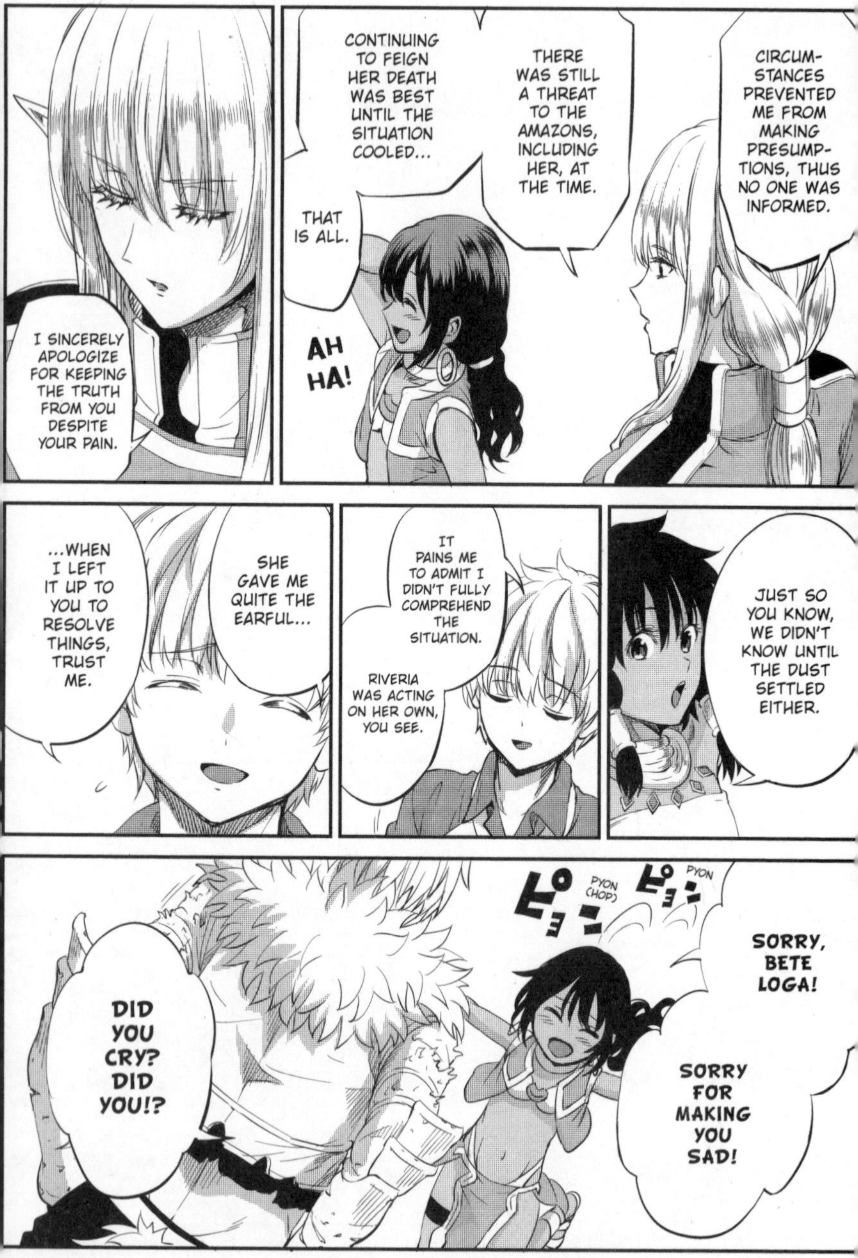
CIRCUM-STANCES PREVENTED ME FROM MAKING PRESUMP-TIONS, THUS NO ONE WAS INFORMED.
THERE WAS STILL A THREAT TO THE AMAZONS, INCLUDING HER, AT THE TIME.
CONTINUING TO FEIGN HER DEATH WAS BEST UNTIL THE SITUATION COOLED...
THAT IS ALL.
AH HA!
I SINCERELY APOLOGIZE FOR KEEPING THE TRUTH FROM YOU DESPITE YOUR PAIN.
JUST SO YOU KNOW, WE DIDN'T KNOW UNTIL THE DUST SETTLED EITHER.
IT PAINS ME TO ADMIT I DIDN'T FULLY COMPREHEND THE SITUATION.
RIVERIA WAS ACTING ON HER OWN, YOU SEE.
SHE GAVE ME QUITE THE EARFUL...
...WHEN I LEFT IT UP TO YOU TO RESOLVE THINGS, TRUST ME.
PYON
PYON (HOP)
SORRY, BETE LOGA!
SORRY FOR MAKING YOU SAD!
DID YOU CRY? DID YOU!?

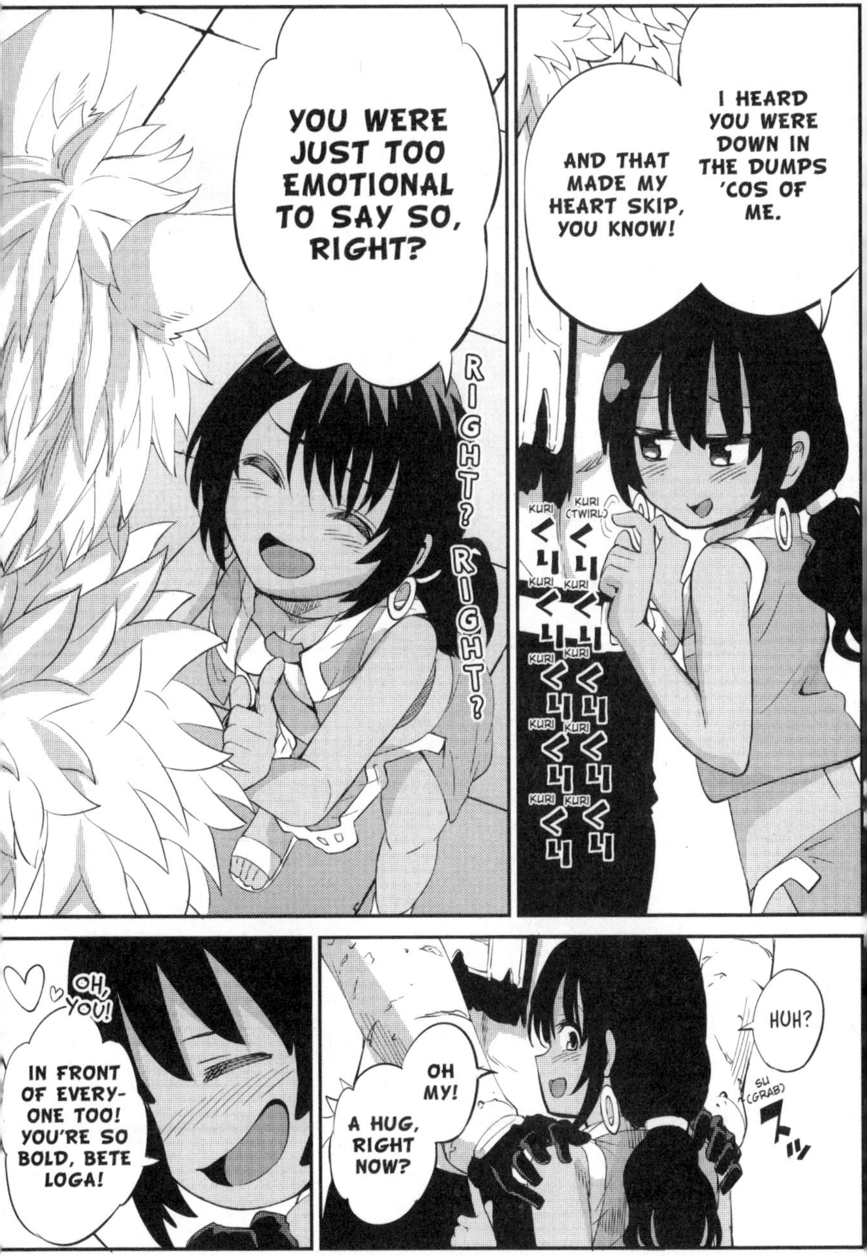
I HEARD YOU WERE DOWN IN THE DUMPS 'COS OF ME.
AND THAT MADE MY HEART SKIP, YOU KNOW!
KURI (TWIRL)
KURI KURI KURI KURI KURI KURI KURI KURI KURI
YOU WERE JUST TOO EMOTIONAL TO SAY SO, RIGHT?
RIGHT? RIGHT? RIGHT?
HUH?
SU (GRAB)
OH MY!
A HUG, RIGHT NOW?
OH, YOU!
IN FRONT OF EVERY-ONE TOO! YOU'RE SO BOLD, BETE LOGA!

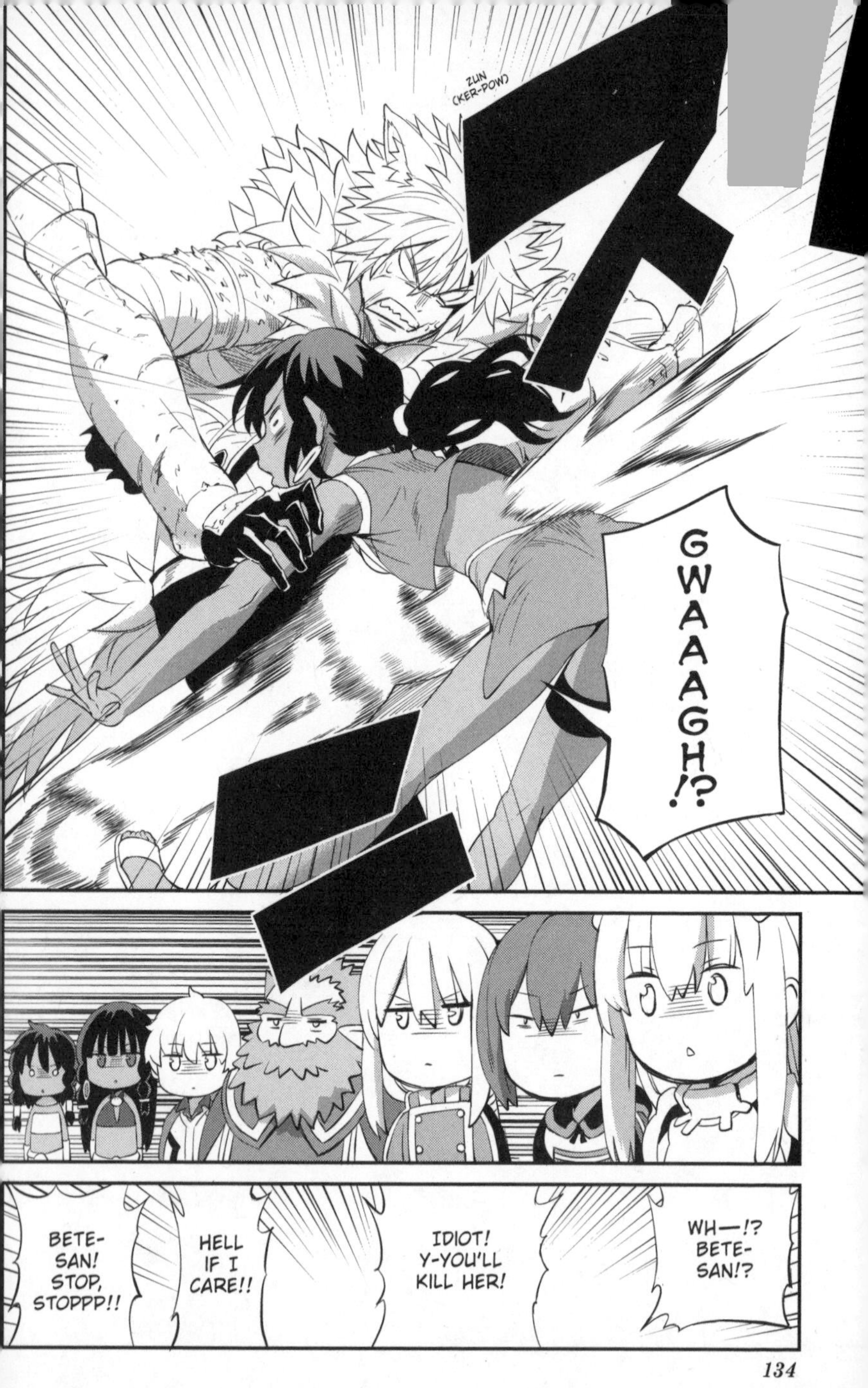
ZUN (KER-POW)
GWAAAGH!?
WH—!? BETE-SAN!?
IDIOT! Y-YOU'LL KILL HER!
HELL IF I CARE!!
BETE-SAN! STOP, STOPPP!!

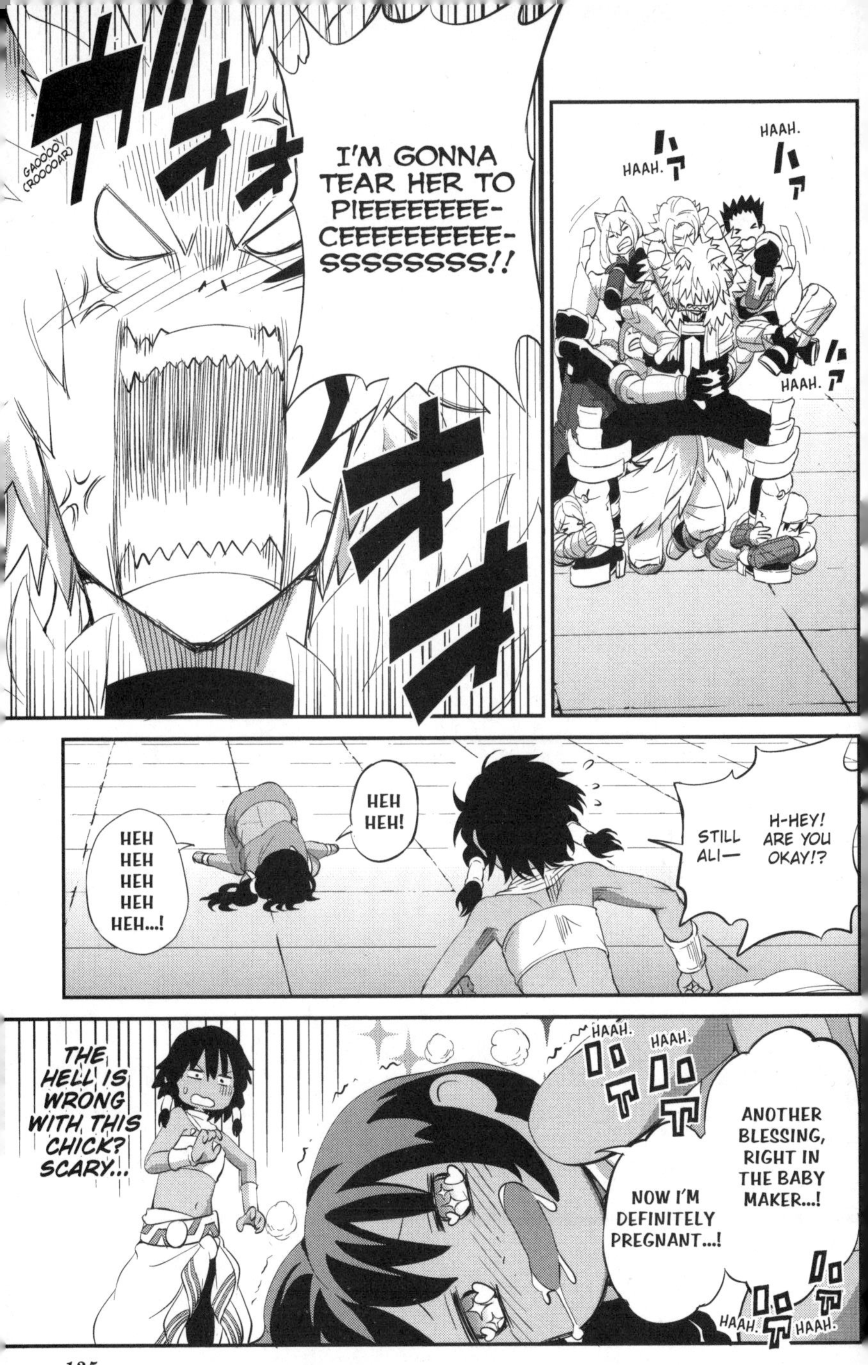
HAAH.
HAAH.
HAAH.
GAOOOOOY (ROOOOAR)
I'M GONNA TEAR HER TO PIEEEEEEEE-CEEEEEEEEEE-SSSSSSSS!!
H-HEY! ARE YOU OKAY!?
STILL ALI—
HEH HEH!
HEH HEH HEH HEH HEH...!
HAAH.
HAAH.
ANOTHER BLESSING, RIGHT IN THE BABY MAKER...!
NOW I'M DEFINITELY PREGNANT...!
HAAH.
HAAH.
THE HELL IS WRONG WITH THIS CHICK? SCARY...

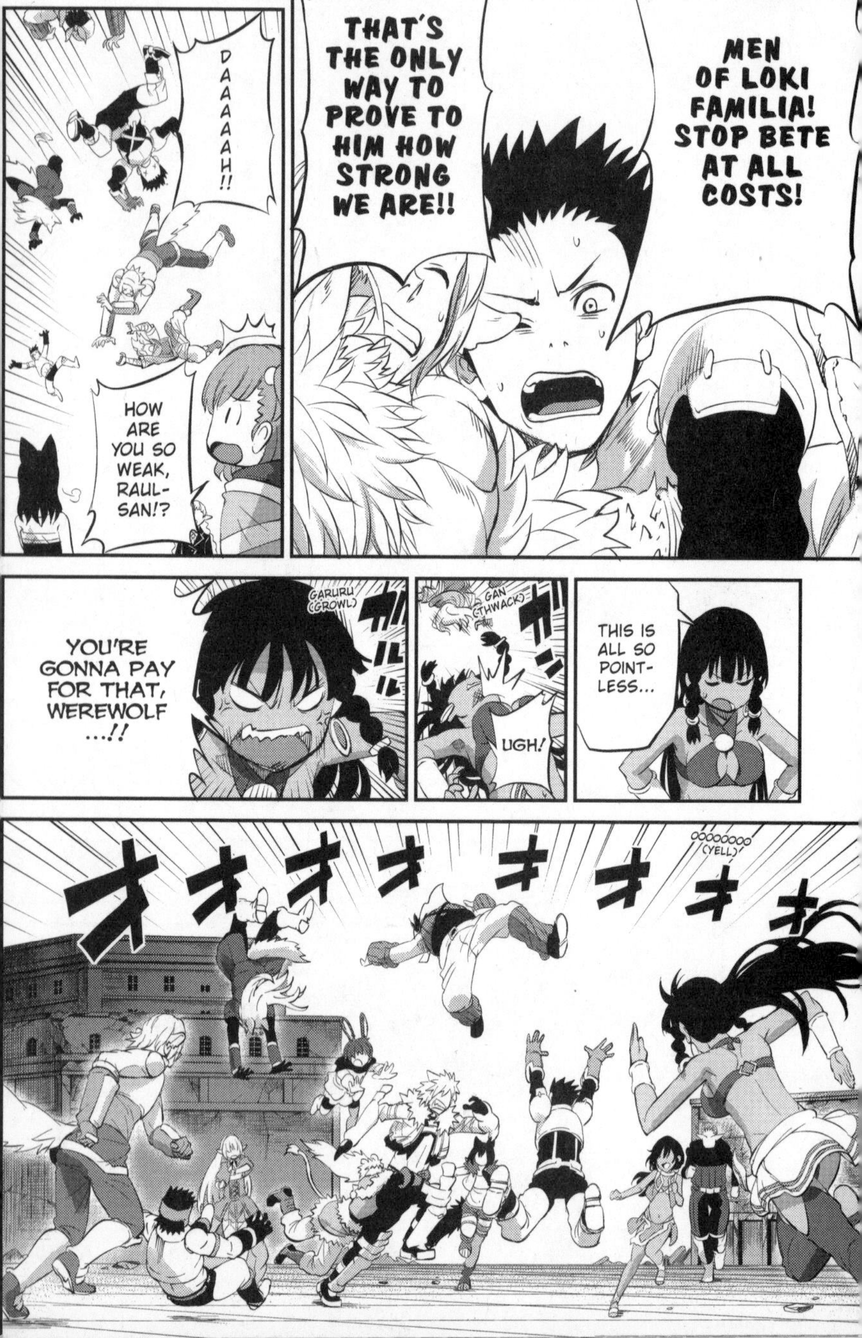
MEN OF LOKI FAMILIA! STOP BETE AT ALL COSTS!
THAT'S THE ONLY WAY TO PROVE TO HIM HOW STRONG WE ARE!!
DAAAAAH!!
HOW ARE YOU SO WEAK, RAUL-SAN!?
THIS IS ALL SO POINTLESS...
GAN (THWACK)
UGH!
GARURU (GROWL)
YOU'RE GONNA PAY FOR THAT, WEREWOLF ...!!
OOOOOOOO (YELL)

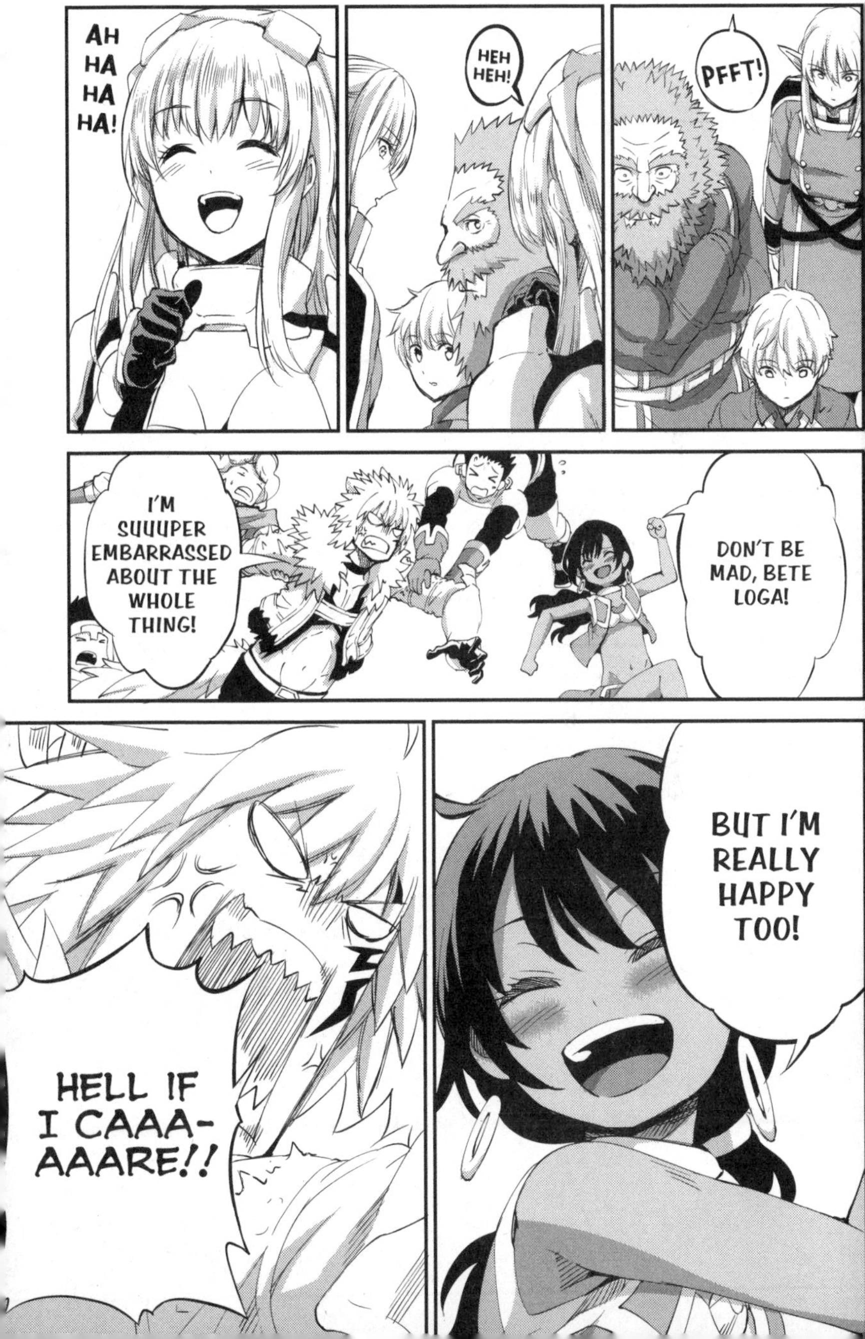
PFFT!
HEH HEH!
AH HA HA HA!
DON'T BE MAD, BETE LOGA!
I'M SUUUPER EMBARRASSED ABOUT THE WHOLE THING!
BUT I'M REALLY HAPPY TOO!
HELL IF I CAAA-AAARE!!

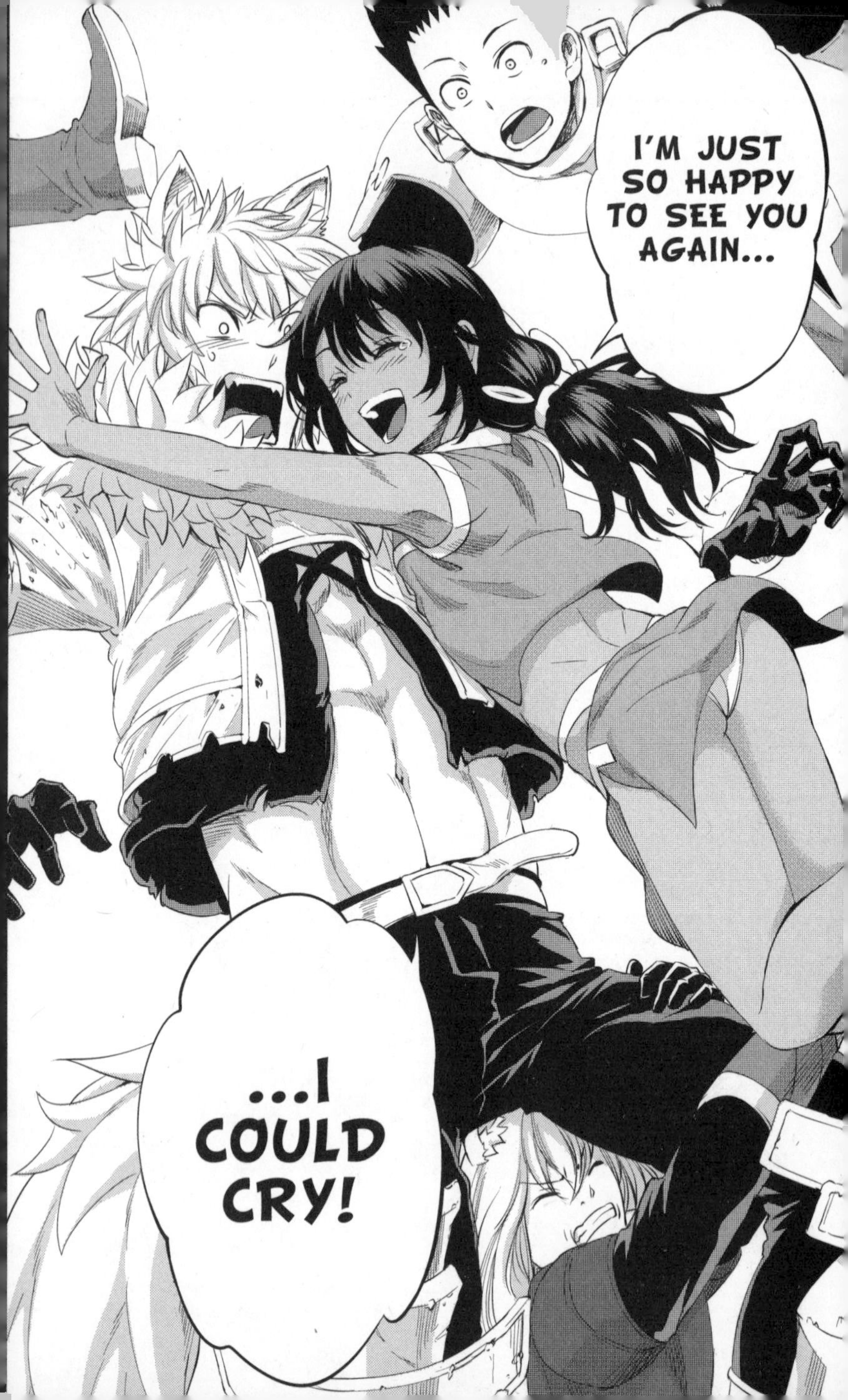
I'M JUST SO HAPPY TO SEE YOU AGAIN...
...I COULD CRY!

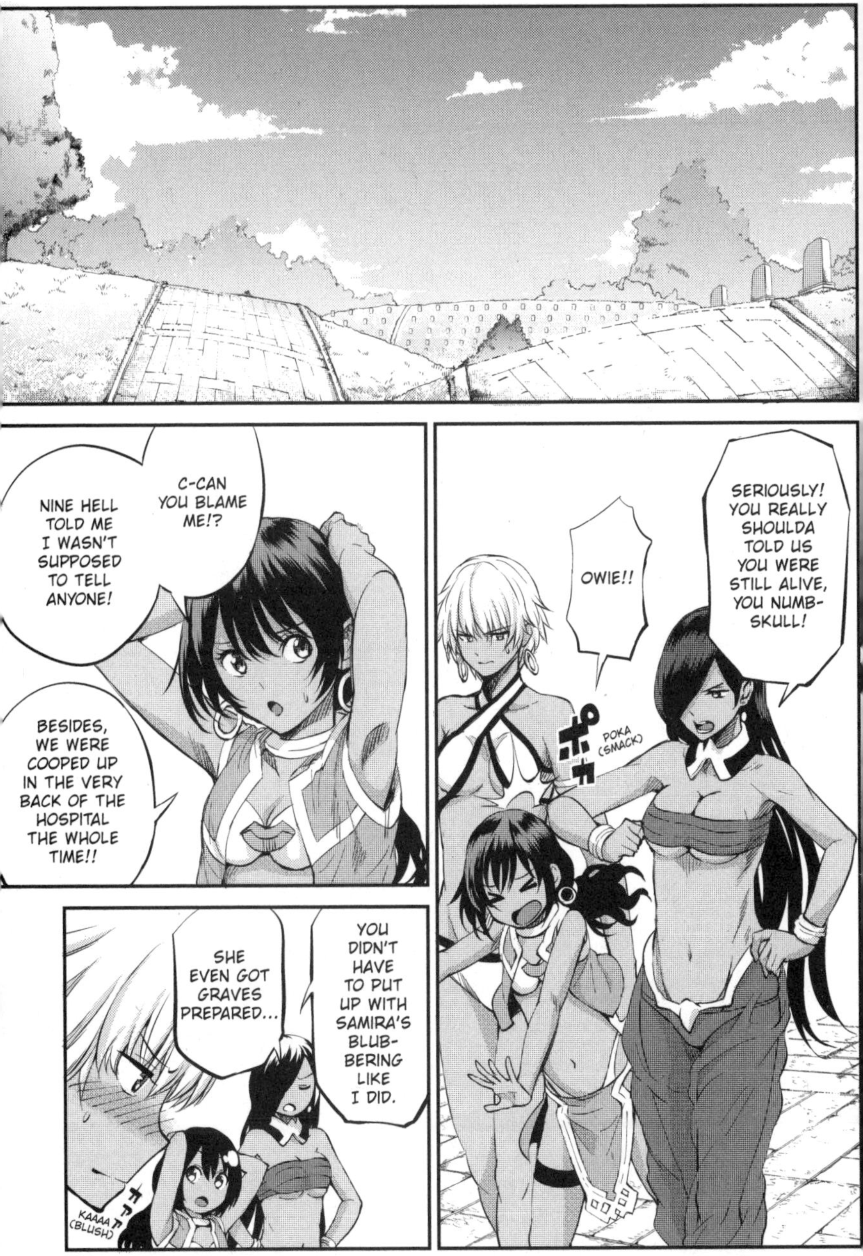

SERIOUSLY! YOU REALLY SHOULDA TOLD US YOU WERE STILL ALIVE, YOU NUMB-SKULL!
OWIE!!
POKA (SMACK)
C-CAN YOU BLAME ME!?
NINE HELL TOLD ME I WASN'T SUPPOSED TO TELL ANYONE!
BESIDES, WE WERE COOPED UP IN THE VERY BACK OF THE HOSPITAL THE WHOLE TIME!!
YOU DIDN'T HAVE TO PUT UP WITH SAMIRA'S BLUB-BERING LIKE I DID.
SHE EVEN GOT GRAVES PREPARED...
KAAAA (BLUSH)

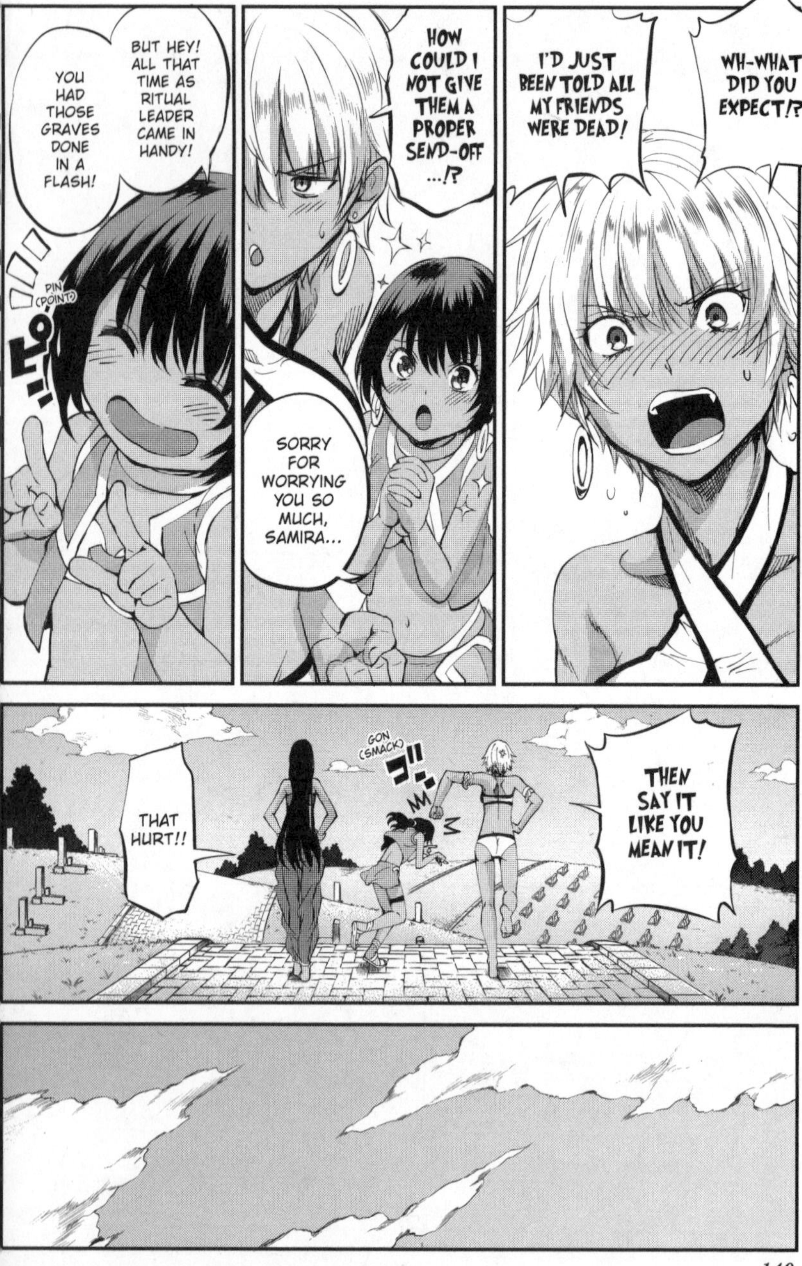
WH-WHAT DID YOU EXPECT!?
I'D JUST BEEN TOLD ALL MY FRIENDS WERE DEAD!
HOW COULD I NOT GIVE THEM A PROPER SEND-OFF ...!?
SORRY FOR WORRYING YOU SO MUCH, SAMIRA...
BUT HEY! ALL THAT TIME AS RITUAL LEADER CAME IN HANDY!
YOU HAD THOSE GRAVES DONE IN A FLASH!
PIN (POINT)
THEN SAY IT LIKE YOU MEAN IT!
GON (SMACK)
THAT HURT!!

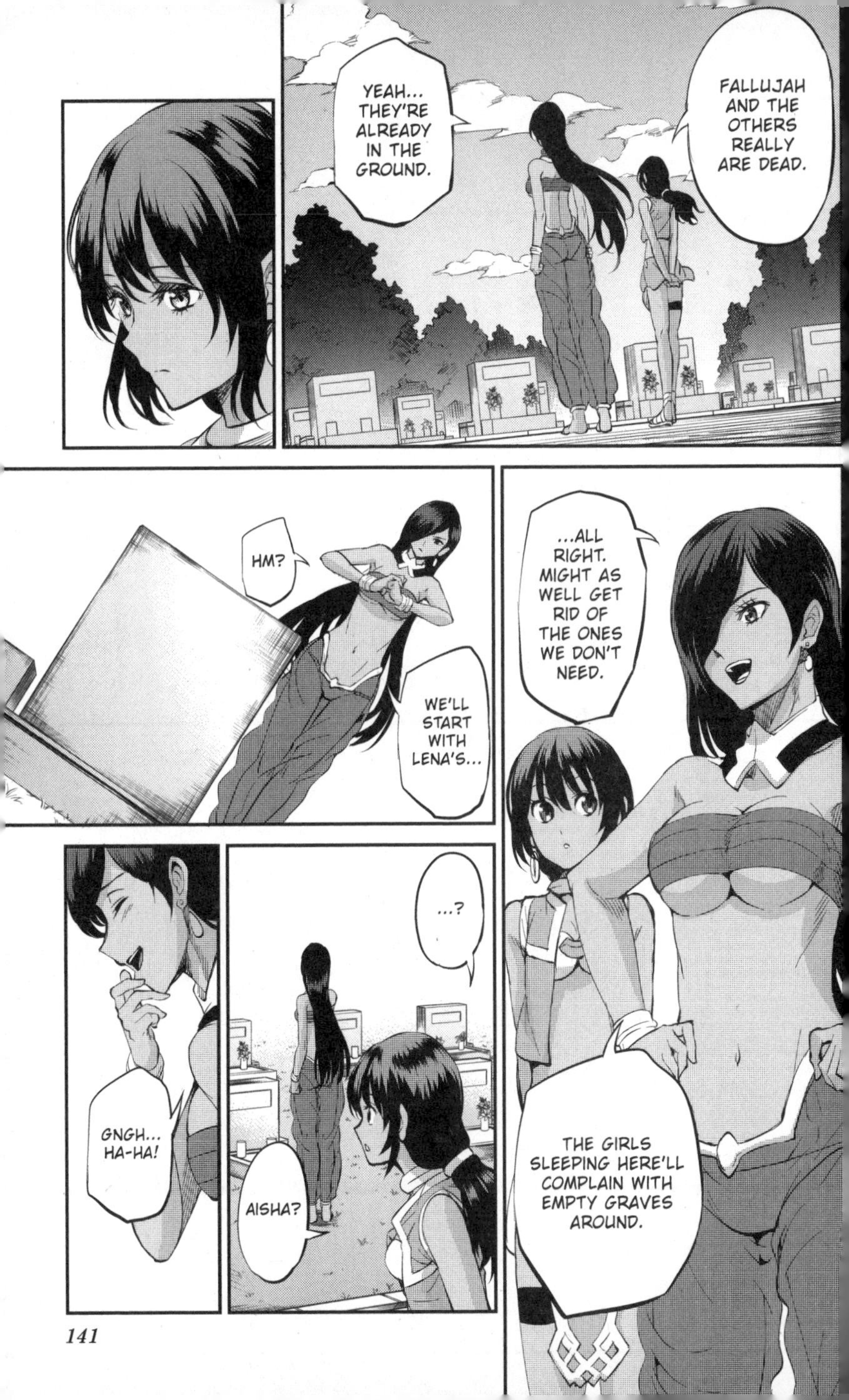
FALLUJAH AND THE OTHERS REALLY ARE DEAD.
YEAH... THEY'RE ALREADY IN THE GROUND.
...ALL RIGHT. MIGHT AS WELL GET RID OF THE ONES WE DON'T NEED.
THE GIRLS SLEEPING HERE'LL COMPLAIN WITH EMPTY GRAVES AROUND.
HM?
WE'LL START WITH LENA'S...
...?
AISHA?
GNGH... HA-HA!

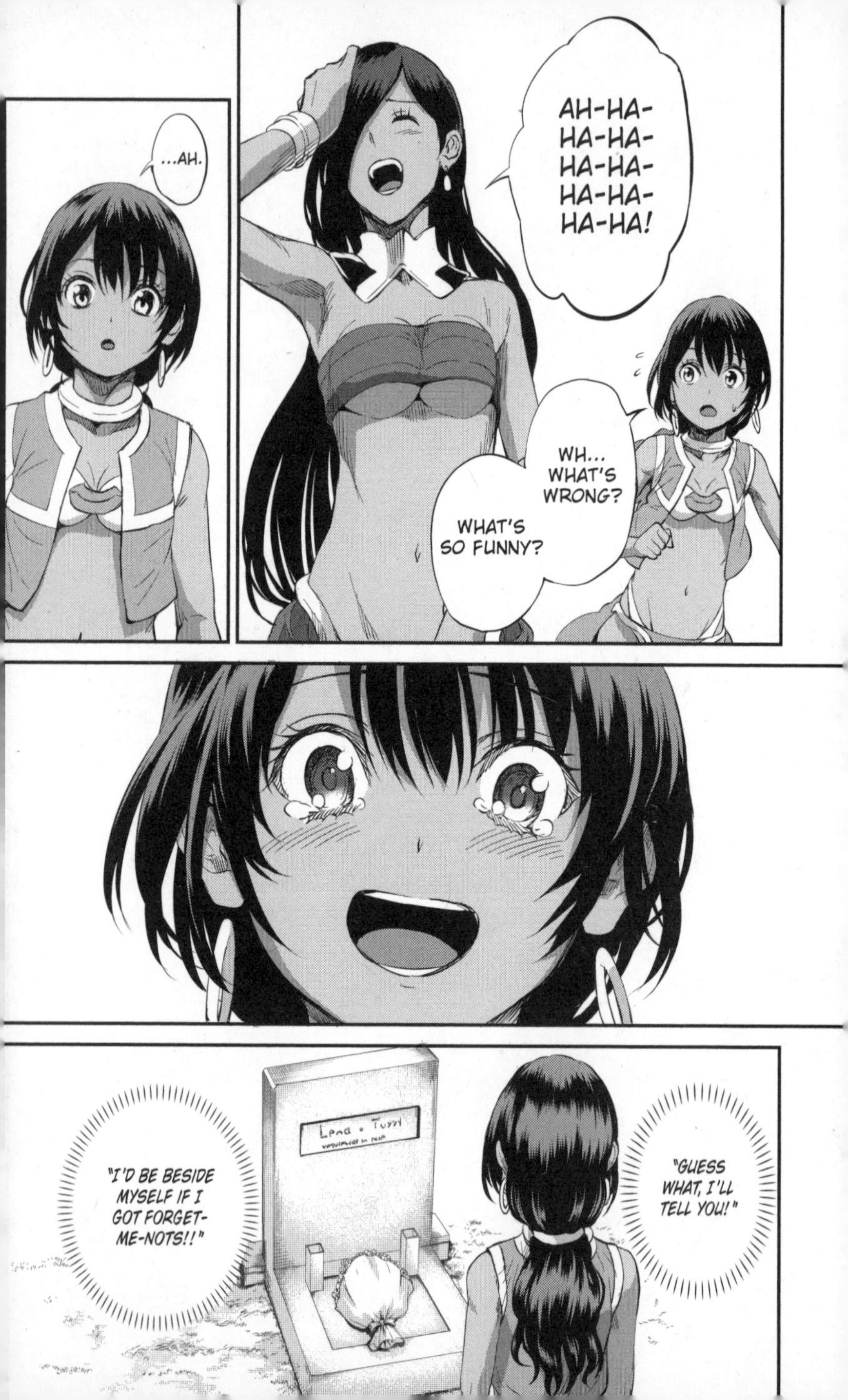
AH-HA-HA-HA-HA-HA-HA-HA-HA-HA!
WH... WHAT'S WRONG?
WHAT'S SO FUNNY?
...AH.
"GUESS WHAT, I'LL TELL YOU!"
"I'D BE BESIDE MYSELF IF I GOT FORGET-ME-NOTS!!"

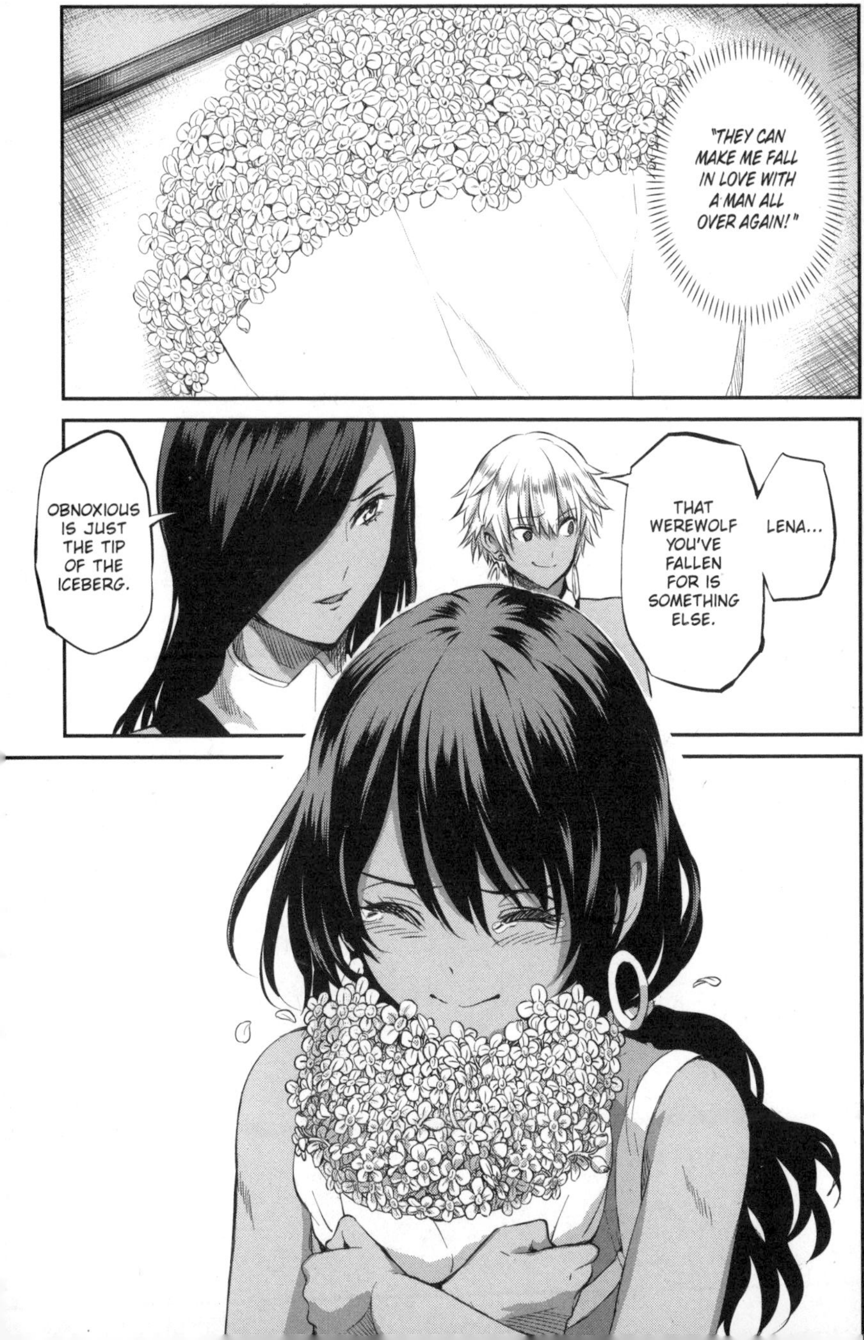
"THEY CAN MAKE ME FALL IN LOVE WITH A MAN ALL OVER AGAIN!"
LENA...
THAT WEREWOLF YOU'VE FALLEN FOR IS SOMETHING ELSE.
OBNOXIOUS IS JUST THE TIP OF THE ICEBERG.

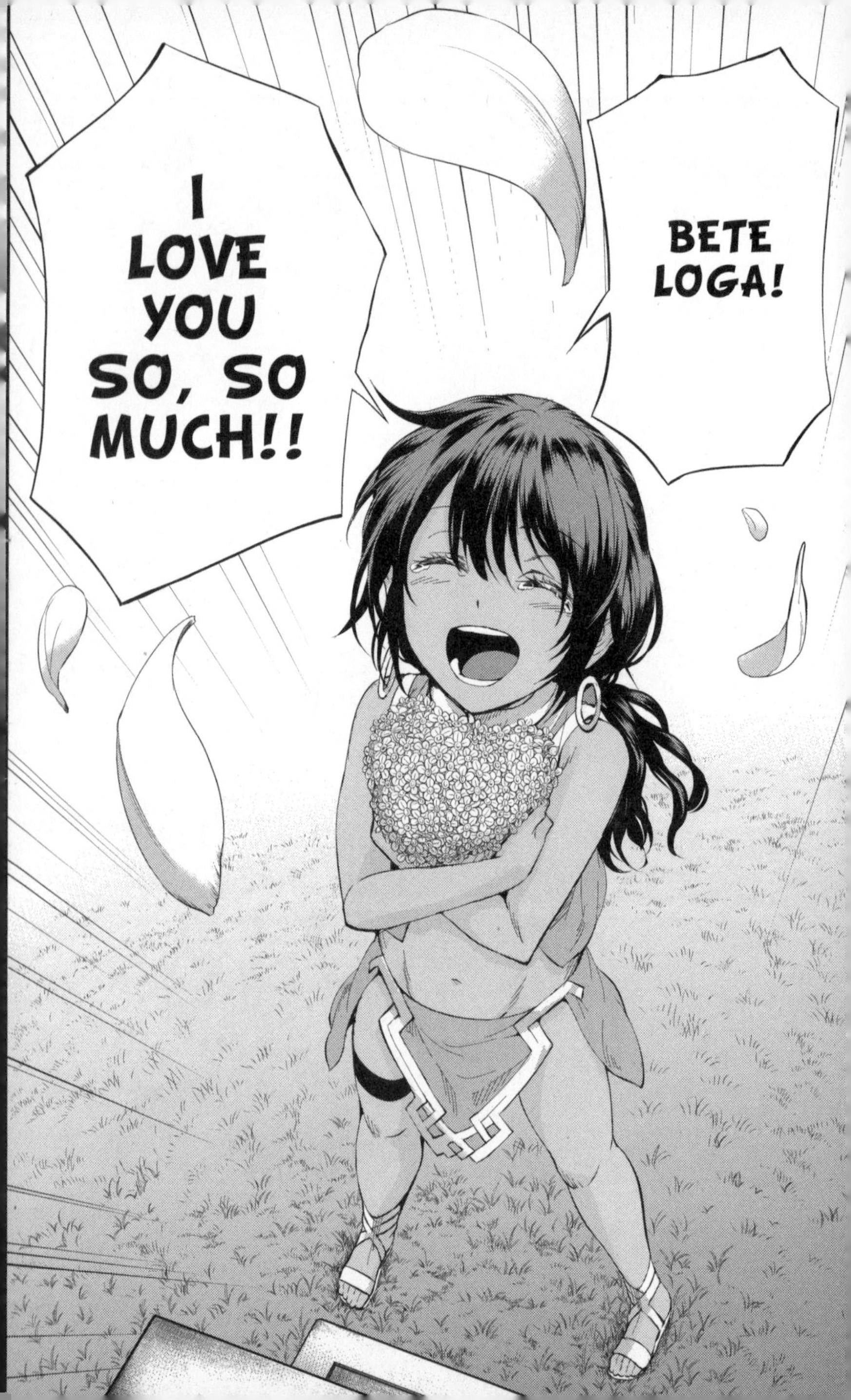
BETE LOGA!
I LOVE YOU SO, SO MUCH!!

Is it WRONG to try to PICK-UP GIRLS in A DUNGEON? ON THE SIDE

Sword Oratoria

quest 78. Break

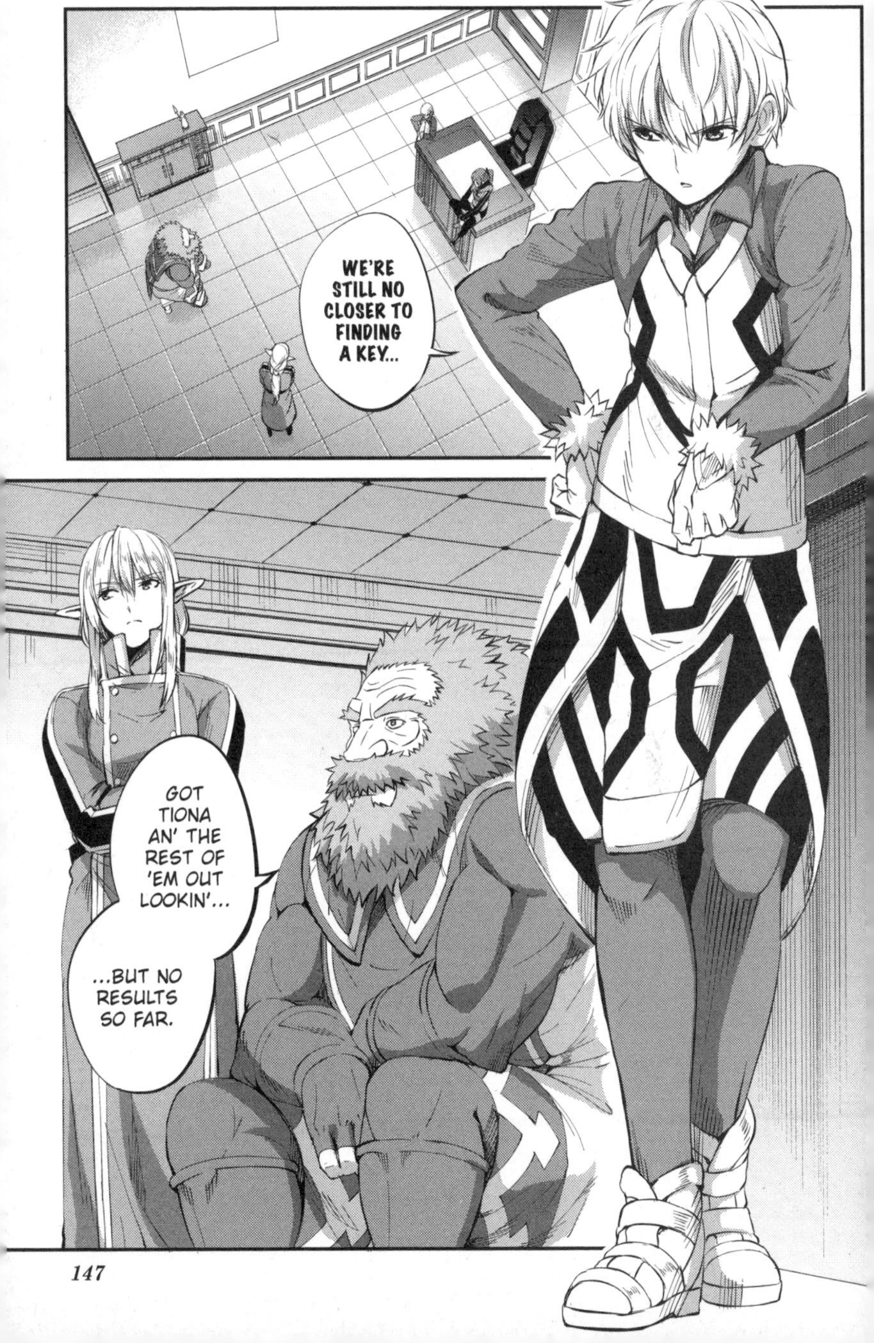
WE'RE STILL NO CLOSER TO FINDING A KEY...
GOT TIONA AN' THE REST OF 'EM OUT LOOKIN'...
...BUT NO RESULTS SO FAR.

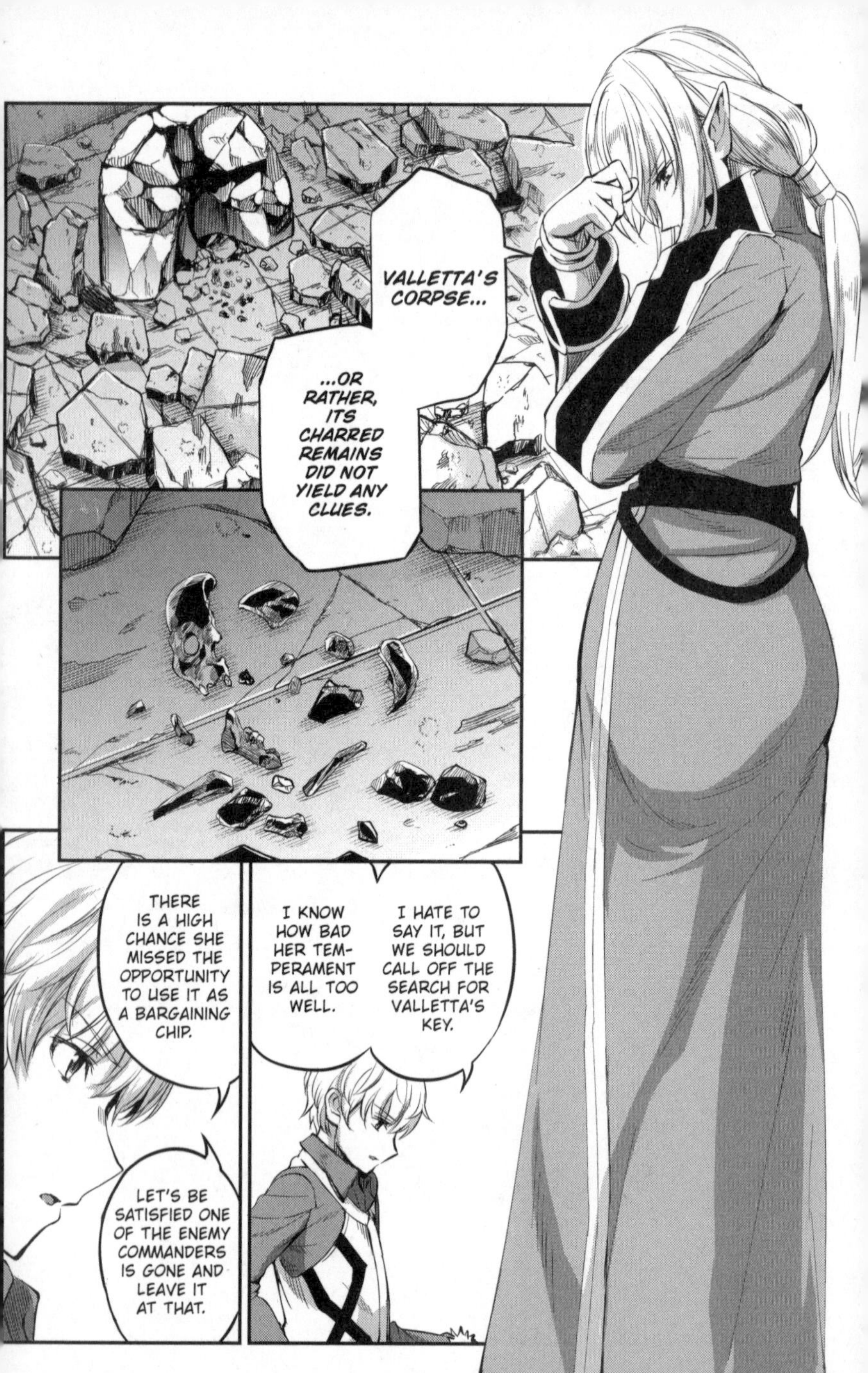
VALLETTA'S CORPSE...
...OR RATHER, ITS CHARRED REMAINS DID NOT YIELD ANY CLUES.
I HATE TO SAY IT, BUT WE SHOULD CALL OFF THE SEARCH FOR VALLETTA'S KEY.
I KNOW HOW BAD HER TEMPERAMENT IS ALL TOO WELL.
THERE IS A HIGH CHANCE SHE MISSED THE OPPORTUNITY TO USE IT AS A BARGAINING CHIP.
LET'S BE SATISFIED ONE OF THE ENEMY COMMANDERS IS GONE AND LEAVE IT AT THAT.

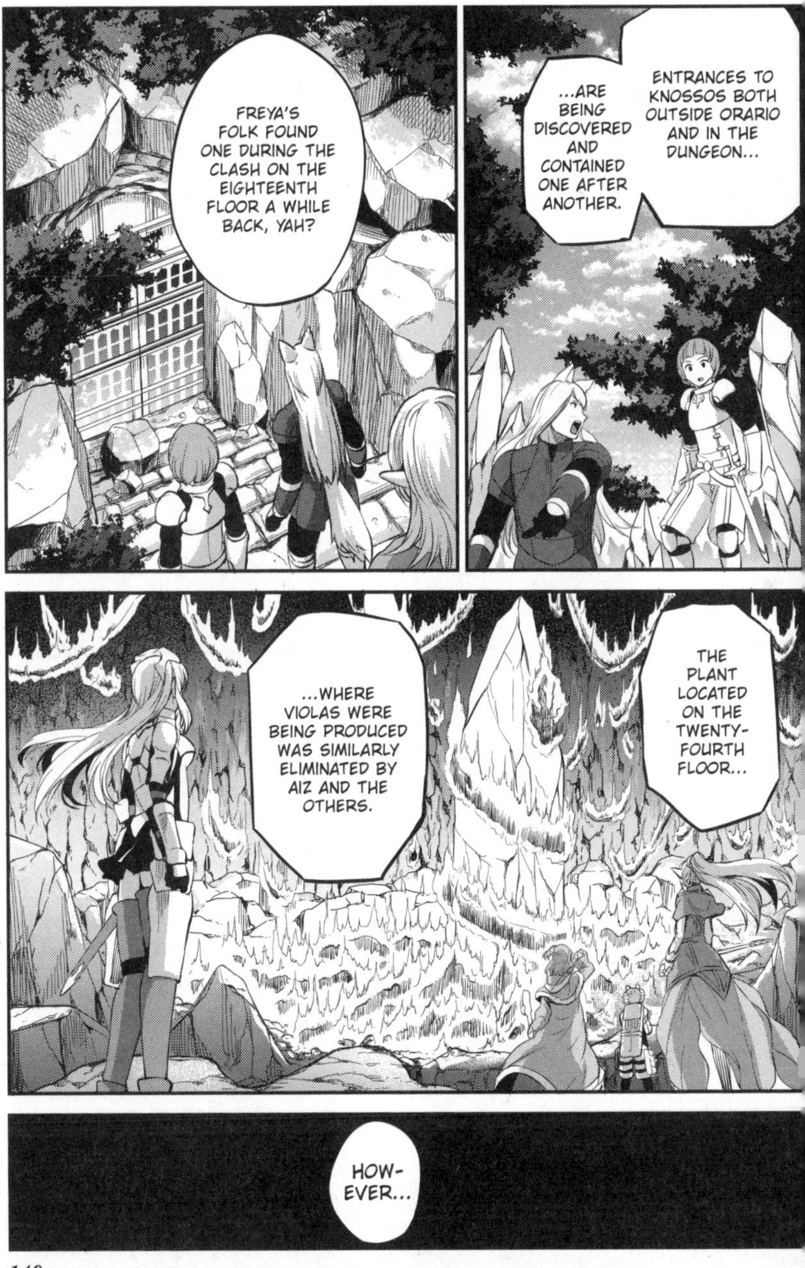
ENTRANCES TO KNOSSOS BOTH OUTSIDE ORARIO AND IN THE DUNGEON...
...ARE BEING DISCOVERED AND CONTAINED ONE AFTER ANOTHER.
FREYA'S FOLK FOUND ONE DURING THE CLASH ON THE EIGHTEENTH FLOOR A WHILE BACK, YAH?
THE PLANT LOCATED ON THE TWENTY-FOURTH FLOOR...
...WHERE VIOLAS WERE BEING PRODUCED WAS SIMILARLY ELIMINATED BY AIZ AND THE OTHERS.
HOW-EVER...

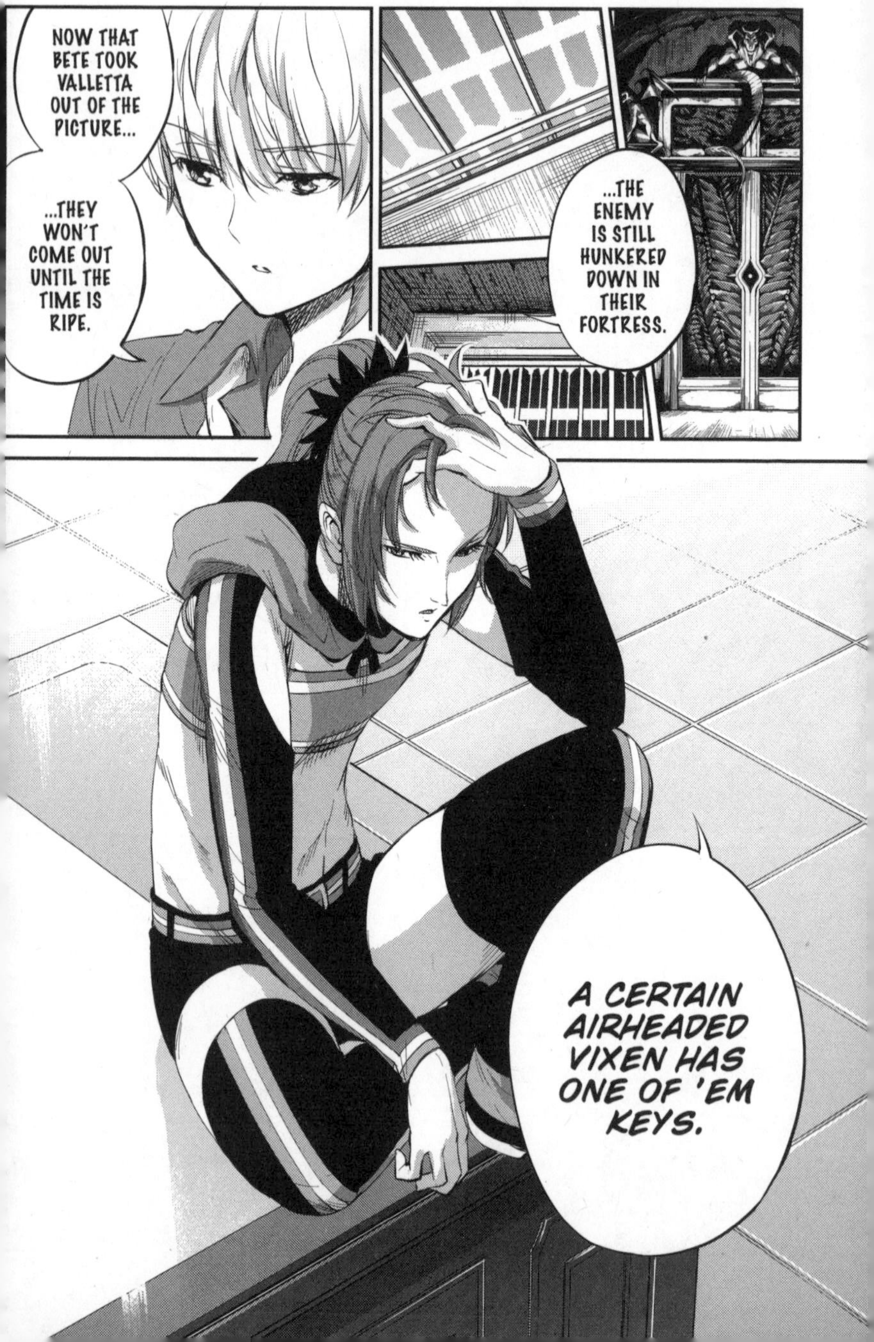
...THE ENEMY IS STILL HUNKERED DOWN IN THEIR FORTRESS.
NOW THAT BETE TOOK VALLETTA OUT OF THE PICTURE...
...THEY WON'T COME OUT UNTIL THE TIME IS RIPE.
A CERTAIN AIRHEADED VIXEN HAS ONE OF 'EM KEYS.

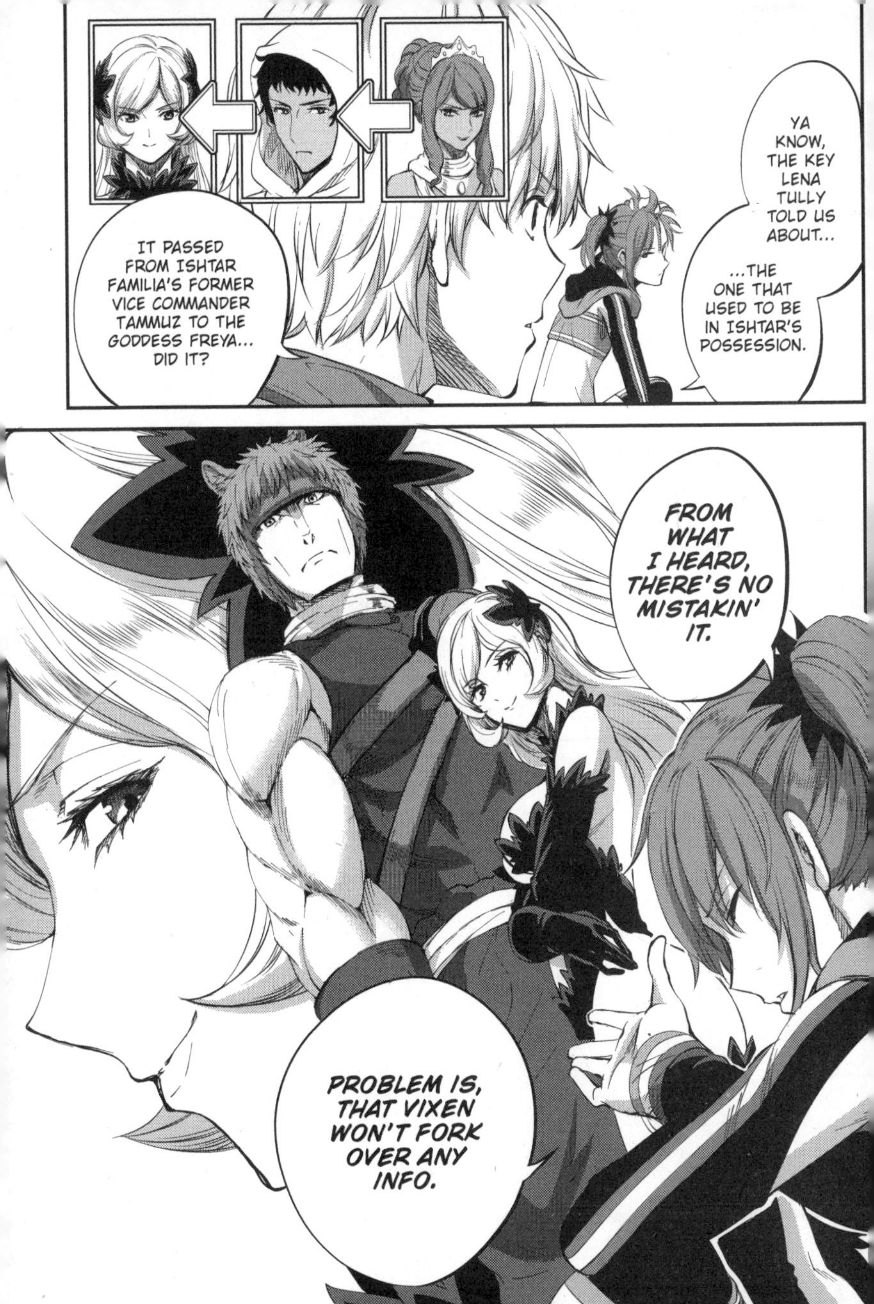
YA KNOW, THE KEY LENA TULLY TOLD US ABOUT...
...THE ONE THAT USED TO BE IN ISHTAR'S POSSESSION.
IT PASSED FROM ISHTAR FAMILIA'S FORMER VICE COMMANDER TAMMUZ TO THE GODDESS FREYA... DID IT?
FROM WHAT I HEARD, THERE'S NO MISTAKIN' IT.
PROBLEM IS, THAT VIXEN WON'T FORK OVER ANY INFO.

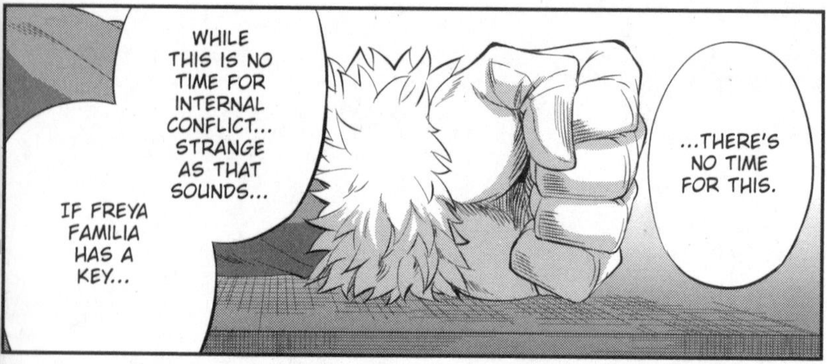
...THERE'S NO TIME FOR THIS.
WHILE THIS IS NO TIME FOR INTERNAL CONFLICT... STRANGE AS THAT SOUNDS...
IF FREYA FAMILIA HAS A KEY...
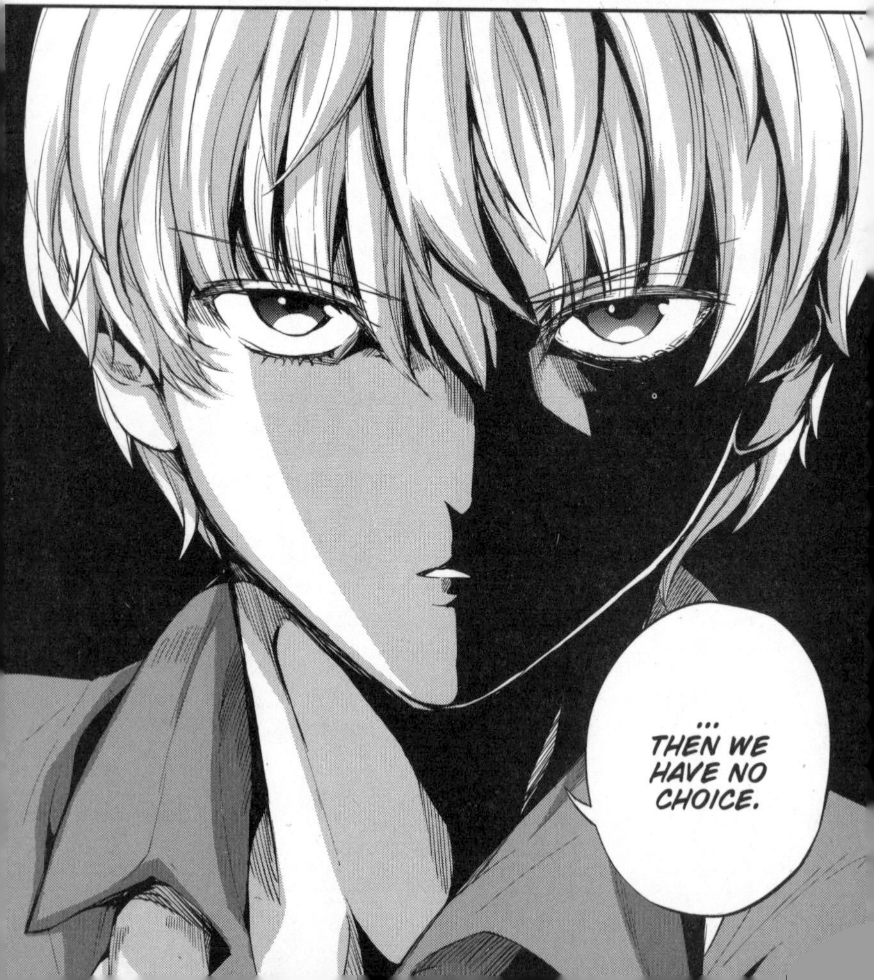
... THEN WE HAVE NO CHOICE.

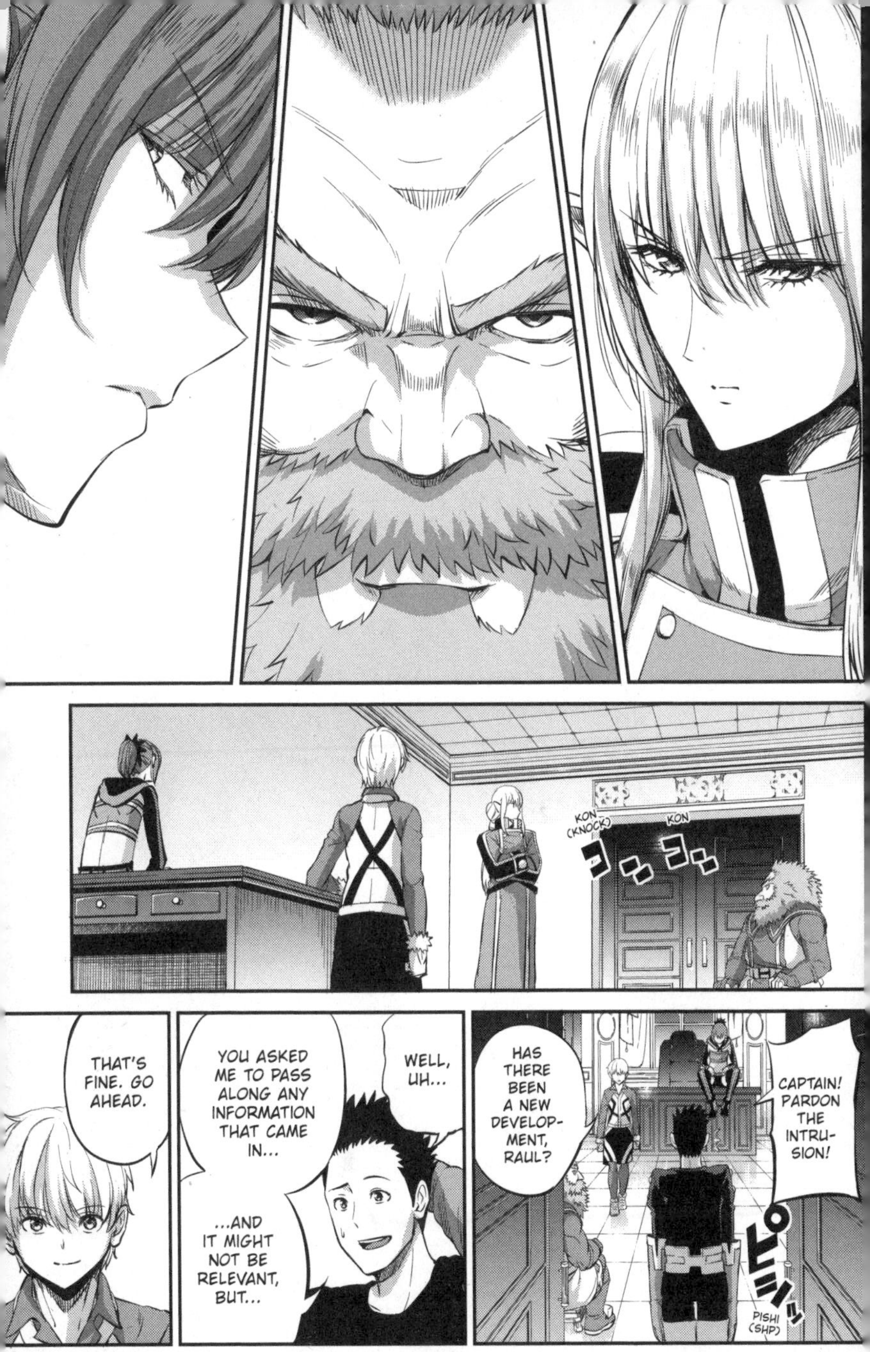

KON (KNOCK)
KON
CAPTAIN! PARDON THE INTRUSION!
PISHI (SHP)
HAS THERE BEEN A NEW DEVELOPMENT, RAUL?
WELL, UH...
YOU ASKED ME TO PASS ALONG ANY INFORMATION THAT CAME IN...
...AND IT MIGHT NOT BE RELEVANT, BUT...
THAT'S FINE. GO AHEAD.

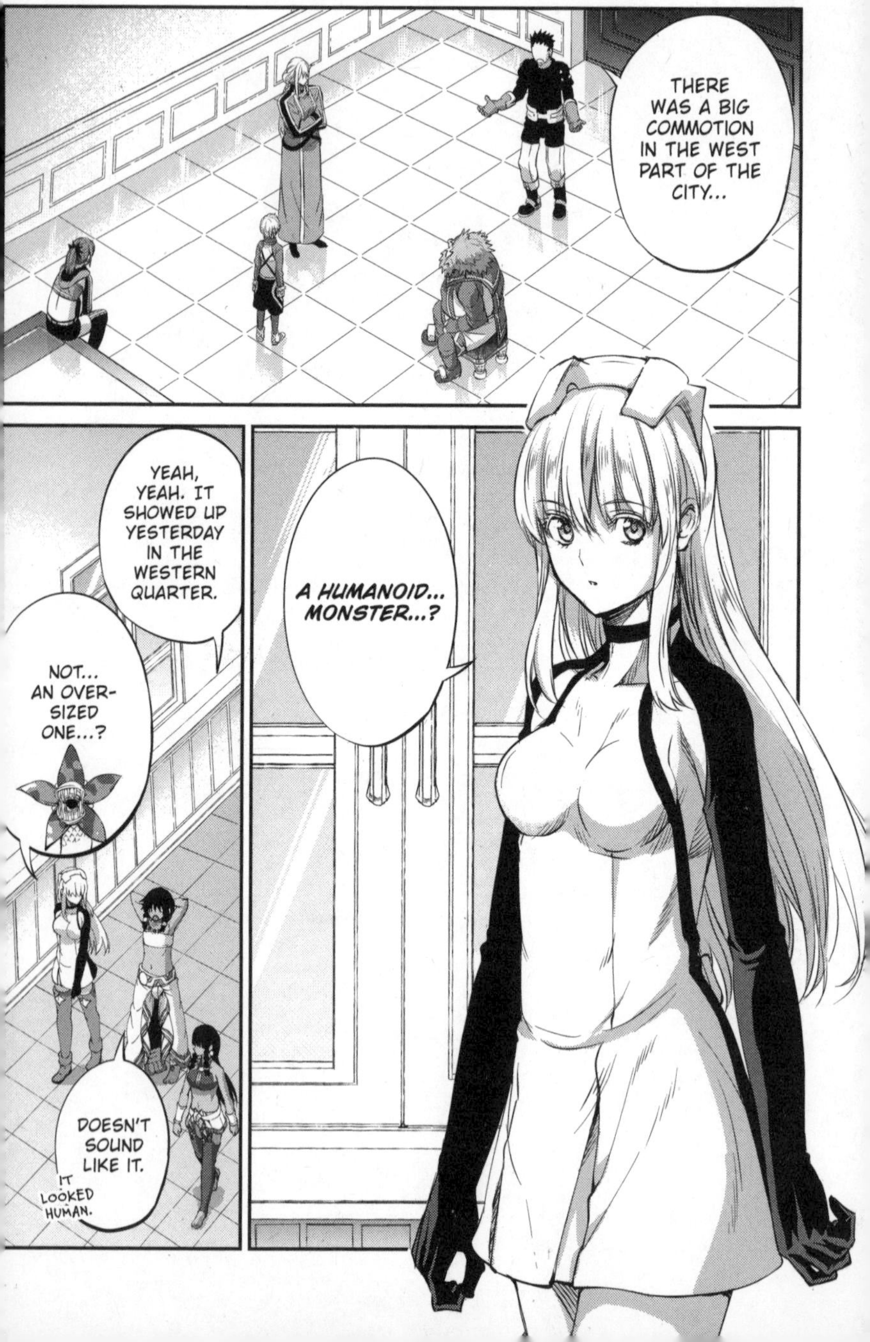
THERE WAS A BIG COMMOTION IN THE WEST PART OF THE CITY...
A HUMANOID... MONSTER...?
YEAH, YEAH. IT SHOWED UP YESTERDAY IN THE WESTERN QUARTER.
NOT... AN OVER-SIZED ONE...?
DOESN'T SOUND LIKE IT.
IT LOOKED HUMAN.

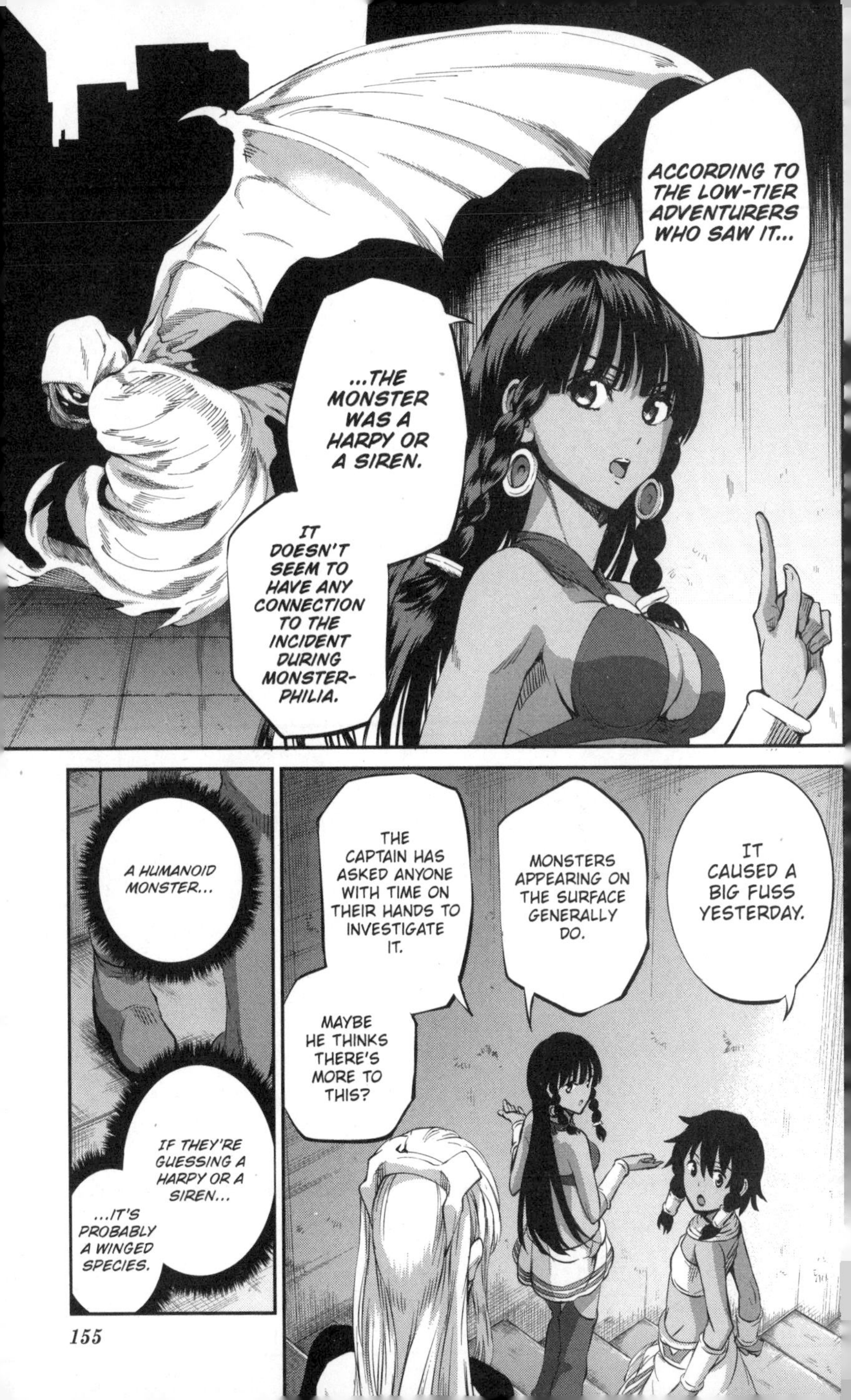
ACCORDING TO THE LOW-TIER ADVENTURERS WHO SAW IT...
...THE MONSTER WAS A HARPY OR A SIREN.
IT DOESN'T SEEM TO HAVE ANY CONNECTION TO THE INCIDENT DURING MONSTER-PHILIA.
IT CAUSED A BIG FUSS YESTERDAY.
MONSTERS APPEARING ON THE SURFACE GENERALLY DO.
THE CAPTAIN HAS ASKED ANYONE WITH TIME ON THEIR HANDS TO INVESTIGATE IT.
MAYBE HE THINKS THERE'S MORE TO THIS?
A HUMANOID MONSTER...
IF THEY'RE GUESSING A HARPY OR A SIREN...
...IT'S PROBABLY A WINGED SPECIES.

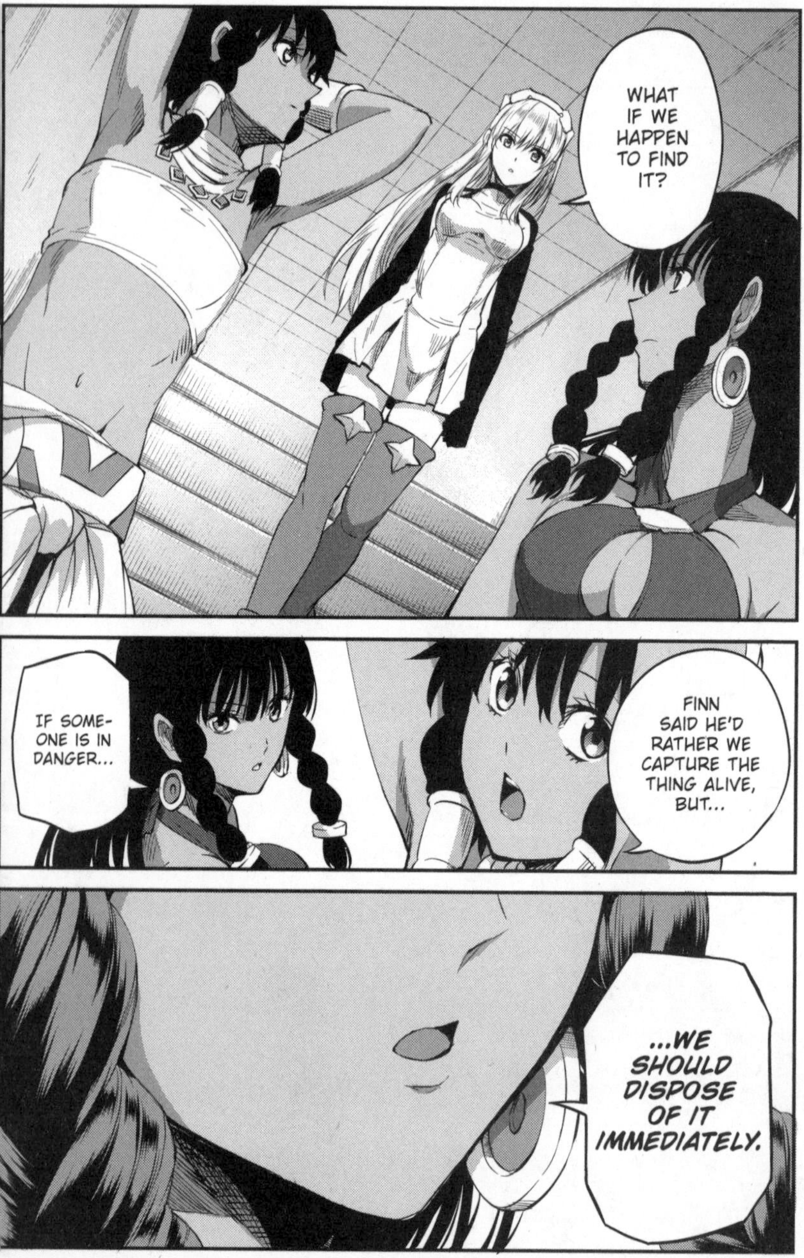
WHAT IF WE HAPPEN TO FIND IT?
FINN SAID HE'D RATHER WE CAPTURE THE THING ALIVE, BUT...
IF SOME-ONE IS IN DANGER...
...WE SHOULD DISPOSE OF IT IMMEDIATELY.

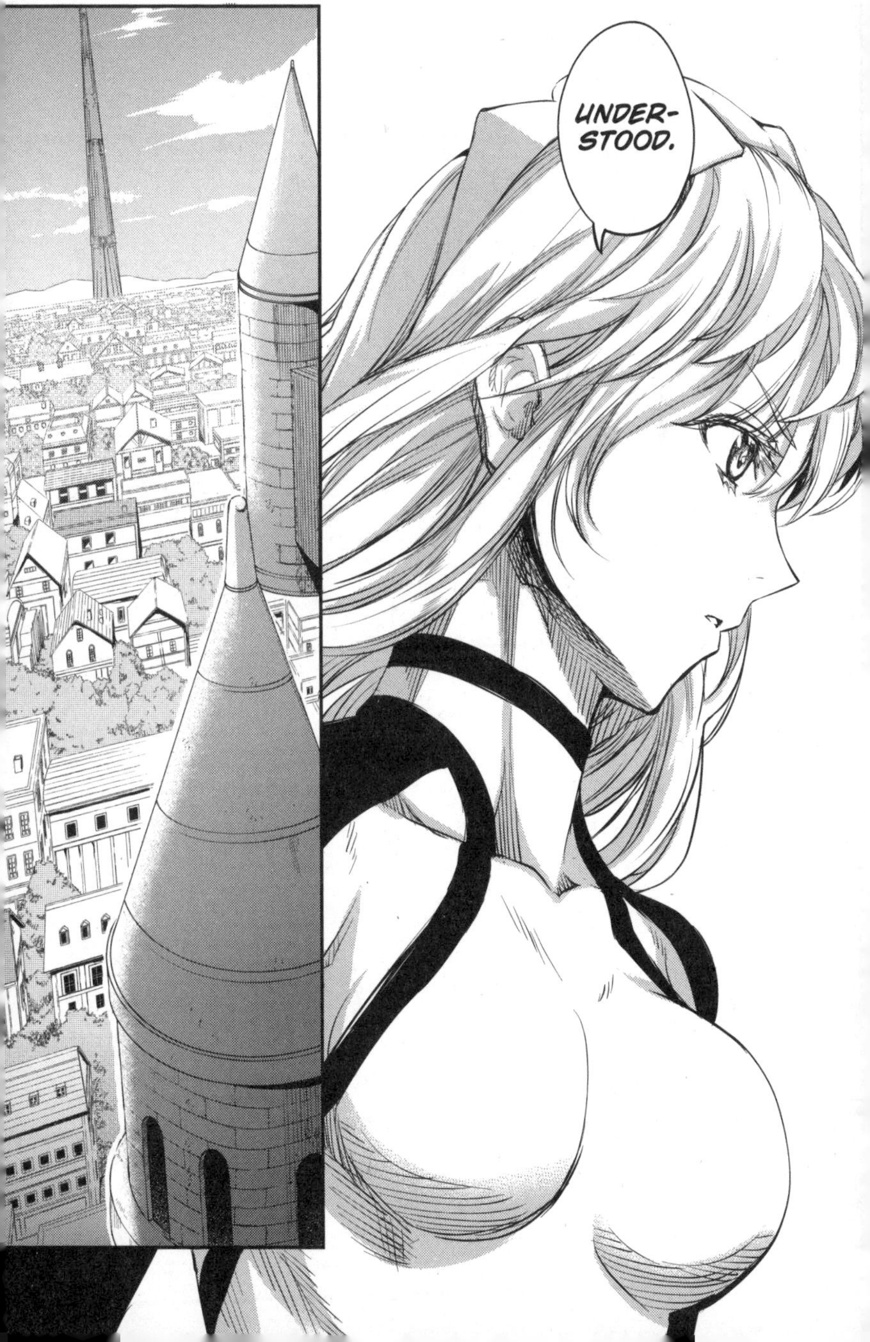
UNDER-STOOD.

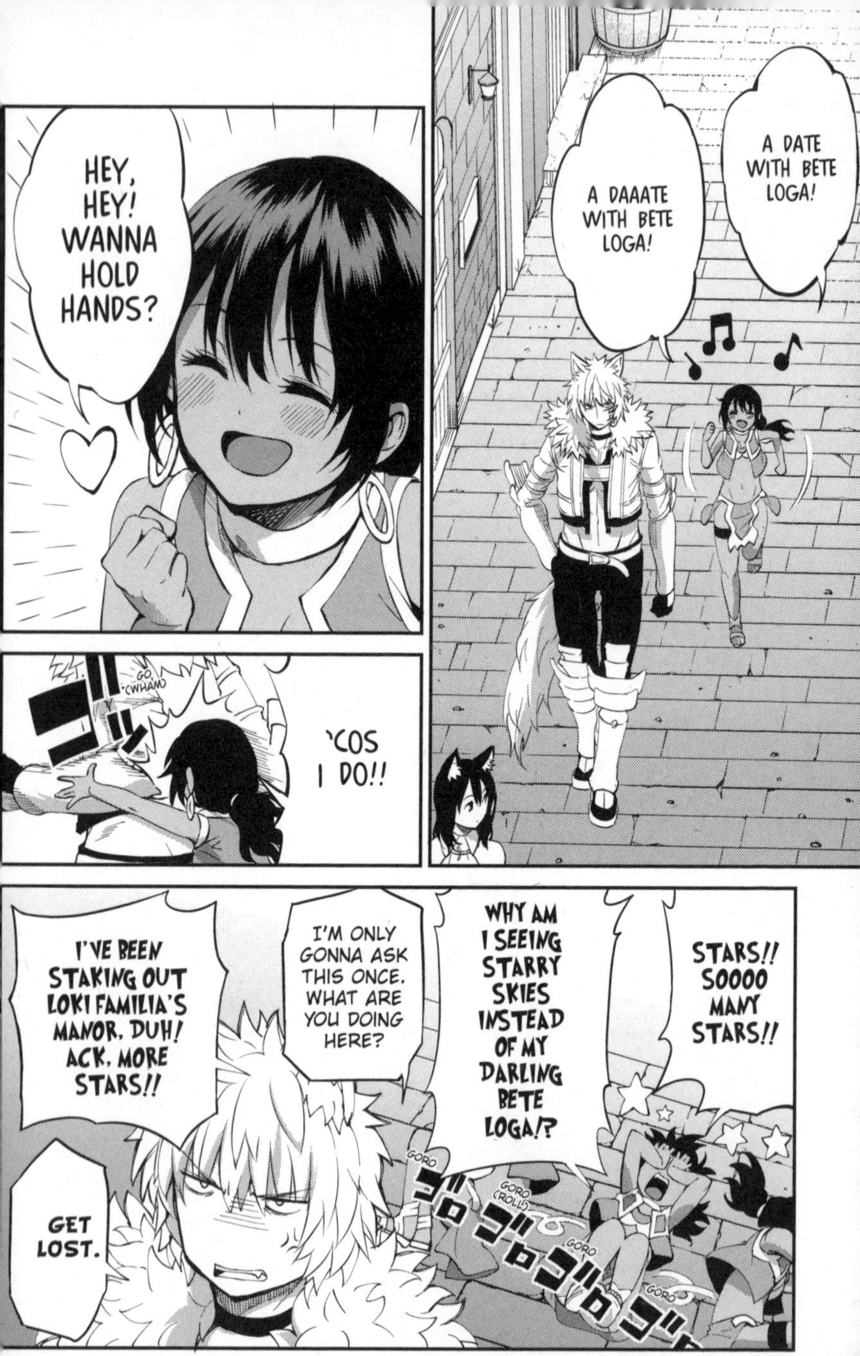
A DATE WITH BETE LOGA!
A DAAATE WITH BETE LOGA!
HEY, HEY! WANNA HOLD HANDS?
GO (WHAM)
'COS I DO!!
STARS!! SOOOO MANY STARS!!
WHY AM I SEEING STARRY SKIES INSTEAD OF MY DARLING BETE LOGA!?
I'M ONLY GONNA ASK THIS ONCE. WHAT ARE YOU DOING HERE?
I'VE BEEN STAKING OUT LOKI FAMILIA'S MANOR, DUH! ACK, MORE STARS!!
GORO GORO (ROLL) GORO GORO
GET LOST.

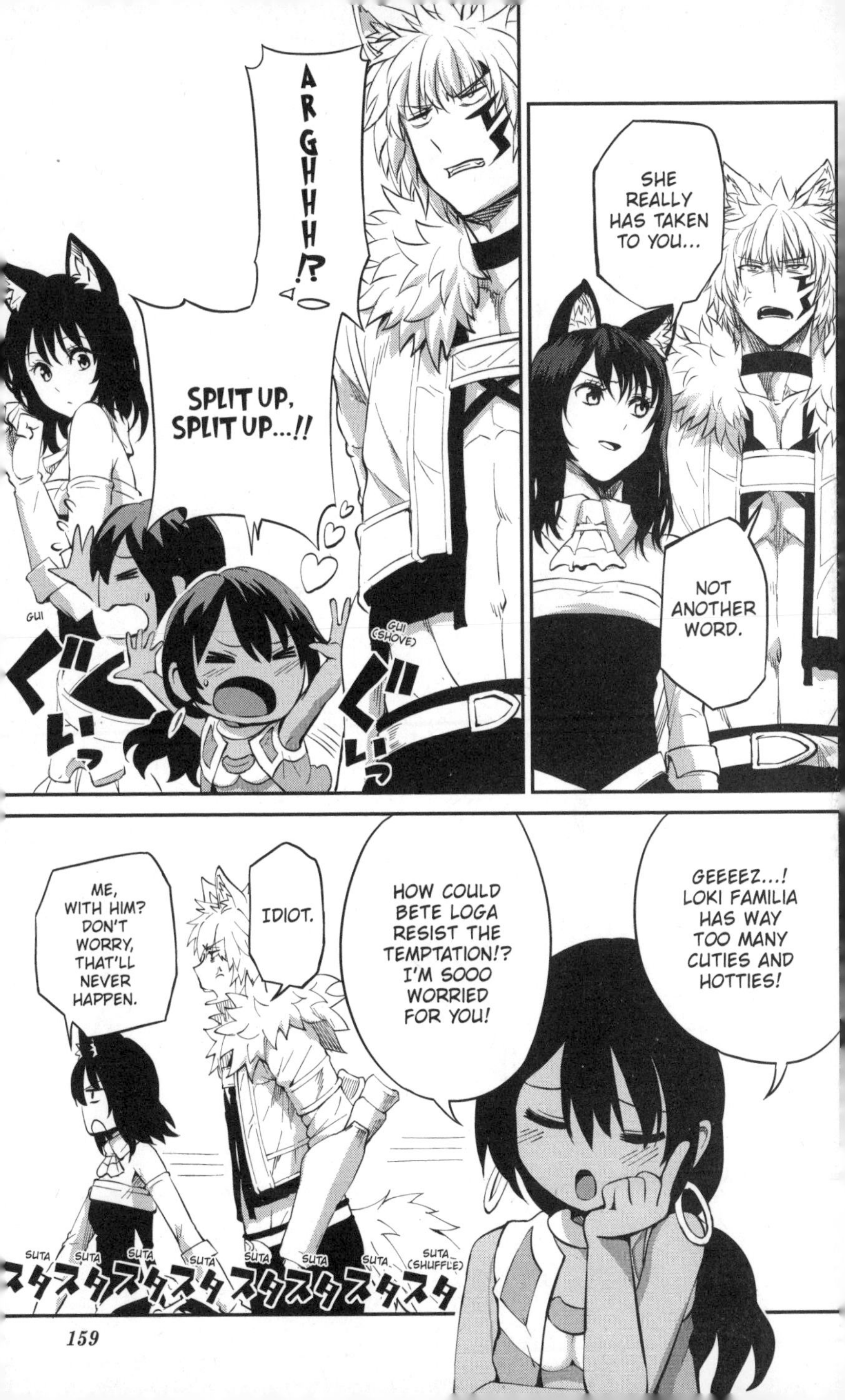
SHE REALLY HAS TAKEN TO YOU...
NOT ANOTHER WORD.
ARGHHHH!?
SPLIT UP, SPLIT UP...!!
GUI (SHOVE)
GUI
GEEEEZ...! LOKI FAMILIA HAS WAY TOO MANY CUTIES AND HOTTIES!
HOW COULD BETE LOGA RESIST THE TEMPTATION!? I'M SOOO WORRIED FOR YOU!
IDIOT.
ME, WITH HIM? DON'T WORRY, THAT'LL NEVER HAPPEN.
SUTA SUTA SUTA SUTA SUTA SUTA SUTA SUTA (SHUFFLE)

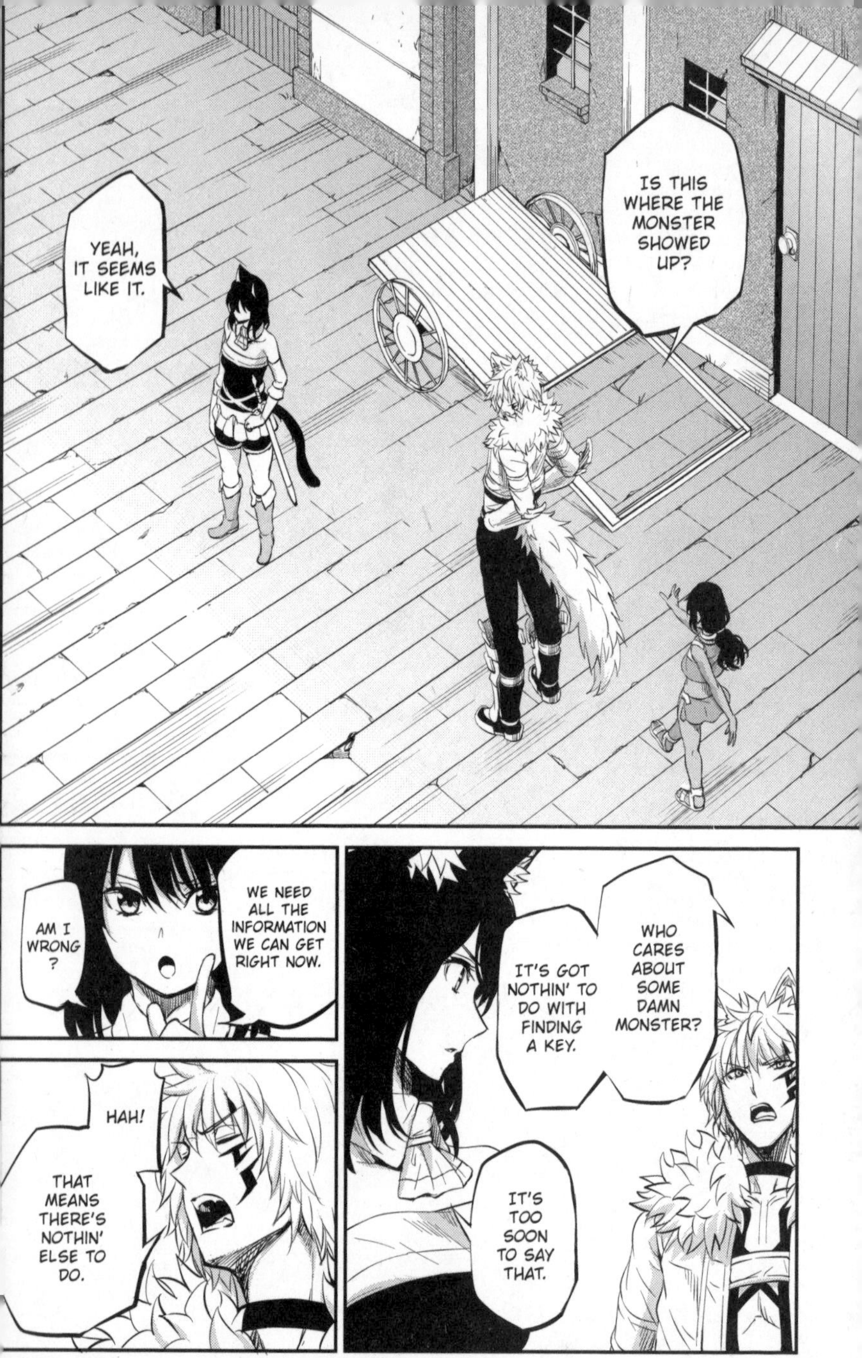
IS THIS WHERE THE MONSTER SHOWED UP?
YEAH, IT SEEMS LIKE IT.
WHO CARES ABOUT SOME DAMN MONSTER?
IT'S GOT NOTHIN' TO DO WITH FINDING A KEY.
IT'S TOO SOON TO SAY THAT.
WE NEED ALL THE INFORMATION WE CAN GET RIGHT NOW.
AM I WRONG?
HAH!
THAT MEANS THERE'S NOTHIN' ELSE TO DO.

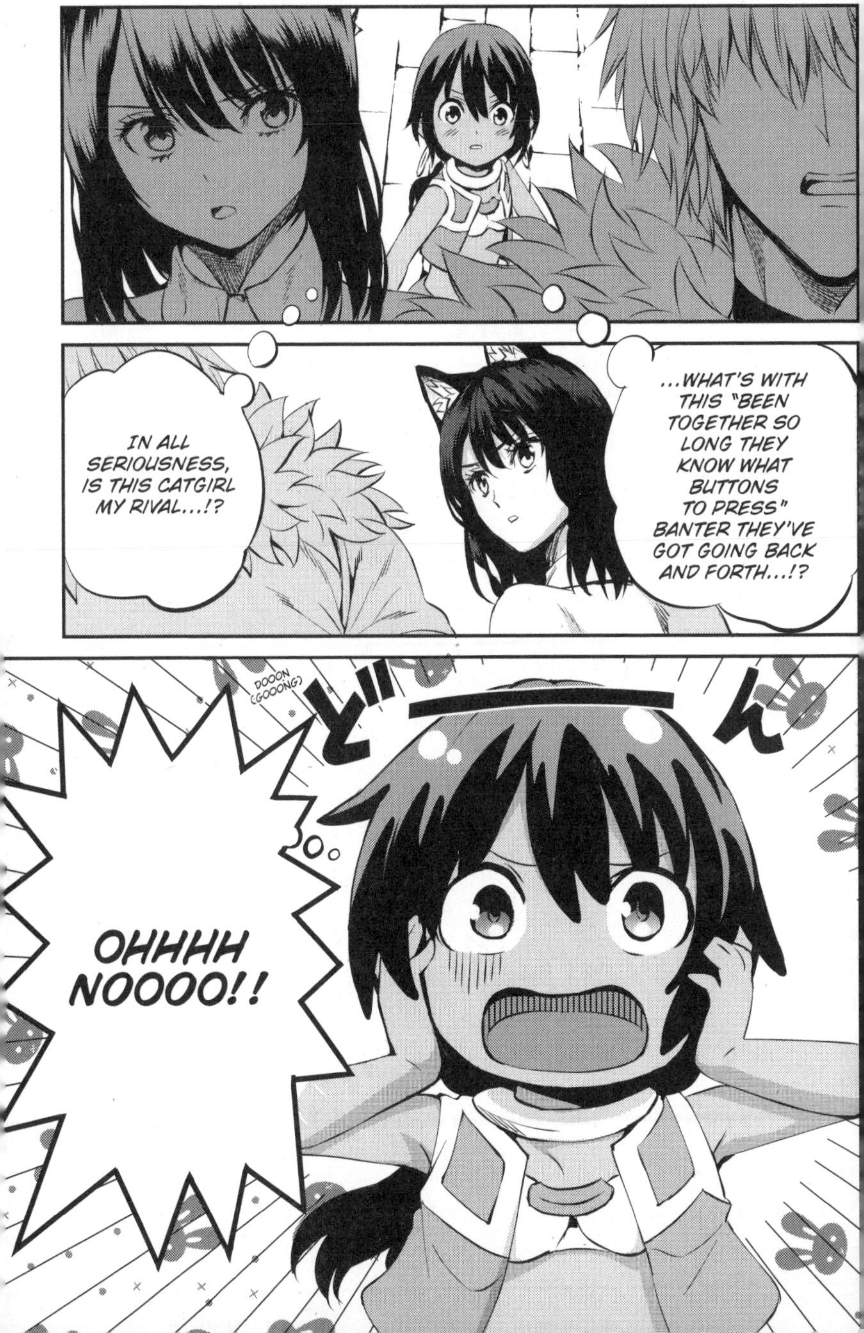
...WHAT'S WITH THIS "BEEN TOGETHER SO LONG THEY KNOW WHAT BUTTONS TO PRESS" BANTER THEY'VE GOT GOING BACK AND FORTH...!?
IN ALL SERIOUSNESS, IS THIS CATGIRL MY RIVAL...!?
どーーん
DOOON (GOOONG)
OHHHH NOOOO!!

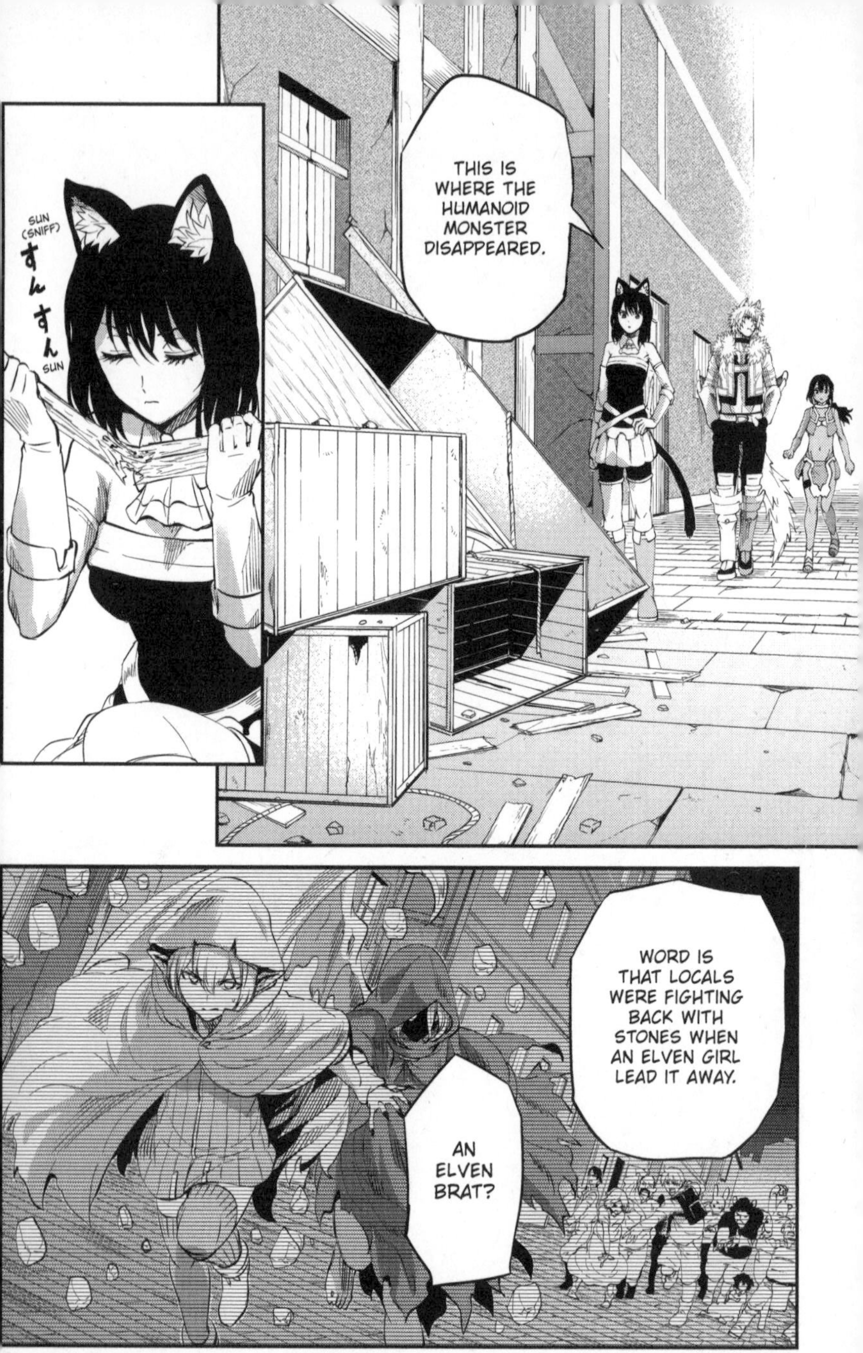
THIS IS WHERE THE HUMANOID MONSTER DISAPPEARED.
SUN (SNIFF)
すんすん
SUN
WORD IS THAT LOCALS WERE FIGHTING BACK WITH STONES WHEN AN ELVEN GIRL LEAD IT AWAY.
AN ELVEN BRAT?

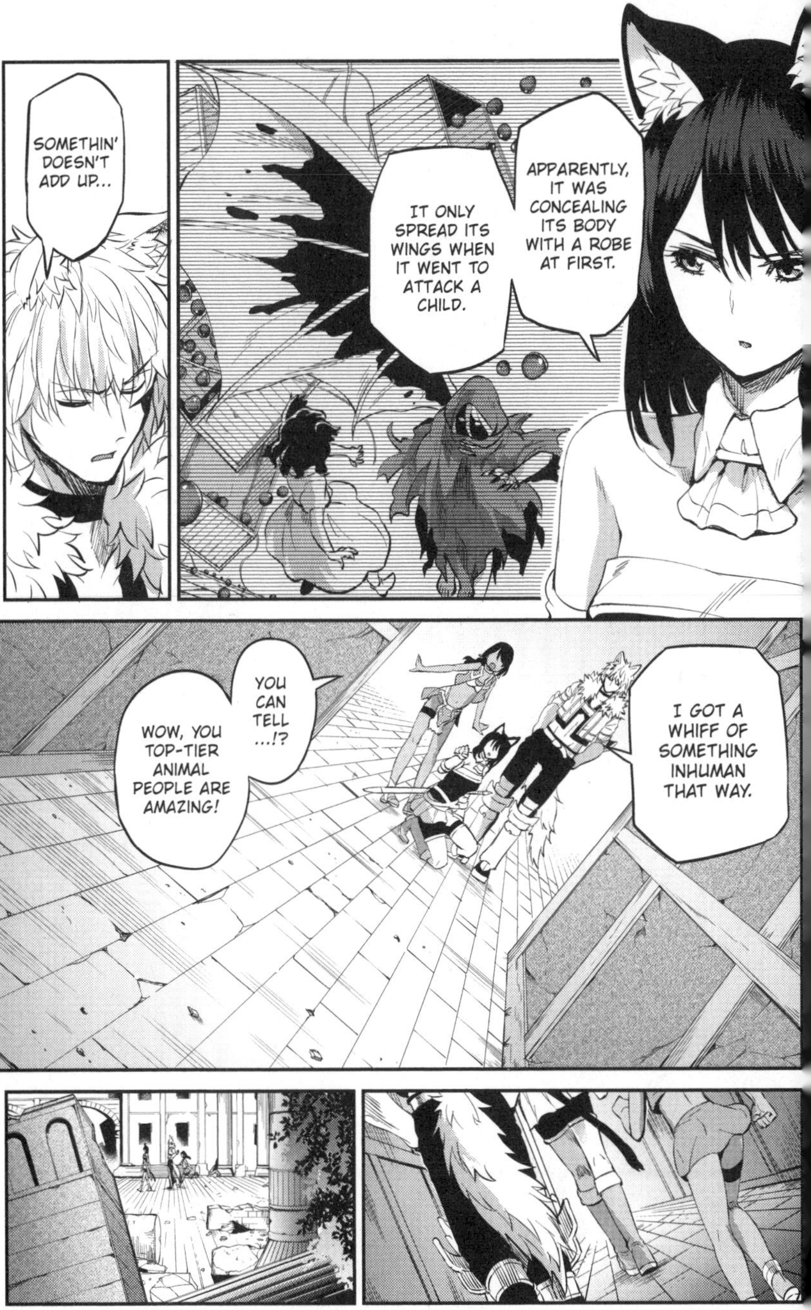
APPARENTLY, IT WAS CONCEALING ITS BODY WITH A ROBE AT FIRST.
IT ONLY SPREAD ITS WINGS WHEN IT WENT TO ATTACK A CHILD.
SOMETHIN' DOESN'T ADD UP...
I GOT A WHIFF OF SOMETHING INHUMAN THAT WAY.
YOU CAN TELL ...!?
WOW, YOU TOP-TIER ANIMAL PEOPLE ARE AMAZING!

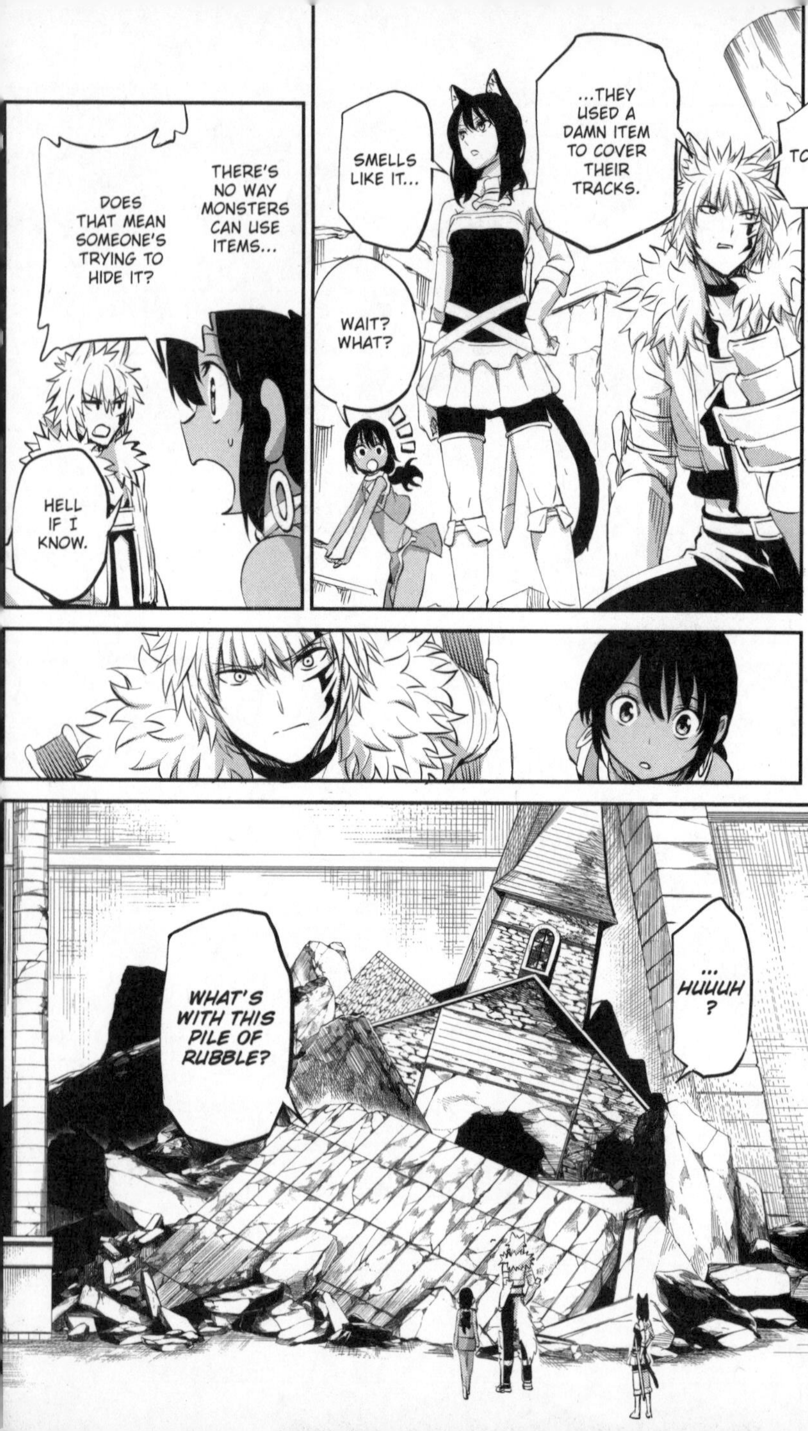
TCH!
...THEY USED A DAMN ITEM TO COVER THEIR TRACKS.
SMELLS LIKE IT...
WAIT? WHAT?
THERE'S NO WAY MONSTERS CAN USE ITEMS...
DOES THAT MEAN SOMEONE'S TRYING TO HIDE IT?
HELL IF I KNOW.
...HUUUH?
WHAT'S WITH THIS PILE OF RUBBLE?

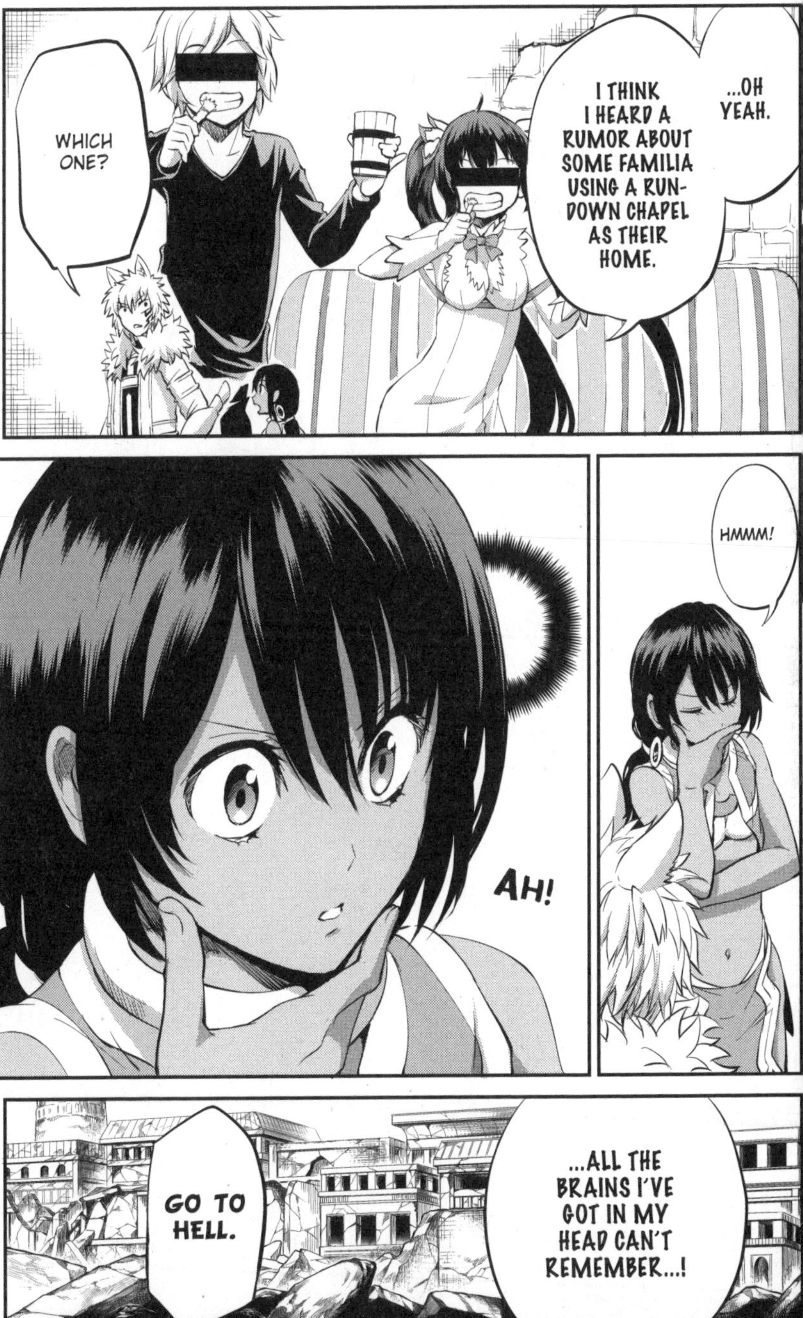
...OH YEAH.
I THINK I HEARD A RUMOR ABOUT SOME FAMILIA USING A RUN-DOWN CHAPEL AS THEIR HOME.
WHICH ONE?
HMMM!
AH!
...ALL THE BRAINS I'VE GOT IN MY HEAD CAN'T REMEMBER...!
GO TO HELL.

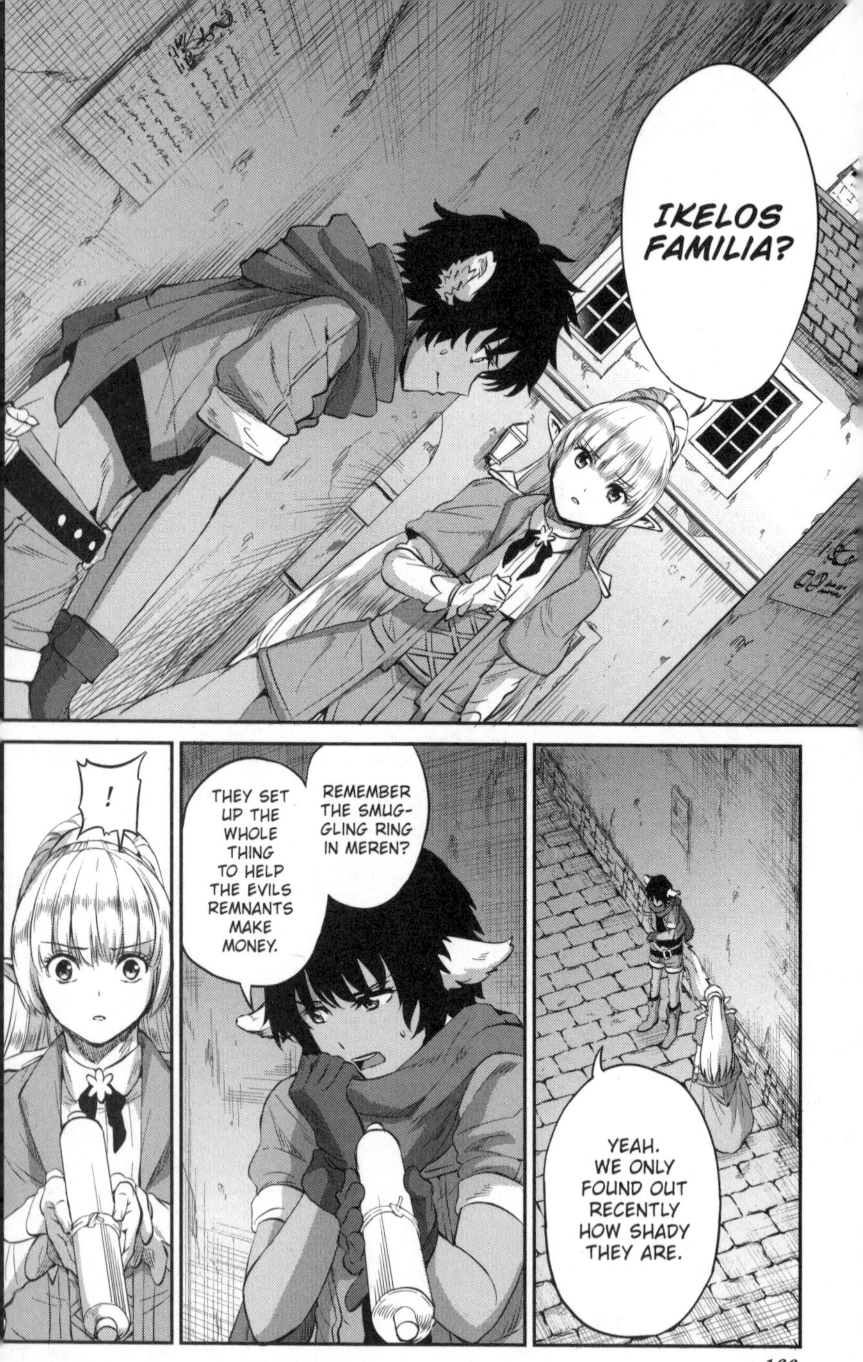
IKELOS FAMILIA?
YEAH. WE ONLY FOUND OUT RECENTLY HOW SHADY THEY ARE.
REMEMBER THE SMUG-GLING RING IN MEREN?
THEY SET UP THE WHOLE THING TO HELP THE EVILS REMNANTS MAKE MONEY.
!

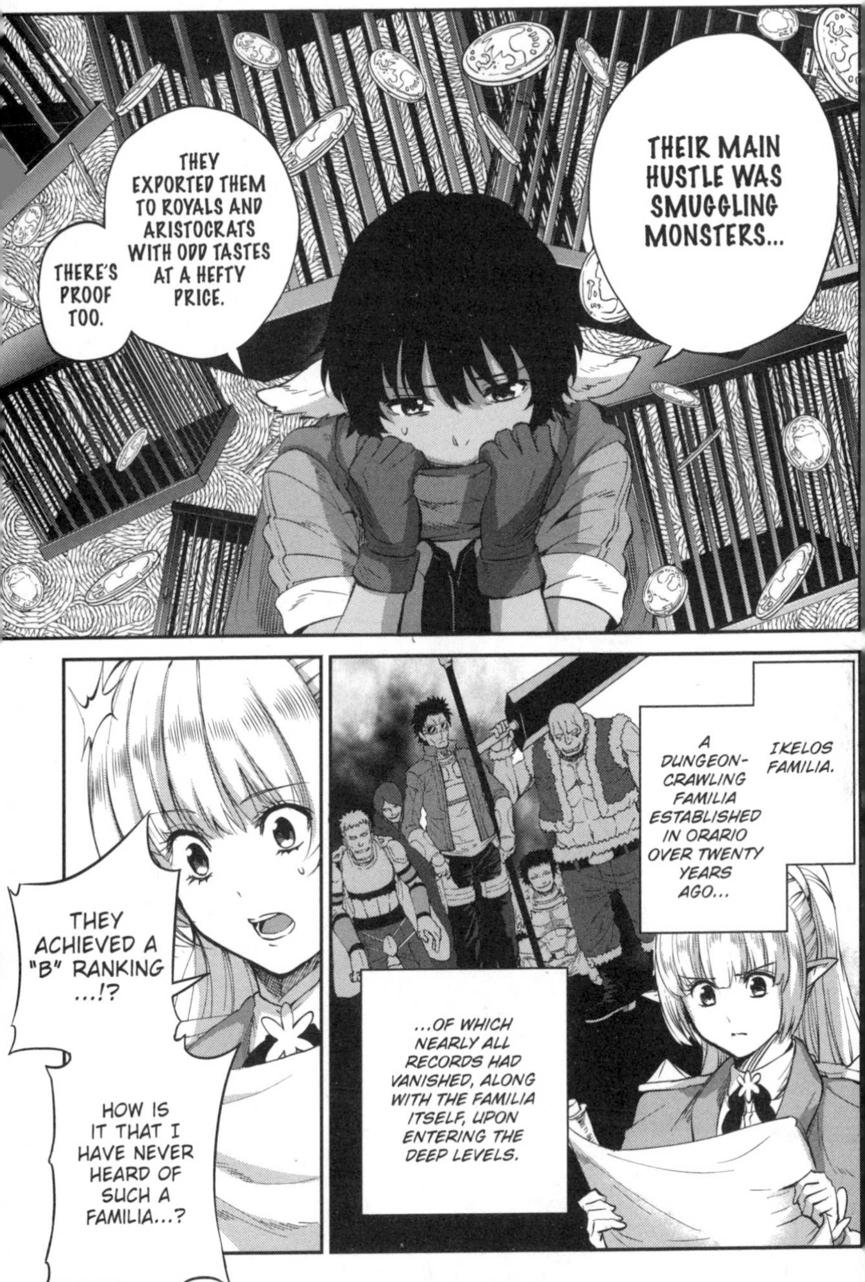
THEIR MAIN HUSTLE WAS SMUGGLING MONSTERS...
THEY EXPORTED THEM TO ROYALS AND ARISTOCRATS WITH ODD TASTES AT A HEFTY PRICE.
THERE'S PROOF TOO.
IKELOS FAMILIA.
A DUNGEON-CRAWLING FAMILIA ESTABLISHED IN ORARIO OVER TWENTY YEARS AGO...
...OF WHICH NEARLY ALL RECORDS HAD VANISHED, ALONG WITH THE FAMILIA ITSELF, UPON ENTERING THE DEEP LEVELS.
THEY ACHIEVED A "B" RANKING ...!?
HOW IS IT THAT I HAVE NEVER HEARD OF SUCH A FAMILIA...?

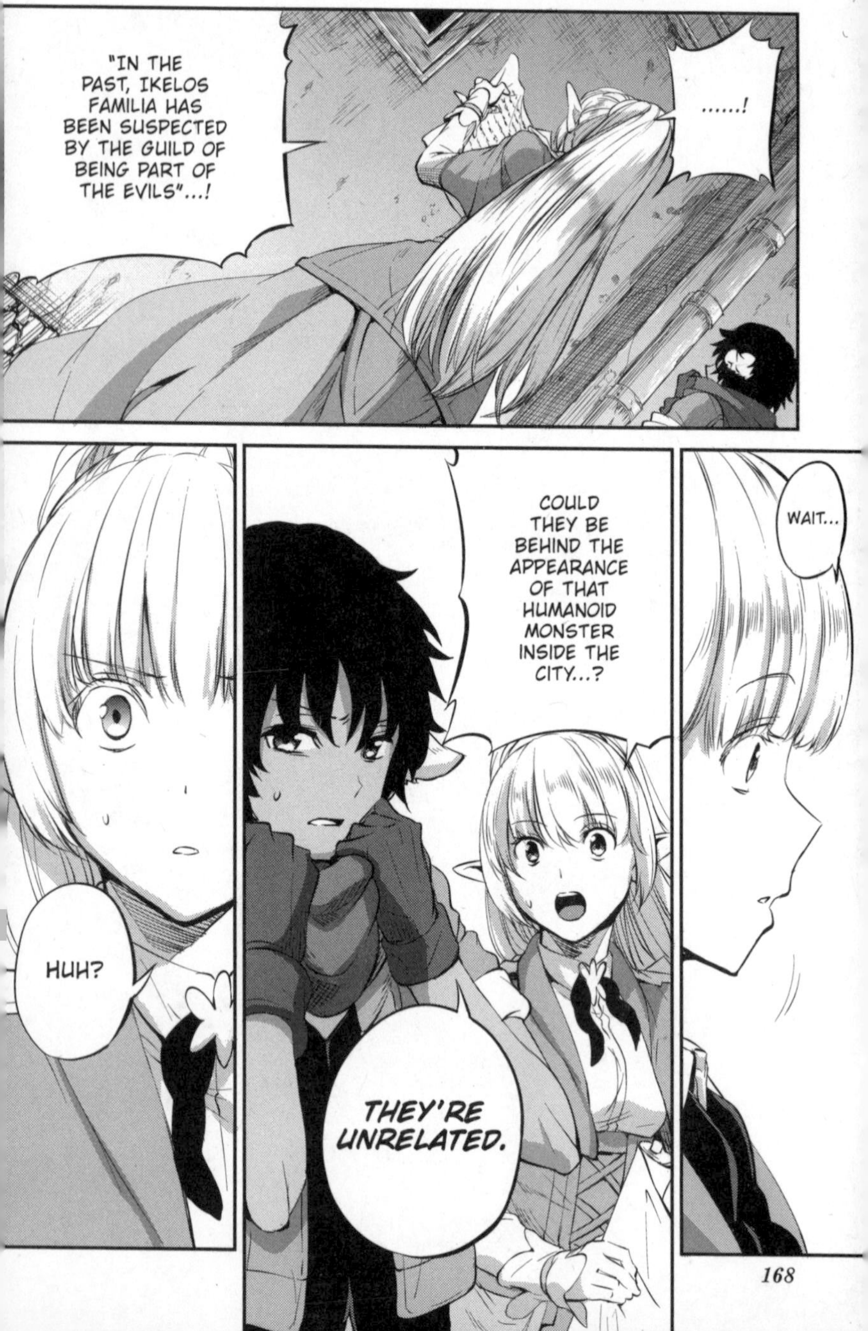
......!
"IN THE PAST, IKELOS FAMILIA HAS BEEN SUSPECTED BY THE GUILD OF BEING PART OF THE EVILS"...!
WAIT...
COULD THEY BE BEHIND THE APPEARANCE OF THAT HUMANOID MONSTER INSIDE THE CITY...?
THEY'RE UNRELATED.
HUH?

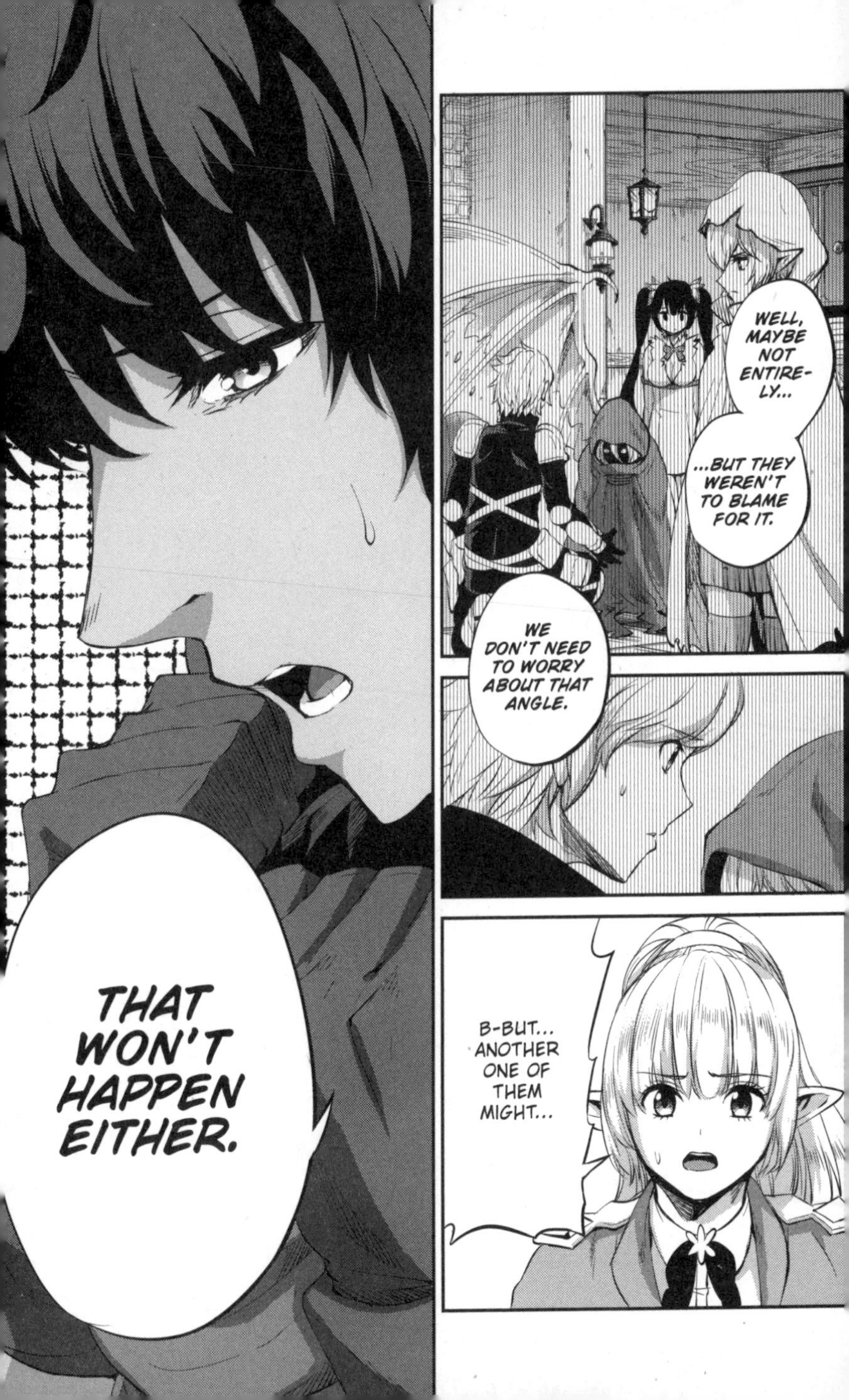
WELL, MAYBE NOT ENTIRE-LY...
...BUT THEY WEREN'T TO BLAME FOR IT.
WE DON'T NEED TO WORRY ABOUT THAT ANGLE.
B-BUT... ANOTHER ONE OF THEM MIGHT...
THAT WON'T HAPPEN EITHER.

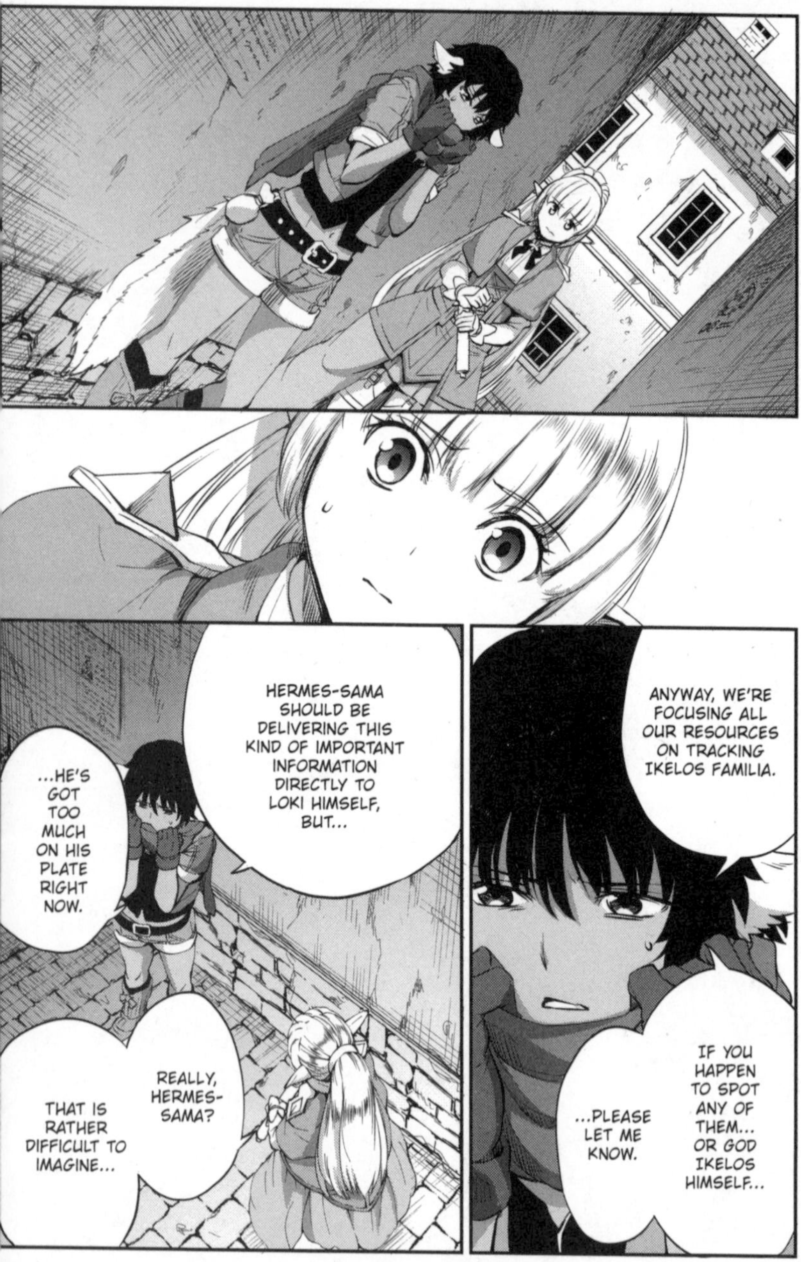
ANYWAY, WE'RE FOCUSING ALL OUR RESOURCES ON TRACKING IKELOS FAMILIA.
IF YOU HAPPEN TO SPOT ANY OF THEM... OR GOD IKELOS HIMSELF...
...PLEASE LET ME KNOW.
HERMES-SAMA SHOULD BE DELIVERING THIS KIND OF IMPORTANT INFORMATION DIRECTLY TO LOKI HIMSELF, BUT...
...HE'S GOT TOO MUCH ON HIS PLATE RIGHT NOW.
REALLY, HERMES-SAMA?
THAT IS RATHER DIFFICULT TO IMAGINE...

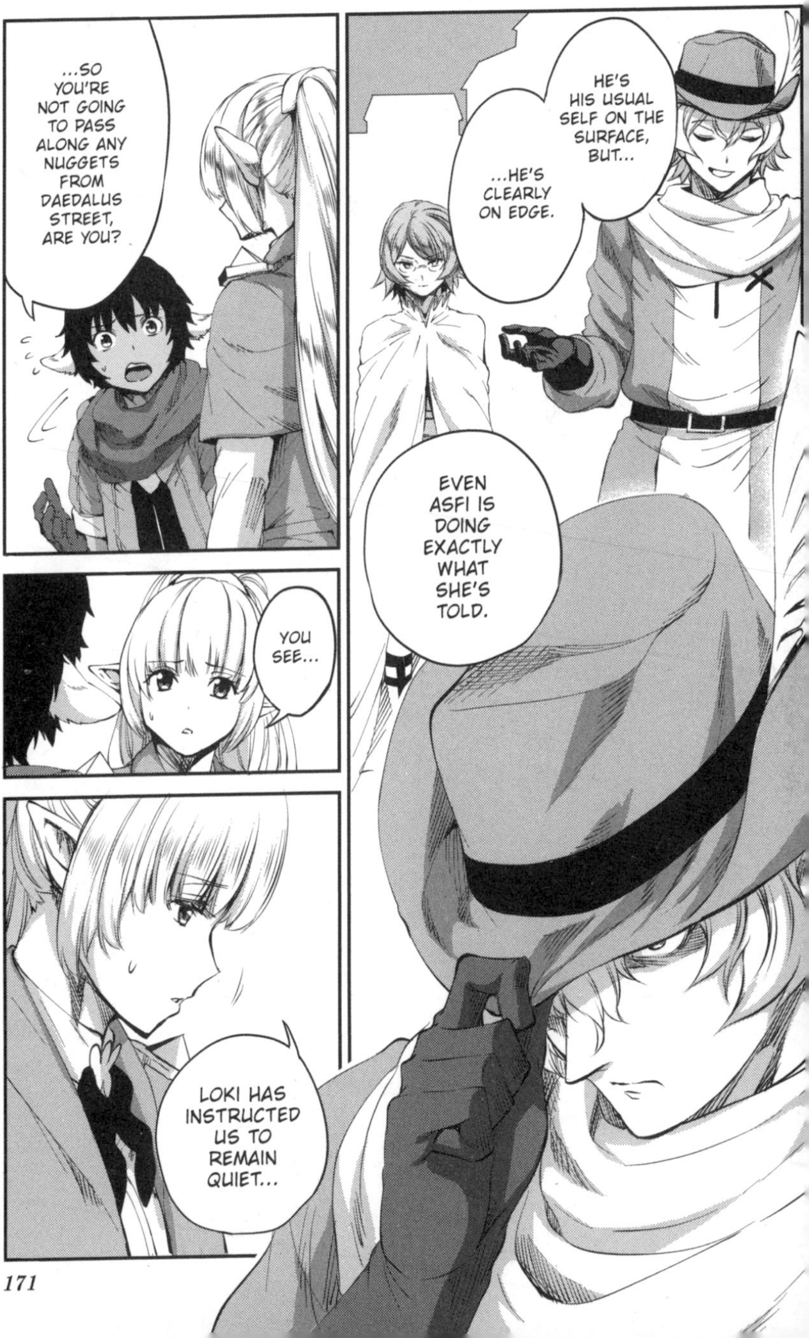
HE'S HIS USUAL SELF ON THE SURFACE, BUT...
...HE'S CLEARLY ON EDGE.
EVEN ASFI IS DOING EXACTLY WHAT SHE'S TOLD.
...SO YOU'RE NOT GOING TO PASS ALONG ANY NUGGETS FROM DAEDALUS STREET, ARE YOU?
YOU SEE...
LOKI HAS INSTRUCTED US TO REMAIN QUIET...

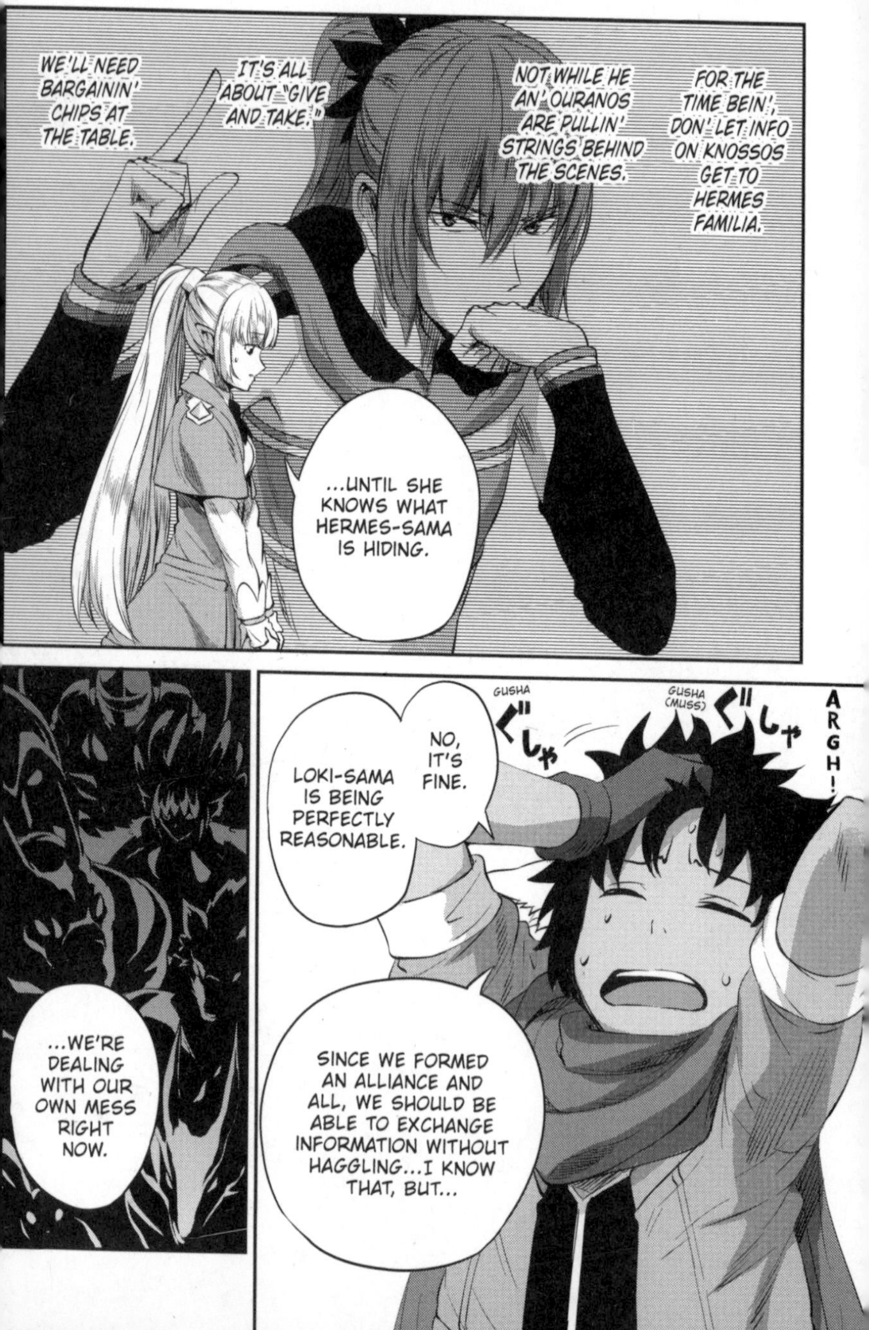
FOR THE TIME BEIN', DON' LET INFO ON KNOSSOS GET TO HERMES FAMILIA.
NOT WHILE HE AN' OURANOS ARE PULLIN' STRINGS BEHIND THE SCENES.
IT'S ALL ABOUT "GIVE AND TAKE."
WE'LL NEED BARGAININ' CHIPS AT THE TABLE.
...UNTIL SHE KNOWS WHAT HERMES-SAMA IS HIDING.
ARGH!
GUSHA (MUSS)
GUSHA
NO, IT'S FINE. LOKI-SAMA IS BEING PERFECTLY REASONABLE.
SINCE WE FORMED AN ALLIANCE AND ALL, WE SHOULD BE ABLE TO EXCHANGE INFORMATION WITHOUT HAGGLING...I KNOW THAT, BUT...
...WE'RE DEALING WITH OUR OWN MESS RIGHT NOW.

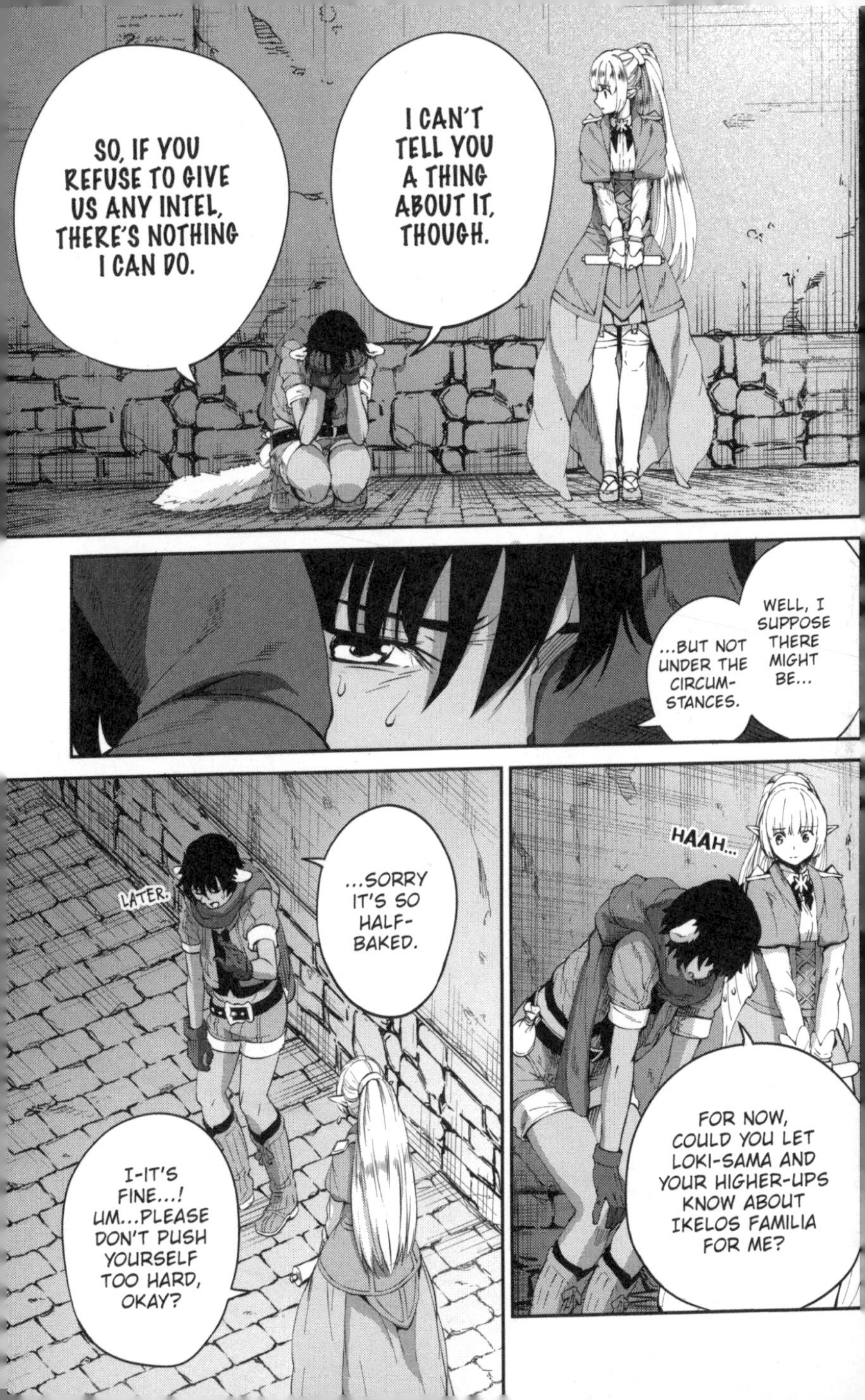
I CAN'T TELL YOU A THING ABOUT IT, THOUGH.
SO, IF YOU REFUSE TO GIVE US ANY INTEL, THERE'S NOTHING I CAN DO.
WELL, I SUPPOSE THERE MIGHT BE...
...BUT NOT UNDER THE CIRCUM-STANCES.
HAAH...
FOR NOW, COULD YOU LET LOKI-SAMA AND YOUR HIGHER-UPS KNOW ABOUT IKELOS FAMILIA FOR ME?
...SORRY IT'S SO HALF-BAKED.
LATER.
I-IT'S FINE...! UM...PLEASE DON'T PUSH YOURSELF TOO HARD, OKAY?

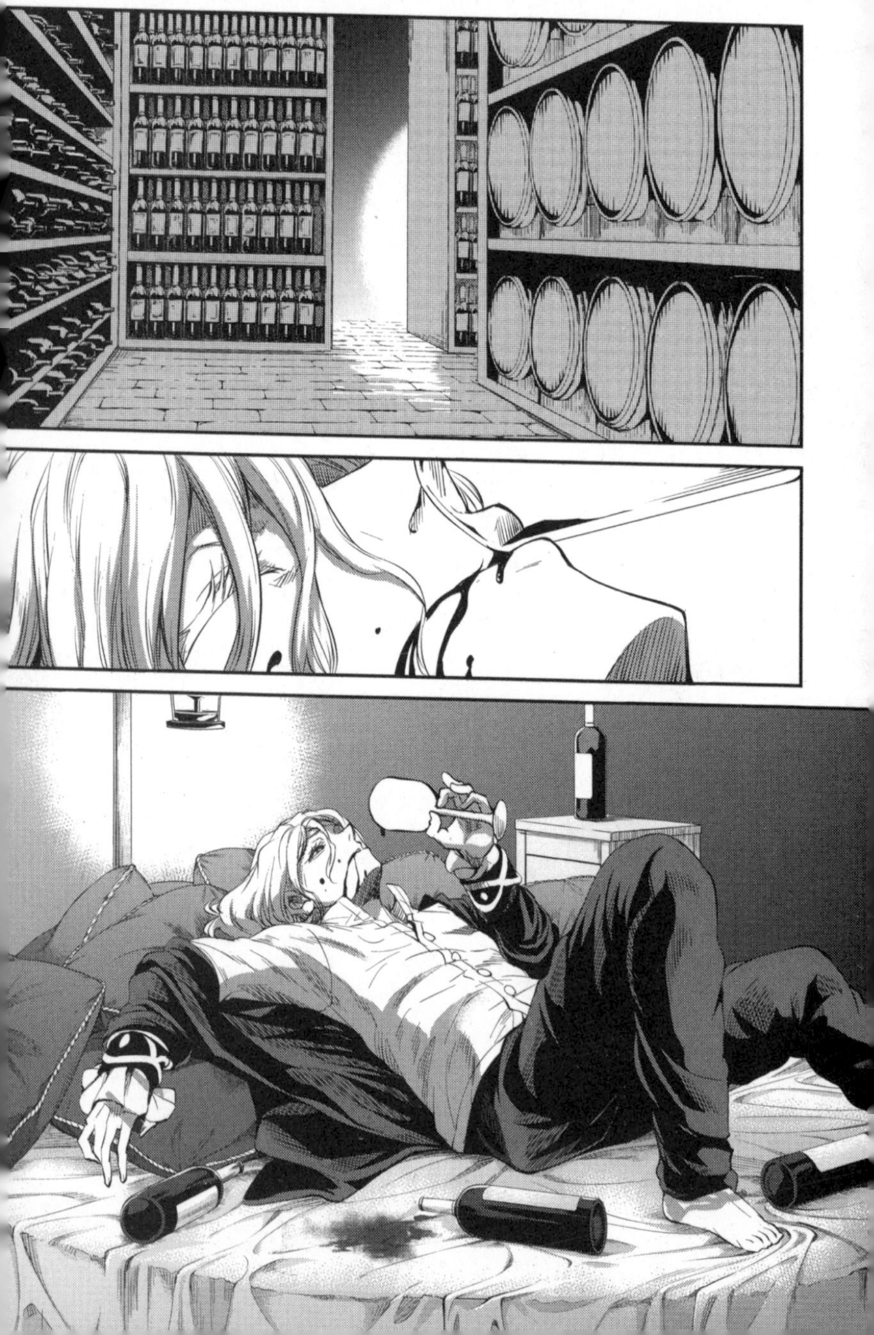

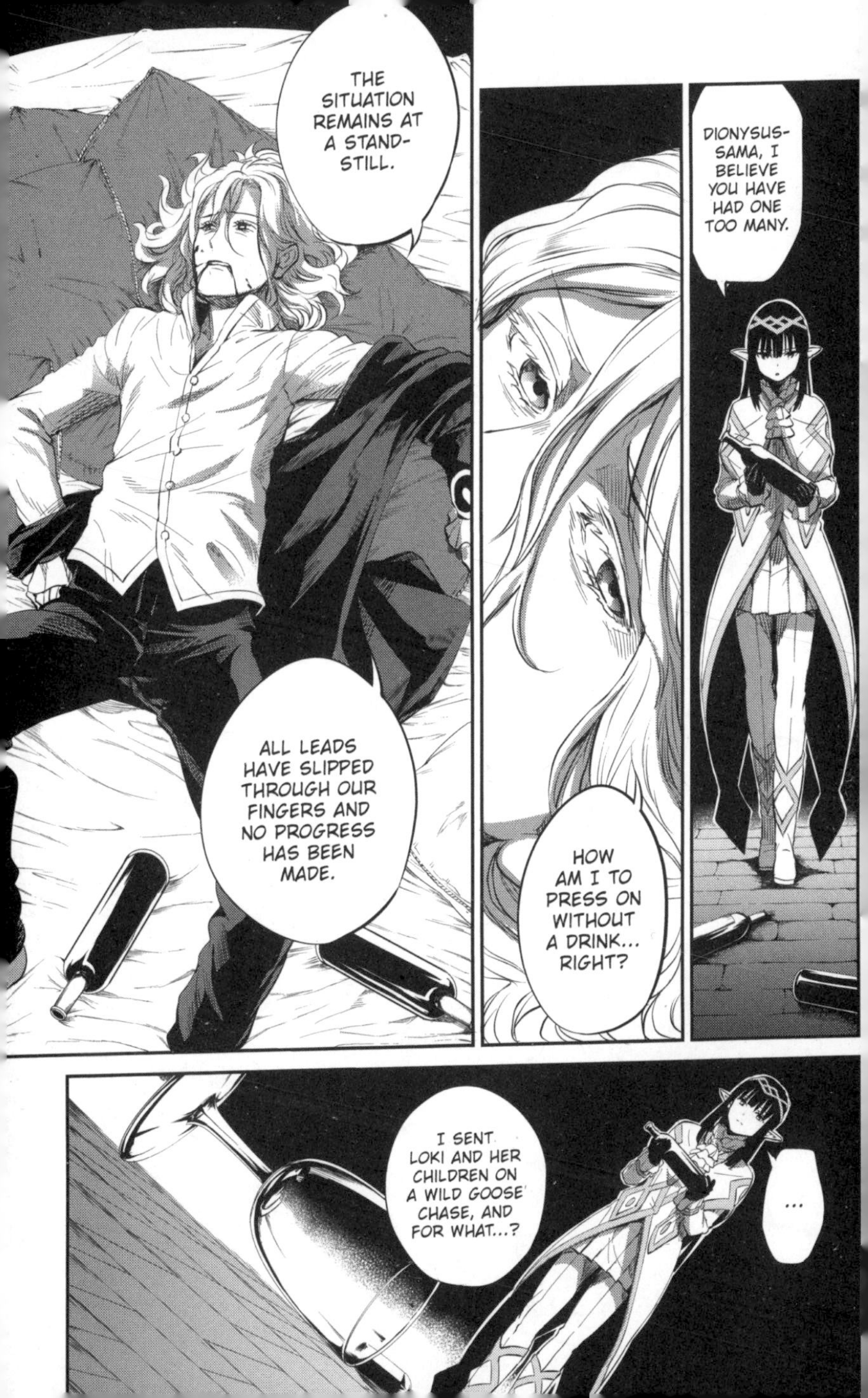

DIONYSUS-SAMA, I BELIEVE YOU HAVE HAD ONE TOO MANY.
HOW AM I TO PRESS ON WITHOUT A DRINK... RIGHT?
THE SITUATION REMAINS AT A STAND-STILL.
ALL LEADS HAVE SLIPPED THROUGH OUR FINGERS AND NO PROGRESS HAS BEEN MADE.
...
I SENT LOKI AND HER CHILDREN ON A WILD GOOSE CHASE, AND FOR WHAT...?

I'M A BUFFOON.
AN IMBECILE.
...YET, I HAVE NO CHOICE BUT TO KEEP MOVING FORWARD.

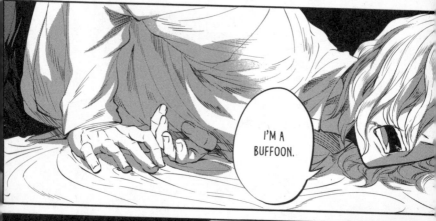

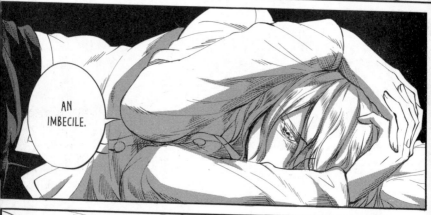

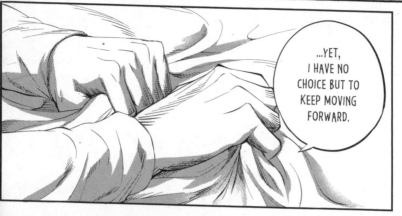

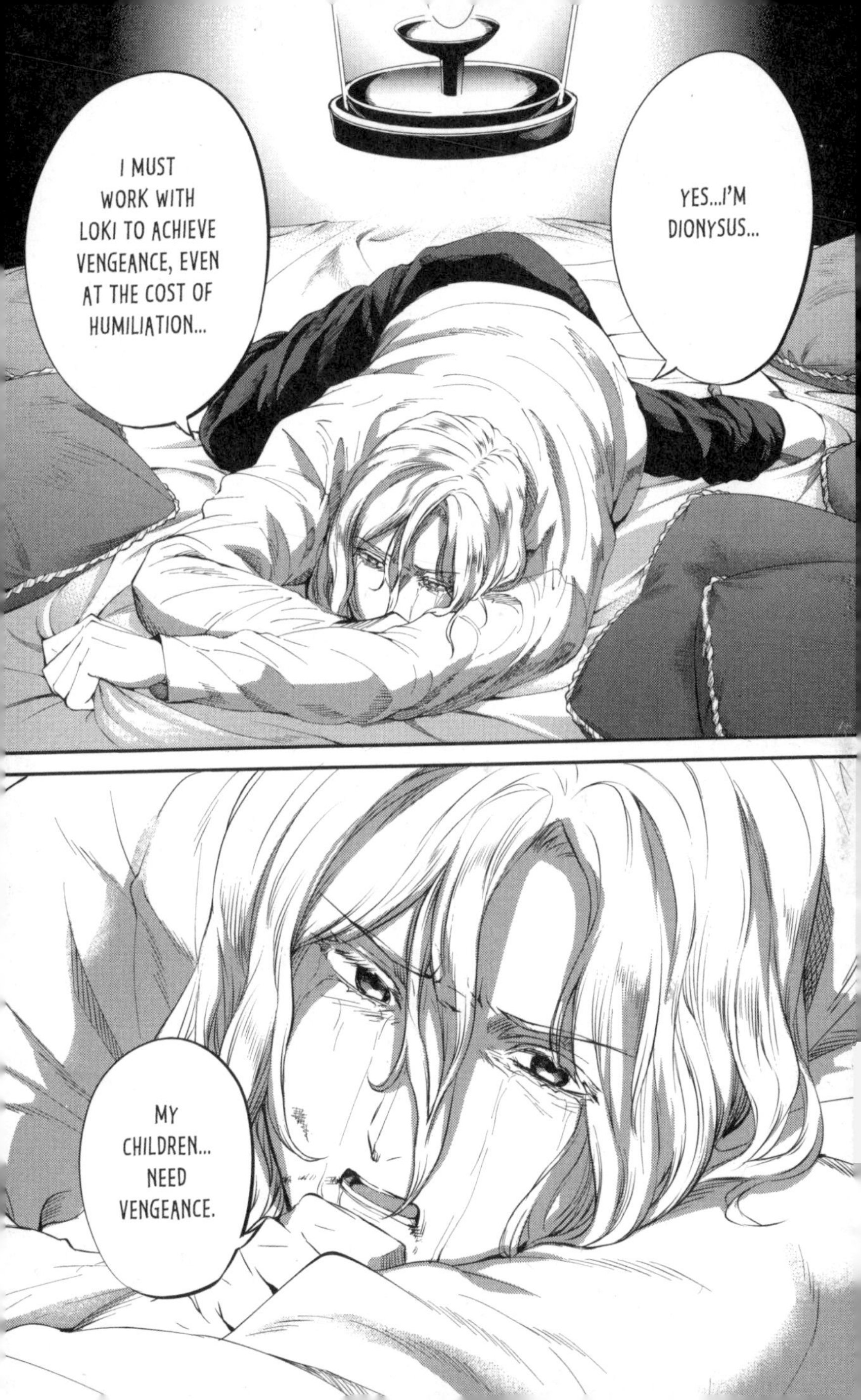
YES...I'M DIONYSUS...
I MUST WORK WITH LOKI TO ACHIEVE VENGEANCE, EVEN AT THE COST OF HUMILIATION...
MY CHILDREN... NEED VENGEANCE.

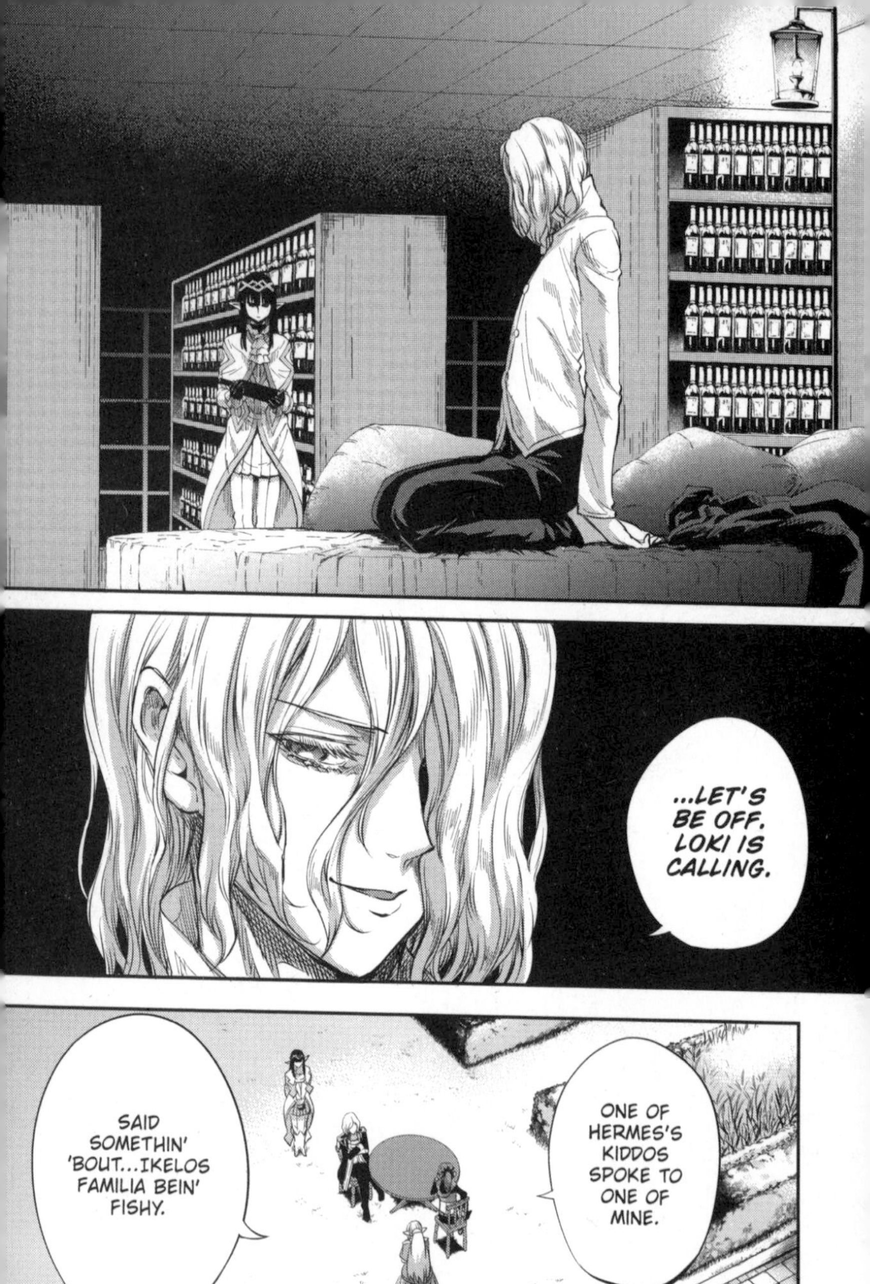
...LET'S BE OFF. LOKI IS CALLING.
ONE OF HERMES'S KIDDOS SPOKE TO ONE OF MINE.
SAID SOMETHIN' 'BOUT...IKELOS FAMILIA BEIN' FISHY.

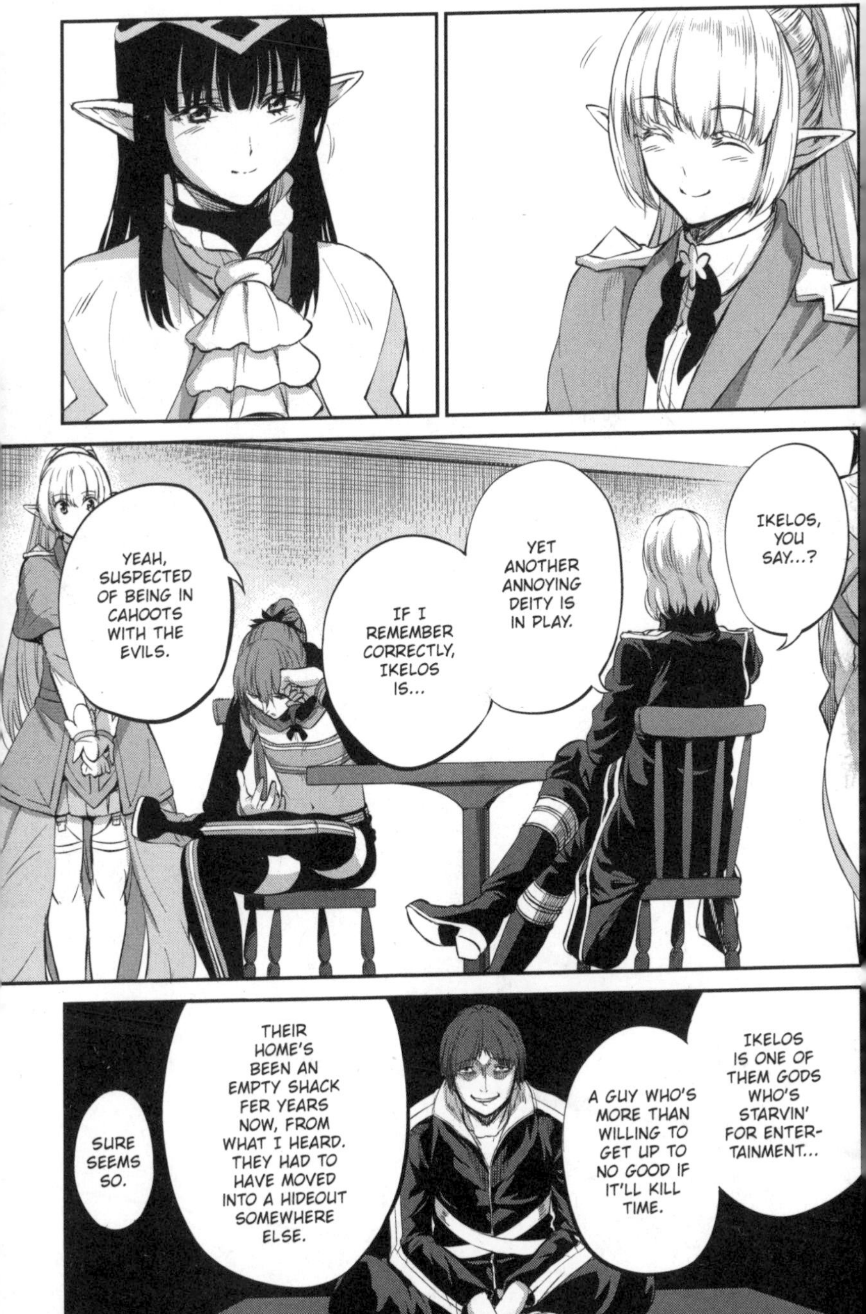
IKELOS, YOU SAY...?
YET ANOTHER ANNOYING DEITY IS IN PLAY.
IF I REMEMBER CORRECTLY, IKELOS IS...
YEAH, SUSPECTED OF BEING IN CAHOOTS WITH THE EVILS.
IKELOS IS ONE OF THEM GODS WHO'S STARVIN' FOR ENTER-TAINMENT...
A GUY WHO'S MORE THAN WILLING TO GET UP TO NO GOOD IF IT'LL KILL TIME.
THEIR HOME'S BEEN AN EMPTY SHACK FER YEARS NOW, FROM WHAT I HEARD. THEY HAD TO HAVE MOVED INTO A HIDEOUT SOMEWHERE ELSE.
SURE SEEMS SO.

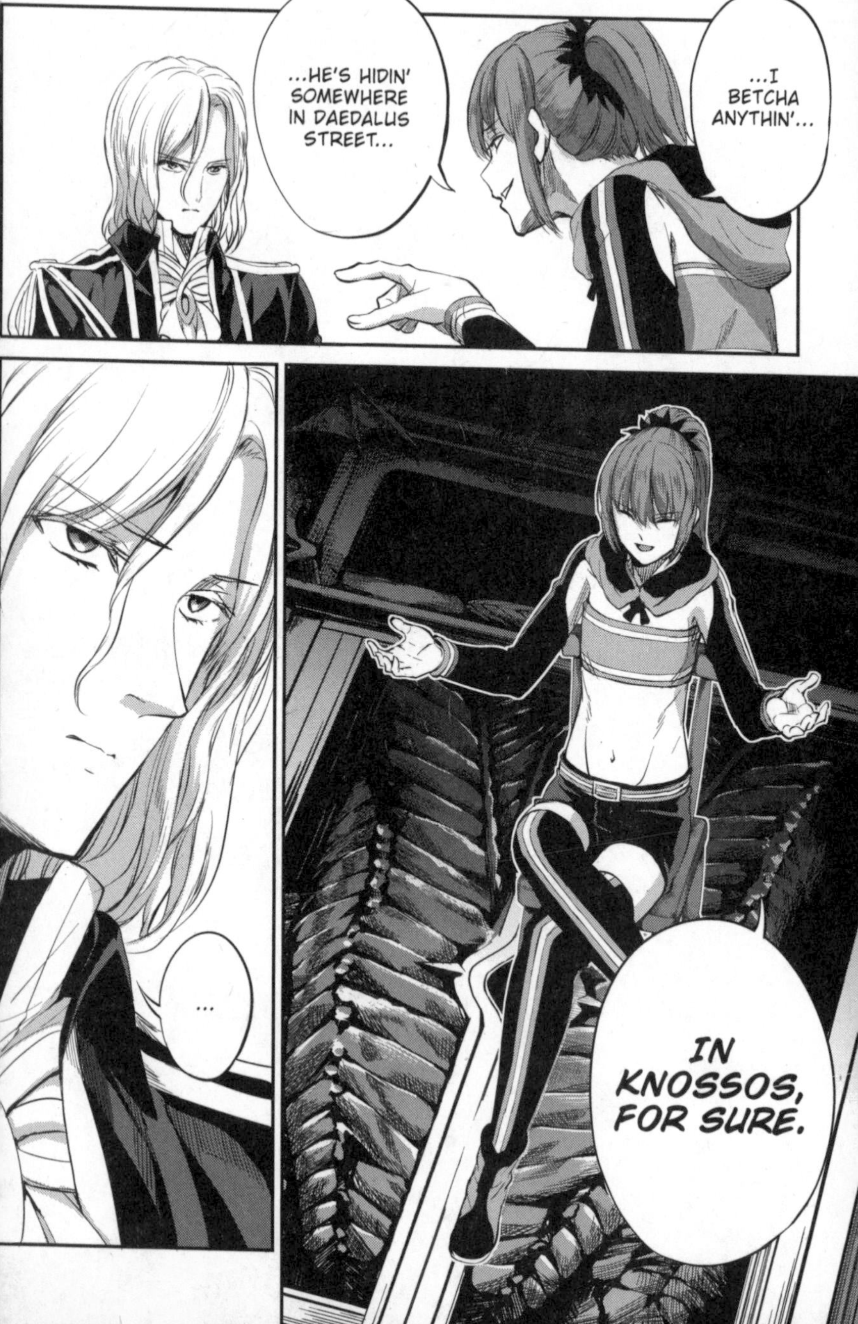
...I BETCHA ANYTHIN'...
...HE'S HIDIN' SOMEWHERE IN DAEDALUS STREET...
IN KNOSSOS, FOR SURE.
...

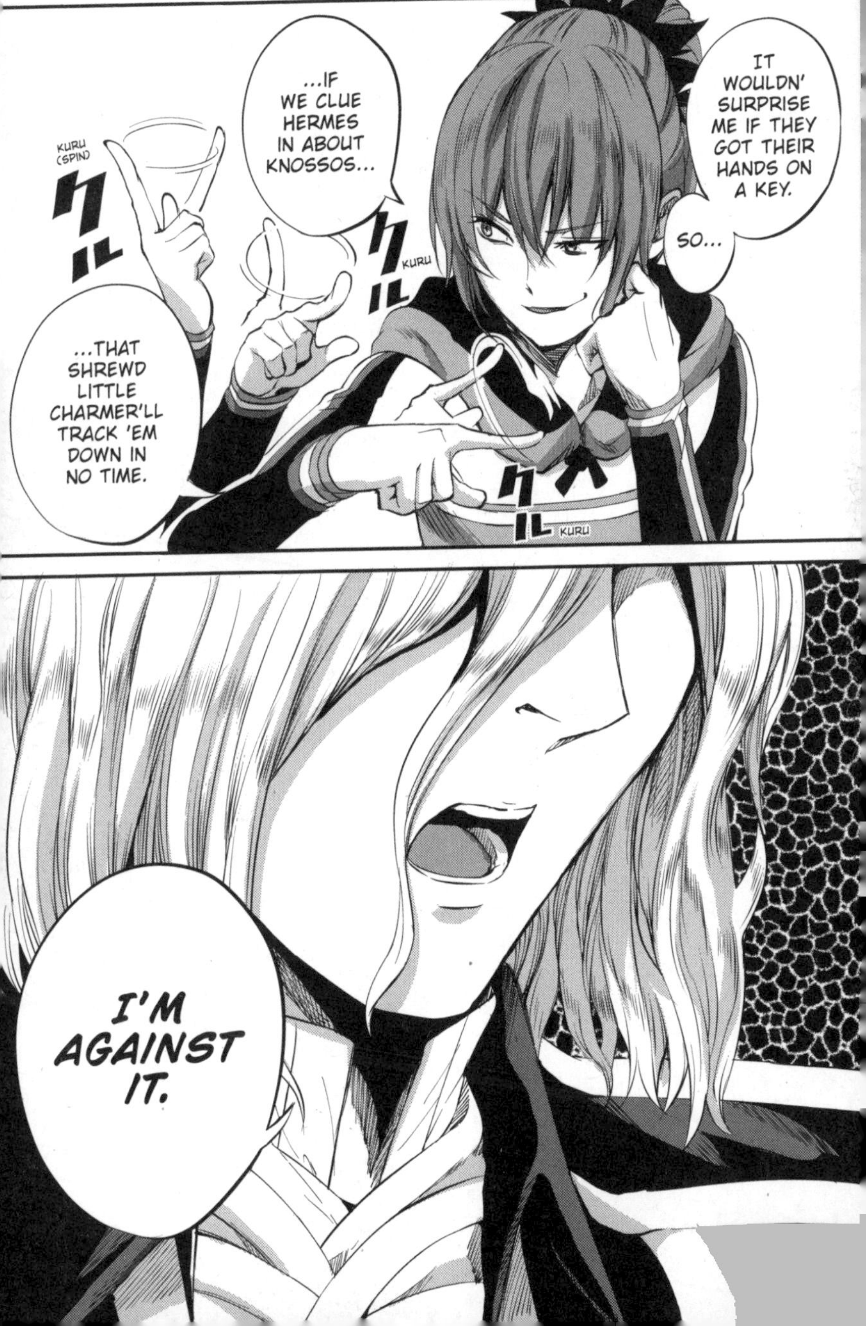

IT WOULDN' SURPRISE ME IF THEY GOT THEIR HANDS ON A KEY.
SO...
...IF WE CLUE HERMES IN ABOUT KNOSSOS...
KURU
KURU
KURU (SPIN)
...THAT SHREWD LITTLE CHARMER'LL TRACK 'EM DOWN IN NO TIME.
I'M AGAINST IT.

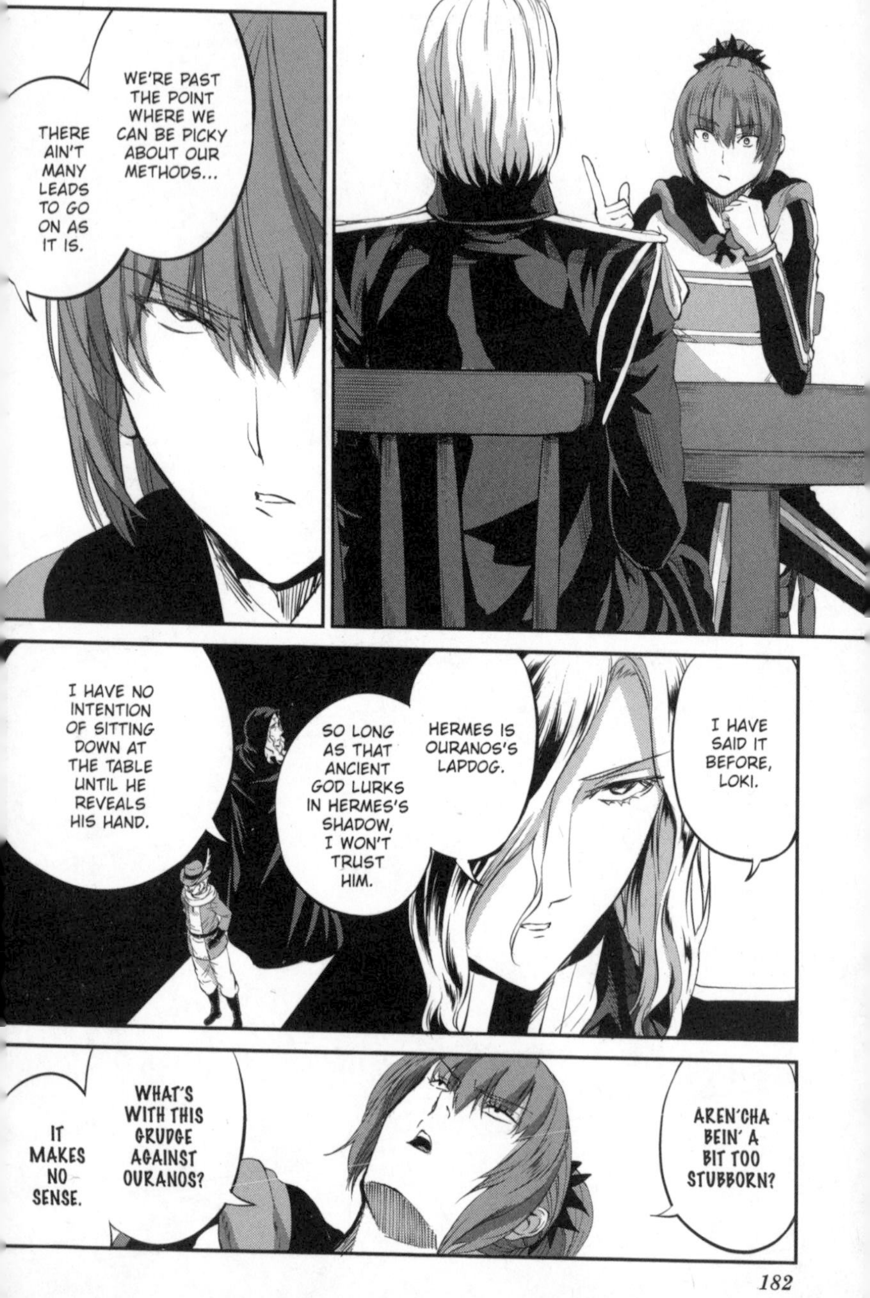
WE'RE PAST THE POINT WHERE WE CAN BE PICKY ABOUT OUR METHODS...
THERE AIN'T MANY LEADS TO GO ON AS IT IS.
I HAVE SAID IT BEFORE, LOKI.
HERMES IS OURANOS'S LAPDOG.
SO LONG AS THAT ANCIENT GOD LURKS IN HERMES'S SHADOW, I WON'T TRUST HIM.
I HAVE NO INTENTION OF SITTING DOWN AT THE TABLE UNTIL HE REVEALS HIS HAND.
AREN'CHA BEIN' A BIT TOO STUBBORN?
WHAT'S WITH THIS GRUDGE AGAINST OURANOS?
IT MAKES NO SENSE.

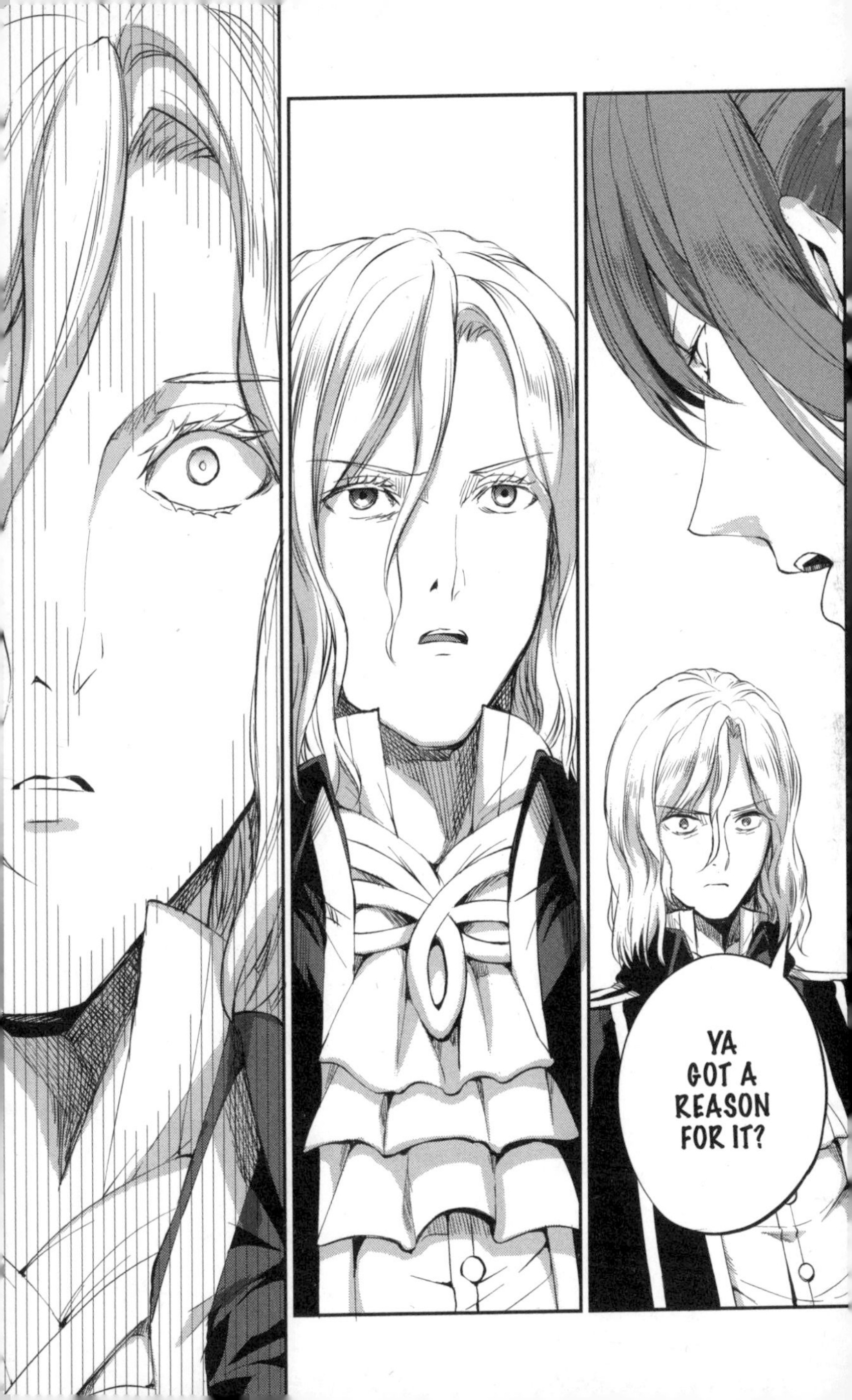
YA GOT A REASON FOR IT?

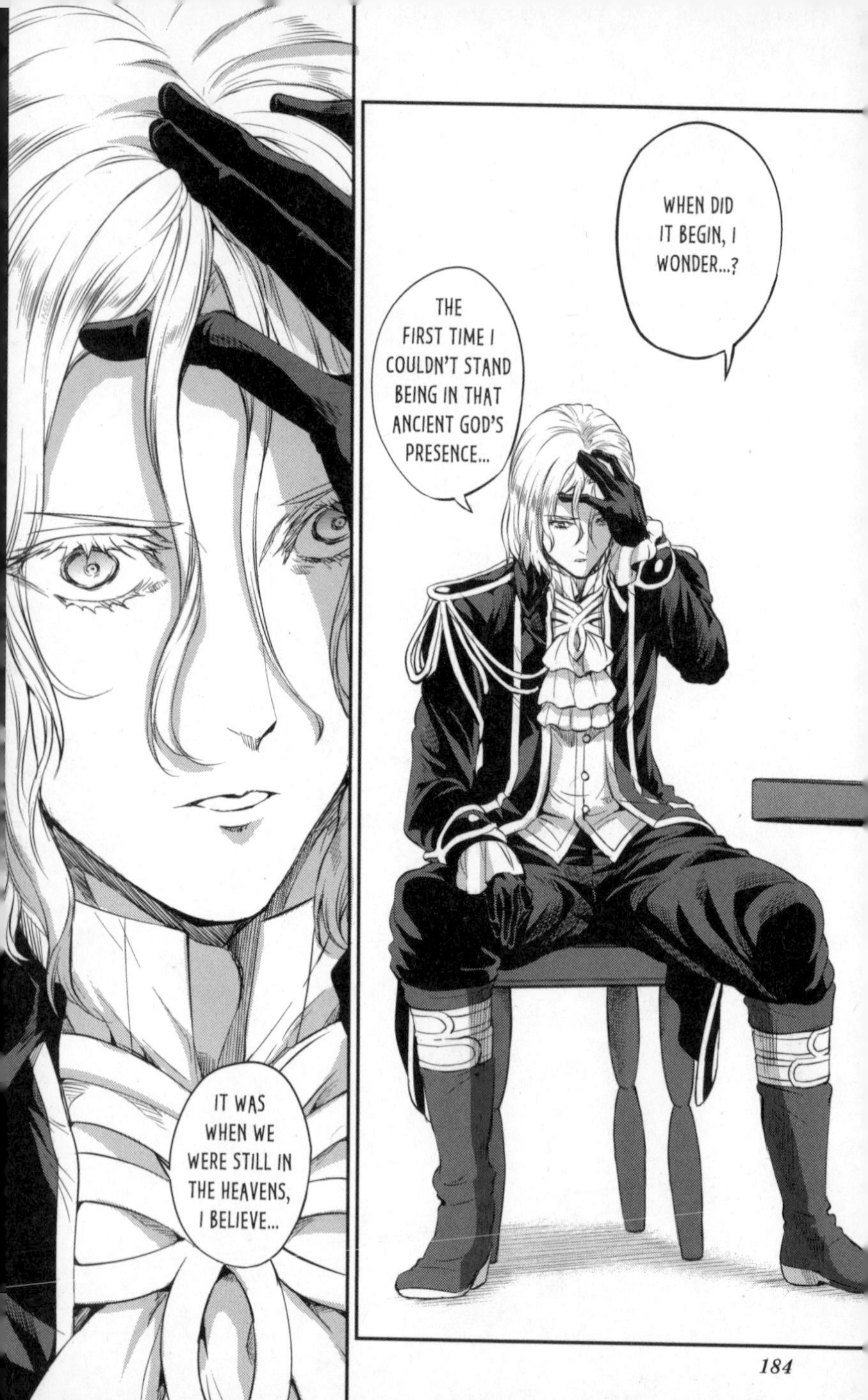
WHEN DID IT BEGIN, I WONDER...?
THE FIRST TIME I COULDN'T STAND BEING IN THAT ANCIENT GOD'S PRESENCE...
IT WAS WHEN WE WERE STILL IN THE HEAVENS, I BELIEVE...

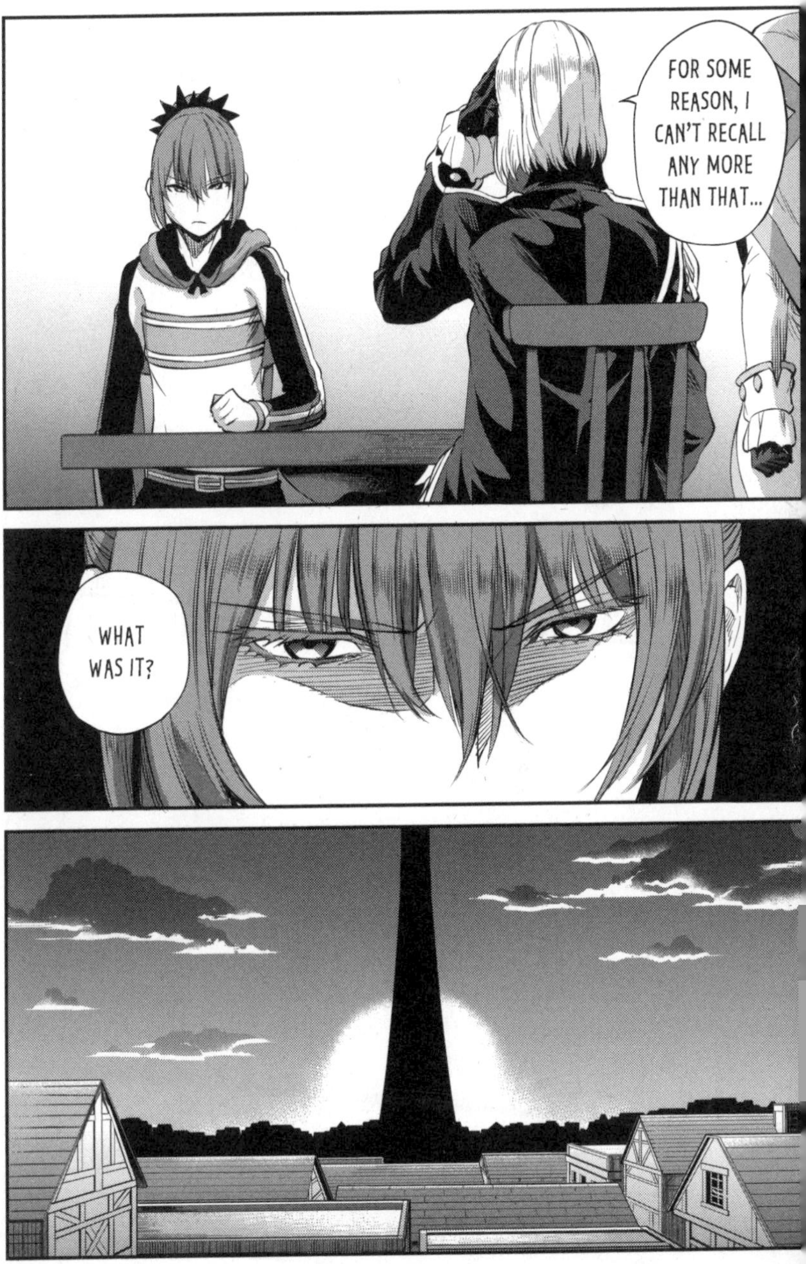
FOR SOME REASON, I CAN'T RECALL ANY MORE THAN THAT...
WHAT WAS IT?

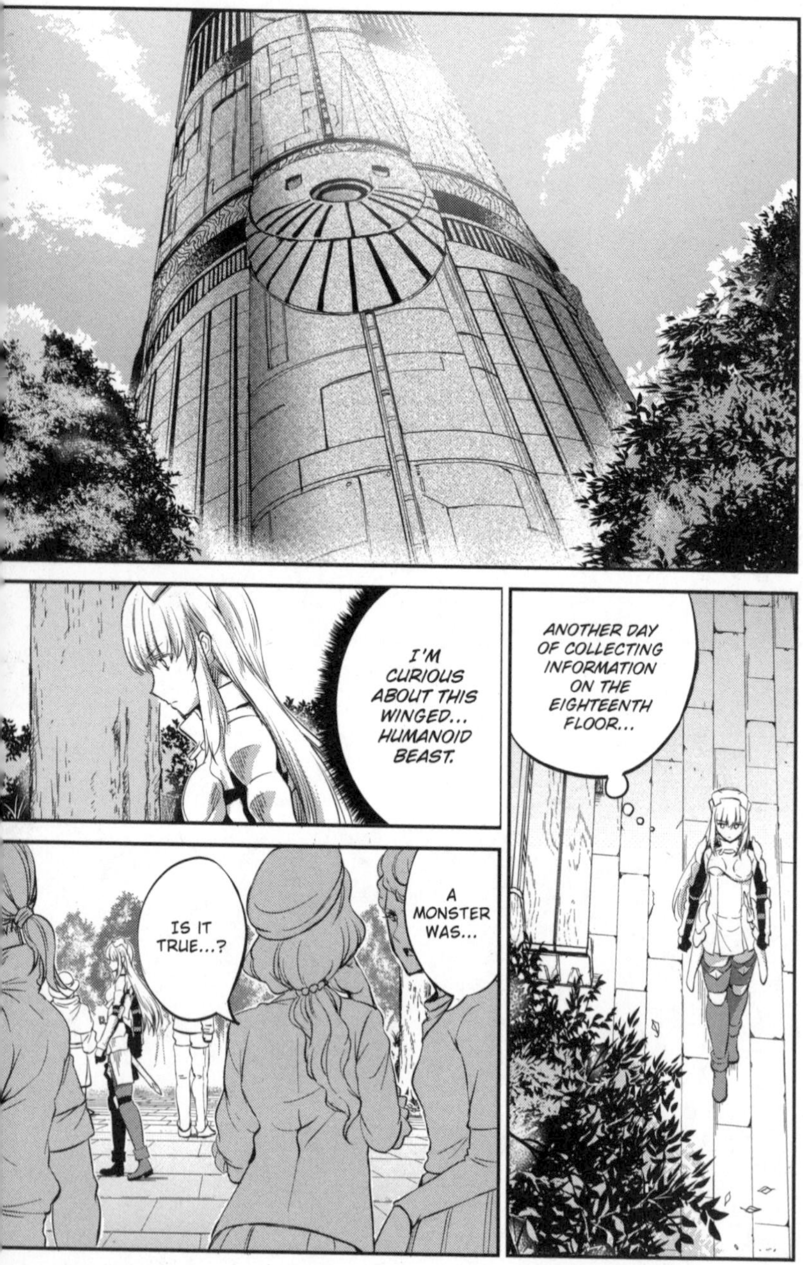

ANOTHER DAY OF COLLECTING INFORMATION ON THE EIGHTEENTH FLOOR...
I'M CURIOUS ABOUT THIS WINGED... HUMANOID BEAST.
A MONSTER WAS...
IS IT TRUE...?

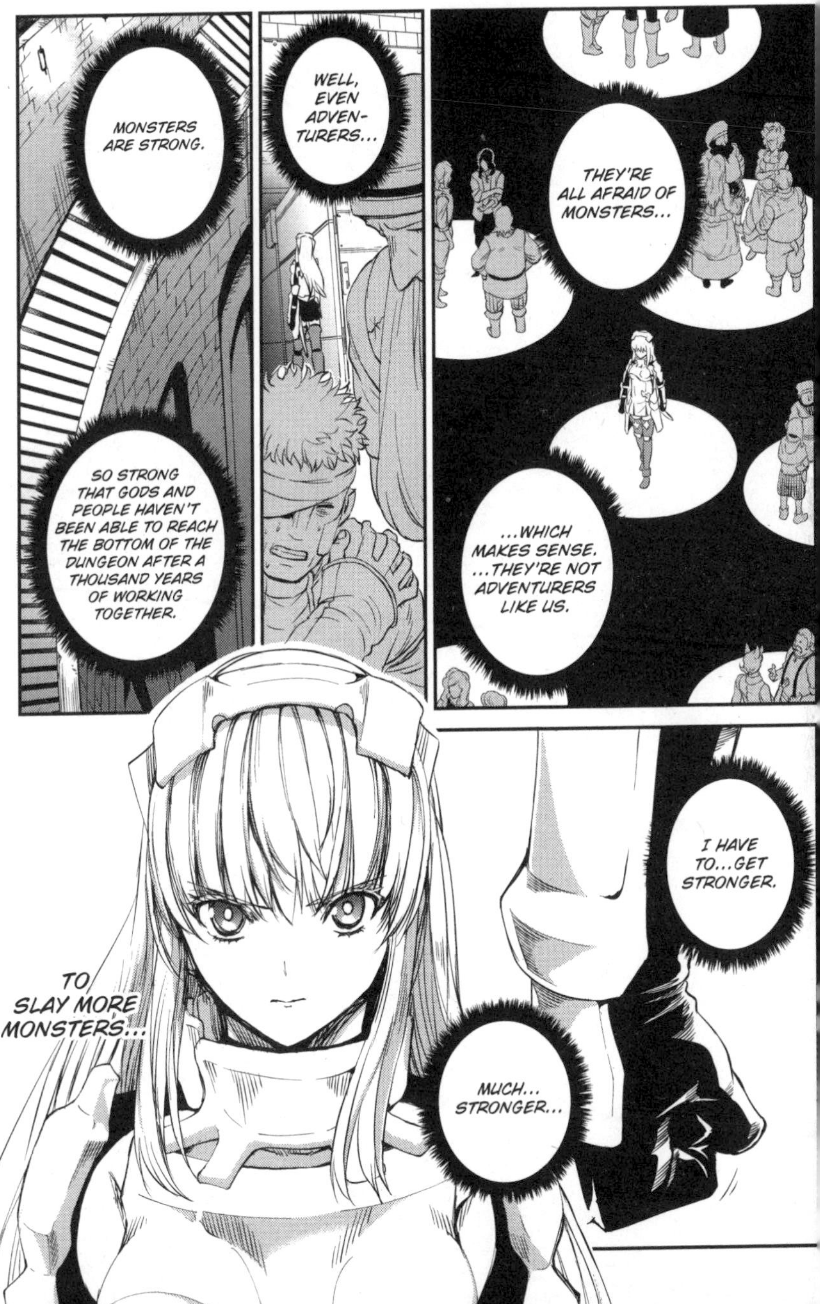
THEY'RE ALL AFRAID OF MONSTERS...
...WHICH MAKES SENSE. ...THEY'RE NOT ADVENTURERS LIKE US.
WELL, EVEN ADVENTURERS...
MONSTERS ARE STRONG.
SO STRONG THAT GODS AND PEOPLE HAVEN'T BEEN ABLE TO REACH THE BOTTOM OF THE DUNGEON AFTER A THOUSAND YEARS OF WORKING TOGETHER.
I HAVE TO...GET STRONGER.
MUCH... STRONGER...
TO SLAY MORE MONSTERS...

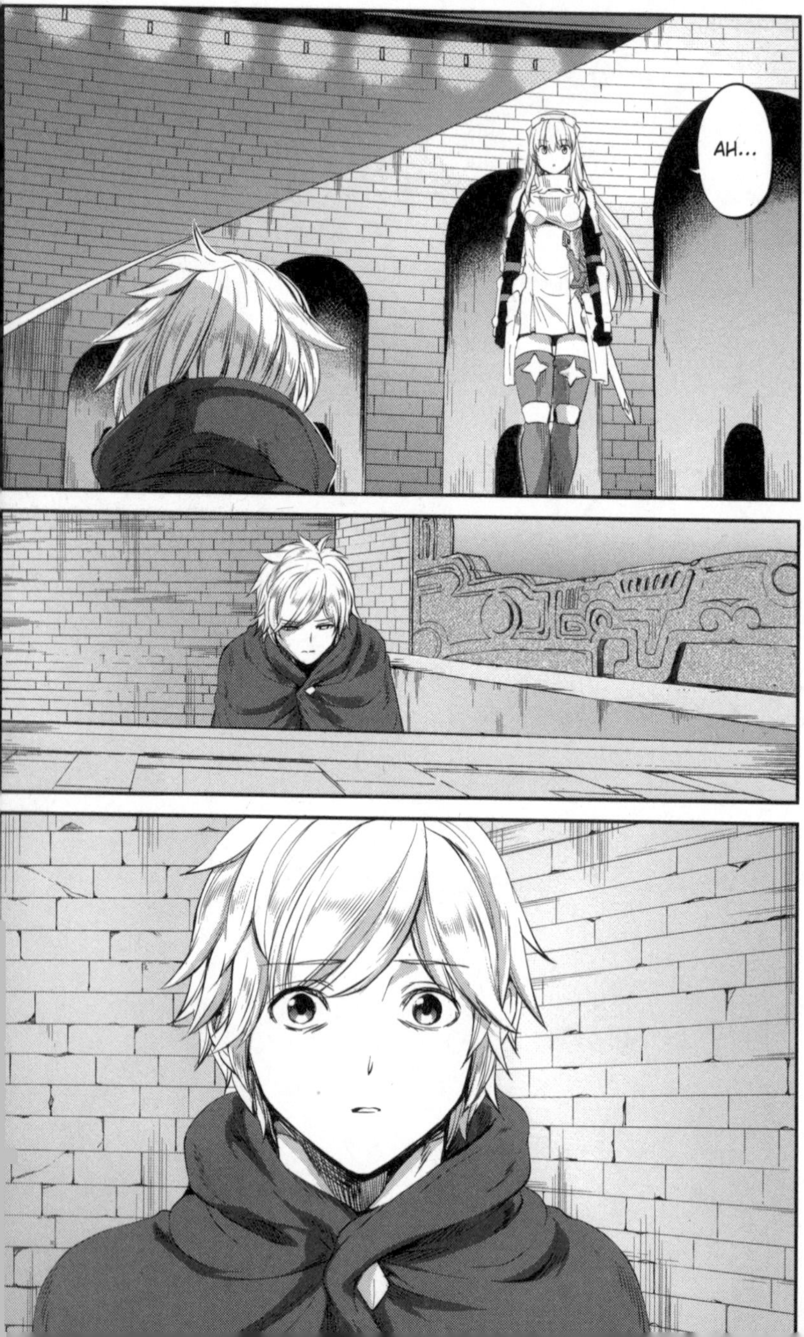
AH...

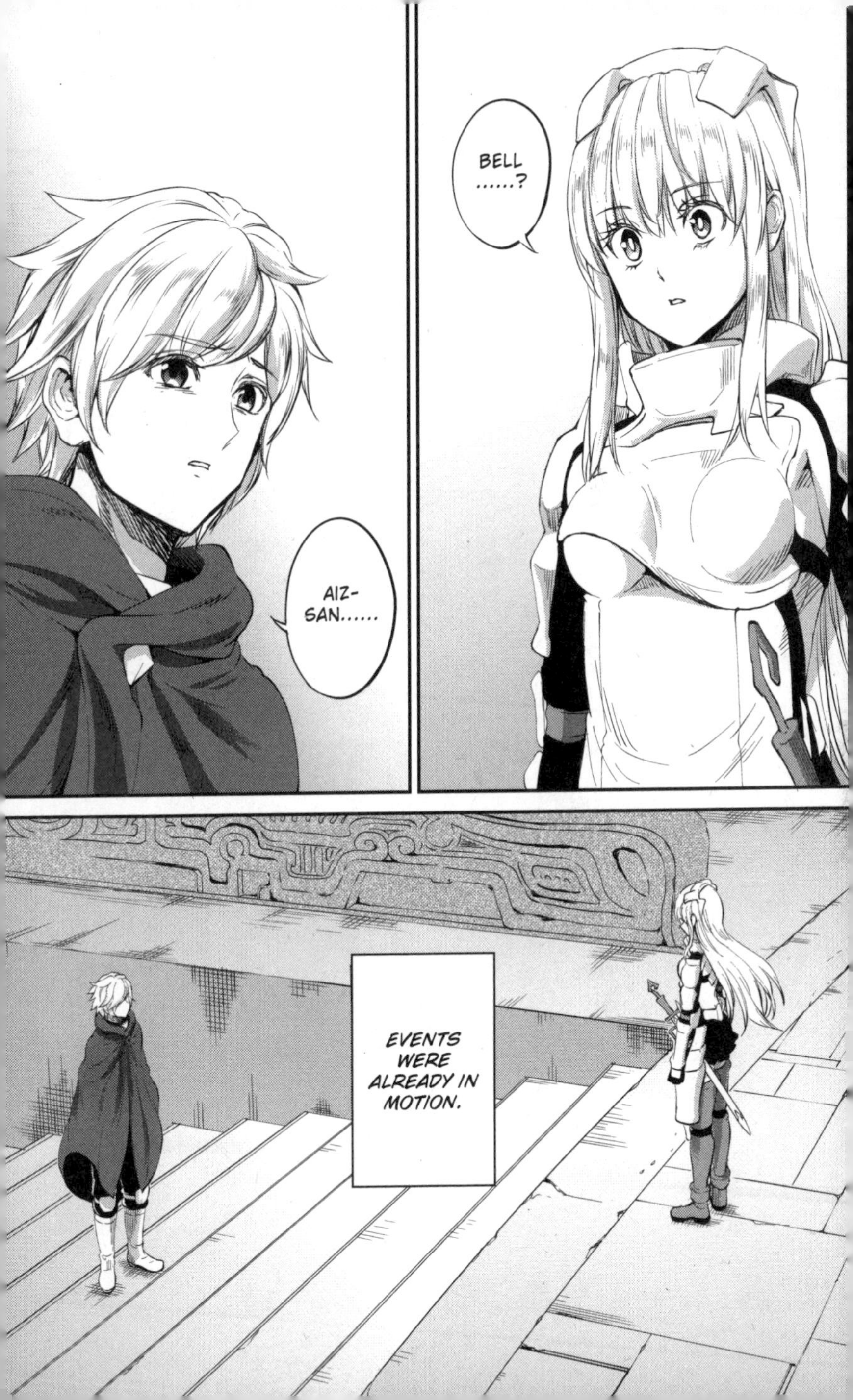
BELL ......?
AIZ-SAN......
EVENTS WERE ALREADY IN MOTION.

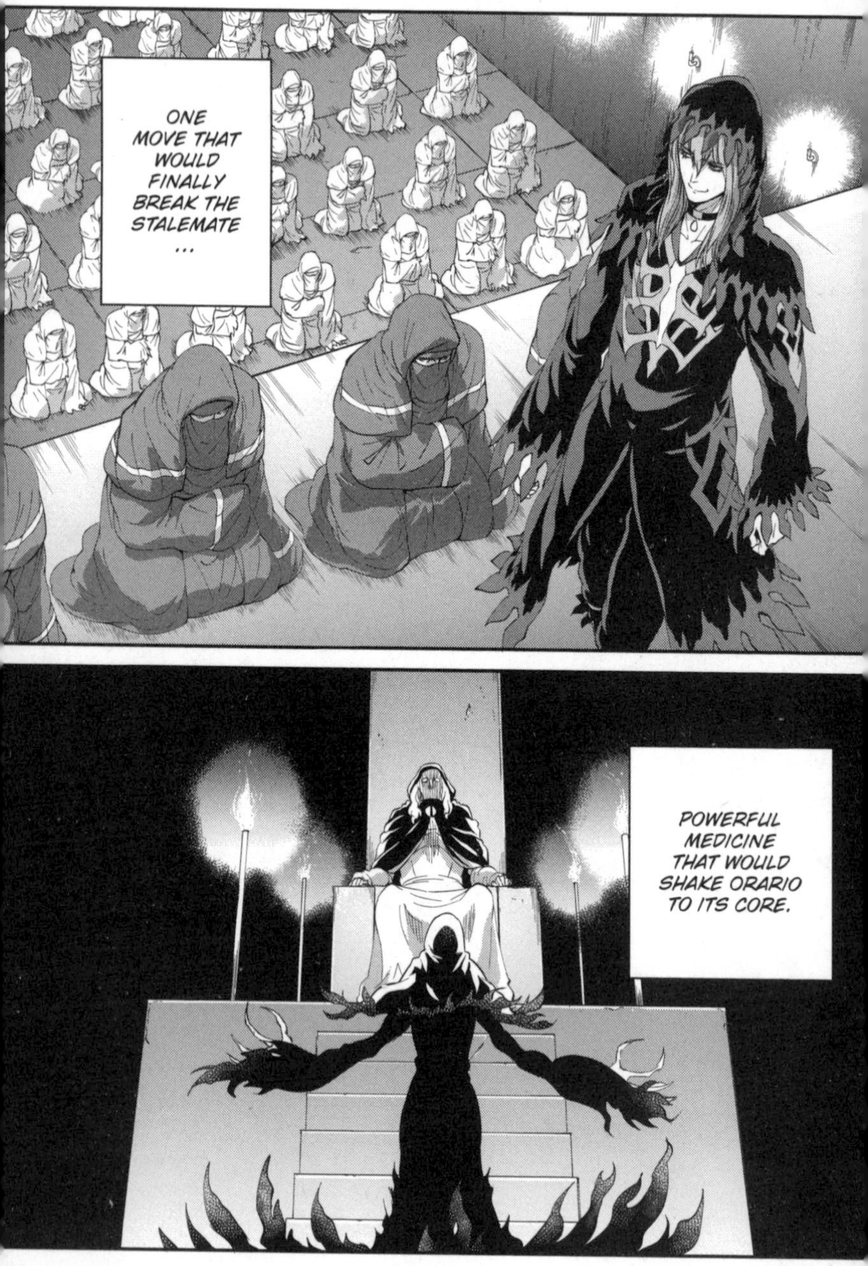
ONE MOVE THAT WOULD FINALLY BREAK THE STALEMATE...
POWERFUL MEDICINE THAT WOULD SHAKE ORARIO TO ITS CORE.

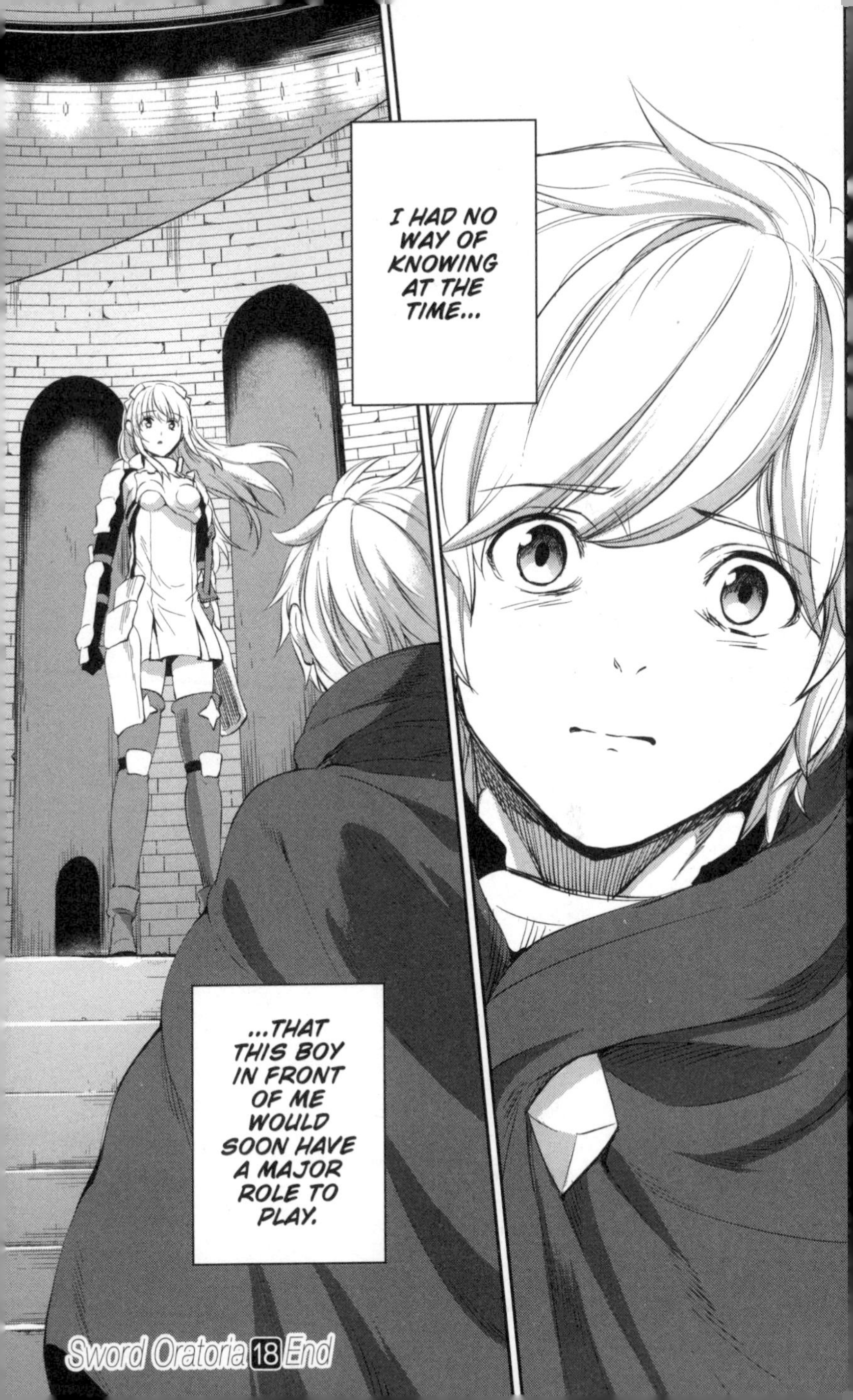
I HAD NO WAY OF KNOWING AT THE TIME...
...THAT THIS BOY IN FRONT OF ME WOULD SOON HAVE A MAJOR ROLE TO PLAY.
Sword Oratoria 18 End

AFTERWORD

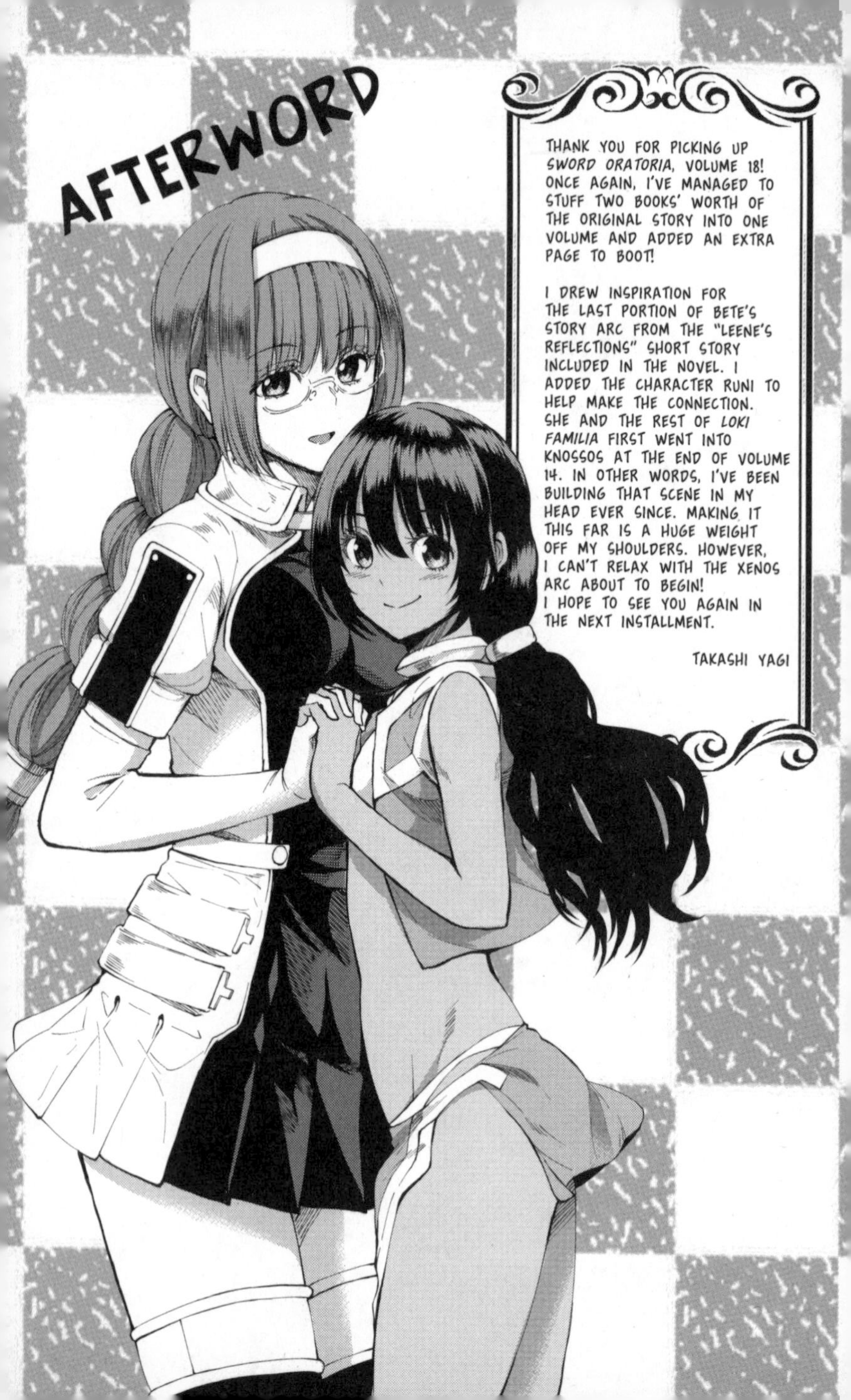

THANK YOU FOR PICKING UP *SWORD ORATORIA*, VOLUME 18! ONCE AGAIN, I'VE MANAGED TO STUFF TWO BOOKS' WORTH OF THE ORIGINAL STORY INTO ONE VOLUME AND ADDED AN EXTRA PAGE TO BOOT!

I DREW INSPIRATION FOR THE LAST PORTION OF BETE'S STORY ARC FROM THE "LEENE'S REFLECTIONS" SHORT STORY INCLUDED IN THE NOVEL. I ADDED THE CHARACTER RUNI TO HELP MAKE THE CONNECTION. SHE AND THE REST OF *LOKI FAMILIA* FIRST WENT INTO KNOSSOS AT THE END OF VOLUME 14. IN OTHER WORDS, I'VE BEEN BUILDING THAT SCENE IN MY HEAD EVER SINCE. MAKING IT THIS FAR IS A HUGE WEIGHT OFF MY SHOULDERS. HOWEVER, I CAN'T RELAX WITH THE XENOS ARC ABOUT TO BEGIN!
I HOPE TO SEE YOU AGAIN IN THE NEXT INSTALLMENT.

TAKASHI YAGI

Is it Wrong to Try to Pick Up Girls in a Dungeon? On the Side

Sword Oratoria

CEYA

IS IT WRONG TO TRY TO PICK UP GIRLS IN A DUNGEON? ON THE SIDE: SWORD ORATORIA ⑱

Fujino Omori
Takashi Yagi
Haimura Kiyotaka, Yasuda Suzuhito

Translation: Andrew Gaippe • Lettering: Phil Christie

DUNGEON NI DEAI WO MOTOMERU NO WA MACHIGATTEIRUDAROUKA GAIDEN SWORD ORATORIA vol. 18
©Fujino Omori/SB Creative Corp.
Original Character Designs:©Kiyotaka Haimura/SB Creative Corp.
Original Character Designs:©Suzuhito Yasuda/SB Creative Corp.
© 2021 Takashi Yagi/SQUARE ENIX CO., LTD.
First published in Japan in 2021 by SQUARE ENIX CO., LTD.
English translation rights arranged with SQUARE ENIX CO., LTD. and Yen Press, LLC through Tuttle-Mori Agency, Inc.

English translation © 2022 by SQUARE ENIX CO., LTD.

Yen Press
150 West 30th Street, 19th Floor
New York, NY 10001

Visit us at yenpress.com
facebook.com/yenpress
twitter.com/yenpress
yenpress.tumblr.com
instagram.com/yenpress

First Yen Press Edition: August 2022
Edited by Yen Press Editorial: Mark Gallucci
Designed by Yen Press Design: Jane Sohn, Andy Swist

Yen Press is an imprint of Yen Press, LLC.
The Yen Press name and logo are trademarks of Yen Press, LLC.

Library of Congress Control Number: 2016946068

ISBNs: 978-1-9753-3842-8 (paperback)
        978-1-9753-3843-5 (ebook)

10 9 8 7 6 5 4 3 2 1

WOR

Printed in the United States of America

OCT - - 2022